Burma

WORLD BIBLIOGRAPHICAL SERIES

General Editors:
Robert G. Neville (Executive Editor)
John J. Horton

Robert A. Myers   Ian Wallace
Hans H. Wellisch   Ralph Lee Woodward, Jr.

John J. Horton is Deputy Librarian of the University of Bradford and currently Chairman of its Academic Board of Studies in Social Sciences. He has maintained a longstanding interest in the discipline of area studies and its associated bibliographical problems, with special reference to European Studies. In particular he has published in the field of Icelandic and of Yugoslav studies, including the two relevant volumes in the World Bibliographical Series.

Robert A. Myers is Associate Professor of Anthropology in the Division of Social Sciences and Director of Study Abroad Programs at Alfred University, Alfred, New York. He has studied post-colonial island nations of the Caribbean and has spent two years in Nigeria on a Fulbright Lectureship. His interests include international public health, historical anthropology and developing societies. In addition to *Amerindians of the Lesser Antilles: a bibliography* (1981), *A Resource Guide to Dominica, 1493–1986* (1987) and numerous articles, he has compiled the World Bibliographical Series volumes on *Dominica* (1987) and *Nigeria* (1989).

Ian Wallace is Professor of German at the University of Bath. A graduate of Oxford in French and German, he also studied in Tübingen, Heidelberg and Lausanne before taking teaching posts at universities in the USA, Scotland and England. He specializes in contemporary German affairs, especially literature and culture, on which he has published numerous articles and books. In 1979 he founded the journal *GDR Monitor*, which he continues to edit under its new title *German Monitor*.

Hans H. Wellisch is Professor emeritus at the College of Library and Information Services, University of Maryland. He was President of the American Society of Indexers and was a member of the International Federation for Documentation. He is the author of numerous articles and several books on indexing and abstracting, and has published *The Conversion of Scripts* and *Indexing and Abstracting: an International Bibliography*. He also contributes frequently to *Journal of the American Society for Information Science*, *The Indexer* and other professional journals.

Ralph Lee Woodward, Jr. is Chairman of the Department of History at Tulane University, New Orleans, where he has been Professor of History since 1970. He is the author of *Central America, a Nation Divided*, 2nd ed. (1985), as well as several monographs and more than sixty scholarly articles on modern Latin America. He has also compiled volumes in the World Bibliographical Series on *Belize* (1980), *Nicaragua* (1983), and *El Salvador* (1988). Dr. Woodward edited the Central American section of the *Research Guide to Central America and the Caribbean* (1985) and is currently editor of the Central American history section of the *Handbook of Latin American Studies*.

VOLUME 132

Burma

Patricia M. Herbert

Compiler

CLIO PRESS

OXFORD, ENGLAND · SANTA BARBARA, CALIFORNIA
DENVER, COLORADO

© Copyright 1991 by Clio Press Ltd.

All rights reserved. No part of this publication may be reproduced, stored in any
retrieval system, or transmitted in any form or by any means, electronic, mechanical,
photocopying or otherwise, without the prior permission in writing of the publishers.

British Library Cataloguing in Publication Data

Herbert, Patricia M.
Burma. – (World bibliographical series; 132)
I. Title
016.591

ISBN 1–85109–088–6

Clio Press Ltd.,
55 St. Thomas' Street,
Oxford OX1 1JG, England.

ABC-CLIO,
130 Cremona Drive,
Santa Barbara,
CA 93117, USA.

Designed by Bernard Crossland.
Typeset by Columns Design and Production Services, Reading, England.
Printed and bound in Great Britain by
Billing and Sons Ltd., Worcester.

THE WORLD BIBLIOGRAPHICAL SERIES

This series, which is principally designed for the English speaker, will eventually cover every country (and many of the world's principal regions), each in a separate volume comprising annotated entries on works dealing with its history, geography, economy and politics; and with its people, their culture, customs, religion and social organization. Attention will also be paid to current living conditions – housing, education, newspapers, clothing, etc.– that are all too often ignored in standard bibliographies; and to those particular aspects relevant to individual countries. Each volume seeks to achieve, by use of careful selectivity and critical assessment of the literature, an expression of the country and an appreciation of its nature and national aspirations, to guide the reader towards an understanding of its importance. The keynote of the series is to provide, in a uniform format, an interpretation of each country that will express its culture, its place in the world, and the qualities and background that make it unique. The views expressed in individual volumes, however, are not necessarily those of the publisher.

VOLUMES IN THE SERIES

For Juliette Eliane Mya
and in memory of
Daw Khin Kyi

Contents

Contents

Contents

Preface

Burma, often dubbed the hermit nation of Asia and portrayed in tourist guides and coffee-table books as a beautiful land of smiling people and Buddhist temples, has, since 1988, come more closely into world focus and attracted critical attention. In 1988, after twenty-six years of authoritarian socialist rule and, anticipating more successful movements for change in Eastern Europe, a series of pro-democracy demonstrations rocked Burma. The movement, seen by many as Burma's second struggle for independence, was – a year before the events of Tiananmen Square in China – ruthlessly suppressed by the military who seized power on 18 September 1988, and established rule by the State Law and Order Restoration Council (SLORC). Although multi-party general elections were held on 27 May 1990 in which the main opposition party, the National League for Democracy, won a landslide victory gaining 392 out of 485 contested seats, the State Law and Order Restoration Council has signally failed to transfer power to a duly elected civilian government. SLORC's continuing repressive rule and abuse of human rights have been highlighted by the award of the 1991 Nobel Peace Prize to Daw Aung San Suu Kyi who emerged in 1988 to become the focus of the people's aspirations for peaceful democratic change in Burma and who has been held under house arrest in Rangoon since July 1989.

This bibliography contains references to these dramatic recent political events in Burma as well as to the wealth of older source material on this little-known country. It constitutes the first and most fully annotated multi-disciplinary guide to English-language publications about Burma to appear in twenty years. It mirrors Burma's past and present in the sense that a substantial number of entries reflect British colonial and wartime connections with Burma as well as pioneering scholarship in general, while Burma's isolation from the world for over thirty years is reflected in the relatively few modern anthropological, economic and technical studies. Particular care has been taken in the annotation of entries to make connections as well as evaluations with the aim of helping both general and specialist readers to make further discoveries. Where specialized bibliographical compilations already exist, for example in the areas of language, linguistics, periodical articles and doctoral dissertations on Burma, I have cut down on detailed references, but in certain areas where there are no existing subject bibliographies, for example on Western fiction set in Burma and on art, I have tried to give more extensive coverage. Some may consider that undue weight has been given to certain topics such as Christian missionary titles and colonial period and military memoirs, but I felt it was valid to reference such varied endeavours as, for many Western users of this bibliography, these represent strong links with Burma. It is a matter of personal regret but of utmost practicality that Burmese-language works had to be excluded from this compilation. I similarly regret the loss of many other references which in the extreme pressure of cutting and amalgamating entries had to be dropped from my original over-large compilation in order to conform with the length, guidelines and selection criteria of the World Bibliographical Series.

Altogether the bibliography contains over 1,500 references in 850 numbered main entries, and is divided into thirty subject headings, eight of which are further subdivided. Within each chapter heading, entries are arranged alphabetically by author, except in the periodicals and yearbooks chapters where entry is by order of title. For many works which encompass several subjects, a choice of entry under a single subject heading had to be made but the use of cross referencing and the provision of separate author, title and subject indexes should enable the reader to access all references. Burmese names are entered in direct order and the honorific terms of address (U, Daw, Maung etc.) have – for the most part and with no discourtesy intended – been omitted both in the author entry and in the annotations. In the romanization of Burmese names and words, that of the original author has generally been adhered to, and elsewhere a standard conventional transcription without accented tones has been used. It remains to comment upon the bibliography's title in the light of the announcement in mid-1989 by Burma's ruling military junta, the State Law and Order Restoration Council, that the country should henceforth be called Myanmar (the Burmese word for Burma). Since the underlying logic for this name change was unclear, I have chosen to view it as for internal consumption only and as no more imperative in English-speaking international terms than it is to call Japan Nippon, Germany Deutschland, Florence Firenze or Munich München. I have therefore adhered to the use of Burma as the name of the country, Burman to denote the ethnic majority population, and to Burmese to denote both the language and the peoples of Burma as a whole.

Acknowledgements

I am grateful to John Randall of Books of Asia for making available at an early stage of the bibliography's compilation a listing of his extensive collection of books on Burma. For the most part in compiling this bibliography I have been able to rely upon the incomparable Burma collections of my place of work, The British Library, supplemented by those of the School of Oriental and African Studies. I am indebted to U Thaw Kaung, Universities' Central Library, Rangoon, for providing me with details of Burma reprint editions of some titles, and to my library colleagues Henry Ginsburg, Xiao Wei Bond and Hamish Todd for advice on entry of Thai, Chinese and Japanese names respectively. For their help in responding to some last minute queries, I wish to thank particularly Anna Allott, Michael Aris, Michael Aung-Thwin, Gertrude Barns, Barry Bloomfield, John Guy, Gustaaf Houtman, John Okell, Martin Smith and Robert Taylor. For any inadvertent errors and omissions I alone remain responsible. The compilation of this bibliography has been, like my feelings for Burma, an expression of love tinged with despair. It has occupied virtually all my spare time and I have to thank my family for being so supportive and tolerant – from my husband Ariel who typed many of the entries, to grown-up daughter Christine and her husband Robert for help with my small daughter in the school holidays and to Olga and Thomas and family for excusing my absence on several occasions. Special thanks are due too to Katrina McClintock of Clio Press for her patient editing and for, appropriately, not flinching from the insertion of such eleventh hour items as Aung San Suu Kyi's *Freedom from fear*.

Patricia M. Herbert
London
October 1991

Introduction

Burma, endowed with great natural resources and ethnic diversity, is the largest country in mainland Southeast Asia with a land area of over 260,000 square miles. It is roughly diamond shaped, measuring some 500 miles from east to west and some 800 miles long from north to south, with a long narrow coastal strip (Tenasserim) extending a further 500 miles southwards into the Malay Peninsula. The coastline of the Indian Ocean from the Bay of Bengal to the Andaman Sea forms a natural boundary to the south and southwest, while Burma is bordered to the northwest by Bangladesh and India, to the north and northeast by China (and Tibet) and by Laos and Thailand to the southeast and south. Separated from neighbouring countries by high mountain barriers and lying off the main shipping routes, Burma's natural geographic fastness has been reinforced at various periods by the isolationist and inward-looking policies of the country's rulers.

The interior of the country comprises a series of river valleys – those of the Irrawaddy, Chindwin, Sittang and Salween rivers – running from north to south and divided from one another by mountain ranges and plateaux. The highland areas are inhabited by the hill peoples of Burma – of which the largest groups are the Kachin, Chin, Shan (the latter in the highland plateau of the Shan Hills), and the Karen (who are also extensively settled in the lowlands). The Irrawaddy River forms the country's main artery – Kipling's 'road' to Mandalay – and is navigable from the coast for some 900 miles as far as Bhamo, while its tributary the Chindwin is navigable for some 400 miles. The lowland area subdivides into a dry zone (Upper and Central Burma), and the fertile plain and delta of Lower Burma which forms the principal rice growing area and supports the bulk of the country's population. Burma's climate is predominantly tropical, with annual rainfall varying between as much as 200 inches along the coastlands which receive the brunt of the monsoon winds (from May to October), to between 25 to 50 inches in the dry zone and an average of 100 inches in the lowland plains. It is the dry zone, centred at the confluence of the Irrawaddy and Chindwin Rivers, which forms the historic heartland of the Burmans, the largest of Burma's ethnic groups, constituting approximately sixty-five per cent of a total population of over forty-one million (1991 estimate).

History

The Burmans migrating from the northeast moved into the dry zone and established settlements and irrigation works from about the 9th century AD. They came into contact with, and absorbed, an early people known as the Pyu whose ancient cities – Sri Ksetra (near Prome), Beikthano (Vishnu city) and Halin – attest to the influence of Indian Hinduism and Buddhism and to a high degree of civilization. The Burmans' southward expansion also brought them into contact with the highly cultured Mon, an ethnically and linguistically distinct people. There were important Mon settlements in Lower Burma (classically known as Ramannadesa) at Thaton and Pegu, although the centre of Mon civilization lay further to the east in the lower Menam valley of present day Thailand where the ancient Mon kingdom of Dvaravati flourished until the 11th century. The Shan, a Tai people who were part of a general southward migration into the Menam basin, form a third important group, dominating central Burma from the 13th to the early 16th centuries.

In the mid-11th century, the early Burman settlements in the dry zone were consolidated at Pagan under one ruler, King Anawrahta (1044-77), the founder of the Pagan dynasty and empire. He was the first king to establish Burman rule over much of the country. His conquest of the Mon kingdom of Thaton opened Pagan to Mon cultural influence and, above all, to Theravada Buddhism. A golden age of art and architecture followed and Theravada Buddhism became firmly established as a popular – rather than just as a court cult – religion, while Mahayana, Tantric and Hindu religious elements diminished. A stupendous programme of temple building, religious patronage and endowments followed and Pagan became a centre for Pali and Buddhist scholarship. To this day, hundreds of huge brick-built Buddhist temples, many with ornate stucco decoration and interior wall paintings, still stand, spreading from the eastern bank of the Irrawaddy over an area of sixteen square miles.

Following the Mongol invasion of 1287-88, Pagan declined (for reasons that are still the subject of scholarly debate) and its empire fragmented into smaller Shan, Mon and Burman kingdoms or states which vied with each other for ascendancy and control of resources. Early European travellers' acounts of the 16th century onward attest to the wealth and growing trade of the Mon kingdom of Pegu and of the ports of Syriam, Martaban and Bassein. Foreign adventurers and trading companies competed for a foothold and sometimes became embroiled in internal politics and clashes between the Mon, Burman and Arakanese kingdoms. In this period, too, the centre of power fluctuated between Upper and Lower Burma, with the capital of the early Toungoo (Taung-ngu) dynasty first at Toungoo, then at Pegu until in 1635 it moved to Ava in the dry zone. Upper Burma was to remain the political and cultural heartland of the Burman empire – with the capital shifting from Ava to Amarapura to Mandalay – until 1885.

The Burmans were only gradually able to reassert their hegemony over the Mons and the Shans. In the 16th century, Kings Tabinshweti and Bayinnaung of the Toungoo dynasty briefly reunited Burma but it was only in the 18th century that the kings of the Kon-baung dynasty (founded in 1752 by King Alaung-hpaya) by vigorous military campaigns and by administrative consolidation asserted Burman control over an area roughly equivalent to the boundaries of modern Burma. The ancient independent kingdom of Arakan, centred from the 15th century at Mrohaung, was conquered by King Bagyidaw in 1784 and annexed to the Burmese empire. War was also waged against neighbouring Thailand whose capital Ayutthaya was besieged and plundered by the Burmese in 1767.

In the 19th century, bitter disputes with the British about commercial and diplomatic relations resulted in three Anglo-Burmese Wars (1824-26, 1852 and 1885) as a result of which the British took over Burma in three stages: Arakan and Tenasserim provinces in 1826, Lower Burma in 1852-53 and the remaining kingdom of Upper Burma in 1885-86. Of the kings of the last Kon-baung dynasty of Burma, King Mindon (r. 1853-78) stands out as an enlightened ruler, but his modernizing reforms could not safeguard his truncated kingdom of Upper Burma from the onward tide of British imperialist and commercial ambitions which engulfed his ineffective successor, King Thibaw, who was deposed in 1885 and exiled with his family to India. There followed several years of 'pacification' campaigns and military expeditions by the British to subdue resistance to British rule and to persuade the hereditary rulers of other ethnic groups such as the Shans to acknowledge British suzerainty.

British Burma was ruled as a province of British India. From 1862 the principal colonial officer was a Chief Commissioner responsible to the Government of India. After 1897 rule was exercised by a Lieutenant-Governor and, beginning in 1923, by a Governor and a Legislative Council with a majority of elected members in a system known as dyarchy. The Legislative Council, however, controlled only certain limited aspects of government and administration. Burma under British rule underwent rapid institutional, economic and social change. The society that developed under British colonialism has been aptly termed (by J. S. Furnivall) a 'plural society' – a three-tiered structure with the British occupying élite positions in the administration and professions, immigrant Indians (and to a lesser extent the Chinese) monopolizing retail trade and money lending, the lower levels of the administration and the labour market, and the majority indigenous Burmese being left as peasant cultivators who, in the unstable economic conditions and unrestrained market forces of the early 20th century, became increasingly indebted and landless.

The roots of 20th-century Burmese nationalism lay in British 'divide and rule' policies and the loss of traditional authority structures, in the encouragement of Indian migrant labour, in the exploitation by foreigners of Burma's rich natural resources and in growing Burmese perceptions that they were second-class citizens in their own country and judged by the British as less ready for self-government than India. Buddhism proved a powerful rallying and unifying factor in the early nationalist movement which was led by a small educated Burmese élite and in which politicized monks played an important part. In the 1920s nationalist politics were dominated by the General Council of Burmese Associations (GCBA) which had evolved from the Young Men's Buddhist Association (YMBA) but split into factions over the issue of whether to participate in, or boycott, the Legislative Council and whether to support, or oppose, separation from India. In 1937, as provided for in the Government of Burma Act of 1935, the administration of Burma was separated from that of India and a bicameral legislature was introduced under the premiership of Dr. Ba Maw. The 1930s saw the rise of the *Do-bama Asi-ayon* ('We Burmans Association') of the *Thahkin* ('master') nationalists who, taking inspiration from the failed peasant uprising of Hsaya San in 1930-32, resolved that military training and organization was necessary to defeat the British and regain Burma's independence. Several young leaders who later became known as the 'Thirty Comrades' – among them Aung San and Ne Win – received military training in Japan and became important figures in shaping Burma's future. The experience of the Japanese occupation of Burma from 1942 and the formation under General Aung San of the Burma Independence Army ensured that the British, after a bitter Burma Campaign to reconquer Burma from the Japanese, would find it impossible at the end of the Second World War to deny for long Burmese demands for immediate and complete independence.

Modern Burma
In accordance with the Aung San–Attlee Agreement of January 1947, elections were held in which General Aung San's Anti-Fascist People's Freedom League (AFPFL) won a large majority. Before the

new Constitutent Assembly could prepare for independence, however, Aung San and six members of his Executive Council were assassinated on 19 July 1947 at the instigation of a jealous rival politician, U Saw. General Aung San's memory is revered to this day as the architect of Burma's independence and of the Panglong Agreement of 1947 whereby Burma's diverse ethnic groups joined the Union of Burma. On 4 January 1948 Burma became a fully independent state and chose not to join the British Commonwealth. However, at the outset before Burma could rebuild her war-shattered economy, the unity of the newly independent state, with U Nu as Prime Minister, was threatened by communist and other insurrections and, above all, by the rebellion of the Karen National Defence Organization

Burma's relatively brief period of constitutional democracy ended in 1958 when, following irrevocable splits in the AFPFL, U Nu asked the head of the Burma Army, General Ne Win, to form a 'Caretaker Government'. Army rule restored some law and order to the country and General Ne Win at that time went on record as abhorring 'interference in the political field by government servants or armed forces'. Elections were held in February 1960 and U Nu's 'Clean' AFPFL faction, renamed the Pyeidaungsu (Union) Party, formed another government. Notwithstanding this, political, religious and minority tensions were mounting and U Nu's government was overthrown by General Ne Win's military coup of 2 March 1962. Henceforth, power was invested in the military's Revolutionary Council and the country set on the rigid political and economic path outlined in *The Burmese way to socialism* and formulated by a single political party, the Burma Socialist Programme Party (BSPP). The nation was isolated from the outside world, foreign and large private business concerns were nationalized, an economic programme designed to ensure self-sufficiency was launched, and a neutralist foreign policy adhered to strictly. In 1971, Ne Win and other leading military figures renounced their military rank. Three years later a new constitution, a Council of State and a People's Assembly (*Pyeithu Hlutdaw*) were introduced. Political conflict, underground communist movements and ethnic insurgencies remained unresolved, with the Burma Army absorbing a large proportion of the country's budget and resources. By 1987, Burma – a fertile country rich in natural resources and once the world's major exporter of rice – had been reduced to applying to the United Nations for 'least developed nation' status.

The deteriorating economy, rising inflation, two demonetizations in two years and mounting student protest and public disaffection culminated in U Ne Win's resignation as Chairman of the Burma

Introduction

Socialist Programme Party on 23 July 1988. These events triggered mass demonstrations calling for a multi-party system and the end of socialism, and Burma seemed on the brink of change. For several weeks Burma – so long isolated from the world – was in the news as demonstrators took to the streets and for a brief period the Burmese media found freedom of expression. U Ne Win's immediate and short term successors, military hardliner General Sein Lwin (26 July-12 August) and the more moderate civilian, Dr. Maung Maung (19 August-18 September), tried to control the escalating situation – the former by a 'shoot to kill' policy (against unarmed demonstrators and participants in a nationwide general strike on the 8 August 1988), and the latter by some conciliatory measures – but on 18 September 1988 the Burma Army under General Saw Maung staged a military takeover, established rule by the State Law and Order Restoration Council (SLORC), and systematically crushed the pro-democracy movement, causing several thousand deaths and arrests. The country's name was changed to Myanmar, socialism abandoned and some foreign investment encouraged.

SLORC to some extent confounded critics by holding on 27 May 1990 what are generally acknowledged to have been on the day free and fair multi-party elections, but subsequently all of SLORC's actions have aroused intense international opprobrium. Despite severe restrictions on election campaigning and the placing under house arrest of Aung San Suu Kyi (daughter of Burma's national hero, General Aung San, who emerged in this period as an inspirational figure of indomitable courage and ideals), and the detention of other key figures, the main opposition party, the National League for Democracy, won the elections by a huge majority. SLORC's complete failure to honour the election results and to transfer power to a duly elected civilian government, its prevarications on this issue and increasing repression and abuse of human rights, its selling off of the nation's natural resources and devotion of the proceeds largely to the military can hardly inspire optimism about Burma's future. The Burma Army's longstanding conviction that it alone can safeguard the Union of Burma and maintain law and order has since 1962 turned into political and economic dominance of the country by the military. Moreover, this has led its leaders down an increasingly repressive and isolated path, thereby eliminating their chances of effecting national reconciliation and unity and of initiating progressive economic and political programmes for the benefit of all the peoples of Burma.

The Country and its People

1 Let's visit Burma.
Aung San Suu Kyi. London: Burke, 1985. 96p. map.
Despite its title, this is not a guide book but a well-written introduction to Burma for the general reader and for school room use. It covers Burma's geographical setting and natural resources, history, ethnic groups, and Burmese crafts, and is illustrated by colour and black-and-white photographs. Another introductory work with good details of everyday life, customs and beliefs is Saw Myat Yin's *Burma* (Singapore: Times Editions, 1991. 128p. [Cultures of the World]).

2 Essays offered to G. H. Luce by his colleagues and friends in honour of his seventy-fifth birthday.
Edited by Ba Shin, Jean Boisselier, Alexander B. Griswold. Ascona, Switzerland: Artibus Asiae, 1966. 2 vols. bibliog. (Artibus Asiae Supplementum 23).
A collection of forty-two papers by distinguished scholars on aspects of Asian history, religion, literature and the arts, offered to Gordon Luce, foremost scholar of early Burma and author of *Old Burma – early Pagan* (q.v.), of which the most relevant to Burma are, in volume one: 'Etes-vous fâchée, belle-mère? Conte marma' ('Are you angry, mother-in-law? A Marma story'), by Denise Bernot (p. 59-66); 'Relations between Ceylon and Burma in the 11th century AD' by Bokay (p. 93-96); 'A problem in the phonology of Lahu' by Robbins Burling (p. 97-101); 'Les Mons de Dvāravatī' by George Coedès, (p. 112-16); 'The Chinese in Rangoon during the 18th and 19th centuries' by Chen Yi Sein (p. 107-11); 'A folk song collector's letter from the Mon country in Lower Burma' (1941) by Khin Zaw (p. 164-66); 'Contribution à la géographie historique de la Haute Birmanie (Mein, Pong, Kosambi et Kamboja)' by Jean Rispaud (p. 213-24); 'A translation of three shield-dance songs attributed to the Lord of Myinzaing' by Wun (p. 240-41); and, in volume two: 'Buddha images of Tai Yuan types found in Burma' by Ba Shin (p. 1-5); 'The Jatakas in Burma' by Lu Pe Win (p. 94-108); 'The devatā plaques of the Ananda basement' by Harry L. Shorto (p. 156-65); and 'The old city of Pagan' by Thin Kyi (p. 179-88). In addition, there is at the beginning of volume one a poem 'Pagan and Velu' by Wun in Burmese, and translated into English by Khin Zaw (p. viii-ix), and a select bibliography of the

1

writings of Gordon Luce, listing over sixty items, compiled by Ba Shin and Alexander B. Griswold (p. xi-xvi). Ba Shin (1914-70), a distinguished historian and epigraphist, worked closely with Gordon Luce and was the author of *Lokahteikpan: an early Burmese culture in a Pagan temple* (Rangoon: Burma Historical Commission, Ministry of Union Culture, 1962. 198p. map) and other studies.

3 Burma: a country study.

Edited by Frederica M. Bunge, prepared by Foreign Area Studies, The American University. Washington, DC: US Government Printing Office, 1983. 3rd ed. 326p. maps. biblipg. (Area Handbook Series, DA Pam 550-61).

This study updates and replaces the *Area handbook for Burma* (originally published in 1968, and revised in 1971). It is a compact reference work on Burma, providing an exposition and analysis of the country's dominant social, political and economic aspects, with chapters contributed by different researchers, as follows: 'Historical setting' by Donald M. Seekins. 'Society and its environment' by John P. Ferguson; 'The economy' by Stephen B. Wickman: 'Government and politics' by Rinn-Sup Shinn; 'National security' by Melinda W. Cook. An appendix contains fifteen statistical tables based mostly on information from official Burma publications, and there is an extensive bibliography for each chapter.

4 Burma, a profile.

Norma Bixler. London: Pall Mall, 1971. 244p. 4 maps. bibliog.

A descriptive rather than analytical account of Burma in the pre-1970 period, with introductory chapters on Burma's geography and history. The author accompanied her husband on a Ford Foundation library assignment to Burma in the late 1950s and in an earlier book, *Burmese journey* (Yellow Springs, Ohio: Antioch, 1967. 238p.), gives an engaging account of an American family's adjustment to a different culture.

5 A letter from Burma.

Françoise Boudignon. Rangoon: UNICEF, 1984. 98p. map.

This charming description of everyday village life at Pagan is in the form of a sketch book and accompanying narrative sent by the author to her nephews in France.

6 Burma and Japan: basic studies on their cultural and social structure.

Edited by The Burma Research Group. Tokyo: Burma Research Group, Tokyo University of Foreign Studies, 1987. 312p.

A collection of twenty-seven short essays, the majority by Japanese scholars but also some by visiting Burmese scholars, on a variety of subjects including linguistics, literature, religion, history, politics, economics and comparative culture. Intended for non-Japanese language readers these essays give an idea of the range of research and publications on Burma in contemporary Japan. Among the longer essays are 'Socio-political currents in Burmese literature 1910-1940' by Aung San Suu Kyi (p. 65-83); 'On Anti-Fascist writings of Thein Pe Myint' by Midori Minamida (p. 84-101); 'Some aspects of 'modernization' in *Story of Maung Hmaing, the Roselle Seller*' by Keiko Hotta (p. 102-15); 'Nine sects (gaings) of Theravada Buddhism' by Zenno Ikuno (p. 117-34); 'A report on the Taungbyoûn Na' festival' by Tetsuya Hamada (p. 145-60); 'A note on Zambudipa Ok Saung Zambu island in a nutshell' by Than Tun (p. 175-88); 'Some problems in the study of the Burmese legal literature with special reference to the Dhanmatha's (Dhammathats) or the traditional law texts' by Ryuji

Okudaira (p. 199-207); 'U Thuriya's rebellion – the anti-colonial uprising in late 19th century Lower Burma' by Toshikatsu Ito (p. 209-30); and 'A note on the Burmese peasant rebellion, 1930-32 – some features of the forming process of the rebel bands' by Kenji Ino (p. 231-46). *Shiroku* (Kagoshima, Japan: Center for Historical Research, 1968-. annual) contains many articles on Burma (mostly in Japanese but some in English).

7 Special Burma Studies Issue.

Crossroads: An Interdisciplinary Journal of Southeast Asian Studies, vol. 4, no. 1 (Fall 1988). 151p.

This special Burma issue of the scholarly journal *Crossroads* (published twice yearly by the Center for Southeast Asian Studies, Northern Illinois University, DeKalb, Illinois) contains ten papers primarily on religion, originally presented at the inauguration of the Center for Burmese Studies at Northern Illinois University on 29 July 1987, and mostly rewritten for publication. The papers presented are: 'Nats' by U Nu (p. 1-12); 'The path to Buddahood: the spiritual mission and social organization of mysticism in contemporary Burma' by Juliane Schober (p. 13-30); 'Bhikkhuni, Thilashin, Mae-chii: women who renounce the world in Burma, Thailand, and the classical Pali Buddhist texts' by Ingrid Jordt (p. 31-39); 'Transformation of the nats: the humanization process in the depiction of the thirty-seven lords of Burma' by Sarah M. Bekker (p. 40-45); 'Cakravartin: ideology, reason, and manifestation of Siamese and Burmese kings in traditional warfare (1538-1854)' by Sunait Chutintaranond) (p. 46-56); 'When one wheel stops: Theravada Buddhism and the British raj in Upper Burma' by Mark R. Woodward (p. 57-90); 'Observations on the translation and annotation of the royal orders of Burma' by Than Tun (p. 91-99); 'Status of women in family law in Burma and Indonesia' by Aye Kyaw (p. 100-20); 'Contemporary Burmese earthenware' by H. Leedom Lefferts (p. 121-27); 'A survey of selected resources for the study of Burma' by William Tuchrello (p. 128-51).

8 In the shadow of the pagoda: sketches of Burmese life and character.

Edward William Dirom Cuming. London: W. H. Allen, 1893. 362p.

Stories of Burmese life which attempt to portray the scene through both Burmese and British eyes. Subjects covered include the Shwe Dagon pagoda, Karen life, tiger hunting, dacoits and convicts. With illustrations from photographs by P. Klier and Watts & Skeen of Rangoon. Cuming (1862-1942) spent some years in Burma in the rice export business. He also wrote a fictionalized account of village life and dacoits, *With the jungle folk: a sketch of Burmese village life* (London: Osgood, McIlvaine, 1897. 400p.), with illustrations by a Burmese artist.

9 Burma.

Frank Siegfried Vernon Donnison. London: Ernest Benn, 1970. 252p. map. bibliog. (Nations of the Modern World).

A well-written introduction to Burma for the general reader which concentrates on history and political developments (up to the 1960s period). The author's views and convictions have been shaped by his long and distinguished Indian civil service (ICS) career in Burma from 1922 to 1947. When assessing the first years of government by General Ne Win, the author finds no grounds for optimism about Burma's future progress under a military dictatorship.

10 **Essays on Burma.**
Edited by John P. Ferguson. Leiden, The Netherlands: E. J. Brill, 1981. 167p. map. (Contributions to Asian Studies, vol. 16).

A distinctly mixed bag of essays by members of the Burma Studies group based in America, as follows: 'Dr. Ba Maw of Burma' by Edward M. Law-Yone (p. 1-18); 'The concept of Anade: personal, social and political implications' by Sarah M. Bekker (p. 19-37); 'Jambudipa: classical Burma's Camelot' by Michael Aung-Thwin (p. 38-61); 'Masters of the Buddhist occult: the Burmese weikzas' by John P. Ferguson and E. Michael Mendelson (p. 62-80); 'Contemporary Burmese literature' by Thaung (the novelist Aung Bala) (p. 81-101); 'On the vocabulary and semantics of "field" in Theravada Buddhist society' by F. K. Lehman (p. 101-11); 'The Pagan period (1044-1287): a bibliographic note' by Bardwell L. Smith (p. 112-30); 'Our Burma experience of 1935-1938' by John F. Cady (p. 131-65).

11 **Burma.**
Max Ferrars, Bertha Ferrars. London: Sampson, Low, Marston, 1900. 237p.

This rare publication remains in many ways an unsurpassed photographic compendium and introduction to different aspects of Burmese life at the turn of the century. The text is arranged thematically with chapters on childhood, adolescence, manhood, trades, occupations and crafts, ethnic groups, festivals, old age and funeral observances, etc. and is illustrated with 455 black-and-white photographs (mostly small sized but with some full plate). Appendixes to the book include a chronology (to 1885), notes on Burmese measurements, and specimens of Burmese music.

12 **A people at school.**
Harold Fielding Hall. London: Macmillan, 1906. 286p.

Fielding Hall (1859-1917) arrived in Burma before the Third Anglo-Burmese War and entered government service following the British annexation of Upper Burma in 1886. His book is an affectionate, if distinctly paternalistic, description of Burma and the Burmese in the period both before and after the 1886 annexation. As well as his first work, *The soul of a people* (q.v.), Fielding Hall also published (under the name of Fielding) two volumes of oral memories and stories of Mandalay palace life, *Thibaw's queen* (London; New York: Harper & Brothers, 1899. 294p.) and *Palace tales* (London; New York: Harper & Brothers, 1900. 262p.), collected by the author in 'an attempt to rescue from complete oblivion one phase of life in the Palace in the times of the Burmese Kings'. In addition, he wrote a romantic novel featuring a honeymoon in Burma, *Love's legend* (London: Constable, 1914. 325p.).

13 **The soul of a people.**
Harold Fielding Hall. London: Richard Bentley, 1898. 363p.

A sympathetic attempt to understand and portray the Burmese, their religion and its effect upon them. The author's guiding principle was to see things from within rather than without, and to learn about Buddhism from direct observation and conversation. The book was immensely popular and went through several editions and reprints in the decade after its publication. The original edition was published under the name of Fielding, but subsequent editions were published under the name of Fielding Hall. He also wrote two general works on religion and faith, *The hearts of men* (London: Hurst & Blackett, 1904. rev. ed. 312p.) and *The inward light* (London: Macmillan, 1908.

252p.) in which he often gives examples from Burmese Buddhism, considering that the Burmese 'alone of modern people retain the spirit of Buddhism as it was understood'.

14 Burmese personal names.

Gustaaf Houtman. Rangoon: Department of Religious Affairs, 1982. 89p. bibliog.

Anyone new to matters Burmese finds Burmese names and the lack of a family surname confusing. This essay, reproduced directly from the typescript, covers the principles and astrological rules governing the choice of names. It also examines selected Burmese authors' use of names and terms of address to convey the social status of their fictional characters.

15 Perspective of Burma: an Atlantic Monthly supplment.

New York: Intercultural Publications, 1958. 73p. map. bibliog.

This collection of short essays by Burmese writers, scholars and politicians is primarily on aspects of Burmese culture, and also contains biographical details of the contributors. Among the contributions are 'Continuity in Burma: the survival of historical forces' by Kyaw Thet (p. 19-23); 'The women of Burma' by Mya Sein (p. 24-27); 'The concept of neutralism: what lies behind Burma's foreign policy' by James Barrington (p. 28-30); 'Modern Burmese literature: its background in the independence movement' by On Pe (p. 56-60); 'Burma's socialist democracy: some problems of practical politics' by Law Yone (p. 61-66); and, 'Burmese music' by Khin Zaw (p. 67-69). Of most value – on account of the accompanying colour and black-and-white illustrations – are two articles (p. 33-45) on art: 'The early art of Burma' by Thaw Ka and 'Contemporary Burmese art' by Thein Han, while there are also drawings (p. 70-71) by Wun Tha of traditional dances of Burma.

16 Colourful Burma.

Khin Myo Chit. Rangoon: University Press, 1988. 2 vols.

This pot-pourri of articles, reminiscences and stories by a leading Burmese writer, Khin Myo Chit (1915-), has sections on the Buddhist way of life, Burmese customs, language, trees, fruits and vegetables, cuisine (with recipes), women, the performing arts, and also includes eight short stories. It is illustrated by Ba Kyi. Some of these items were included in an earlier collection by Khin Myo Chit, *The Thirteen carat diamond and other stories: a collection of short stories and sketches* (Rangoon: Sarpay Lawka Book House, 1969. 201p.) which contains six short stories and essays on Burmese life and culture.

17 Flowers and festivals round the Burmese year.

Khin Myo Chit. Rangoon: The Author, 1980. 92p.

A description of the festivals and flowers associated with each Burmese month. It also contains (p. 5-16) seasonal poems written by the Burmese court poet, Hpo-thu-daw U Min (1798-1848), translated into English by Tha Noe. Another description of the twelve seasonal festivals of the Burmese lunar calendar, and of *nat* (spirit) festivals, pagoda and other local festivals can be found in Tha Myat, *The twelve festivals of Burma* (Rangoon: Student Press, 1980. 28p. bibliog.). A guide to various Burmese festivals and national holidays, with an account of the traditional ceremonies of *shin-byu* (becoming a Buddhist novice) and ear-boring is given in Phil Scanlon, *Southeast Asia: a cultural study through celebration* (DeKalb, Illinois: Northern Illinois University, Center for Southeast Asian Studies, 1985, p. 112-38).

5

18 **A wonderland of Burmese legends.**
Khin Myo Chit. Bangkok: Tamarind, 1984. 126p. map.

This book provides a brief explanation of what the figures of spirits (*nats*), fabulous beasts and ogres seen in Burmese temples and art represent, and narrates the legends and stories associated with Burmese cities, temples, images and shrines; with colour illustrations by Paw Oo Thet, one of Burma's best known contemporary artists.

19 **Historical and cultural dictionary of Burma.**
Joel M. Maring, Ester G. Maring. Metuchen, New Jersey: Scarecrow, 1973. 290p. bibliog. (Historical and Cultural Dictionaries of Asia, no. 4).

An alphabetical listing of approximately 1,600 entries pertaining to Burmese history, culture, physical geography, natural history, economics, politics and demography, with the primary focus on culture and history.

20 **Burmese family.**
Mi Mi Khaing. Bombay, India; Calcutta, India: Longmans, Green, 1946. 140p.; Bombay: Orient Longmans, 1956; Bloomington, Indiana: Indiana University Press, 1962; New York: AMS, 1979. 200p.

Written in wartime exile in India in 1945, this is a nostalgic portrayal of a Burmese childhood in the 1920s and 1930s. Although the privileged world of a civil service family in colonial Burma has long disappeared, the author's evocation of everyday family life makes this book a classic.

21 **The world of Burmese women.**
Mi Mi Khaing. London: Zed, 1984; Singapore: Times Books International, 1986. 198p. bibliog.

This wide-ranging study of women in Burmese society covers the kinship system, family law and practices, women at home and at work, women in religion, and their education, training and social problems. The book is full of insights, anecdotes, case histories and examples drawn from the author's own research, experiences and family circle. Mi Mi Khaing (1916-90), a much respected Burmese writer, is best known for her first book, *Burmese family* (q.v.). Also relevant is a case study of the role of Burmese women in socioeconomic life, based on data collected in 1980-81 from a village in Lower Burma, by Mya Than, 'The role of women in rural Burma: a case study', *Sojourn: Social Issues in Southeast Asia*, vol. 1, no. 1 (Feb. 1986), p. 97-108.

22 **Cultural heritage of Burma.**
Krishna Murari. New Delhi: Inter-India Publications, 1985. 312p. map. bibliog.

Compiled from secondary sources, this study presents a synthesis of Burma's history, religion, art and architecture.

23 **Burma under British rule and before.**
John Nisbet.   Westminster, England: Archibald Constable, 1901.
2 vols. maps.
The author, a former conservator of forests with twenty-five years' service in Burma, aimed to provide the first comprehensive book on Burma since it came entirely under British rule in 1886. With chapters on pre-British Burma, Burmese Buddhism, customs, festivals, science, language and literature, and an emphasis on Burma's 'material progress' in chapters on the British administration, trade, railways and forestry. Nisbet incorporates much first-hand observation – for example, of tattooing, boat races, chess playing – and includes a plan of the Mandalay palace buildings, and extracts from Burmese literature and law.

24 **Burmese vignettes.**
C. Harcourt Robertson.   London: Luzac, 1949. 146p.
First published in 1930 (London: W. Thacker) as a reprint of articles that originally appeared in the *Madras Mail*, this book presents twenty-four sketches of Burmese life and characters (a monk, cigar roller, magistrate, dacoit, astrologer, lacquer maker, silk weaver, etc.). With pen-and-ink illustrations by the author, and a brief glossary at the end of each chapter.

25 **A description of the Burmese empire, compiled chiefly from Burmese documents.**
Father Vincentius Sangermano, translated from the Italian and Latin by William Tandy, with a preface and note by John Jardine.   London: Susil Gupta, 1966. 5th ed. 311p. map.
Sangermano was an Italian Barnabite missionary in Burma from 1783 to 1808. His account of Burma was compiled partly during his residence there and partly after his return to Italy, where he died in 1819. His manuscript was translated into English and first published in Rome in 1833 (for the Oriental Translation Fund of Great Britain and Ireland). Sangermano's account has chapters on Burmese cosmography, history, government, religion, literature, customs, and law. The value of his work is that much of it is based on first-hand observation and on Burmese sources – Sangermano also provides the first Western translation of a Burmese law code. His work was much used and quoted by 19th-century British officials and retains its value to this day as a careful observation of late 18th-century Burma. The judicial commissioner of British Burma, John Jardine, had the work reprinted in 1885 (by the Government Press, Rangoon) and brought out a new edition in 1893. The 1893 edition (published by Archibald Constable in Westminster) has a twenty-nine-page introduction, five appendixes and lengthy footnotes, all compiled by Jardine. It was published under the title, *The Burmese empire a hundred years ago, as described by Father Sangermano*, and it is from this edition that the 1966 reprint was made. There is also an Indian reprint (New Delhi: BR Publishing, 1984) of the 1893 edition under the title, *The Burmese empire a hundred years ago.*

26 **Burma: a handbook of practical information.**
James George Scott. London: Daniel O'Connor, 1921. 3rd rev. ed.
536p. map. bibliog.

An illustrated general guide – and now a period piece – to Burma (described on the first page as 'a sort of recess, a blind alley, a back reach') with chapters on the country and its peoples, government, industries, archaeology, arts and music, religion, language and literature, and a section 'hints to new residents' (which includes the intruiging advice 'Do not drink lemon squashes, even when they are offered you by your dentist'). With lists of the districts and divisions of Burma and the Shan States, and of flora and fauna, minerals and gems in the appendixes. Scott's first and best work on Burma, published under the pseudonym 'Shway Yoe', was *The Burman, his life and notions* (q.v.). Among his many other works on Burma are *Burma as it was, as it is, and as it will be* (London: George Redway, 1886. 184p.) – an imperialistic general sketch of 'our new province' – and a descriptive, rather than analytical, history, *Burma from the earliest times to the present day* (London: T. Fisher Unwin, 1924. 372p.). Details of Scott's life and career in Burma can be found in G. E. Mitton, *Scott of the Shan hills* (q.v.).

27 **The Burman, his life and notions.**
James George Scott (Shway Yoe). London: Macmillan, 1882. 2 vols;
New York: W. W. Norton, 1963; Whiting Bay, Isle of Arran: Kiscadale
Publications, 1989. 609p.

'Shway Yoe' was the pseudonym under which Sir James George Scott (1851-1935) who spent nearly thirty years in Burma published his first and most famous work on Burma. The 1882 edition was reissued in 1896 and 1910; the 1963 paperback reprint contains an introduction by John K. Musgrave which gives biographical details of the author and an appreciation of his work; while the 1989 hardback reprint has a new foreword by John Falconer who draws attention to revisions made in the 1910 edition and sets Scott's work in context. The Burma Scott so evocatively describes is Burma as he first experienced it in the late 1870s, but his book remains a classic which still has relevance today for understanding the Burmese way of life and culture. In the book's sixty-four short chapters can be found details on such matters as the Burmese system of name giving according to the day of the week upon which one is born, horoscopes, Buddhist ceremonies, marriage and family life, *nats* and spirit worship, festival and games, death and funeral rites.

28 **Burma: a socialist nation of Southeast Asia.**
David I. Steinberg. Boulder, Colorado: Westview, 1982. 150p. 4 maps.
bibliog. (Westview Profiles/Nations of Contemporary Asia).

A good general introduction to modern Burma. Steinberg describes the country's diverse ethnic and geographical characteristics, and surveys Burmese history, emphasizing continuing themes, and examining the effects of the colonial period on the structures of post-independence Burma, and the causes of the military coup of 1962. His analysis of Ne Win's government is current through to 1981.

29 **Burmese sketches.**
Taw Sein Ko. Rangoon: British Burma Press, 1913, 1920. 2 vols.

A collection of over 300 pieces, described by the author as 'fugitive essays', originally published in various (now defunct) journals from 1883-1919 by Taw Sein Ko (1864-1930) whose long and distinguished service to the government of Burma included appointments as assistant secretary, examiner in Chinese, and superintendent of the Archaeological Survey. Among the subjects covered in his essays are ethnology, philology, archaeology, biography, folklore, fiction, religion, education, Chinese matters, and numismatics. Also included are some details of Taw Sein Ko's own life and career. Taw Sein Ko's major publication was the compilation in Burmese of *Selections from the records of the Hlutdaw* (Rangoon: Government Printing, 1901, 1909. 2 vols. Latest reprint, edited by Aung Thein: Rangoon, 1977).

30 **The Union of Burma: a study of the first years of independence.**
Hugh Tinker. London: Oxford University Press, issued under the auspices of the Royal Institute of International Affairs, 1967. 4th rev. ed. 423p. maps. bibliog.

First published in 1957, this study is primarily devoted to the turbulent period of the Karen uprising and civil war in newly independent Burma, with a good survey of the country's political, military, economic, and religious spheres. It has been updated by a brief account of the first years of Ne Win's rule and concludes that the military government is failing to restore peace and order or to realize its objectives. Tinker assesses Nu's premiership favourably, seeing it as an attempt 'to create a genuinely democratic community'.

31 **We the Burmese: voices from Burma.**
Edited by Helen G. Trager. New York: Frederick A. Praeger, 1969. 297p.

A collection of Burmese views of Burma and the Burmese way of life presented in various forms – short stories, essays, biographies, poetry, folk tales, speeches, cartoons, comics and photos, news items and editorials – and intended to serve as an introduction to most aspects of (pre-1970) Burmese society and culture.

Gazetteer of Upper Burma and the Shan States.
See item no. 111.

British Burma gazetteer.
See item no. 112.

An account of an embassy to the kingdom of Ava: sent by the Governor-General of India in the year 1795.
See item no. 179.

Burma and the Japanese invader.
See item no. 184.

Journal of an embassy from the Governor-General of India to the court of Ava in the year 1827: with an appendix containing a description of fossil remains by Professor Buckland and Mr. Clift.
See item no. 185.

Twentieth century impressions of Burma: its history, people, commerce, industries and resources.
See item no. 214.

A narrative of the mission to the court of Ava in 1855: together with the journal of Arthur Phayre envoy. . .
See item no. 215.

Forgotten land: a rediscovery of Burma.
See item no. 328.

Ethnic groups of mainland Southeast Asia.
See item no. 407.

Burma, nationalism and ideology: an analysis of society, culture and politics.
See item no. 550.

The state in Burma.
See item no. 562.

Travellers' Accounts and Guidebooks

Pre-20th century travellers

32 Narrative of an official visit to the king of Burmah, in March 1875, from notes made at the time.
C. H. E. Adamson.   Newcastle upon Tyne, England: J. Bell, 1878. 26p.

This account belongs to a tense period in Anglo-Burmese relations when the author, later the assistant commissioner of British Burma, was sent to Mandalay to convey a letter announcing a forthcoming diplomatic mission by Sir Douglas Forsythe. Adamson was accompanied for part of the trip by Ney Elias who joined Horace Browne's and John Anderson's Burma–Yunnan expedition – for an account see John Anderson, *Mandalay to Momien* [sic] (q.v.). Elias (1844-97) wrote an *Introductory sketch of the history of the Shans in Upper Burmah and Western Yunnan* (Calcutta, India: Foreign Dept. Press, 1876. 63p.) and his links with Burma are related in the biography by Gerald Morgan, *Ney Elias: explorer and envoy extraordinary in high Asia* (London: George Allen & Unwin, 1971. 194p. 7 maps. bibliog.). Adamson later published *A short account of an expedition to the jade mines in Upper Burma, in 1887-1888* (Newcastle upon Tyne, England: J. Bell, 1889. 65p. map.).

33 Mandalay to Momien [sic]: a narrative of the two expeditions to Western China of 1868 and 1875 under Colonel Edward B. Sladen and Colonel Horace Browne.
John Anderson.   London: Macmillan, 1876. 479p. 3 maps.

An account of Britain's last attempts during Burmese rule of Upper Burma to explore an overland trade route to China via Bhamo, with descriptions of the Kachins, Shans and Chinese Shans, and route maps. A brief account is given of the murder in February 1875 of Augustus Margary who was conducting a counterpart survey of the route from Shanghai to Bhamo. Anderson published a separate detailed report on Colonel Sladen's 1868 expedition entitled *A report on the expedition to Western Yunan via Bhamo* (Calcutta, India: Office of the Superintendent of Government Printing,

1871. 458p. 2 maps) which included historical background (drawn from previous British reports) and descriptions of the geology and other physical features of the country, the Irrawaddy and its sources, the Shans, Kachins and other races to the east of Bhamo, with routes and vocabularies of the hill tribes in the appendixes. Edward Bosc Sladen (1827-90), British Political Resident at Mandalay, 1864-68, and Chief Political Officer, British Expeditionary Forces in 1885, published an *Official narrative of the expedition to explore trade routes to China via Bhamo* Calcutta, India: Government Printing, 1870) and an article, 'Expedition from Burma, via the Irrawaddy and Bhamo, to South Western China', *Royal Geographical Society Journal*, vol. 41 (1871), p. 257-81. John Anderson (1833-1900), who became superintendent of the Indian Museum in Calcutta in 1866, also published a separate scientific report of his Yunnan expeditions, *Anatomical and zoological researches: comprising an account of the two expeditions to western Yunnan in 1868 and 1875* (London: Bernard Quaritch, 1878. 2 vols.).

34 **Our viceregal life in India: selections from my journal 1884-1888.**
Hariot Georgina Blackwood, Marchioness of Dufferin and Ava.
London: John Murray, 1890. 408p. map.

The author, wife of Frederick Temple Blackwood, Lord Dufferin (1826-1902) who as governor-general of India presided over the Third Anglo-Burmese War and decided upon the 'annexation pure and simple' of Upper Burma on 1 January 1886, accompanied Lord Dufferin on a visit to Burma in February 1886. One chapter (p. 173-205) gives impressions of Upper Burma and describes Mandalay palace – 'a marvellous place it is . . . golden roofs beautifully carved, and more gold and glass palings, acres of gilt roofing and shining pinnacles, and forests of teak pillars all gold!' – and also gives gossip of life at the Burmese court. Their visit to Burma and the Third Anglo-Burmese War are also covered in the standard biography of Lord Dufferin by Alfred Lyall, *The life of the Marquis of Dufferin and Ava* (London: John Murray, 1905. 2 vols.).

35 **Bhamo expedition: report on the practicability of re-opening the trade route between Burmah and Western China.**
Alexander Bowers. Rangoon: American Mission Press, 1869. 2 maps.

This account by a member of Sladen's 1868 expedition – concerning which see John Anderson, *Mandalay to Momien* [*sic*] (q.v.) – emphasizes commercial matters and gives current prices of goods at Momien and in the Shan States during the progress of the expedition. An important feature of the book is the inclusion of Captain Bowers' sketches – reproduced in eighty-nine pages of lithographs – of local scenes and people and, above all, of ornamental motifs copied from monasteries and temples.

36 **A narrative of sport and travel in Burmah, Siam and the Malay peninsula.**
John Bradley. London: Samuel Tinsley, 1876. 338p.

The author claims to belong to the class of travellers who 'travel principally for the gratification of their love of adventure and change of scenery', but his account is principally of shooting his way around Burma (p. 1-89) in 1869, with everything from elephants and tigers to birds forming the 'sport'. Bradley survived being mauled by a tiger in Burma.

37   **The grand peregrination: being the life and adventures of Fernão Mendes Pinto.**
Maurice Collis.   London: Faber & Faber, 1949. 313p. map. bibliog.
Collis bases his narrative on the text of Pinto's *Peregrinaçao* (Lisbon: Pedro Crasbeeck, 1614) and scholarly commentaries to produce a clear and readable account of Pinto's 16th-century travels. Collis considers Pinto's literary and historical work 'a masterpiece which enlarges, by transcending, truth' and comments on Pinto's Burma narrative (p. 166-228): 'That he should have been able to grasp its politics so well, describe in his objective manner, as in a drama, its unification under Tabin Shwe-ti and Bayin Naung, and lay bare so clearly the Talaing question, the most abiding in Burmese history, is truly extraordinary when one remembers that at the time he composed the *Peregrination* nothing had been published about the country in a European language'.

38   **The land of the great image: being experiences of Friar Manrique in Araken.**
Maurice Collis.   London: Faber & Faber, 1953. 317p. map.
Sebastien Manrique was a Portuguese Augustinian missionary who spent much of the period 1629-37 in Arakan, and also visited the Philippines, China and India. His account of his travels was originally written in Spanish and published in 1649 and 1653. Collis' retelling of Manrique's travels is enhanced by his own knowledge of Arakan and by his considerable gift for historical narrative. Manrique's vivid account of the Arakanese court, the coronation of King Thirithudhamma in 1635 and of the intrigues of Portuguese adventurers can be found on p. 127-272. Collis adds from Arakanese sources supplementary historical details and goes on to describe how Manrique survived years of adventure in the east only to be murdered in London. This was originally published in 1946 (London: Faber & Faber. 259p.). Collis based his account on the Hakluyt Society edition, *Travels of Fray Sebastien Manrique 1629-1643: a translation of the Itinerario de las Missiones Orientales with introduction and notes by C. Eckford Luard, assisted by Father F. Hosten* (Oxford: Hakluyt Society, 1927. 2 vols. maps.), volume one of which contains Manrique's 'Journey to Arakan', prefaced by an introduction to his life and work, with a chronology and map of Manrique's travels.

39   **Marco Polo.**
Maurice Collis.   London: Faber & Faber, 1950. 190p.
This popular biography and retelling of the travels of the celebrated 13th-century Venetian, Marco Polo, includes Polo's description of the battle between the Burmese war elephants and the Chinese (p. 99-114) and of the city of Pagan. There is also an earlier fully annotated translation by Henry Yule, author of *A narrative of the mission to the court of Ava in 1855* (q.v.), entitled *The book of Ser [sic] Marco Polo, the Venetian, concerning the kingdom and marvels of the East* (London: John Murray, 1871. 2 vols. maps.).

40 **Report on the railway connexion of Burmah and China: with account of exploration-survey.**
Archibald Ross Colquhoun, Holt S. Hallett.   London: Allen, Scott, 1888. 239p. 15 maps.

This publication contains more detailed geographical data than is to be found in Colquhoun's earlier publications *Across Chryse* and *Amongst the Shans* (q.v.). It is in several parts: the first (p. 1-46), by Colquhoun, summarizes attempts from the 1820s to open up communications between Burma and China, and past explorations executed and routes proposed. The second part (p. 47-220) consists of Hallett's detailed and most readable account of his 1884 expedition through southeastern Burma to Chieng Mai and Bangkok. Hallett does not confine himself to geographical matters but is a mine of information on many aspects of daily life with sketches of Shan weapons, utensils, fishing implements, houses, etc. Hallett was accompanied by the missionary and Shan language scholar, Josiah Nelson Cushing and appendixes to the book (p. 221-39) give vocabularies collected from different tribal groups en route. The folding maps incorporate detailed survey data of the area and routes.

41 **Ralph Fitch, Elizabethan in the Indies.**
Michael Edwardes.   London: Faber & Faber, 1972. 184p.

This account of Fitch's travels in the east from 1583 to 1591 contains plentiful quotations from Fitch's own account of his voyages and from other contemporary sources (printed in the not very accessible *Hakluytus posthumus or Purchas his pilgrims*, edited by Samuel Purchas in the 17th century and reprinted in Glasgow, 1905). Fitch was the first Englishman to visit Burma (in 1586-88) and his travels and observations are given in a chapter entlted 'Lord of the White Elephant' (p. 96-124). Fitch's description of the Shwe dagon – '. . . of a wonderfull bignesse, and all gilded from the foot to the toppe. It is the fairest place, as I suppose, that is in the world' – is much quoted. For a guide to Fitch and other 16th-century travellers in Burma, see Donald F. Lach, *Southeast Asia in the eyes of Europe* (q.v.).

42 **Among pagodas and fair ladies: an account of a tour through Burma.**
Gwendolen Trench Gascoigne.   London: A. D. Innes, 1896. 312p.

These sketches of a 'land of rubies and pearls and gold – the home of a merry, kindly, laughing people . . .' include photographs and a description of Mandalay palace.

43 **Burma after the conquest.**
Grattan Geary.   London: Sampson Low, Marston, Searle, & Rivington, 1886. 345p.

The author, editor of the *Bombay Gazette*, presents a keenly observed description of Upper Burma at the time of its annexation by the British in 1885-86 and, after debating the pros and cons of annexation, comes down in favour of British rule, concluding: 'It will be the fault of our citizens and our administrators if they do not avail themselves of the opportunity to benefit Burma and the Empire alike, and unite them in the bonds of a growing civilization'.

44 **The river of golden sand: the narrative of a journey through China and Eastern Tibet to Burmah.**
William John Gill, introduction by Henry Yule. London: John Murray, 1880; Farnborough, England: Gregg International, 1969. 2 vols. 10 maps.

This account of a survey of river and land routes undertaken in 1876-77 by Captain Gill (1843-82) of the Royal Engineers ends in Bhamo in Upper Burma, the end-point of Chinese overland trade routes. With detailed route maps and itineraries.

45 **Our trip to Burmah: with notes on that country.**
Charles Alexander Gordon. London: Baillière, Tindall & Cox, 1877. 265p. maps.

The author, an army surgeon-general, accompanied the commander-in-chief of the Madras Army on a trip to Burma from 23 December 1874 to 23 February 1875. The book consists of his informative Burma travel diary, and a supplementary section of extensive notes on aspects of Burma (history, customs, medical practices, etc.) drawn from articles and reports by fellow British officers and travellers. A feature of this work is its illustrations which consist of contemporary sketches and woodcuts of Burmese games and scenes, twelve fine, mounted sepia photographs (from studios of Messrs. Jackson, Shepherd & Bourne, and of Nicholas & Company) and six chromo-lithographs of works by a Burmese artist.

46 **Rough pencillings of a rough trip to Rangoon.**
[Colesworthy Grant]. Calcutta, India: Thacker, Spink; London: W. Thacker, 1853. 49p. map.

Published anonymously, this work comprises the journal and lithographed sketches made by the artist Colesworthy Grant (1813-80) on a visit to Rangoon, with footnotes updating events to the time of the Second Anglo-Burmese War (1852). Its interest lies in his description of meetings with various British and Armenian residents of Burma and his drawings of their houses and other contemporary scenes (temples, boats, the grave of the wife of the first American Baptist missionary to the country, Mrs. Ann Judson, at Amherst, etc.). Also reproduced is a sketch map of old Rangoon. Grant later accompanied Sir Arthur Phayre's mission to Upper Burma as official artist and some of his paintings are reproduced in Henry Yule, *A narrative of the mission to the court of Ava in 1855* (q.v.).

47 **Jahangir and the Jesuits: with an account of the travels of Benedict Goes and the mission to Pegu from the Relations of Father Fernão Guerreiro, S.J.**
Fernão Guerreiro, translated by C. H. Payne, edited by E. Denison Ross, Eileen Power. London: George Routledge, 1930. 287p. maps. (The Broadway Travellers).

This book consists of three narratives extracted from Fernão Guerreiro's *Relations*, a history of the missionary undertakings of the Society of Jesus in Asia and Africa during the first nine years of the 17th century (and originally published in Portugal between 1603 and 1611). Part three (p. 185-276) contains Guerreiro's account of the mission of Benedict de Goes (d. 1608) to Pegu, supplemented by copious editorial notes and by an account of Antonio Bocarro for the period 1609-13. The narrative provides a graphic contemporary account of the rise and fall of the Portuguese adventurer, Philippe de Brito, who conquered and ruled the port of Syriam from 1600 to 1613 until besieged and put to death by the Burmese king.

48   **A thousand miles on an elephant in the Shan States.**
Holt S. Hallett.   Edinburgh, London: William Blackwood & Sons, 1890; Bangkok: White Lotus, 1988. 484p. maps.

A careful compilation narrating Hallett's travels in Thailand and the Shan States in 1876 to survey possible railway routes from Burma. He was accompanied by two American missionaries, Rev. Dr. Josiah Nelson Cushing and Rev. Dr. Daniel McGilvary, and dedicated his work to 'the American missionaries in Burmah, Siam and the Shan States'. Hallett was a lively observer of the local topography, people, trade and customs, and recorded his impressions not only in words but in detailed illustrations that are included in this book, together with route maps. The 1988 reprint has an added twelve-page preface by Virginia M. Di Crocco. Another account by Hallett of a further survey trip is contained in Archibald Ross Colquhoun and Holt S. Hallett, *Report on the railway connexion of Burmah and China* (q.v.).

49   **Picturesque Burma.**
Alice M. Hart (Mrs. Ernest Hart).   London: J. M. Dent, 1897. 400p. maps. bibliog.

A well-observed account of a visit to Burma in 1895 with over a 100 illustrations including sketches by the author, ten photogravures and excellent photos by Beato and by Johannes of Mandalay and by Bourne & Shepherd of Calcutta.

50   **A concise account of the kingdom of Pegu, its climate, produce, trade and government; the manners and customs of its inhabitants, interspersed with remarks moral and political.**
William Hunter.   Calcutta, India: John Hay, 1785; London: J. Sewell, Cornhill, J. Debritt, 1789. 110p.

The author, an army surgeon in the service of the East India Company, spent from August to September 1782 in Burma after his ship was dismasted in a storm and forced to put into Rangoon for a refit. He diligently set about collecting information on Burma with the aim of arousing the East India Company's interest in the trade of Pegu (Lower Burma). His account is not restricted to economic matters and contains astute observations on all aspects of the kingdom. The Burmese, commented Hunter, 'rather chuse to resign the advantage they might derive from an extensive commerce, than endanger their existence as an independent people'. A description of Hunter's work with extensive quotations from it can be found in the article by Yi Yi, 'A rare and little known work on Burma', *Naing-ngan Thamaing Thu-tei-thana Sa-Zaung = Researches in Burmese History*, no. 5 (1985), p. 117-49.

51   **Southeast Asia in the eyes of Europe: the sixteenth century.**
Donald F. Lach.   Chicago; London: University of Chicago Press Phoenix Books, 1968. [157p.].

A reprint, retaining the original pagination, of chapter seven on 'Southeast Asia' of volume one (entitled 'The century of discovery'), book two of Lach's magisterial five-part study *Asia in the making of Europe* (Chicago; London: University of Chicago

Press, 1965-77). It depicts, on the basis of extant printed sources, what Europeans of the 16th century reported about Southeast Asia. After an introductory review of the sources, there are separate country sections with Burma covered on p. 539-59. Lach describes Portuguese and other contacts with Burma and draws on ten substantial accounts published between 1510 and 1599 by Varthema, Pires, Barbosa, Castanheda, Barros, Fedrici, Maffei, Balbi, Fitch, and Linschoten. The full bibliographical references for these works are not provided in this paperback reprint, and for these the bibliography in the original edition would need to be consulted. While references to Burma in the rest of Lach's work are relatively scarce the whole is worth consulting for its comprehensive survey of the impact of the discovery of Asia on the development of the arts, institutions, literatures, technology and ideas of Europe.

52 **Travels in the Burman empire.**
Howard Malcom. Edinburgh: William & Robert Chambers, 1840. 82p. map.

The author who was 'engaged in the philanthropic object of exploring new fields of missionary enterprise' (for the American Baptist Mission) visited Burma from February to November 1836. The first part of his account records, in diary form, his visits to Amherst, Moulmein, Rangoon, Ava and Arakan; the second part contains 'digested notes' on all aspects of the country. Malcom was a diligent and accurate observer who generally took care to record only what he had himself observed or could verify. His account is illustrated with wood engravings made from his own sketches. It was originally published as the first section of the author's *Travels in South-Eastern Asia* (Boston, Massachusetts: Gould, Kendall & Lincoln, 1839).

53 **The silken East: a record of life and travel in Burma.**
Vincent Clarence Scott O'Connor. London: Hutchinson, 1904. 2 vols. map.

The author lived and travelled in Burma in the 1890s and writes with sentimental affection of his travels there and its people. Well-illustrated with approximately 380 black-and-white photographs (by Klier, Beato, and others), and 20 colour plates of paintings by J. R. Middleton, Mrs. Otway Wheeler Cuffe and Saya Chone.

54 **Report on the eastern frontier of British India: with a supplement on the British political relations with Ava.**
Robert Boileau Pemberton, supplement by George Thomas Bayfield. Calcutta, India: Baptist Mission Press, 1835. 261p. [+97p.]; Gauhati, India: Government of Assam, Department of Historical and Antiquarian Studies, 1966. 269p. [+147p.].

Pemberton (1798-1840) in 1830 explored military and commercial routes from India to Upper Burma, crossing the mountains from Manipur by the Akui route to Kindat and making his way down the Chindwin to Ava. He draws on this experience in his detailed account of the geography, ethnology and history of India's eastern borders with Arakan, Manipur, Assam and Cachar. Statistical information is given in nineteen supplementary tables. See also the article by D. G. E. Hall, 'Notes on R. B. Pemberton's journey from Munipoor to Ava, and from thence across the Yoma mountains to Arracan (14 Jul. – 1 Oct. 1830)', *Journal of the Burma Research Society*, vol. 43, no. 2 (Dec. 1960), p. 1-96. Pemberton's work is published with a supplement entitled *Historical review of the political relations between the British government in India and the empire of Ava*, compiled by George Thomas Bayfield (1806-40), an assistant-surgeon who accompanied Henry Burney on his posting as British Resident at Ava. Bayfield's account had some influence and, unlike Burney, he was contemptuous of the Burmese. For a critique of Bayfield's writing – described as 'a polemical pamphlet aimed at exposing Burmese perfidy' – see D. G. E. Hall's 'British writers of Burmese history from Dalrymple to Bayfield', in *Historians of South-East Asia* (q.v.), edited by D. G. E. Hall, p. 255-66.

55 **The travels of Mendes Pinto.**
Fernão Mendes Pinto, edited and translated by Rebecca D. Catz.
Chicago, Illinois; London: University of Chicago Press, 1989. 663p. map. bibliog.

The first complete English translation and critically annotated edition of the *Peregrinaçao* (Travels) of Fernão Mendes Pinto (1510?-83), first published in Lisbon in 1614. Pinto's work, which describes his travels in Asia between 1537 and 1558 is, in the words of his translator, 'purportedly autobiographical' and a 'corrosive satire' in which Pinto 'took the essence of history and extracted from it a moral lesson urgent in his own time and still valid today'. Pinto's adventures in Burma form some of the most dramatic episodes in the book. He describes the Burmese siege of Martaban in 1545, the betrayal of its king by Portuguese mercenaries and the cruel executions and sack of the city that followed (p. 310-36); also the Burmese siege of Prome and Sandoway (p. 378-80), and the Burmese invasion of Thailand and siege of Ayutthaya in 1548 (p. 411-55). An appreciation and retelling of Pinto's passages on Burma can be found in Maurice Collis, *The grand peregrination* (q.v.).

56 **The land of the white elephant: sights and scenes in south-eastern Asia, a personal narrative of travel and adventure in Farther India embracing the countries of Burma, Siam, Cambodia, and Cochin-China (1871-2).**
Frank Vincent. London: Sampson, Low, Marston, Low & Searle, 1873; New York: Harper & Brothers, 1874. 316p.; Singapore; Oxford; New York: Oxford University Press in association with The Siam Society, Bangkok, 1988. 316p. map. (Oxford in Asia Hardback Reprints).

This record of an American's travels in Southeast Asia includes a section on Burma (p. 1-87) with details of the author's audience with King Mindon who invited him to enter his service (Vincent's comment on which was: 'perhaps he wished Americans to settle in Burma as a sort of political offset to the English'). The reprint edition has an introduction by William L. Bradley giving details of the life and travels of Vincent (1848-1916), and has been slightly retitled *The land of the white elephant: sights and scenes in South-East Asia 1871-1872*.

57 **Journal of a voyage up the Irrawaddy to Mandalay and Bhamo.**
J. Talboys Wheeler. Rangoon: J. W. Baynes; London: Trubner, 1871. 102p.

As secretary to Albert Fytche, chief commissioner of British Burma, Wheeler made a 1,000 mile trip up the Irrawaddy from 6 November to 19 December 1870. He gives a portrait of the Burmese ministers and of King Mindon with whom he had an audience as well as of various Europeans at Mandalay including the Italian priest Father Abbona and the Rev. Marks, whose school he visited.

58 **Through Burma to western China: being notes of a journey in 1863 to
   establish the practicability of a trade-route between the Irawaddi and the
   Yang-tse-kiang.**
   Clement Williams.   Edinburgh, London: William Blackwood & Sons,
   1868. 213p. 2 maps.
   The author, an assistant surgeon in the 68th Light Infantry and the first British political
   agent at Mandalay (whose medical skills found favour with the Burmese court), was
   concerned to find a practical trade route between Burma and China and to point out
   the impracticability of railway route proposals. His diary of the journey to test a route
   is given on p. 47-174 and covers the period from January to April 1863, describing his
   journey up the Irrawaddy from Mandalay to Bhamo, his residence at Bhamo,
   explorations and return to Mandalay. He gives much information on life at Bhamo,
   particularly on the Chinese, Shans and Kachins, Burmese officials, and Burmese
   dramatic performances with an outline of two plays. The volume is illustrated with
   engravings from his own drawings and photographs. The appendixes contain extracts
   from published articles on routes to western China, and outlines of three further plays
   witnessed by Dr. Williams (p. 205-13).

59 **Sunny days in Burma.**
   A. W. Wills.   Birmingham, England: Midland Counties Herald Press,
   1905. 200p. 2 maps.
   This account of a visit to Burma in 1899-1900 is handsomely illustrated with a hundred
   superb black-and-white photographs by the author, including many of Toungoo taken
   while visiting relatives and several of Mandalay. Among the subjects photographed are
   pottery production, Burmese musicians, woodcarving, a Buddhist initiation, temples,
   monasteries and houses.

60 **Eighteen hundred miles on a Burmese tat: through Burmah, Siam, and
   the Eastern Shan States.**
   George John Younghusband.   London: W. H. Allen, 1888. 162p. map.
   This account of a six-month journey on horseback from Moulmein to Kengtung and
   Bangkok via Chiang Mai in 1887 has some information on the Shans and Karens and is
   illustrated with the author's poor sketches.

**The Ficus Elastica in Burma proper or a narrative of my journey in search of
it: a descriptive account of its habits of growth and the process followed by the
Kakhyens in the preparation of caoutchoue.**
See item no. 131.

19

20th-century travellers

61 Invitation to an Eastern feast.
Austin Coates. London: Hutchinson, 1953. 270p.

This travelogue includes a chapter (p. 154-93) on two visits to Burma in the days when foreigners could travel without restrictions and stay in Burmese homes; with observations on the Karen and other insurrections in the period 1948-50. Coates' *Personal and Oriental* (New York: Harper & Brothers, 1957. 260p.) contains an account of a further visit to Burma (p. 157-90).

62 Lords of the sunset: a tour in the Shan States.
Maurice Collis. London: Faber& Faber, 1938. 326p. map.

Collis wanted to write about the Shan States because they 'are in the imperial attic and I want to bring them into the drawing-room'. His account concentrates on the eccentricities and charm of the Shan *sawbwa* (hereditary rulers) and their consorts, and portrays the Shan States on the threshold of modernization and change (with no mention of the opium, war lords or insurgency that have come to be associated with the Shan States in the post-Second World war period).

63 Into the east: notes on Burma and Malaya.
Richard Henry Parnell Curle, preface by Joseph Conrad. London: Macmillan, 1923. 224p.

This travelogue by an inveterate traveller and writer on Joseph Conrad and his works, includes an account of five months' travel in Burma (p. 22-118). Notable for a particularly unappreciative description of the Shwe Dagon.

64 Peacocks and pagodas.
Paul Edmonds. London: George Routledge, 1924. 282p.

The author was inspired to visit Burma by reading H. Fielding Hall's *The soul of a people* (q.v.) and has produced a happy, anecdotal travelogue of his experiences there in 1922-23; with forty-four block print illustrations.

65 A Burmese enchantment.
Colin Metcalf Dallas Enriquez. Calcutta, India: Thacker, Spink, 1916. 319p. map.

The author, who also wrote under the pen name 'Theophilus', explains his purpose as follows: 'having fallen under a Burmese enchantment, I want to perpetuate the influence of it'. He gives entertaining accounts of life in Upper Burma and of travels in the frontier districts. He pays particular attention to Buddhist matters and describes and illustrates several Burmese temples, and gives an account of the legend of the *chinthei* (mythical lion) figures that guard them. Enriquez (b. 1884) published further books giving his impressions of different regions and peoples of Burma, among them: *A Burmese loneliness: a tale of travel in Burma, the Southern Shan States and Keng Tung* (Calcutta, India: Thacker, Spink, 1918. 283p. map.), *A Burmese wonderland: a tale of travel in Lower and Upper Burma* (Calcutta, India: Thacker, Spink, 1922. 261p. map.) and *A Burmese arcady* (q.v.).

66 **Burma painted and described.**
Robert Talbot Kelly. London: Charles Black, 1905. 261p. map.
Impressions of seven months' extensive travel in Burma in 1904 with reproductions of seventy-five of the author's watercolours. Kelly (1861-1934) brought out other editions of his work: a much shorter version with twelve illustrations (London: A. & C. Black, 1929. 85p. [Peeps at Many Lands]), and a revised edition with thirty-two illustrations (London: A. & C. Black, 1933, 256p.).

67 **Mogok: the valley of rubies.**
Joseph Kessel, translated from the French by Stella Rodway. London: MacGibbon & Kee, 1960. 199p.
These travellers' tales of the ruby mines of Mogok, Upper Burma, were first published under the title *La vallée des rubis* (Paris: Librairie Gallimard, 1955).

68 **The Burma Road.**
Miles Kington. In: *Great journeys*. By Philip Jones Griffiths, (et al.). London: BBC Books, 1989, p. 119-64.
This entertaining account of a visit to Burma and to Kunming, China, to research and film a television programme on the old Burma Road captures more than most travelogues the flavour of Burma in the 1980s. The text is complemented by photographs by Tom Owen Edmunds. For earlier accounts of the Burma Road, see Nicol Smith, *Burma Road* (q.v.).

69 **A holiday in Burma: with a chapter on a visit to Calcutta.**
C. M. Leicester. Exeter, England: A. Wheaton, 1928. 191p.
A narrative of travel by train and on the Salween River through Burma in the cool season of 1926-27, with photos of local life by Seabury Edwardes.

70 **Golden earth: travels in Burma.**
Norman Lewis. London: Jonathan Cape, 1952. 270p. map; London: Eland Books, 1984.
Lewis explored Burma in 1951 and, predicting it would become a hermit nation, explicitly set out to capture the 'old' Burma before it became inaccessible and changed. His work is an accomplished travelogue, with a gentle touch of irony, and still worth reading by any would-be traveller to Burma.

71 **Land of jade: a journey through insurgent Burma.**
Bertil Lintner. Edinburgh: Kiscadale Publications; Bangkok: White Lotus, 1990. 315p. maps.
An account of a perilous eighteen-months' journey, mostly on foot, across the insurgent areas of northern Burma from the Naga Hills, through Kachin State and the Golden Triangle in 1985-87. Lintner interviewed the leaders and followers of the various insurgent forces (Naga, Kachin, Communist and Shan) and his work provides a unique perspective on Burma's forty-year-long civil war about which the author observes: 'Burma, with its rich natural and human resources, deserves a better fate than being torn apart by a civil war which neither side can win by military means'. The

book is illustrated by over sixty black-and-white and colour photographs taken by the author's Shan wife, Hseng Noung.

72 **The gentleman in the parlour: a record of a journey from Rangoon to Haiphong.**
William Somerset Maugham. London: William Heinemann, 1930; New York: Paragon House, 1989. 300p. map.

The first part of this superior leisurely travelogue covers the novelist's journey upriver from Rangoon to Pagan and Mandalay, and his travels on horseback through the Shan States to Kengtung. Maugham (1874-1965), who described the Shwe Dagon as like 'a sudden hope in the dark night of the soul', later stated that his book was written as an 'exercise in style'.

73 **Where Burma meets China: life and travels in the Burma–China border lands.**
Beatrix Metford. London; Glasgow: Blackie, 1935. 231p. map.

Observations on travel between Bhamo and Tengyueh in Yunnan, with descriptions and photographs of the Kachin, Palaung, Lisu and Shan hill peoples.

74 **A bachelor girl in Burma.**
Geraldine Edith Mitton. London: Adam & Charles Black, 1907. 275p. map.

Impressions of a two-months' stay in Burma, the text enlivened by ninety-five photographs. The author in 1920 renounced bachelor girlhood for marriage to Sir James George Scott (Shway Yoe) and produced a biography of her husband, *Scott of the Shan Hills* (q.v.). They collaborated on writing fiction set in Burma and published under their joint names the following books: *The green moth* (London: John Murray, 1922. 302p.), *A frontier man* (London: John Murray, 1923. 308p.), *Under an eastern sky* (Allahabad: A. H. Wheeler, 1924. 286p.), and a story for children written from an elephant's point of view about life under the Burmese kings and the British, entitled *The life story of an elephant* (London: A. & C. Black, 1930. 216p.). Mitton also published under her name alone two earlier works set in Burma, a children's adventure story, *In the grip of the wild Wa* (London: Adam and Charles Black, 1913. 296p.) and a novel, *The two-stringed fiddle* (London: John Murray, 1919. 320p.).

75 **From Edinburgh to India and Burmah.**
William G. Burn Murdoch. London: George Routledge, 1908. 403p.

Record of a journey in 1905-06 illustrated with twenty-four colour reproductions of paintings by the author, and numerous other black-and-white sketches.

76 **Canoe to Mandalay.**
R. Raven-Hart. London: The Book Club, 1939. 2nd ed. 245p.

A lively travelogue of an unusual journey.

77　**A turning wheel: three decades of an Asian revolution as witnessed by a correspondent for the New Yorker.**
Robert Shaplen.　London: André Deutsch, 1979. 397p.
Includes a chapter 'Burma – poverty and pride' (p. 119-41) describing personalities, policies and events in Burma from 1962 to 1978. Shaplen concludes that were Kipling to visit Burma today, 'it is doubtful that he would find it worth a song or a sonnet. The return of George Orwell might be more to the point'.

78　**Burma Road: the story of the world's most romantic highway.**
Nicol Smith.　New York: Garden City Publishing, 1940. 333p. map.
A first-hand account with lots of anecdotes of an intrepid American's car journey along the Burma Road from Kunming to Lashio, just before the Second World War. Another account is Neville Bradley, *The old Burma Road: a journey on foot and muleback* (London: William Heinemann, 1945. 138p.) which describes his journey in 1930, and is mostly devoted to China. Robert Lawson Slater's *Guns through arcady: Burma and the Burma Road* (London: Angus & Robertson, 1941; Madras, India: Diocesan Press, 1943. 239p. map) has stories of life in the Shan States and of the supplies sent to China via the Burma Road in the two years leading up to the Japanese invasion of Burma, and contains the (unfulfilled) forecast that 'communication between an industrial India and a rapidly changing China, with Rangoon as the port and the Burma Road as the main highway, may well be one of the major possibilities of the new world'. An account of the Burma Road's construction is Tan Pei-Ying, *The building of the Burma Road* (q.v.).

79　**Far ridges: a record of travel in North-Eastern Burma 1938-39.**
John Keith Stanford.　London: C. & J. Temple, 1944. 208p. map.
The author, a keen ornithologist, was invited to joint the 1938-39 Vernay-Cutting expedition to the remote Hpimaw Hills on the eastern edge of Myitkyina District where he had previously spent four years as a deputy-commissioner. He provides an immediate and informative account of a scientific expedition in action, and of his companion on the expedition, Frank Kingdon-Ward, 'lord of wild flowers'. Another account of the expedition with photographs of the team at work and of Lisu, Maru and Lashi tribal people can be found in Suydam Cutting, *The fire ox and other years* (London: Collins, 1947, p. 298-333).

80　**The great railway bazaar: by train through Asia.**
Paul Theroux.　London: Hamish Hamilton, 1975. 342p. map.
This noted novelist's classic account of a rail journey in the grand tradition contain three humorous chapters (p. 178-206) on his journey from Rangoon via Mandalay and Maymyo to the Shan States in an attempt to travel over the Gokteik viaduct steel bridge (built in 1899 by the Pennsylvania Steel Co.). Another piece on Burma by Theroux which is well-worth reading as an antidote to the 'timeless charm' type of travel writing on Burma is 'Seven Burmese days' in his *Sunrise with sea monsters: travels and discoveries 1964-1984* (London: Hamish Hamilton, 1985), p. 48-57.

Farrer's last journey: Upper Burma, 1919-20.
See item no. 115.

In farthest Burma: the record of an arduous journey of exploration and research through the unknown frontier territory of Burma and Tibet.
See item no. 122.

Guidebooks

81 **Wanderings in Burma.**
George W. Bird. London: Simpkin, Marshall, Hamilton, Kent, 1897.
410p. 19 maps.
A 19th-century travel guide by an Education Service official with twenty years' residence in Burma. Arranged in two parts: the first (p. 1-145) giving a general introduction to Burma, and the second (p. 146-410) describing twenty-four 'routes' or excursion tours throughout Burma with a description of the main sights and practical travel advice of dated charm (for example: 'The best way to get expeditiously to May Myo from Mandalay is to ride. With two ponies, and a bullock-cart for servants and kit, the journey up can be comfortably made in two days'.). The volume includes a large folding map in the cover pocket, maps of sections of the Irrawaddy River, plans of Rangoon, Pegu, Mandalay city and Mandalay palace, Amarapura, Shwebo, Salon and Pagan, and sixty-seven photographs principally by Felice Beato of Mandalay. The accomplished photography of Beato (c. 1825-1908), a Venetian-born naturalized British citizen who in 1889 set up a photographic studio and a Burmese furniture, arts and craft business in Mandalay, features in many British publications of the period.

82 **Collins illustrated guide to Burma.**
Caroline Courtauld. London: Collins, 1988. 207p. maps. bibliog.
(Asian Guide Series).
This beautiful colour illustrated guide is more far-ranging and informative than most travel guides, combining historical, cultural and practical information. By the same author is a stunning colour pictorial album of Burma, *In search of Burma* (London: Frederick Muller, 1984. 112p. 2 maps. bibliog.) which emphasizes Buddhism and Burmese culture and is accompanied by a simple thematic text presenting Burma as a country of captivating charm and timelessness.

83 **Burma.**
John Hoskin. Singapore: Times Editions, 1987. 95p. maps.
A lavishly colour illustrated travel guide to the 'eccentric charm' of Burma. It includes two pages on one of the few surviving puppet theatres of Burma. Photographs by Luca Invernizzi Tettoni.

84   Le guide du routard 1990/1: Thailande-Birmanie, Hong-Kong, Macao.
(The back-packer's guide 1990/91: Thailand – Burma, Hong Kong –
Macao).
Edited by Pierre Josse, assisted by Benoit Lucchini.   Paris: Hachette,
1990. 183p. (Le Guide de Routard: Collection sous direction de Philippe
Gloaguen).

This French travel guide prides itself on giving up-to-date coverage, and combines
practicality and humour, with a good section on Burma (p. 123-54) advocating
discovering Burma 'as quickly as possible as it has yet to be ravaged by mass tourism'.

85   Burma.
Wilhelm Klein, directed and designed by Hans Johannes Hoefer, and
edited by John Anderson.   London: Apa Productions (HK), 1988. 7th
ed. 332p. 15 maps. bibliog. (Insight Guide Series).

One of the best travel guides to Burma, with lavish colour photographs (by Günter
Pfannmüller) and a well-researched text on all aspects of Burma, past and present. An
unusual feature is the inclusion of rare 19th and early 20th-century black-and-white
photographs, and appendixes giving ground plans for ancient sites and temples. An
associated publication is *Burma the golden* by Wilhelm Klein, photographs by Günter
Pfannmüller (Singapore: Apa Productions (HK) for The Bookseller, Bangkok, 1982.
239p.), a sumptuous colour picture album and text on Burma past and present.

86   Thailand & Burma.
Frank Kusy, Frances Capel.   London: Cadogan, 1988. 392p. maps.
(Cadogan Books).

The Burma section (p. 243-385) of this guide is written by Frances Capel and is well-
researched and practical with general and background information, and guides to
Rangoon, Mandalay, Maymyo, Pagan, Inle Lake and their surrounding areas and,
briefly, to other places at present out of bounds to the tourist. The author sees Burma
as a country 'whose magic reaches out to enchant those who are not dependent on the
comforts of the Western world'.

87   South East Asia: the travellers guide.
Stefan Loose, Renate Ramb, translated by David Crawford, Peter
Conolly-Smith.   Huddersfield, England: Springfield, 1988. 3rd ed. 665p.
maps. (The Traveller's Guide)

A revised and updated edition translated from the sixth German edition (published
under the title *Sudostasien Handbuch* [South East Asian handbook]) with general
travel information on the region and a good concise chapter on Burma (p. 39-66) full
of practical advice.

88   Southeast Asia handbook.
Carl Parkes.   Chico. California: Moon, 1990. 873p. maps.

A travel guide with an up-to-date, plain speaking section on 'Myanmar' (p. 65-126),
with colour and black-and-white illustrations, and boxed lists of festivals, main sights
and accommodation.

89　**Burma: a travel survival kit.**
　　Tony Wheeler.　South Yarra, Australia: Lonely Planet, 1989. 5th ed.
　　184p. maps. (Travel Survival Kit Series).
First published in 1979, this excellent, regularly updated guide is well-illustrated with
sixteen colour plates, maps and plans. It goes outside the standard tourist track, with
useful practical tips on how to make the most of a seven-days' visit. Burma is also
included in Tony Wheeler's *South-East Asia on a shoestring* (Hawthorn, Australia:
Lonely Plant, 1989. 6th ed. 679p. 123 maps) with practical advice on accommodation
and food, with tips on behaviour, dress, language, etc. The sixth edition (1989) carries
a one page 'stop press' update on Burma reporting the extension of the hitherto seven-
days' tourist visa to fourteen days.

Site guides

90　**Historical sites in Burma.**
　　Aung Thaw.　Rangoon: Sarpay Beikman, 1972. 157p. map. bibliog.
A brief guide to the principal ancient sites of Burma, arranged chronologically from
Beikthano to Mandalay, with colour and black-and-white illustrations. Written by a
former director of Burma's Archaeology Service.

91　**Glimpses of glorious Pagan.**
　　Department of History, University of Rangoon, Burma.　Rangoon: The
　　Universities' Press, 1986. 60p. map.
This is a good brief general guide to the ancient temples of Pagan, capital of Burma
from the 11th to the 13th centuries. There are colour photographs, site plans and
descriptions of the most important of Pagan's 2,000 brick temples which cover an area
of sixteen square miles on the eastern bank of the Irrawaddy in central Burma. A brief
description of the new Archaeological Museum at Pagan which opened in 1979 is also
included. It is to date the only popular guide to Pagan, and is widely available in
Burma for tourists, but not so easy to find outside Burma. It replaces an earlier guide,
A pictorial guide to Pagan, first produced in 1955 by the director of the Archaeological
Survey, Burma.

92　**Guide to the Mandalay palace.**
　　Charles Duroiselle.　Rangoon: Superintendent, Government Printing,
　　1925. 59p. map.
A detailed guide to the palace of Mandalay built by King Mindon in 1857-58, with
notes on the use of the palace's halls and apartments and descriptions of its wooden
architecture. Duroiselle was superintendent of the Archaeological Survey, Burma, and
prepared the guide with the help of informants who had known the palace in royal
times. The palace was destroyed in the Second World War and today only a wooden
model of the extensive palace buildings may be viewed. Duroiselle's text was reprinted
under the title *The Mandalay Palace* (Rangoon: Directorate of Archaeological Survey,
Ministry of Union Culture, 1963), supplemented with thirty-one plates of photographs,
plans, and measured drawings of the palace structures and architectural motifs as
preserved in the Archaeological Department. A more recent, but very general,

introduction to Mandalay (and other palaces) can be found in chapter one, 'The palaces of Burma' (p. 8-20) of *The palaces of South-East Asia: architecture and customs* by Jacques Dumarçay, edited and translated by Michael Smithies (Singapore: Oxford University Press, 1991. 143p. maps. bibliog.). Mandalay Palace is being rebuilt.

93 **Die goldene Pagoda: Shwedagon – ein Sinnbild des Buddhismus.** (The golden pagoda: the Shwedagon – a Buddhist symbol.)
Annemarie Esche. Hanau, GFR: Muller & Kiepenheuer, 1985. 146p. maps. bibliog.

A description of the great Shwe Dagon temple in Rangoon, plus an account of the Buddha and legends associated with the temple; with over fifty colour photographs. Also by Esche is *Das goldene Kloster zu Mandalay* ('The golden monastery at Mandalay'.) (Leipzig, GDR: Insel-Verlag, 1977. 62p.), primarily a black-and-white photographic record with a descriptive essay, of the elaborately wood-carved Shwei-gyaung (Golden Monastery) in Mandalay.

94 **Ancient Arakan.**
Sylvia Fraser-Lu. *Arts of Asia*, vol. 17, no. 2 (March-April 1987), p. 96.109.

This article surveys the history of Arakan as an independent state until its conquest by the Burmese in 1784, and describes in detail the ancient temples and images at Mrauk-u (Mro-haung) and other sites; well illustrated with over forty black-and-white photographs of Arakanese temples and images.

95 **Mandalay and other cities of the past in Burma.**
Vincent Clarence Scott O'Connor. London: Hutchinson, 1907; Bangkok: White Lotus, 1987. 436p. maps.

A British colonial officer's evocative description of Burma's past written in the form of a guide to twelve Burmese cities and temple sites: Mandalay, Ava, Amarapura, Sagaing, Tagaung, Pagan, Prome, Sri Ksetra, Po-u-daung, Thaton, Pegu, and Mergui. It is full of detail and first-hand observation and can still, despite the passage of time, inform and afford the modern traveller many insights. Illustrated with over 235 black-and-white photographs and 8 colour plates from paintings by J. R. Middleton and the Burmese artist Saya Chone, together with a plan of the palace of Mandalay and maps and plans of Mandalay city, Pagan and Ava.

96 **Shwe Dagon.**
Win Pe. Rangoon: Printing & Publishing Corporation, 1972. 128p. maps. bibliog.

A well-written account of the great Shwe Dagon pagoda in Rangoon which covers its history, architecture, structure and engineering problems, management, its role in the Burmese people's life, and gives a guide to the shrines and many other points of interest on the Shwe Dagon platform. Drawings of the Shwe Dagon's architectural elements and a plan of the platform are provided (in pocket at end). As well as black-

Travellers' Accounts and Guidebooks. Site guides

and-white photographs, it contains several colour close-ups of the jewelled orb and vane at the pagoda's summit.

Pagan: art and architecture of old Burma.
See item no. 742.

Geography and Geology

General

97 **Economic resources of the Union of Burma.**
Nafis Ahmad. Natick, Massachusetts: Earth Sciences Laboratory, US
Army Natick Laboratories, 1971. 307p. 16 maps. bibliog. (Technical
Report 71-61-ES, Series ES-70).

An in-depth study of the economic geography of Burma in four parts: part one
introduces the country and its economy in 1967 and considers population distribution
and ethnic composition; part two outlines Burma's physical base of geology and
geomorphology, climate, vegetation, forests and soils; part three examines agricultural
and mineral resources; and part four industries, transportation, trade and commerce.
Included is an extensive bibliography (p. 255-307), concentrating on economic
resources.

98 **Geology of Burma.**
Friedrich Bender, with contributions by Dietrich Bannert, Jorn
Brinckmann, Franz Gramann, Dietrich Helmcke. Berlin: Borntraeger,
1983. 293p. maps. bibliog. (Beiträge zur Regionalen Geologie der Erde,
vol. 16).

This clearly written, comprehensive and up-to-date geological study is divided into five
sections: general introduction (including a survey of past geological research in
Burma); regional geology; stratigraphy; tectonics and magmatism; palaeographic
evolution; and, energy, metallic and non-metallic raw materials, water and soil. With
an excellent exhaustive bibliography (p. 226-60), over 100 maps, figures and tables,
and, in the end pockets, a separate colour geological map and a black-and-white
structural map, showing faults, structural trends and volcanic structures. See also the
recent work by Charles S. Hutchinson on the region as a whole, *The geological
evolution of South-east Asia* (Oxford: Clarendon, 1989. 368p. [Oxford Monographs on
Geology & Geophysics, no. 13]).

29

99   **The mineral resources of Burma.**
   Harbans Lal Chhibber.   London: Macmillan, 1934. 320p. map.
Burma's extremely rich mineral deposits are surveyed and described in this useful work
which has chapters on gemstones, jade, amber, iron-ore deposits, coal and lignite,
gold, lead, silver and zinc deposits, petroleum, tin, tungsten, salt, other miscellaneous
minerals, soils, water supplies, and road and building minerals. There is no
bibliography as such, but extensive references are given at the end of each chapter.
Chhibber, a former head of the Department of Geology and Geography at Rangoon
University, also produced a classic geological textbook and study, *The geology of
Burma* (London: Macmillan, 1934. 538p. maps) and a well-illustrated textbook on the
physical geography of Burma, *The physiography of Burma* (London: Longmans,
Green, 1933; New York: AMS Press, 1975, 148p. 40 maps. bibliog.).

100   **South-east Asia: a social, economic and political geography.**
   Charles A. Fisher.   London: Methuen, 1966. 2nd ed. 831p. 110 maps.
   bibliog.
The best and most authoritative geography of Southeast Asia. The first part treats the
region as a whole, describes its political geography in the pre-European period and in
the era of Western rule, and assesses the legacy of the West. The remainder of the
book considers each of the countries of Southeast Asia in greater detail. The chapter
on Burma (p. 430-83) describes the refashioning of Burma under British rule and
economic and political geography since independence.

101   **Marine policy in Southeast Asia.**
   Edited by George Kent, Mark J. Valencia.   Berkeley, California;
   London: University of California Press, 1985. 425p. bibliog.
This detailed and wide-ranging study is divided into sections on marine geography,
national marine interests, maritime jurisdictional interests, ocean use (fisheries, etc.),
oil and gas explorations, enforcement of marine jurisdictions, and co-operation.
Includes a brief discussion of Burma's marine interests, boundary issues with India,
fisheries, oil and gas exploration, and defence issues. Also useful is *Atlas for marine
policy in Southeast Asian seas*, edited by Joseph R. Morgan and Mark J. Valencia, for
the East-West Environment & Policy Institute (Berkeley, California: University of
California Press, [1983]. 144p.).

102   **The oil fields of Burma.**
   Edwin Hall Pascoe.   Calcutta, India: Geological Survey of India;
   London: Kegan Paul, Trench, Trübner, 1912. 269p. maps. (Geological
   Survey of India, Memoirs, vol. 40, part 1).
A detailed study (with over seventy plates) describing and analysing the physical
features, rocks, structure, geological faults and commercially significant petroleum
deposits of Burma on a district by district basis. Pascoe used data collected between
1905 and 1909 while working as a government supervisor in the oil fields of Burma and
as assistant superintendent of the Geological Survey of India. He also published other
geological studies and reports on fossils and shells. For more recent mapping of
Burma's oil and gas reserves, see *The South East Asia oil and gas activity and
concession map* (Ledbury, England: Oilfield Publications Ltd., [1984]. 2 maps.).

103   **The world weather guide.**
R. A. Pearce, C. G. Smith.   London: Hutchinson. 1990. 2nd ed. 480p.
map.
Burma's climate is briefly described (p. 213-15) and monthly temperatures given for
the towns of Akyab, Lashio, Mandalay and Rangoon. A detailed study of Burma's
rainfall and temperature patterns, with a listing of often obscure articles on Burma's
climate can be found in Robert E. Huke, edited by Don C. Bennett, *Temperature
change with elevation in Burma: a study* (Bloomington, Indiana: Indiana University
Foundation Research Division, 1962. 143p. maps. bibliog.) and in Robert E. Huke,
Rainfall in Burma (Hanover, New Hampshire: Dartmouth College, 1966. 93p.). A
19th-century description of (Lower) Burma's climate, with statistical appendixes, is
given in Henry F. Blanford. *A practical guide to the climates and weather of India,
Ceylon and Burmah and the storms of the Indian seas* (London: Macmillan, 1889,
p. 189-97).

104   **The mineral resources of Burma.**
Norman Mosley Penzer.   London: George Routledge; New York:
E. P. Dalton, 1922. 176p. maps. bibliog.
A feature of this work is its bibliography, which is comprehensive for the period. The
bibliographical references and the text attempt to incorporate and summarize all the
known information on Burma's mineral resources. Accompanied by a folding map
showing the distribution of mineral resources, sketch maps of different mineral
regions, and an appendix giving a glossary of Burmese geological and mineralogical
words.

105   **Southeast Asian seas: oil under troubled waters – hydrocarbon potential,
jurisdictional issues, and international relations.**
Mark J. Valencia.   Singapore: Oxford University Press, 1985. 155p.
maps. bibliog.
An examination of major trends in hydrocarbon exploration in the Southeast Asian
region, with an analysis of the oil and gas factor in jurisdictional disputes and
international relations. It contains some data on Burma and discusses maritime claims,
petroleum geology in the Andaman Sea and maritime boundaries with India.

Maps, atlases and gazetteers

106   **Atlas of South-East Asia.**
Introduction by Daniel George Edward Hall.   London: Macmillan;
New York: St. Martin's, 1964. 84p. 130 maps.
A useful, basic atlas with colour maps of the individual countries of the region and
thematic maps illustrating climate and vegetation, land use, agriculture, irrigation,
minerals, industries, communications, population, etc., with plans of major cities.
Maps of Burma, including a plan of Rangoon and a large-scale map of the Irrawaddy
Delta are on p. 51-60. Hall's introduction (p. 62-82) emphasizes historical and political
developments.

107 **Burma: official standard names approved by the United States Board on Geographic Names.**
Washington, DC: Department of the Interior, Office of Geography, 1966. 725p. map. (Gazetteer no. 96).

Contains 52,000 entries for places and features with cross-references from variant to standard names, with coded locational map references, and a glossary of generic terms.

108 **Early maps of South-East Asia.**
R. T. Fell. Singapore; Oxford; New York: Oxford University Press, 1988. 103p. bibliog. (Images of Asia).

A good introduction to the earliest European maps of the region, their artistic and historical significance, and to notable map-makers and publishers. The chapter on Burma (p. 63-70) covers cartography of Burma up to the late 19th century.

109 **Burma.**
Munich, GFR: Nelles Verlag, [1985]. (Nelles Maps).

A good folding map of Burma for general use, with Upper Burma on one side and Lower Burma on the reverse, and an inset giving maps of Rangoon and Mandalay cities. It has very clear print, and marks in red such features as ancient sites and capitals, airports, war cemeteries, tribal markets. The scale is 1:1,500,000. Available from Nelles Verlag, D-8000, Munich 45, Germany, and from APA Press, Hong Kong (for distribution in Asia and the Pacific region).

110 **A historical atlas of South Asia.**
Edited by Joseph E. Schwartzberg. Chicago, Illinois; London: University of Chicago Press, 1978. 352p. bibliog.

This comprehensive cartographic record of the history of South Asia covers Burma for the period from the mid-18th century until its independence in 1948, and also includes a short treatment of the Southeast Asian region as a whole. The atlas is divided into five sections: maps and photographic plates, text elucidating the maps, bibliography, index, and inserts (two overlay maps and three chronological charts in the end pockets). Among the material on Burma covered and mapped is the growth of the Burman empire, the expansion of British power, major events in Burma 1857-1935, political and constitutional developments, Burma during the Second World War (with insets on the Burma–India front 1943-44 and on the reconquest of Burma 1944-45), together with ethnographic, demographic and cultural data. A revised edition is forthcoming from Oxford University Press.

111 **Gazetteer of Upper Burma and the Shan States.**
James George Scott, assisted by John Percival Hardiman. Rangoon: Government Printing. 1900-1901. 5 vols; New York: AMS Press, [1983]. 5 vols. map.

This massive (over 3,000p.) work is arranged in two parts: the first part (in two volumes) contains, in the first volume, an introduction to the physical geography of Burma, an account of Burmese history from 1852 (taken from Burmese sources), and of the British annexation and 'pacfication' of Upper Burma (from 1885 through to the late 1890s), with chapters on the Shan States, Kachin Hills and Chin Hills, and a detailed ethnographic section with alphabets and vocabularies; in the second volume are chapters on religion (including cosmology, the spirits, invulnerability from physical dangers, talismans and tattooing), palace customs (including court language, titles, royal and monastic architecture and the temples and images of Pagan and other ancient cities), geology and mineralogy, forestry, agriculture and industrial arts (including weaving, dyeing, pottery, brass, and paper making), revenue administration (past and present), population and trade, and government and administration under the kings. Part two (in three volumes) consists of the gazetteer proper arranged in alphabetical order of place name with often quite extensive notes and statistical data. The indexes to each volume of part one help access this material, and there is also a geographical index to each volume of part two, a glossary, plans (of Mandalay Palace and Mingun), good photographs (particularly of ethnic minorities), and drawings of cabbalistic designs, spinning and weaving implements, pottery and costume. All in all, a monumental compilation of particular value for its ethnographic and historical information.

112 **British Burma gazetteer.**

Compiled by Horace Ralph Spearman.   Rangoon: Government Press, 1880. 2 vols.

A large official compilation (reprinted in 1983 as *Gazetteer of Burma* by Cultural Publishing in Delhi) covering geography, geology, forestry, ethnology, religion, history, customs, the arts, etc., with a gazetteer by alphabetical order of place name in volume two. Between 1911 and 1935 an invaluable series of illustrated district-by-district *Burma Gazetteers*, mostly in two volumes, and compiled by individual colonial administrators was published – and, for the most part, reprinted in the 1950s and '60s (Rangoon: Government Printing) – covering the history, inhabitants, agriculture and irrigation, forestry and minerals, occupations and trade, communications systems, general and revenue administration, education, public health, etc. of each district. A listing of these can be found in Henry Scholberg, *The district gazetteers of British India: a bibliography* (Geneva: Zug, 1970. [Bibliotheca Asiatica, 3]).

113 **Atlas of Southeast Asia.**

Richard Ulack, Gyula Pauer.   New York: Macmillan Publishing; London: Collier Macmillan, 1989. 171p. bibliog.

This is more of a geographical handbook than an atlas providing colour maps and a general guide to the physical, social, political, economic, cultural, and human geography of the region. Part one gives a regional overview, briefly surveying Southeast Asia's physical environment and resources, historical and political background, cultural characteristics and population patterns. Part two gives a country-by-country survey noting distinctive features of each nation. Burma is covered on p. 111-22, using data current to 1988.

Flora and Fauna

114 **The fauna of British India, including Ceylon and Burma.**
Edited by William Thomas Blanford (1906-08 by C. T. Bingham,
1908-27 by A. E. Shipley, 1928-30 by E. C. Stuart Baker, 1929-32 by
J. Stephenson, 1933-64 by R. B. S. Sewell). London: Taylor &
Francis, 1888-[1950]. Multi-vols.

Under this title, and with different editorships, there appeared from the late 19th
century through to the 1950s and into the 1970s (when the title was changed to read
The fauna of India, including Pakistan, Ceylon, Burma and Malaya, and was published
by Government Press in Delhi and Calcutta, India), a series of detailed and fully
illustrated biological studies that stand today as an unsurpassed monument of scientific
investigation and classification of a vast region. Some forty individual titles were
published in this series often as multi-volume works, and many appeared in revised and
expanded editions. Although centred on the fauna of India, they draw on and
incorporate data from research in Burma, and have invaluable bibliographies. Species
covered by this exensive series include mammalia, fish, birds, reptiles, marine life,
lepidoptera, to mention but a few. Several of these titles were reprinted in the 1970s
and 1980s in New Delhi by Today & Tomorrow's Printers & Publishers.

115 **Farrer's last journey: Upper Burma, 1919-20.**
Euan Hillhouse Methven Cox. London: Dulau, 1926; Sakonnet,
Rhode Island: Theophrastus, 1977. 244p. map.

The author accompanied the botanist Reginald Farrer on his last plant-hunting
expedition to the extreme north of Burma. Farrer died there in 1920 and Cox draws on
his letters and articles to produce this account of the expedition. The appendix contains
a complete list, compiled by Helen T. Maxwell, of all rhododendrons collected by
Farrer, together with his field notes. Also relevant is *The plant introductions of
Reginald Farrer*, edited by Cox (London: New Flora & Silva, 1930. 113p.) which
contains a section 'Farrer's notes on plants sent home from Upper Burma' (p. 57-92)
and a bibliography of Farrer's writings compiled by W. T. Stearn (p. 101-13).

116 **Some common Burmese timbers: and other relevant information.**
V. Desraj. Rangoon: Student Press, 1961. 170p.

A handbook describing and assessing the most common commercial timbers of Burma, with sections on timber conversion, grading, seasoing, preserving, pricing and measuring.

117 **Elephants and their diseases: a treatise on elephants.**
Griffith H. Evans. Rangoon: Superintendent, Government Printing & Stationery, 1961. 323p. bibliog.

A reprint of the 1910 edition (Rangoon: Government Printing), itself a reprint and rearrangement of the original 1901 publication. A classic and comprehensive handbook on elephants in Burma giving general information on working elephants, with more detailed sections on their anatomy, diseases and veterinary care. Designed primarily for use by self-reliant forestry officials.

118 **Burmese earthworms: an introduction to the systematics and biology of megadrile Oligochaetes with special reference to Southeast Asia.**
Gordon Enoch Gates. Philadelphia: American Philosophical Society, 1972. 326p. maps. bibliog. (Transactions of the American Philosophical Society, New Series, vol. 62, part 7).

The origins of this definitive study are described by the author as 'the war-induced abortion of a project parthenogenetically conceived in the mind of an unsophisticated MA, ignorant of systematics, who had to identify Rangoon earthworms for use in laboratory sections of the first biology course of university grade to be taught in Burma'.

119 **The orchids of Burma (including the Andaman Islands).**
Bartle Grant. Rangoon: Hanthawaddy Press, 1895; Dehra Dun, India: Bishen Singh Mahendra Pal Singh, [1976]. 424p.

A standard, but unillustrated, reference work on Burmese orchids, taking as its starting point the classificatory system used by the Reverend Charles Parish in his account of orchids published in the revised 1883-84 edition of Francis Mason's *Burma, its people and productions* (q.v.). With indexes of technical terms and of genera and species. Some references to the orchids of Burma may also be found in the more recent and colour illustrated *An introduction to the orchids of Asia* by Mark L. Isaac Williams (London: Angus & Robertson, 1988. 261p. maps. bibliog.).

120 **List of trees, shrubs, herbs, and principal climbers, etc. recorded from Burma: with vernacular names.**
H. G. Hundley, Chit Ko Ko. Rangoon: Superintendent, Government Printing & Stationery, 1961. 3rd rev. ed. 532p.

A listing of nearly 7,000 species with Burmese (and some Chin, Kachin, Karen, Mon and Shan) vernacular names and botanical names. It is a revision and considerable expansion of an earlier compilation by Forestry Conservation officials, James Henry Lace (1857-1918) and Alexander Rodger, *List of trees, shrubs, and principal climbers, etc. recorded from Burma: with vernacular names* (Rangoon: Superintendent, Government Printing, 1922. 2nd ed. 366p.; Dehra Dun, India: Bishen Singh Mahendra

Pal Singh, 1984), and incorporates the species discovered and collected from the 1920s to the 1950s.

121 **The Collins field guide to the birds of South-East Asia.**
Ben King, Edward C. Dickinson, illustrated by Martin W.
Woodcock.   Lexington, Massachusetts: Stephen Greene Press, 1988.
480p. maps. bibliog.

This book was first published (London: William Collins, 1975) under the title *A field guide to the birds of South-East Asia*. It covers all the 1,198 ornithological species identified up to 1971 in Burma, Malaysia, Thailand, Laos, Cambodia, Vietnam and Hong Kong. The listing of birds gives the English name and scientific name, identification, range and habitat. There are black-and-white and colour illustrations of all the commoner species and all the main types of Southeast Asian birds, with 869 species illustrated in all. The introductory material describes the principles by which the data has been arranged, and gives a guide to identifying birds and a glossary. Also relevant is *A field guide to the bird songs of South-East Asia*, compiled and edited by Terry White (London: British Library National Sound Archive, 1984. 16p. including two cassettes of recordings of 138 bird species), providing a sound guide for bird-watchers in the field.

122 **In farthest Burma: the record of an arduous journey of exploration and research through the unknown frontier territory of Burma and Tibet.**
Frank Kingdon-Ward.   London: Seeley, Service, 1921. 311p.

Kingdon-Ward (1885-1958), a noted plant-collector and explorer made twenty-three expeditions to Assam, Burma, China and Tibet between 1909 and 1957. This, the first of his many books about plant-hunting in Burma, records an expedition made in 1914 up the eastern branch of the Irrawaddy. Other Kingdon-Ward books on Burma are as follows: *From China to Hkamti Long* (London: Edward Arnold, 1924. 312p. map.), an account of a 1922 journey from the Yangtze across to the jungles surrounding the Irrawaddy's headwaters; *Plant hunting on the edge of the world* (London: Victor Gollancz, 1930; reprinted, with introduction by Geoffrey Smith, London: Cadogan Books, 1985. 383p. maps.), a botanical travel book of which part two covers plant-hunting in remote regions of Burma in 1926; *Plant-hunter's paradise* (London: Jonathan Cape, 1937. 347p. 2 maps.) describing a 1930-31 expedition to the Burma–Tibet frontier; *Burma's icy mountains* (London: Jonathan Cape, 1937. 287p.); and, his last book, *Return to the Irrawaddy* (London: Andrew Melrose, 1956. 224p. map.) describing his 1953 expedition to northern Burma's Kachin State, with three chapters giving details of the rhododendrons of the region. All Kingdon-Ward's books are characterized by their vivid descriptions of the scenery and plants of Burma's remotest regions, and of the discomforts and dangers encountered. Also by Kingdon-Ward is a collection of autobiographical and botanical essays, *Pilgrimage for plants* (London: George G. Harrap, 1960. 191p. map. bibliog.) which includes his observations on land utilization and ecological recommendations for Burma, and contains an introduction and bibliography (p. 180-86) of Kingdon-Ward's many publications compiled by William T. Stearn. A recent compilation of extracts from Kingdon-Ward's books and articles, chosen, edited and with an introduction by John Whitehead, is *Himalayan enchantment: an anthology* (London: Serindia Publications, 1990. 254p. map). For a portrait of Kingdon-Ward at work, see John Keith Stanford, *Far ridges* (q.v.) and, above all, the fine biography by Charles Lyte, *Frank Kingdon-Ward: the last of the great plant hunters* (London: John Murray, 1989. 218p. maps. bibliog.) which draws on Kingdon-Ward's diaries and letters and includes details of his reconnaissance of swift and safe escape routes for refugees and the military at the time of the Japanese invasion of Burma. In his later years, Kingdon-Ward used the hyphenated form of his name, while his earlier works were published under the name of Ward.

123 **Forest flora of British Burma.**
Sulpiz Kurz.   Calcutta, India: Office of the Superintendent of
Government Printing, 1877; Dehra Dun, India: Bishen Singh
Mahendra Pal Singh & Periodical Experts, Delhi, 1974. 2 vols.

Sulpiz Kurz (1833-78) was curator of the Herbarium, Royal Botanical Gardens, Calcutta. His book provides an extremely detailed botanical description of some 2,000 species of trees and shrubs identified in Burma. The introduction gives a useful description of the different types of forests found in Burma and the species associated with them. An index of plant names in the vernacular and in English is given, and there is a separate index of botanical orders, genera and species.

124 **Burma, its people and productions: or, notes on the fauna, flora and
minerals of Tenasserim, Pegu and Burma.**
Francis Mason, rewritten and enlarged by William Theobald.
Hertford, England: Stephen Austin & Sons, published by order of the
Chief Commissioner of British Burma, 1882-83. rev. ed. 2 vols.

This work has a complex history and has expanded greatly in scope and size (to over 1,300p.) from its first edition published under the title *The natural productions of Burmah: or, notes on the fauna, flora and minerals of the Tenasserim provinces and the Burman empire* (Maulmain, Burma: American Mission Press, Thos. S Ranney, 1850. 220p.). Mason, an English-born American Baptist missionary to the Karens, was inspired to produce his scientific compilation by the difficulty he experienced when translating the Bible into Karen in rendering botanical terms exactly. Mason enlarged his original 1850 compilation to incorporate data acquired following the British annexation of Lower Burma and he drew on, and acknowledged, the work of a host of fellow scientifically minded Europeans in Burma and on pioneer Burma botanists such as Francis Buchanan, who accompanied Michael Symes on his 1795 embassy to Ava, the English missionary Felix Carey, and Dr. Wallich, a member of John Crawfurd's embassy to Ava in 1826-27. The enlarged editions were published under the titles *Tenasserim or notes on the fauna, flora, minerals, and nations of British Burma and Pegu* (Maulmain, Burma: American Mission Press, Thos. S. Ranney, 1852. 712p.) and *Burma, its people or natural productions: or notes on the nations, flora, and minerals of Tenasserim, Pegu and Burmah, with systematic catalogues of the known mammals, birds, fish, reptiles, insects, mollusks, crustaceans, annalids, radiates, plants and minerals, with vernacular names* (Rangoon: Thomas Stowe Ranney; London: Trübner; New York: Phinney, Blakeman & Mason, 1860. 913p.). There is also an offshoot of his 1850 publication entitled *Flora Burmanica: or a catalogue of plants indigenous and cultivated in the valleys of the Irrawaddy, Salwen, and Tenasserim, from notes on the fauna, flora and minerals of the Tenasserim provinces and the Burman empire* (Tavoy, Burma: Karen Mission Press, C. Bennett, 1851. [paginated p. 545-676]). For the 1882 edition, Theobald (a deputy-superintendent of the Geological Survey of India) revised and rewrote extensively Mason's 1860 edition, particularly the zoological and botanical sections, losing in the process much of Mason's distinctive language and style, and making a different arrangement of the material, incorporating much new information (for example, the Rev. Charles Parish's observations and lists of orchids [vol. 2, part 1,

p. 148-202]). The 1882 revised edition has dropped entries in Burmese and Karen scripts used in the earlier editions for giving the indigenous names of fauna and flora, etc.

125 **Botanical survey of the Southern Shan States: with a note on the vegetation of the Inle Lake.**
Mohinder Nath.   Rangoon: Burma Research Society Fiftieth Anniversary Publications, no. 1 (1961), p. 157-418. maps.
A detailed monograph listing the finds of a survey made in 1957-59.

126 **A game-book for Burma and adjoining territories: the types, distribution and habits of large and small game, together with notes on game preservation, photography, tracking, still-hunting and the care and measurement of trophies.**
Edgar Henry Peacock.   London: H. F. & G. Witherby, 1933. 292p.;
New Delhi: International Books & Periodicals Supply Service, 1985.
292p. map.
The author, a deputy conservator of forests and a game warden in British Burma, offers in his introduction an explanation for the apparent paradox of one whose duty it is to conserve wild life writing a book on the sport of shooting it. The book contains a good deal of natural history information as well as practical advice to hunters. Geraldine Peacock's biography of Peacock (1893-1955), *The life of a jungle walla: reminiscences in the life of Lieut.-Col. E. H. Peacock, D.S.O., M.C.* (Ilfracombe, England: Arthur H. Stockwell, 1958. 134p.) contains chapters on their life in Burma and on Peacock's distinguished wartime service with Force 136 and Karen guerrillas, and a section on trapping and training wild elephants by the stockade method. Another 'game book', well illustrated with colour and black-and-white plates, and giving information on, and vernacular names of, animal species, is R. Lydekker's *The great and small game of India, Burma, and Tibet* (London: Rowland Ward, 1900. 416p.).

127 **Medicinal plants of East and Southeast Asia: attributed properties and their uses.**
Lily M. Perry, with the assistance of Judith Metzger.   Cambridge, Massachusetts; London: MIT Press, 1980. 620p. bibliog.
A massive compilation listing officinal uses of flowering plants and ferns (p. 1-446) including many from Burma, with a bibliography (p. 447-94), and indexes of therapeutic properties, plants, disorders, plant remedies and scientific names. It can be used in conjunction with a series produced by the Burma Medical Research Institute of which the first volume *Burmese indigenous medicinal plants: 1, Plants with reputed hypoglycemic action* by Mya Bwin, Sein Gwan (Rangoon: Burma Medical Research Institute, 1967. 157p.) gives an illustrated systematic description of plants useful in the treatment of diabetes. Also relevant is the bilingual (English and Burmese) publication *Some medicinal and useful palnts, both indigenous and exotic, of Burma* by San Khin, edited by Tha Myat (Rangoon: Student Press, 1970. 147p. bibliog.).

128   **The Burmese cat.**
Robine Pocock, Dorothy Silkstone Richards, Moira Swift, Vic
Watson.   London; Sydney: B. T. Batsford, 1975. 182p.
Full of feline information, this book contains a brief discussion of the breed's tenuous
links with Burma.

129   **The grasses of Burma.**
D. Rhind.   Calcutta, India: American Mission Press, 1945. 99p.
A detailed botanical compilation of known Burmese grass flora. An earlier work,
which has the advantage of being illustrated, is A. McKerral, *The commoner grasses of
Burma: with notes on their agricultural importance and distribution* (Rangoon:
Superintendant, Government Printing & Stationery, 1937. 23p. [+23p. of plates].
[Department of Agriculture, Burma, Bulletin no. 20]). Also relevant is Norman Loftus
Bor, *The grasses of Burma, Ceylon, India and Pakistan, excluding Bambusae* (New
York: Pergamon, 1960. 767p. bibliog.) in the 'International Series of Monographs on
Pure and Applied Biology; Division: Botany', vol. 1.

130   **The birds of Burma.**
Bertram Evelyn Smythies.   Edinburgh, London: Oliver & Boyd, 1953.
2nd ed. 688p. map. bibliog.; Dehradun, India: International Book
Distributors, 1984. 589p. map. bibliog.
This massive, authoritative book was first published in an edition of 1000 copies in
Rangoon by the American Baptist Mission Press in 1940. The author, in his preface to
the second edition, tells how the original paintings and blocks for printing the colour
plates (by A. M. Hughes) of the first edition were rescued on the eve of the Japanese
occupation of Rangoon. Originally intended as a concise field guide, the author,
believing that in independent Burma the study of birds seemed 'doomed to stagnate',
expanded his original work into as full and accurate as possible account of the birds of
Burma. The bibliography is invaluable for its listing of 20th-century publications on
Burmese ornithology, including many articles published in the *Journal of the Bombay
Natural History Society*. For earlier publications, Smythies refers the reader, to the
bibliography in *Birds* by E. W. Oates and W. T. Blanford (London: Taylor & Francis,
1889-98. 4 vols.) published as part of the massive series *The Fauna of British India,
including Ceylon and Burma*, edited by W. T. Blanford (q.v.).

131   **The Ficus Elastica in Burma proper or a narrative of my journey in
search of it: a descriptive account of its habits of growth and the process
followed by the Kakhyens in the preparation of caoutchouc.**
G. W. Strettell.   Rangoon: Government Press, 1876. 222p. map.
An intrepid botanist's account of a journey through Upper Burma in 1873 with much
observation of local scenes, and a map showing the geographical distribution of the
rubber plant.

132 Burmese timber elephant.

Toke Gale. Rangoon: Trade Corporation, 1974. 162p. map. bibliog.

The author, a retired Burmese forestry official, has distilled nearly thirty years' experience, study and observations into this useful illustrated book on Burmese elephants. It covers elephant physiology and life cycle, the capture and training of elephants, white elephants, and working elephant equipment, with a glossary of terms.

133 Wild animals of Burma.

Tun Yin. Rangoon: Rangoon Gazette, 1967. 301p. bibliog.

A useful, fully illustrated compilation incorporating scientific data and the accumulated experience of many observers. The introduction surveys 19th and 20th-century scientific expeditions in Burma, with details of various western naturalists and explorers and their publications; with an invaluable bibliography (p. 281-95). More comprehensive than H. C. Smith's *Wild animals of Burma* (Rangoon: British Burma Press, 1936. 2 vols.) which summarizes information on twenty-four larger mammals (vol. 1. 54p.) and twenty-eight smaller mammals (vol. 2. 99p.). Also relevant is *Riches of the wild: land mammals of South-East Asia* by the Earl of Cranbrook, with colour plates by A. M. Hughes (Singapore; Oxford; New York: Oxford University Press, 1987. 95p. map. bibliog.) in the series 'Images of Asia' which describes 660 species and gives an indication by country, or region, of the distribution of each species.

134 Tropical rain forests of the Far East.

T. C. Whitmore. Oxford: English Language Book Society/Oxford University Press, 1986. 2nd rev. ed. 352p. maps. bibliog.

An authoritative work which draws together scattered specialized individual research into a coherent account for a wider general audience. The book highlights the serious, escalating ecological damage in progress and developments in the study of rain forest ecology. First published in 1975, the bibliography of the revised edition has doubled in size, making it an extensive research aid. References to Burma may be found throughout the index, and the book also has a detailed index of plant names. Also relevant is Philip Hurst's *Rainforest politics: ecological destruction in South East Asia*, (London: Zed, 1991).

Far ridges: a record of travel in North-Eastern Burma 1938-39.
See item no. 79.

The forests of India.
See item no. 234.

Elephant Bill.
See item no. 339.

Seafood of South-East Asia.
See item no. 787.

Prehistory and Archaeology

135   **The 'neolithic' culture of Padahlin caves.**
Aung Thaw.   *Asian Perspectives*, vol. 14 (1971), p. 123-33.
A report on excavations at a neolithic site in the Shan States and of the discovery of more than 1,600 stone tools and of red-ochre cave illustrations. Previously published in *Journal of the Burma Research Society*, vol. 52, pt. 1 (June 1969), p. 9-23 [+25p. of plates and drawings of the finds].

136   **Report of the excavations at Beikthano.**
Aung Thaw.   Rangoon: Ministry of Union Culture, 1968. 220p.
A detailed account of the excavations conducted by the Archaeological Survey of Burma at the ancient Pyu city, Beikthano, in Magwe District, during the years 1959-63; with sixty-five black-and-white plates, illustrations of burial urns, pottery and metal objects excavated, and site plans and sections. On Pyu sites, see also Myint Aung's 'The excavations at Halin', *Journal of the Burma Research Society*, vol. 53, pt. 2 (1970), p. 53-63; Tha Hla and Nyi Nyi's 'Report on the fieldwork at Hmawza (Sri-Ksetra) and Prome', *Journal of the Burma Research Society*, vol. 61, pts. 1 and 2 (1958), p. 83-99; and Than Tun's 'A forgotten town of Burma', *Shiroku*, vol. 12 (1979), p. 51-56. On Mon sites, see Myint Aung's 'The capital of Suvannabhumi unearthed?' *Shiroku*, vol. 10 (1977), p. 41-53, while Saimong Mangrai's 'Did Sona and Uttara come to Lower Burma?' *Journal of the Burma Research Society*, vol. 59, pts. 1-2 (1976), p. 155-66 discusses Buddhism at Sriksetra and has a note on excavations at Thaton.

137   **Burma before Pagan: the status of archaeology today.**
Michael Aung-Thwin.   *Asian Perspectives*, vol. 35, no. 2 (1982-83),
p. 1-21.
This useful article traces the development of archaeology in Burma and summarizes findings to date, placing them in the larger Southeast Asian context. Aung-Thwin describes the publications series of the Archaeological Survey of Burma (previously of India) and of published inscriptions, and of more recent Burmese works publishing the results of archaeological research in Burma at various sites. His article focuses on the Pyu culture of Burma (from 200 BC to the 9th century AD) and excavations at Pyu sites, describing and illustrating the finds, and outlining a new chronology for Burmese

prehistory. Also included is a description of the Stone Age culture of Burma, with a map of Stone Age sites and drawings of artifacts.

138 **Ancient Arakan: with special reference to its cultural history between the 5th and 11th centuries.**
Pamela C. Gutman. PhD thesis. Australian National University, Canberra 1977. 376p. bibliog.

An important study (including ninety-two plates) of the ancient kingdom of Arakan before the rise of the Burmese empire, based on Sanskrit and other extant inscriptions coins, sculpture and architecture. See also Thin Kyi's 'Arakanese capitals: a preliminary survey of their geographical setting', *Journal of the Burma Research Society*, vol. 53, pt. 2 (1970), p. 1-13.

139 **The ancient Pyu.**
Gordon H. Luce. *Journal of the Burma Research Society*, vol. 27, pt. 3 (Dec. 1937), p. 239-53. Reprinted, Rangoon: Burma Research Society, *Fiftieth Anniversary Publications*, no. 2 (1961), p. 307-21.

This is one of the first of many pioneering studies based on epigraphic and linguistic research by Gordon H. Luce (1889-1979), culminating in his major study, *Old Burma – early Pagan* (q.v.). Among Luce's other articles are: 'A century of progress in Burmese history and archaeology', *Journal of the Burma Research Society*, vol. 32, pt. 1 (June 1949), p. 79-94 summarizing work done before 1942 and citing important studies by Emil Forchhammer, Taw Sein Ko, Charles Duroiselle, Pe Maung Tin, Paul Pelliot Charles Otto Blagden and others; 'Mons of the Pagan dynasty', *Journal of the Burma Research Society*, vol. 36, pt. 1 (June 1953), p. 1-19; 'Old Kyaukse and the coming of the Burman', *Journal of the Burma Research Society*, vol. 42, pt. 1 (June 1959), p. 59-101; 'The early Syám in Burma's history', *Journal of the Siam Society*, vol. 46, pt. 1 (Aug. 1958), p. 123-214 and vol. 47, pt. 1 (June 1959), p. 59-101. 'Dvaravati and old Burma', *Journal of the Siam Society*, vol. 53 (1965), p. 10-26; and, 'The career of Htilaing Min (Kyanzittha)', *Journal of the Royal Asiatic Society*, new series, vol. 1-2 (1966), p. 53-68. A select bibliography of Luce's writings can be found in *Essays offered to G. H. Luce by his colleagues and friends in honour of his seventy-fifth birthday*, edited by Ba Shin, Jean Boisselier, Alexander B. Griswold (q.v.), while the appreciation by Pan Hla, 'Gordon Hannington Luce 1889-1979'. *Journal of the Burma Research Society*, vol. 62, pts. 1-2 (Dec. 1979), p. 215-34, also lists many of Luce's publications. A warm portrait of Luce describing his great contribution to Burmese scholarship is given in Hugh Tinker's article, 'The place of Gordon Luce in research and education in Burma during the last decades of British rule', *Journal of the Royal Asiatic Society* (1986), no. 2, p. 174-60.

140 **Phases of pre-Pagan Burma: languages and history.**
Gordon H. Luce. Oxford: Oxford University Press, 1985. 2 vols. 2 maps.

This is the last work, published posthumously, of the doyen of Burmese archaeological studies, Gordon Luce (1889-1979). It deals with the early history of Burma to the founding of Pagan (c. AD 856), and thus complements his massive study of the early Pagan period, *Old Burma – early Pagan* (q.v.). What shines through this learned densely footnoted study is Luce's enthusiasm and excitement at parting the mists of time to reveal 'partial glimpses of various phases of genuine history'. To do this Luce combines a study of the limited inscriptional and documentary evidence with archaeological findings and, above all, with analysis of the languages of the hills and plains peoples of Burma. Volume one is arranged into chapters on the early peoples of Burma (and their languages), as follows: the Mon-Khmer, Karen, Thet-Kadu, Pyu, Chin, Mru and K'umi (North Arakan), and the Burma-Lolo. These are followed by an index of words in language charts, an index of Chinese characters, and a detailed catalogue of plates. Volumes two contains 26 language charts and 100 pages of black-and-white plates. Also relevant is Luce's philological compilation, reproduced from his handwritten manuscript, *A comparative word-list of Old Burmese, Chinese and Tibetan*, with an introduction by Eugénie J. A. Henderson, and references and sources by Tin Htway (London: School of Oriental & African Studies, University of London, 1981. 88p.).

141 **The ancient Pyu of Burma: vol. 1, Early Pyu cities in a man-made landscape.**
Janice Stargardt. Cambridge, England: Publications on Ancient Civilizations in Southeast Asia (PACSEA), in association with the Institute of Southeast Asian Studies, Singapore, 1990. 416p. maps.
This, the first major study of the early Pyu civilization in Burma, examines Pyu economic and social development over a period of more than one thousand years, to the 9th century AD. Volume one begins with the antecedents to urbanization, the environment and prehistoric background, and then examines the extensive irrigation work of the Pyu, focusing on three major Pyu sites, Beikthano, Halin and Sri Ksetra. Other early irrigated sites in Burma are also discussed within the wider context of the realtionship between hydraulic systems and urbanization. Volume one concentrates on Beikthano covering its pre-Buddhist phase, Buddhist culture, architecture and artifacts, and examining the wider regional significance of Beikthano, with over 100 figures, tables and maps, plus three separate maps in the end pockets showing archaeological and ancient hydraulic features at Beikthano, Sri Ksetra and Halin from aerial surveys. There are sixteen pages of plates. To be followed by Volume two, *Pyu kingdoms of the north and south*.

142 **Research on early man in Burma.**
Helmut de Terra, Hallam L. Movius, with supplementary reports by Edwin H. Colbert, J. Bequaert. *Transactions of the American Philosophical Society*, new series, vol. 32, pt. 3 (1943), p. 267-464.
This report of an American scientific expedition to Burma in 1937-38 is divided into two main sections: 'The Pleistocene of Burma' by de Terra (p. 271-340) giving geological data on the Irrawaddy Basin and the Northern Shan highlands and the Pleistocene history of Burma; and, 'The stone age of Burma' by Movius (p. 341-91), with a bibliography (p. 392-94) of valuable references for the prehistory of Burma. Also included are the following supplementary reports 'Pleistocene vertebrates collected in Burma' by Edwin H. Colbert (p. 395-430), and 'Fresh-water shells from cave deposits in the Southern Shan States' by J. Bequaert (p. 431-36). The expedition went on to Idonesia and the final section of the report is on early man in Java (p. 437-64). See also the article by Russell L. Ciochan, Donald E. Savage, Thaw Tint and Ba Maw, 'Anthropoid origins in Asia? New discovery of amphipethecus from the Eocene of Burma', *Science*, no. 229 (Aug. 1985), p. 756-59, on the discovery of the fossil Amphipethecus Mogaungensis.

Historical sites in Burma.
See item no. 90.

The advent of Buddhism in Burma.
See item no. 479.

History

General

143 The British 'pacification' of Burma: order without meaning.

Michael Aung-Thwin. *Journal of Southeast Asian Studies*, vol. 16, no. 2 (Sept. 1985), p. 245-61.

Conventional (Western) intellectual parameters for evaluating the colonial and post-independence periods are challenged in this article. Burmese criteria for defining order and indigenous methods of 'pacification' are examined and contrasted with the pacification policies and methods pursued by the British in the post-1885 period. The 1962 military coup and the policies of the Ne Win era are also interpreted in the light of underlying Burmese criteria and viewed as more of a 'resurrection than a true revolution'. Among other interpretative and historiographical essays by Aung-Thwin are 'Prophecies, omens and dialogue: tools of the trade in Burmese historiography' in *Moral order and the question of change: essays on Southeast Asian thought*, edited by David K. Wyatt, Alexander Woodside (New Haven, Connecticut: Yale University Southeast Asia Studies, 1982, p. 78-103), 'Divinity, spirit, and human: conceptions of classical Burmese kingship' in *Centers, symbols, and hierarchies: essays on the classical states of Southeast Asia*, edited by Lorraine Gesick (New Haven, Connecticut: Yale University Southeast Asia Studies, 1983, p. 45-86, and 'Heaven, earth, and the supernatural world: dimensions of the exemplary center in Burmese history' in *The city as a sacred center: essays on six Asian contexts*, edited by Bardwell Smith, Holly Baker Reynolds (Leiden, The Netherlands: E. J. Brill, 1987, p. 88-102).

144 Conference under the tamarind tree: three essays in Burmese history.

Paul J. Bennett. New Haven, Connecticut: Yale University, Southeast Asian Studies, 1971. 152p. 4 maps. bibliog. (Yale University Southeast Asia Studies Monograph Series, no. 15).

An American Foreign Service officer's stimulating reappraisal and analysis of different periods in Burmese history. The three essays are 'The fall of Pagan: continuity and change in 14th-century Burma' (p. 3-53); 'The conference under the tamarind tree'

Burmese politics and the accession of King Thibaw, 1878-1882' (p. 57-99); and 'Two Southeast Asian ministers and reactions to European conquest: the Kinwun Mingyi and Phan-Thanh-Gian (p. 103-42). As well as a separate bibliography at the end of the book, each essay is followed by a 'bibliographic comment' which includes a discussion of the Burmese sources used.

145   A history of modern Burma.
John Frank Cady.   Ithaca, New York: Cornell University Press, 1958. 682p. map. bibliog.

This magisterial study of Burma from the late 18th century to the mid-1950s is based largely on western source materials and has long been a standard history of the period. Cady's was the first history of Burma to present a systematic account of Burmese–British relations and political developments and, above all, to give a connected account of Burmese nationalist politics and the struggle for independence. A second printing of the book was done in 1960 with a separate added thirty-four page supplement entitled 'The swing of the pendulum' covering the political events of 1957-60. Cady's *The history of post-war Southeast Asia* (Athens, Ohio: Ohio University Press, 1974. 720p. 3 maps. bibliog.) has sections on Burma's governmental and economic problems in the period 1951-62, and on Burma under military rule. Cady's *The United States and Burma* (Cambridge, Massachusetts; London: Harvard University Press, 1976. 303p. 5 maps.) in the 'American Foreign Policy Library' series is not, as its title seems to suggest, a study of American–Burmese relations, but a basic introductory history of Burma from the 11th century to the early 1970s. A bibliographical essay surveying published English-language sources on Burma is appended.

146   In search of Southeast Asia: a modern history.
Edited by David Joel Steinberg.   Honolulu: University of Hawaii Press, 1987. rev. ed. 590p. 5 maps. bibliog.

First published in 1971, this book has become a popular textbook in universities and colleges and is indispensable for an understanding of modern Southeast Asian history. Its main concern is to identify unifying themes that have shaped the history of the region as a whole. The book is divided into sections (the 18th-century world, new challenges to old authorities, frameworks for nations, social change and the emergence of nationalism, Southeast Asian nations in a new world order) which establish leading themes. Within this framework the process of change is examined in more detail for each country. The original edition was written without the participation of a Burma specialist and for this revised edition, a political scientist, Robert H. Taylor, was recruited to rewrite all the Burma portions of the text. Other authors involved in this study include David P. Chandler, William R. Roff, John R. W. Smail, Alexander Woodside, David K. Wyatt. The whole book and its extensive annotated bibliography has been revised and updated for this edition.

147 **Southeast Asian history and historiography: essays presented to
D. G. E. Hall.**
Edited by Charles Donald Cowan, Oliver William Wolters, foreword
by John M. Echols. Ithaca, New York; London: Cornell University
Press, 1976. 436p. bibliog.

Daniel George Edward Hall (1891-1979) was the doyen of Southeast Asian historians.
Over a period of more than fifty years his research and teaching influenced generations
of students and his *A history of South-East Asia* (q.v.) pioneered an integrated regional
approach and framework for understanding Southeast Asian history. This collection of
essays by Professor Hall's students, colleagues and friends was made to honour him in
his eighty-fifth year. It contains four articles of Burma interest: 'Sources of early
Burma history' by Gordon H. Luce (p. 31-42); 'Prolegomena to a phonology of Old
Burmese' by Robert H. Jones (p. 43-50); 'Dalhousie and the Burmese war of 1852' by
Sir Cyril Philips (p. 51-58); and 'A short history of a Burmese–English dictionary,
1913-1963' by Hla Pe (p. 86-99). In addition, there is a biographical sketch of D. G. E.
Hall by C. D. Cowan (p. 11-23) and a bibliography compiled by Helen Cordell (p. 25-
27) of Professor Hall's writings, of which the greatest proportion is on Burma.

148 **Encyclopaedia of Asian history.**
Edited by Ainslie T. Embree (chief editor), prepared under the
auspices of the Asia Society. New York: Charles Scribner's;
London: Collier Macmillan, 1988. 4 vols.

This contains much of relevance to Burma, and provides a convenient means of
accessing basic historical information on Burma, with entries under the headings of
'Burma' and under the names of individual kings, politicians, cities and dynasties, etc.
contributed by Burma specialists Michael Aung-Thwin, John P. Ferguson, Victor B.
Lieberman, William J. Koenig, Myo Myint, Robert H. Taylor, and others. Brief
bibliographical references are given at the end of each entry. Volume four contains a
list of entries and contributors, and an index.

149 **Historians of South-East Asia.**
Edited by Daniel George Edward Hall. London: Oxford University
Press, 1961. 342p. (Historical Writing on the Peoples of Asia).

This volume contains twenty-five papers on various aspects of Southeast Asian
historiography, among which are the following five on Burma: 'The nature of the
Burmese chronicles' by Tet Htoot (p. 50-62); 'A Mon genealogy of kings: observations
on the *Nidana Arambhakatha*' by Harry L. Shorto (p. 63-72); 'Modern historical
writing in Burmese, 1724-1942' by Tin Ohn (p. 85-93); 'British writers of Burmese
history from Dalrymple to Bayfield' by D. G. E. Hall (p. 255-66); and 'Arthur Phayre
and Henry Yule: two soldier-administrator historians' by Hugh Tinker (p. 267-78).

150 **History of South-East Asia.**
Daniel George Edward Hall. London: Macmillan, 1981. 4th rev. ed.
1070p. maps. bibliog. (Macmillan Asian History Series).

First published in 1955, this massive study was the first history of Southeast Asia both
to view the region as an integrated whole with its own perspective and framework, and
to present the history of individual countries within the region. Hall revised and
updated each edition to incorporate the latest research findings and his work remains a

standard history of Southeast Asia. The history of Burma and other countries is presented chronologically in four broad sections: Southeast Asian history to the 16th century; from the beginning of the 16th to the end of the 18th century; the period of European territorial expansion; nationalism and the challenge to European domination. Dynastic lists of rulers, together with colonial governors and governors-general, are given in the appendix. Among Hall's many other studies are a concise general history of Burma to the 1950s, *Burma* (London: Hutchinson's University Library, 1960. 3rd ed. 198p. map. bibliog.; New York: AMS Press, 1974. 184p.) and a review of early Western relations with Burma and of the diplomatic and commercial rivalries that culminated in the British annexation of Burma, *Europe and Burma: a study of European relations with Burma to the annexation of Thibaw's kingdom 1886* (London; New York: Oxford University Press, 1945. 190p. map. bibliog.).

151 History of Burma: from the earliest times to 10 March 1824, the beginning of the English conquest.

Godfrey Eric Harvey, preface by Richard Carnac Temple. London: Longmans, Green, 1925; London: Frank Cass, 1967. 415p. 5 maps. bibliog.

This standard history of Burma, based on Burmese chronicles and on Western archival sources, focuses on political and dynastic events. Harvey incorporates much information not available to Arthur Phayre when writing his pioneering *History of Burma* (q.v.) and, in particular when dealing with the early history of Burma, depends heavily upon the research of Charles Duroiselle. The long appendix (p. 307-90) contains invaluable supplementary notes as well as dynastic tables and the bibliography. An abridged, unreferenced version of Harvey's *History*, with added sections covering the period 1824 to 1885, was published under the title, *Outline of Burmese history* (Bombay, India: Longmans, Green, 1926, 1947. 210p.). Also by Harvey is *British rule in Burma, 1824-1942* (q.v.), and he also contributed succinct sections on Burmese history, covering the period 1287 to 1918, to volumes three to six of *The Cambridge history of British India*, edited by H. H. Dodwell, (et al.) (Cambridge: Cambridge University Press, 1928-37; Delhi: S. Chandra, 1958 [vol.6]). Harvey (1889-1965) was in the Indian Civil Service in Burma from 1912 to 1932, and later became lecturer in Burmese history and law at Oxford University. An examination of changes in Harvey's interpretation of Burmese history, moving from an 'imperialist justification' of the British annexation of Burma to a more liberal and critical approach can be found in an article by Htin Aung, 'Three unpublished papers by Harvey, introduced, explained and commented upon', *Journal of the Burma Resarch Society*, vol. 58, pt. 1 (Oct. 1975), p. 1-52.

152 A history of Burma.

Htin Aung. New York; London: Columbia University Press, 1967. 363p. map.

A general history of Burma from the earliest times to 1962, based primarily on the Burmese chronicles; with bibliographical notes for each chapter providing a critique of western sources. Htin Aung (1909-70), one of four distinguished brothers (Tin Tut, Kyaw Myint and Myint Thein), followed an academic career and did much in his historical and legal writings to champion a 'Burmese' interpretation of history. His *Burmese history before 1287: a defence of the chronicles* (Oxford: Asoka Society, 1970. 46p. bibliog.) is a contentious critique of the theories of Gordon H. Luce, comparing evidence from the Burmese chronicles with that from the inscriptions as analysed by Luce.

153 **The stricken peacock: Anglo-Burmese relations 1752-1948.**
Htin Aung. The Hague: Martinus Nijhoff, 1965. 135p. bibliog.
The author's view is that Western historians have, with the honourable exception of Dorothy Woodman in *The making of Burma* (q.v.), given no consideration 'to the Burmese point of view or to the Burmese sources of history'. His study traces Anglo-Burmese relations from 1619 to 1886, and attempts an assessment of the consequences of British rule and, while still using substantially Western sources, provides a counterpoint to them. Also relevant is his article, 'First Burmese mission to the court of St. James: Kinwun Mingyi's diaries, 1872-74', *Journal of the Burma Research Society*, vol. 57, pts. 1-2 (Dec. 1974), p. 1-198.

154 **The Burmese and Arakanese calendars.**
Alfred Macdonald Bulteel Irwin. Rangoon: Hanthawaddy Printing Works. 1909. 92p.
A general description of the calendrical system and methods of calculation and conversion of dates from the Burmese era, followed by ten tables. In Burma one-hundred-year almanacs giving charts of English and Burmese dates are published regularly under the title *Hnit taya pyet-hkadein*, while for historians the compilation by Yi Yi, *Myan-ma Ingaleik pyet-hkadein* (Rangoon: Burma Historical Commission, 1965. 480p.) giving charts of dates for the period 1701-1820 is useful. A recent specialist work that enables the verification of dates in Southeast Asian inscriptions and historical records, is J. C. Eade, *Southeast Asian ephemeris: solar and planetary positions*, AD 638-2000 (Ithaca, New York: Cornell University Southeast Asia Program, 1989. 175p.). The work by R. L. Soni, *A cultural study of the Burmese era* (Mandalay, Burma: World Institute of Buddhist Culture, 1955. 200p.) purports to be a study of the Burmese era and calendar, but is really a rambling discourse on 'the Indo-Burmese cultural relationship'.

155 **Historical and cultural studies in Burma.**
Edited by Yoshiaki Ishizawa. Tokyo: Institute of Asian Cultures, Sophia University, 1988. 259p.
This research report contains eight papers by four Japanese scholars, as follows: three papers by Yoshiaki Ishizawa, 'Antimonies of Japan: realities of Asia' (p. 9-18), 'Considerations regarding the basic framework of Burmese history and Buddhism' (p. 19-64), and 'Report for a historical and cultural study in Lower Burma' (p. 229-51); two papers by Katsumi Tamura, 'Rethinking spirit-belief in Burma' (p. 169-96), and 'Ethnic issues and national integration' (p. 197-228); 'A preliminary report on the study of the Maru, Lashi, and Atsi languages of Burma' by Shiro Yabu (p. 65-132); and, 'Development of high yielding rice program in Burma' by Teruko Saito (p. 133-68).

156 **Reinterpreting Burmese history.**
Victor B. Lieberman. *Comparative Studies in Society and History*, vol. 29 (1987), p. 162-94.
This important historiographical article on the problems of periodization and interpretation of Burmese history discusses such factors as inter-Asian trade, the siting of Burmese capitals, the political implications of religious donations, ethnic politics and the legacies of colonial rule. Lieberman challenges the view that, despite its revolutionary and anti-feudal rhetoric, the military government of contemporary

Burma draws substantially on pre-colonial traditions. Lieberman argues that 'the emphasis on continuity in style between precolonial and postcolonial regimes ignores crucial changes in structure that the British introduced and that contemporary governments of the Union of Burma are determined, indeed compelled, to preserve'. He does, however, see a basic continuity residing in 'the long highly uneven process of state formation and centralization' that started in the precolonial period and has continued through the colonial and contemporary periods.

57 **Southeast Asia: an illustrated introductory history.**
Milton Osborne. Sydney: London; Boston, Massachusetts: Allen & Unwin, 1988. rev. ed. 263p. maps. bibliog.

A lively thematic treatment of events and developments in the history of modern Southeast Asia, dealing with the region as a whole and designed as an introduction to the region for non-specialists. Since its first publication in 1979, the author has revised and expanded the work and in particular added a chapter on 'discovering Southeast Asia through art and literature' which briefly reviews Southeast Asian art history and fictional writing on Southeast Asia.

58 **History of Burma, including Burma proper, Pegu, Taungu, Tenasserim and Arakan: from the earliest time to the end of the first war with British India.**
Arthur Purves Phayre. London: Trübner, 1883. 311p.; New York: Augustus M. Kelley, 1969. 311p. map.

Phayre (1812-85) served in Tenasserim and Arakan before becoming commissioner of Pegu following its annexation in 1852 and chief commissioner of British Burma from 1862 to 1867. His pioneering *History*, based substantially on Burmese source materials, established a framework, nomenclature, chronology and periodization for Burmese history that has, for the most part, remained unmodified by subsequent generations of scholars. For details of Phayre's career, his source materials and a list of his writings which included studies on the ancient coinage of Burma and Arakan) see the article by Patricia M. Herbert, 'The Sir Arthur Phayre collection of Burmese manuscripts', *British Library Journal*, vol. 1, no. 1 (Spring, 1975), p. 62-70, and that by Hugh Tinker, 'Arthur Phayre and Henry Yule: two soldier-administrator historians', in *Historians of South-East Asia*, edited by D. G. E. Hall (q.v.).

59 **Peacocks, pagodas and Professor Hall: a critique of the persisting use of historiography as an apology for British empire building in Burma.**
Manuel Sarkisyanz. Athens, Ohio: Ohio University Center for International Studies, Southeast Asia Program, 1972. 57p. (Papers in International Studies, Southeast Asia Series, no. 24).

A forceful attack on the writings of Professor D. G. E. Hall on Burma, accusing Hall of imperialist bias and of making value judgements. Also by Sarkisyanz, with Kyaw Than, is *'Myanmar': Burma's killing fields, their military managers and academic whitewashers* ([Heidelberg, Germany]: German–Burmese Association, 1990. [46p.]) – a disjointed attack principally upon Benedict Anderson and Robert H. Taylor whose 1987 statements defending the Ne Win régime are countered by accounts of the suppression of the pro-democracy movement in Burma in 1988, drawn mostly from Bertil Lintner's *Outrage* (q.v.). Sarkisyanz is best known in the Burma context for his study, *Buddhist backgrounds of the Burmese revolution* (q.v.). See also *Festschrift für*

Prof. Manuel Sarkisyanz ('Festschrift to Prof. Manuel Sarkisyanz') edited by Barbar
Diehl-Eli, Emmanuel Sevrugian, Tin Htway (Frankfurt-am-Main, GFR: Verlag Pete
Lang, 1987. 458p. bibliog.) which contains a bibliography of Sarkisyanz's writing
(p. 21-28) and the following contributions on aspects of Burma: 'First impressions c
our first sojourn in Burma and other letters', by Frank N. Trager and Helen Trage
(p. 235-87); 'Leadership and mass response in Java, Burma and in Vietnam' b
B. Dahm (p. 305-40); 'The use and mis-use of the term *Porana* by Burmese scholars
by Hla Pe (p. 381-410); and, 'A preliminary note on the Vinayadharas of Pagan perio
in Burma' by Tin Htway (p. 411-58).

160   **The royal orders of Burma, AD 1598-1885.**
      Edited with introduction, notes and English summary by Than Tun.
      Kyoto, Japan: Center for Southeast Asian Studies, Kyoto University,
      1983-90. 10 vols.

This mammoth compilation (over 4,000p.) represents a major source of information o
Burmese political, social, economic and cultural history over a period of 300 year
Each volume is in two parts: introduction, notes and English translation of the roy
orders, followed by the Burmese text. Volumes one to nine present the orders i
chronological order, while volume ten consists of an 'epilogue' giving Than Tun
observations on the land, people, ruler, law and religion (drawing on material from th
royal orders), a glossary and subject index to the contents of the preceding volume
Dr. Than Tun's 'Observations on the translation and annotation of the royal orders
Burma' can be found in the *Special Burma Studies Issue of Crossroads* (q.v.).
bibliography of Than Tun's writings and a short biography can be found in *Studies c
Burmese history* by 'Colleagues of Dr. Than Tun' (Mandalay, Burma: Histor
Department, Mandalay University, 1982, p. 1-14), issued to mark his retirement fro
Mandalay University.

161   **Burmese historical literature and native and foreign scholarship.**
      Thaung Blackmore. In: *Symposium on historical, archaeological and
      linguistic studies on Southern China, South-East Asia and the Hong
      Kong region*. Edited by F. S. Drake. Hong Kong: Hong Kong
      University Press, 1967, p. 311-19.

A useful survey of Burmese historical writings from the inscriptions to 20th-centu
publications, with a brief review of scholarly works on Burma in English.

162   **Burma from kingdom to republic: a historical and political analysis.**
      Frank N. Trager.   London: Pall Mall Press, 1966. 455p. map.

The basic theme of this study is the independence of Burma – its loss and recovery.
secondary theme is Burma's foreign relations, and Burma's neutralist policy ar
relations with China, Russia and the United States are examined. The book has
bibliography *per se*, but contains extensive bibliographical information and comment
the notes section.

63   **The universe around them: cosmology and cosmic renewal in Indianized
      South-east Asia.**
      Horace Geoffrey Quaritch Wales.   London: Arthur Probsthain, 1977.
      168p. (Probsthain's Oriental Series, vol. 30).

An introduction to Hindu and Buddhist cosmogony and to how cosmological concepts
are interpreted and adapted in Southeast Asian architecture, administration and
ceremonies. Wales summarizes and re-evaluates previous scholarly theories concerning
early Southeast Asian conceptual systems and postulates that Southeast Asian
cosmogony can be traced to a pre-Indian indigenous Dong-son (Bronze Age) culture of
ancient Southeast Asia. Chapter seven (p. 134-63) discusses the application of R. von
Heine-Geldern's theories of state and kingship in Southeast Asia – as first formulated
in a pioneering article in German – to Burma, Thailand and Cambodia.

64   **The making of Burma.**
      Dorothy Woodman.   London: Cresset Press, 1962. 594p. 12 maps.
      bibliog.

This authoritative political history traces Burma's early contacts with China and the
West and examines in detail the background to the three Anglo-Burmese Wars and the
period of resistance following the British annexation of Upper Burma in 1886. The
theme of the book is the fixing of Burma's frontiers and particular attention is paid
throughout to frontier issues and to the affairs of the minority peoples of Burma. The
final part of the book contains a detailed account of the Burma–China boundary
demarcation issue encompassing the Anglo-Chinese negotiations of the late 19th
century, the controversy over the McMahon Line and the resolution of the problem in
1960 with the Burma–China Boundary Treaty. A feature of the work is the author's
extensive quotations from original source materials in the India Office, particularly
from eye-witness reports, which are used to good effect as a corrective to the
perspective found in published official policy papers and narratives based on them.
Many original documents are reproduced in the appendixes, including the text of the
1960 Boundary Treaty.

A historical atlas of South Asia.
See item no. 110.

Pre-19th century

65   **Pagan: the origins of modern Burma.**
      Michael Aung-Thwin.   Honolulu, Hawaii: University of Hawaii Press,
      1985. 264p. 4 maps. bibliog.

An important study of the institutions of the kingdom of Pagan and of the
interrelationships and underlying concepts of politics, economics and religion in the
11th to 13th centuries AD. Aung-Thwin focuses on the relationship between
patronage, religious endowments and redistribution of wealth and examines how these
affected social organization, administration, legal institutions and the political
structure, linking the decline of Pagan to a loss of crown wealth to the Buddhist order.

51

In his concluding chapter Aung Thwin examines continuities between ancient and modern Burmese history. The extensive bibliography contains useful comments on primary sources, inscriptions, etc. A shorter analysis of the dynamics of the Pagan period can be found in Michael Aung-Thwin's article, 'Kingship, the sangha and society in Pagan', in *Explorations in early Southeast Asian statescraft*, edited by Kenneth R. Hall, John K. Whitmore (Ann Arbor, Michigan: University of Michigan Center for South and Southeast Asian Studies, 1976, p. 205-56). Aung-Thwin's theories concerning a linkage between the rise and fall of Burmese dynasties and the pattern of religious endowments have also been formulated in his article, 'The role of Sasana reform in Burmese history: economic dimensions of a religious purification' *Journal of Asian Studies*, vol. 38, no. 4 (Aug. 1979), p. 671-88. This article generated a vigorous academic exchange between Aung-Thwin and Victor B. Lieberman, a follows: Victor B. Lieberman, 'The political significance of religious wealth in Burmese history: some further thoughts', *Journal of Asian Studies*, vol. 39, no. 4 (Aug. 1980) p. 753-69; M. Aung-Thwin, 'A reply to Lieberman', *Journal of Asian Studies*, vol. 40 no. 1 (Nov. 1980), p. 87-90'; and, V. B. Lieberman, 'A note on Burmese religious land holdings', *Journal of Asian Studies*, vol. 40, no. 4 (Aug. 1981), p. 745-46.

166 **Journal of a residence in the Burmhan empire and more particularly at the court of Amarapoorah.**
Hiram Cox. London: John Warren, & G. & W. B. Whittaker, 1821. 431p. Reprinted with introduction by Daniel George Edward Hall. Farnborough, England: Gregg International, 1971. 431p.

Cox (1760-99) was sent to Burma in 1796 as British Resident at Rangoon in accordance with an agreement made by Michael Symes during his 1795 mission to Burma Overpreoccupied with his status, Cox believed Symes had been insulted and manipulated by the Burmese, and he spent an unhappy fruitless period at the Burmese Court which he described (elsewhere) as 'an assembly of clowns', endeavouring to get proper recognition by the Burmese government. His Residency was anything but success and he was recalled from Burma in April 1798. Cox died in Chittagong, where Cox's Bazaar is named after him as a memorial to his work there supervising relief measures for Arakanese refugees in 1799. Following his death, his journal was edited for publication by his son, Henry Cox, and presents a more favourable impression of Cox's conduct than is obtainable from the official records which reveal how Cox disregarded his instructions and courted diplomatic disaster. It should be noted that the 1821 edition has five hand-coloured engraved plates of Burmese court officials by I. M Newton which are reproduced only in black-and-white in the reprint edition. D. G. E Hall, who provided an introduction to the 1971 edition, gave a fuller historical account in his introduction to *Michael Symes, journal of his second embassy to Ava in 1802* (q.v.). For an analysis of Cox's psychology which concludes that the 'Burmese displayed great restraint in the face of importunate and even pathological behaviour on the envoy's part', see: 'Captain Hiram Cox's mission to Burma, 1796-1798: a case of irrational behaviour in diplomacy' by G. P. Ramachandra, in *Journal of Southeast Asian Studies*, vol. 12, no. 2 (Sept. 1981), p. 433-51. Supplementary and statistical material on Burma derived from Cox's papers can be found in a rare early compilation of documents by William Francklin, *Tracts, political, geographical and commercial: on the dominions of Ava, and the north western parts of Hindostaun* (London: T. Cadell & W. Davies, 1811. 281p.) which contains 'Observations on the instructions of the Envoy to the court of Burma' (p. 1-25); 'On the commerce of Ava' (p. 26-122); and 'Topography and population of Ava' (p. 123-59).

167 **Reprint from Dalrymple's Oriental Repertory, 1791-7 of portions relating to Burma.**
Alexander Dalrymple, selected by Godfrey Eric Harvey.   Rangoon: Superintendent, Government Printing, 1926. 260p. maps.

This work reprints, retaining the original pagination, all sections on Burma contained in Dalrymple's exceedingly rare two-volume publication, *Oriental Repertory* (London: Chapman, 1793, 1808), which covered the countries from India to China. Dalrymple spent from 1752-59 in the East India Company's Service at Fort St. George, Madras, and in his leisure studied the old records there and became inspired to encourage the spread of British commerce eastwards of India. Dalrymple was particularly interested in the ill-fated British settlement at Negrais, but his compilation does not contain all the records relating to Negrais or to other early British relations with Burma. The material in this reprint volume is selected and arranged by the historian Godfrey E. Harvey, and contains original documents concerning English relations with Burma from 1695 to 1761, with contemporary maps of the 'Ava River', i.e. the Irrawaddy.

168 **Early English intercourse with Burma 1587-1743: with the tragedy of Negrais as a new appendix.**
Daniel George Edward Hall.   London: Frank Cass, 1968. 2nd ed. 357p. bibliog.

Originally published for the University of Rangoon (London: Longmans, Green, 1928), this second edition contains a long appendix (p. 277-357) entitled 'The tragedy of Negrais' which was first published as an article in the *Journal of the Burma Research Society* (vol. 21, pt. 3 (1931), p. 59-133). Hall's work is still the most complete account of British relations, settlements and trade with Burma from the earliest English contacts in the 16th century to the mid 18th-century. It is based on extensive archival research at the India Office and quotes extensively from documents of the period, drawing on much material that was not available to Alexander Dalrymple whose *Oriental repertory* (q.v.) represents the first attempt to compile and reproduce original documents on this subject.

169 **Administrative patterns in historical Burma.**
Khin Maung Kyi, Tin Tin.   Singapore: Institute of Southeast Asian Studies, 1973. 67p. (Southeast Asian Perspectives, no. 1).

The first part of this study discusses theoretical, particularly Marxist, models of society; the second part examines the economic structure – irrigation, revenue, etc. – of the administration of Burma under the kings and analyses the administrative structure itself, making comparisons with theoretical models of Western feudalism and of the 'Asiatic mode of production'. Translated from the original Burmese article in *Union of Burma Journal of Education and Science*, vol. 2, no. 2 (1969), p. 223-75.

170 **The Burmese polity, 1752-1819: politics, administration, and social organization in the early Kon-baung period.**
William J. Koenig. Ann Arbor, Michigan: Center for South & Southeast Asian Studies, University of Michigan, 1990. 332p. map. bibliog. (Michigan Papers on South and Southeast Asia, no. 34).

This study, which originated as a thesis submitted to the School of Oriental & African Studies, University of London in 1978, focuses on the early Kon-baung polity and examines the society, the central political institution of the monarchy and its foundation in Burmese political thought, the administrative apparatus and the role of Buddhist monks, officials and the extended royal lineage. Two basic and interrelated areas of political conflict are discussed – the relative distribution of resources and control of the central political institution, the crown and the politics of the royal succession. The appendixes contain comments and data on population and trends in crown service houses in the period 1783 to 1802, and a discussion of Burmese and Western sources.

171 **Burmese administrative cycles: anarchy and conquest, c. 1580-1760.**
Victor B. Lieberman. Princeton, New Jersey: Princeton University Press, 1984. 338p. 4 maps. bibliog.

This important book offers a case study of political and administrative cycles and their relation to institutional and economic change during approximately 180 years of Burmese history, from 1580 to 1760, the era of the Toungoo dynasty and the beginning of the Kon-baung dynasty. This period saw phases of effective leadership and military conquest alternating with periods of administrative collapse and anarchy. Lieberman focuses on the competition for control of resources and the changing distribution of resources between the throne and élites. The role in strengthening control played by such factors as demographic shifts, the introduction of firearms and growth of maritime commerce is also explored. Drawing largely on hitherto unexploited Burmese-language source materials (which are discussed in an appendix to the book), Lieberman's work is a major contribution to Southeast Asian historiography.

172 **Old Burma – early Pagan.**
Gordon H. Luce. Locust Valley, New York: J. J. Augustin, for *Artibus Asiae* and Institute of Fine Arts, New York University, 1969-70. 3 vols. 4 maps. bibliog. (Artibus Asiae Supplementum 25).

This unsurpassed, monumental study of Pagan, capital of Burma from the 11th to the 13th centuries, is the fruit of Gorden Luce's lifetime scholarship and devotion to the study of early Burma. It tells the story of the founding of Pagan in the dry zone of central Burma, how it became the Buddhist capital of a united Burma and experienced a stupendous period of temple building and religious patronage and devotion. In volume one, Luce draws on contemporary inscriptions as well as on later records to establish a chronology of the monuments and a history of their patronage. He also examines the iconography of the period and shows how the sculpture and painting of Pagan, although building on earlier Indian sources, developed its own style. Volume two consists of a very detailed catalogue of plates, a bibliography and numerous indexes. Volume three contains 455 black-and-white plates. Luce's complex text is enhanced by his masterly translations of inscriptions which in prose and poetry vividly convey their authors' deep Buddhist inspiration. In his preface Luce pays tribute to the help of his Burmese colleagues at the Burma Historical Commission and the Burma Archaeological Department, and concludes by paying honour to the people of Pagan 'for the constant daily provision they have made over 900 years, out of their poverty, for the thousand living monuments of their Religion'.

173 **Southeast Asia in the 9th to 14th centuries.**
Edited by David G. Marr, Anthony C. Milner, introduction by Wang Gungwu. Singapore: Institute of Southeast Asian Studies and Research School of Pacific Studies, Australian National University, 1986. 416p.

A collection of twenty essays, originally presented as papers at an international conference at the Australian National University in May 1984, on aspects of early Southeast Asia. It contains two short papers relevant to Burma: one by Helmut Loofs-Wissowa, 'The true and the corbel arch in mainland Southeast Asian monumental architecture' (p. 239-47) which examines and contrasts the use of the true arch in Pagan temples and of the corbel arch in Angkor, Cambodia; and the other by Pamela Gutman, 'Symbolism of kingship in ancient Arakan' (p. 279-88). In addition, a paper by Janice Stargardt, 'Hydraulic works and South East Asian polities' (p. 23-48) contains some observations on early Burman and Pyu sites.

174 **The administration of Burma.**
Mya Sein, introduction by Josef Silverstein. Kuala Lumpur; Singapore; London: Oxford University Press, 1973. 186p. map. bibliog. (Oxford in Asia Historical Reprints).

Published originally in Burma in 1938 (Rangoon: Zabu Meitswe Pitaka Press. 206p.), this is a pioneering study of the indigenous Burmese system of local administration prior to British rule. The author also briefly describes early British changes in village administration. Daw Mya Sein (1904-88) had a distinguished and varied career, primarily in education, and was Burma's only woman delegate to the Round Table Conference held in London in 1931. She also wrote a wartime pamphlet, *Burma* (London: Oxford University Press, 1944. 2nd ed. 32p. [Oxford Pamphlets on Indian Affairs, no. 17]).

175 **The Glass Palace Chronicle of the kings of Burma.**
Translated by Pe Maung Tin, Gordon H. Luce. London: Oxford University Press, 1923; Rangoon: Rangoon University Press, 1960. 227p. map; New York: AMS Press, 1976. 179p. map.

Very few primary sources on Burmese history are available in translation. This work is a translation of parts of the Burmese chronicle. *Hman-nan maha ya-zawin-daw-gyi* compiled by a committee of Burmese scholars in 1829-32. The period covered in this translation is from the foundation of the cities of Tagaung, Sri Ksetra and Pagan down to the fall of Pagan in the 13th century. Pe Maung Tin's introduction gives a useful survey of the different Burmese chronicles and other sources used in the compilation of the chronicle. Indexes of names and events are provided. There is also a free translation into French of this chronicle, *Pagan, l'univers bouddhique: chronique du Palais de Cristal* ('Pagan, Buddhist universe: the Glass Palace Chronicle') by P. H. Cerre and F. Thomas (Paris: Editions Findlaky, 1987. 114p. maps. bibliog.) which includes a brief description of Pagan's architecture and whose chief interest, for English readers, lies in its beautiful black-and-white plates of the temples of Pagan. Pe Maung Tin and his brother-in-law Gordon Luce also published several volumes on the inscriptions of Burma, details of which and of other collections of inscriptions can best be found in the bibliography to Michael Aung-Thwin, *Pagan: the origins of modern Burma* (q.v.).

176 **Les relations entre la France et la Birmanie au XVIIIe et au XIXe siècles.** (Relations between France and Burma in the 18th and 19th centuries.)
Philippe Preschez. Paris: Fondation Nationale des Sciences Politiques, 1967. 209p. 3 maps. bibliog. (Recherches 12).

Researched primarily from French archival sources, this study examines French contacts with Burma in the period 1723-1810, 'the era of adventurers 1830-1840', political intrigues of the 19th century, and territorial and frontier questions and 'adjustments' in the post-1886 period.

177 **Relationship with Burma.**
Bangkok: Siam Society, 1959. 2 vols. (Selected Articles from the Siam Society Journal, vols. 5 & 6).

This consists primarily of a translation of portions of the Burmese Glass Palace Chronicle dealing with wars between Burma and Thailand in the 16th to 18th centuries, supplemented by Arthur Phayre's account of the same events and by other sources. A parallel source giving the Thai point of view is the translation by Aung Thein, 'Our wars with the Burmese: a work in Thai language by Prince Damrong', *Journal of the Burma Research Society*, vol. 38, pt. 2 (Dec. 1955), p. 121-96; vol. 40, pt. 2 (Dec. 1957), p. 135-238; vol. 40, pt. 2a (May 1958), p. 241-347. See also Aung Thein's 'Intercourse between Siam and Burma as recorded in the Royal Autograph edition of the history of Siam', *Journal of the Burma Research Society*, vol. 25, pt. 2 (Dec. 1935), p. 49-108; vol. 28, pt. 1 (June 1938), p. 109-232.

178 **Sri Lanka and South-East Asia.**
W. M. Sirisena. Leiden, The Netherlands: E. J. Brill, 1978. 186p. map. bibliog.

An examination of political, cultural and religious relations between Sri Lanka and Southeast Asia, concentrating on the period from the 11th to the 15th centuries. Two chapters deal with political relations of the Sinhalese Kings Vijayabahu (1055-1110) and Parakramabahu (1153-86) with Burma, and religious contacts between Sri Lanka and Burma. See also the article by Michael Aung-Thwin, 'The problem of Ceylonese–Burmese relations in the 12th century and the question of an interregnum in Pagan, 1164-1174 AD', *Journal of the Siam Society*, vol. 64, pt. 1 (Jan. 1976), p. 53-74.

179 **An account of an embassy to the kingdom of Ava: sent by the Governor-General of India in the year 1795.**
Michael Symes. London: W. Bulmer, 1800. 504p. maps; Farnborough, England: Gregg, 1969.

This account of Symes' first mission to Burma is published in a handsome quarto edition with steel-engraved plates of Burmese scenes and people, with a facsimile reprint published in 1969. It is the forerunner in scope and in format of the major accounts of Burma produced by other British envoys in the 19th century. Symes' book was the first full account of Burma to be published and it contains a mass of

ıformation on the history, religion, government, social system, language, geography
ıd economy of Burma, together with a narrative of his seven months' stay in Burma
ıd journey to the capital and his reception at court. In diplomatic terms Symes'
ıission was a success and he obtained permission to establish a British Resident at
ıangoon to supervise British commercial affairs. For details of Hiram Cox's mission
ıat followed and of Symes' second mission to Burma in 1802, see the historical
ıtroduction by D. G. E. Hall to *Michael Symes: journal of his second embassy to the*
ıurt of Ava in 1802 (q.v.). Symes was accompanied by Dr. Francis Buchanan and his
ıccount contains eight botanical plates and descriptions of 'the most rare and curious'
ıants collected by Buchanan. Other illustrations are engravings of drawings by the
ıdian artist Singey Bey who accompanied the mission and whose accurate
ıpresentational style attracted some attention at the Burmese court.

ı0   Michael Symes: journal of his second embassy to the court of Ava in
**   1802.**
     Michael Symes, edited with an introduction and notes by Daniel
     George Edward Hall.   London: George Allen & Unwin, 1955. 270p.
ıthough Symes published a detailed report of his first mission to Burma in 1795,
ıtitled *An account of an embassy to the kingdom of Ava: sent by the Governor-*
ıeneral of India in 1795 (q.v.), no account was published by Symes of his second
ıission as all the documents relating to it were placed on the secret list. The
ıcuments reproduced in this volume (p. 93-266) from the Bengal Secret and Political
ıoceedings of the India Office Records include, in addition to Symes' journal entries
ım 26 September 1802 to 1 February 1803 (p. 135-234), letters of instruction to
ımes and other official correspondence. Hall's invaluable introduction (p. 1-89)
ıaces Symes' 1802 mission in its historical context and describes Anglo-French rivalry
ı Burma, Burma in the period 1762-95, Symes' first mission, Captain Hiram Cox's
ıission (1796-98), as well as Symes' second mission and its sequel. Hall provides a
ırong defence of Symes against contemporary and later historians' questioning of the
ıundness of his judgement.

ı1   Burmese sit-tans 1764-1826: records of rural life and administration.
     Frank N. Trager, William J. Koenig, with the assistance of Yi Yi;
     translations from the Burmese by William J. Koenig.   Tucson,
     Arizona: University of Arizona Press, for the Association for Asian
     Studies, 1979. 440p. map. bibliog. (Association for Asian Studies
     Monographs, no. 36).
ıis study makes available in translation a corpus of hitherto not easily accessible
ırmese records, the *sit-tan* or revenue records submitted by local officials in response
ı royal revenue inquests conducted in 1765, 1783 and 1802. Koenig has collected and
ınslated some two-thirds of the approximately 500 *sit-tan* thought to be extant, and
ıs provided more accurate translations of some records first translated by J. S.
ırnivall, a pioneer scholar of this material. The translations form part two of the
ıok (p. 63-399), while part one (p. 1-62) provides a succinct historical introduction to
ırma in the period 1764 to 1826. Dynastic lists of the Burmese kings from 1044 to
ı85 are given in the appendix. A fuller treatment of the early Kon-baung dynasty can
ı found in William J. Koenig, *The Burmese polity, 1752-1819* (q.v.).

A concise account of the kingdom of Pegu, its climate, produce, trade and government, the manners and customs of its inhabitants, interspersed with remarks moral and political.
See item no. 50.

Ancient Arakan: with special reference to its cultural history between the 5th and 11th centuries.
See item no. 138.

The ancient Pyu.
See item no. 139.

Essays on the history and Buddhism of Burma.
See item no. 491.

Burma under British colonialism and the struggle for independence (1826-1948)

182 **Burma and India: some aspects of intellectual life under colonialism.**
Aung San Suu Kyi. Simla, India: Indian Institute of Advanced Study, in association with Allied Publishers, New Delhi, 1990. 84p.

This short study, written while the author spent six months as a Fellow at the Indian Institute of Advanced Study in 1987, compares the Indian and Burmese experiences of colonialism and, in particular, the different intellectual response and nationalist leadership that resulted. The author concludes that the Burmese lacked a leadership which could have helped them face the challenge posed by their confrontation with alien values and, looking to Burma's future, sees it as a country 'still awaiting for its true potential to be realised'.

183 **Burma: register of European deaths and burials.**
British Association for Cemeteries in South Asia, edited by R. E. McGuire. London: BACSA, 1983. [184p.] 2nd ed. map. bibliog.

This unusual publication documents European – predominantly British – deaths in Burma as officially reported or obtained through research. It records inscriptions from headstones and memorial plaques, and has photographs of many cemeteries, both military and civil, as well as of individual graves. In date the gravestones range from one of 1682 in Mergui to 1947. A wealth of background and biographical material is included on the past British presence in Burma. Entries are arranged in order of administrative divisions and districts, and an index of names is provided. There is also an update entitled *Burma: supplement to register of European deaths and burials* edited by Maurice H. Rossington (London: BACSA, 1987. [107p.] map.). This is in two parts: the first contains corrections and revisions to the original publication's entries; and the second contains information collected since 1983. Names are listed by administrative division, town and cemetery, and the text is accompanied by black-and-white photographs of Christian churches and cemeteries in Burma. Available from the British Association for Cemeteries in South Asia (BACSA) Secretary, Theon Wilkinson, 76½ Chartfield Avenue, London SW15 6HQ.

184 **Burma and the Japanese invader.**
John Leroy Christian, foreword by Reginald Hugh Dorman-Smith.
Bombay, India: Thacker, 1943. 418p. maps. bibliog.

A slightly revised version of Christian's *Modern Burma: a survey of political and economic development* (Berkeley, California: University of California Press, 1942. 381p.), including two completely new additional chapters on the Japanese in Burma. Although dated in its approach, it provides a useful survey of pre-war Burma with chapters on its history, government under the British, agriculture, commerce, arts, religion, the Burma Road, nationalist politics, foreign relations, the Japanese military campaign, and Burma under the Japanese occupation (taking events up to mid-1944). Statistics and some official and political documents are reproduced in the appendixes and the book has an extensive bibliography (p. 390-408). Christian also wrote a general introductory work on Burma ('to provide the general reader with something less ponderous' than *Modern Burma*), which was published under the title *Burma* (London: Collins, 1945. 176p. maps). Christian (1900-45) was superintendent of the American Burma Mission in the early 1930s and became a leading specialist on Burma. In the war he served in the US Army as a major, general staff corps, and was killed in Burma in 1945.

185 **Journal of an embassy from the Governor-General of India to the court of Ava in the year 1827: with an appendix containing a description of fossil remains by Professor Buckland and Mr. Clift.**
John Crawfurd.   London: Henry Colburn, 1834. 2nd ed. 2 vols. map.

John Crawfurd (1783-1868), a distinguished orientalist with a record of service in Java, Thailand and the Malay States, was appointed British Resident at Ava in the wake of the First Anglo-Burmese War, and resided at the Burmese capital from September 1826 to February 1827. Crawfurd gives a detailed narrative in volume one (541p.) of his journey from Rangoon up the Irrawaddy via Henzada, Prome and Pagan to Ava, of his reception at the capital, the weeks of negotiations over a commercial treaty and the terms of the Yandabo Treaty, and various excursions made. Volume two (319p.) continues with a description of the mission's departure from Ava, and general chapters on Burmese society, religion, trade and history. The appendixes (separately paginated p. 3-163) contain documents concerning the embassy, the Yandabo Treaty, translations of Burmese letters, proclamations and inscriptions, vocabularies, and statements by prisoners of the Burmese during the First Anglo-Burmese War including John Laird, Adoniram Judson, John Barretto, Henry Gouger and Jeronimo de Cruz. Crawfurd was a poor negotiator and his mission accomplished little. His writing is coloured by the many exasperations he experienced, but his account nonetheless ranks alongside those of Michael Symes and Henry Yule as a major description of the kingdom of Burma. The illustrations include engravings (some coloured), a plan of Ava and lithographic plates of fossil remains.

History. Burma under British colonialism and the struggle for independence (1826-1948)

186 The pacification of Burma.

Charles Haukes Todd Crosthwaite.   London: Edward Arnold, 1912; London: Frank Cass, 1968. 355p. 5 maps.

An account of the military 'pacification' operation that followed the British annexation of Upper Burma of 1886. Although it took the British only a month to invade and annex Upper Burma at the end of 1885, it took another nine years and more than 30,000 troops to subjugate the country. The chapters on the military expedition throughout Upper Burma including in the Shan States and the Chin Hills present a clear narrative of a complicated situation. A Burmese view of the same events is given in Ni Ni Myint's *Burma's struggle against British imperialism, 1885-1895* (q.v.). Sir Charles (1835-1915) was chief commissioner of British Burma from 1887-90 and his account takes pride in the establishment of a well organized, peaceful and prosperous province under British rule.

187 Burma under British rule.

Joseph Dautremer, translated and with an introduction by James George Scott.   London: T. Fisher Unwin, 1913. 388p. map.

An enthusiastic introduction to Burma covering its history, peoples and geography, administration under the British, trade, products and industries. The author was French consul at Rangoon from 1904-08 and makes comparative references to French rule in Indochina. With twenty-four good black-and-white photographs, mainly by Johannes & Co. of Mandalay.

188 Troubled days of peace: Mountbatten and South East Asia Command, 1945-46.

Peter Dennis.   Manchester, England: Manchester University Press, 1987. 220p. bibliog. (War, Armed Forces & Society).

This history of South East Asia Command (SEAC) from the Japanese surrender to Mountbatten's departure from SEAC examines the problems of the allies in the Southeast Asian colonies, political attitudes, restoration of law and order, rescue of prisoners-of-war, etc., with a discussion of Mountbatten's policy toward the Burmese nationalists and a comparison with the situation of the Dutch in the Netherlands East Indies. The grand scale biography of Earl Mountbatten of Burma (1900-79) by Philip Ziegler, *Mountbatten of Burma: the official biography* (London: William Collins, 1985. 786p. bibliog.) has an extensive section (p. 227-323) on Mountbatten's whole period as supreme commander of SEAC and on the return of Burma to civil rule and Mountbatten's relations with Aung San.

189 Deposed King Thibaw of Burma in India, 1885-1916.

Walter Sadgun Desai.   Bombay, India: Bharatiya Vidya Bhavan, 1967. 16p. bibliog. (Bharatiya Vidya Series, no. 25).

Thibaw, King of Burma from 1878 to 1885, was only twenty-seven years old when his kingdom was annexed by the British and the Burmese royal family exiled to Ratnagiri in India. The book describes his years of exile until his death in December 1916, and the fate of other members of the royal family, some of whom were later allowed to return to Burma. A constant theme is the financial situation of the royal family and its descendants. Official correspondence and memorials on the subject of their pensions and family jewels and other possessions are reproduced in thirty appendixes.

190 **History of the British Residency in Burma, 1820-1840.**
Walter Sadgun Desai. Farnborough, England: Gregg International,
1972. 491p. bibliog.
This is a facsimile reprint of the 1939 edition published in Rangoon by the University
of Rangoon. The book is a solid study of Anglo-Burmese relations from the close of
the First Anglo-Burmese War (1824-26) up to the early years of the reign of King
Tharrawaddy (1837-46). It chronicles British attempts to maintain diplomatic relations
with Burma by means of a permanent Residency at the royal capital. It throws light on
many interesting characters 'hitherto buried in the record room' including, above all,
the British Residents, Henry Burney and Richard Benson. Appendixes give the terms
of the Treaty of Yandabo (1826) and various official letters and orders.

191 **The fashioning of Leviathan: the beginnings of British rule in Burma.**
John Sydenham Furnivall. *Journal of the Burma Research Society*.
vol. 29, pt. 1 (April 1939), p. 1-137; Rangoon: Zabu Meitswe Pitaka
Press, 1939. 137p.; Canberra: Research School of Pacific Studies,
Australian National University, in association with the Economic
History of Southeast Asia Project and the Thai-Yunnan Project, 1991.
178p. bibliog.
A careful study of the administration of Tenasserim province in the first twenty years
of British rule after annexation in 1826, and of the adaptation of local administration to
the mechanisms of central government. The 1991 reprint (published as an Occasional
Paper of the Department of Anthropology, Research School of Pacific Studies,
Australian National University), is edited with a brief introduction by Gehan
Wijeyewardene and added bibliography, glossary and biographical notes.

192 **Burma past and present with personal reminiscences of the country.**
Albert Fytche. London: C. Kegan Paul, 1878. 2 vols. map.
The author begins 'I landed in India as a young ensign in 1839; I left it as chief
commissioner of British Burma in 1871' and, in the course of the book's 700 pages,
interweaves autobiography with sketches of Burmese history and British relations with
Burma. In the process Fytche provides a substantial amount of information on the
British administration of Burma, and on the country and its inhabitants. Fytche
succeeded Arthur Phayre as chief commissioner of British Burma in 1867 and, the
same year, led a mission to the court of Mandalay and successfully negotiated a new
commercial treaty with King Mindon. Official documents and memoranda are given in
appendixes to volume two, and Appendix C (p. 252-85) contains Fytche's official
narrative of his mission and the text of the treaty. Volume two also reproduces (p. 25-
58) a translation by Edward B. Sladen and T. P. Sparks of a Burmese play, *The silver
hill* (first published in 1856 [Rangoon: Pegu Press, Thos. S. Ranney. 43p.]). An
account that supplements Fytche's narrative of his 1867 mission to Mandalay is that
given by Henry Woodward Crofton, 'English mission to Mandalay, and treaty with
Burmah', in *Illustrated travels: a record of discovery, geography, adventure*, edited by
H. W. Bates (London: Cassell, Petter & Gilpin, 1869, p. 178-84, p. 212-46, p. 234-39).
Crofton, English Chaplain at Rangoon, accompanied Fytche to Mandalay and provides
an informal description of events and of the city and palace of Mandalay.

193 **The Dalhousie–Phayre correspondence 1852-1856.**
Edited with introduction and notes by Daniel George Edward Hall.
London: Oxford University Press. 1932. 426p. map.

The 262 letters reproduced in this book constitute a complete series covering the period from December 1852, when Arthur Phayre became first British commissioner of Pegu (annexed at the end of the Second Anglo-Burmese War), until the departure of Lord Dalhousie, Governor-General of India, for England in March 1856; seventy-nine of the letters are by Thomas Spears, a Scottish merchant and British correspondent at the Burmese court of Amarapura, whose letters and intelligence Phayre forwarded to Dalhousie. The letters are a mine of historical information, and give a vivid picture of Anglo-Burmese relations and of the characters of Dalhousie and Phayre. Professor Hall provides a valuable historical introduction, biographical details and notes, together with two appendixes giving an account of the Burmese administration and of Lord Dalhousie's second visit to Burma (December 1853-January 1954). For a critical account of the Second Anglo-Burmese War and of the British annexation and first years of administration of Lower Burma, see M. A. Rahim, *Lord Dalhousie's administration of the conquered and annexed states* (Delhi: S. Chand, 1963, p. 80-158) while for a biography of Dalhousie (1812-60), see William Lee-Warner, *The life of the Marquis of Dalhousie, KT* (London: Macmillan, 1904. 2 vols.).

194 **British rule in Burma 1824-1942.**
Godfrey Eric Harvey. London: Faber & Faber, 1946; New York:
AMS Press, 1974. 100p. maps.

A concise review of the British in Burma with the theme that 'what we gave Burma was not a government but an administration'. Arranged topically with very brief sections on the civil service, the courts, crime, the army, communications, public health, education, land alienation, indebtedness, revenue, trade and industry, agriculture, minerals, the Indian minority, the 1931 rebellion, constitutional development (dyarchy, local government, separation from India, 1937 constitution, the franchise).

195 **The Hsaya San rebellion (1930-32) reappraised.**
Patricia M. Herbert. Melbourne, Australia: Monash University
Centre of Southeast Asian Studies, 1982. 16p. (Working paper no. 27).

This brief study is based primarily on Burmese source materials and focuses on the growth and organization of the Burmese nationalist movement at the rural level.

196 **The province of Burma: a report prepared on behalf of the University of Chicago.**
Alleyne Ireland. Boston, Massachusetts: Houghton Mifflin, 1907.
2 vols. map. bibliog. (Colonial Administration in the Far East).

A compendium of information on the British colonial administration of Burma, based largely upon official reports, statistics and monographs. The material is arranged under the following subject categories: general description, history of British acquisition of Burma, the people of Burma, form of government, general administration, the civil service, judiciary, police, prison administration, education, financial system, land revenue system, forest administration, public works, municipal and village administration, medical services, harbour administration, administration of the Shan States and of the Chin Hills, trade and shipping. With twenty appendixes of statistics and abstracts of government regulations. The bibliography (p. 976-1001) includes a complete (as of 1906) list of government publications. An earlier compilation of government regulations and acts, with sections on political, judicial, revenue, local institutions, marine, forestry and miscellaneous matters, is George Edward Fryer's *Hand-book for British Burma* (Moulmein, Burma: T. Whittam, 1867. 579p.) and includes, among its vast range of regulations, rules for hackney carriages, for examinations in Burmese and in Karen, for levying fees on toddy trees, for cutting timber, etc.

197 **King Thebaw and the ecological rape of Burma: the political and commercial struggle between British India and French Indo-China in Burma 1878-1886.**
Charles Lee Keeton, foreword by John F. Cady. Delhi: Manohar Book Service, 1974. 436p. map. bibliog.
Based on extensive research into the India Office Records and other archives, this study of the reign of King Thibaw and Queen Supayalat concentrates on the political and commercial relations and rivalries of the period from 1878 to 1886. The British and French race to exploit Upper Burma's timber resources which took place from 1862 onwards is seen as having caused deforestation and ecological changes that in turn generated further economic and political pressures and led to the British annexation of Upper Burma. The appendixes give the full texts of successive treaties between Burma and British India from 1862 and between Burma and France from 1873 and 1885, together with miscellaneous contemporary English and translated Burmese documents.

198 **The Dobama movement in Burma (1930-1938).**
Khin Yi, foreword by Robert H. Taylor. Ithaca, New York: Southeast Asia Program, Cornell University, 1988. 140p. bibliog. (Southeast Asia Program Monographs, no. 2).
This study of the first eight years of the 'Do bama' ('We Burmans') movement of the *Thakhin* ('master') nationalists is based almost entirely on Burmese source materials. It charts the movement's progression from a narrowly nationalist outlook to an international leftist one, and the irrevocable split that developed between the older members and a Marxist-orientated younger generation. The narrative and quotations convey much of the excitement and fervour of the movement which from the outset demanded independence for Burma. There is a Burmese language companion volume (Southeast Asia Program Monographs, no. 2A) consisting of twelve appendixes reproducing some key documents of the period.

199 **The Burma we love.**
Kyaw Min. Calcutta, India: India Book House, 1945. 2nd rev. ed. 143p.
A discourse on Burmese politics and leaders during the late 1930s and early 1940s, by one of the first Burmans to be admitted to the ranks of the Indian Civil Service (in 1922), who followed a political career in the post-independence period and published *The Nation* newspaper. He also wrote a wartime essay discussing education, formation of an élite and economic and social changes, 'Mein kampf à la Kyaw Min' in *Report of the Education Reconstruction Committee* (Rangoon: Government Printing, 1947, p. 60-76) as well as a narrative of his attendance, via China, at an International Economic

History. Burma under British colonialism and the struggle for independence (1826-1948)

Conference held in Moscow in 1952, *Through the iron curtain via the back door* (London: Ernest Benn, 1953. 287p.).

200 **Epilogue in Burma 1945-48: the military dimension of British withdrawal.**
John H. McEnery. Tunbridge Wells, England: Spellmount, 1990. 160p. map. bibliog.

Researched from army and other official records, this study succinctly relates the Imperial Forces' and Burma Army's role in Burma from the Japanese surrender to the Imperial Garrison's final evacuation. It comments on the assassination of Aung San and members of his Cabinet, reappraises Sir Reginald Dorman-Smith and Sir Hubert Rance (the last two governors of Burma), and establishes an accurate statement of forces levels in Burma in 1945-48 (pointing out the misleading picture 'unwittingly' presented in Hugh Tinker's *Burma: the struggle for independence* [q.v.]) and highlights the contribution of General H. R. Briggs, general officer commanding, to ensuring a peaceful transfer of power. The author includes an epilogue 'Burma forty years on' which does not mince words about the present-day state of Burma. Appendixes detail the run-down of the imperial units and the build up of Burma Army units.

201 **Burmese nationalist movements, 1940-1948.**
Maung Maung. Edinburgh: Kiscadale 1989. 395p. bibliog.

This sequel to the author's *From Sangha to laity* (q.v.) presents a broadly researched account of Burma's campaign for independence. Maung Maung offers a fresh and at times controversial interpretation of events, providing a Burmese perspective that acts as a challenging counterpoint to such key documentary sources as Hugh Tinker's *Burma: the struggle for independence* (q.v.). While using much the same Western sources as Nicholas Tarling's *The fourth Anglo-Burmese war* (q.v.), Maung Maung's study is more far-ranging and his use of Burmese sources and interviews adds a dimension lacking from Western studies.

202 **From Sangha to laity: nationalist movements of Burma 1920-1940.**
Maung Maung. New Delhi: Manohar (for the Australian National University), 1980. 311p. 3 maps. bibliog. (Australian National University Monographs on South Asia, no. 4).

This study is based substantially on Burmese sources and traces the origin of the Burmese nationalist movement of the 1930s, showing how it moved away from the influence of the Buddhist Order (*Sangha*) and took on different ideological influence and leadership. The book is based on, and abbreviated from, the author's MA thesis entitled *The rise and fall of the Buddhist Sangha in Burmese politics 1920-1940* (written while serving as Burma's Ambassador to Australia and submitted in 1976 to the Australian National University, Department of Asian Civilization). Maung Maung (b. 1920), an ex-brigadier in the Burma Army is not to be confused with Dr. Maung Maung (b. 1925), author of many legal and political studies.

203 **A trial in Burma: the assassination of Aung San.**
Maung Maung. The Hague: Martinus Nijhoff, 1962. 117p.

The story of Burma's 'huge sacrifice' – the loss by assassination of independence leader, General Aung San and members of his Executive Council – and of the trial of U Saw and nine others for the assassinations, as told through the records of the

criminal trial. Included here is the text of the Judgement of the Special Tribunal
delivered 30 December 1947 on p. 71-117. The work is illustrated with contemporary
photographs of the courtroom and other scenes.

204 Burma in the crucible.
Maung Maung Pye, foreword by George Algernon West.   Rangoon:
Khittaya Publishing House, 1952. 212p.

A Burmese journalist's history of Burmese nationalist politics from 1904 to the
attainment of independence in 1948. With extensive quotations from speeches, political
manifestos and other sources.

205 British policy and the nationalist movement in Burma, 1917-1937.
Albert D. Moscotti.   Honolulu: University Press of Hawaii, 1974.
264p. bibliog. (Asian Studies at Hawaii, no. 11).

This work was submitted as a doctoral thesis at Yale University in 1950 under the title
British policy in Burma, 1917-1937, and has been much cited by leading scholars such
as John Cady in his *A history of modern Burma* (q.v.). Following his retirement from
the US Foreign Service in 1970, Moscotti revised his thesis for its (overdue) publication
taking into account major secondary works that had appeared in the intervening
twenty-year period, but made no substantial changes. A limitation upon his work is
that the author was not able to consult either India Office archival sources or Burmese
language sources. But the book nevertheless has value as a careful study of the
complex political developments relating to Burma in the period 1917 to 1937 and of the
impact of colonialism on Burma.

206 British colonial policy in Burma: an aspect of colonialism in South East Asia 1840-1885.
Aparna Mukherjee.   New Delhi: Abhinav Publications, 1988. 559p.
bibliog.

This thorough study covers the period from the withdrawal of the British Residency in
Burma in 1840 to the deposition of King Thibaw and the British annexation of Upper
Burma in 1885-86. It concentrates on diplomatic policy towards Burma, British
missions and treaties, and Anglo-Burmese political and commercial relations, and does
not deal with the subject of British administrative policy in Burma.

207 The politics of survival in Burma: diplomacy and statecraft in the reign of King Mindon, 1853-1878.
Myo Myint.   PhD thesis, Cornell University, Ithaca, New York, 1987.
(Available from University Microfilms, Ann Arbor, Michigan, order
no. UM8715619).

This thesis constitutes the first detailed study of King Mindon, contrasting his relative
success in external affairs with his difficulties in internal affairs. Myo Myint also
provides a useful survey of historical sources for King Mindon's reign.

History. Burma under British colonialism and the struggle for independence (1826-1948)

208 **Burma's struggle against British imperialism, 1885-1895.**
Ni Ni Myint. Rangoon: The Universities Press, 1983. 243p. map. bibliog.

A well-researched study which provides a Burmese perspective on the events leading to the British conquest of Upper Burma in 1885, and their aftermath. The book chronicles the explosion of national resistance that took the British years to subdue, providing a counterpoint to the standard British account of these operations by Sir Charles Crosthwaite, *The pacification of Burma* (q.v.). Appendixes to the book reproduce the text of the 1873 and 1874 Convention between France and Burma, the 1885 proclamation of the Burmese *Hluttaw* (Council of Ministers), and give profiles of the resistance leaders.

209 **The political legacy of Aung San.**
Compiled, with introductory essay, by Josef Silverstein. Ithaca, New York: Cornell University, 1972. 100p. (Cornell University Southeast Asia Program Data Paper no. 86).

A collection of hitherto largely unpublished or unobtainable speeches and writings by Burma's national hero, General Aung San (1915-47). The documents, and useful introduction (p. 1-12) by Silverstein, contribute greatly to understanding the ideas and influence of this key figure in 20th-century Burmese history. Among the documents reproduced (p. 40-100) is the full text of Aung San's own selection of documents made a year before his death and originally published in Rangoon in 1946 under the title *Burma's challenge* (and reprinted in 1968, with a Burmese translation by Mya Sein). Other documents are taken from the archives of the Defence Services Historical Research Institute in Rangoon.

210 **Growth of nationalism in Burma 1900-1942.**
Surendra Prasad Singh. Calcutta, India: Firma KLM, 1980. 168p. bibliog.

A general and chronological account of the origins and growth of the Burmese nationalist movement. See also the concise account by B. K. Drake, *Burma: nationalist movements and independence* (Kuala Lumpur: Longman Malaysia, 1979. 72p. 2 maps. bibliog.) with clear charts in the appendixes showing political factions and nationalist movements in the period 1919-41.

211 **The fourth Anglo-Burmese war: Britain and the independence of Burma.**
Nicholas Tarling. Gaya, India: South East Asian Review Office, for the Centre for South East Asian Studies, 1987. 346p.

This solidly researched study tells the story of the British–Burmese constitutional negotiations on the post-war future of Burma and of Burma's attainment of independence. Copious quotations from the original archives and some odd punning chapter titles (for example, 'Unhonoured and Aung San') leaven a complex text. For a Burmese perspective on the subject, see Maung Maung, *Burmese nationalist movements, 1940-1948* (q.v.). Also relevant are two articles by Tarling focusing on the ideas and policies of Sir Reginald Hugh Dorman-Smith, Governor of Burma, 1941-46 as follows: ' "A new and better cunning": British wartime planning for post-war Burma, 1942-43' in *Journal of Southeast Asian Studies* vol. 13, no. 1 (March 1982), p. 33-59; and, ' "An empire gem": British wartime planning for post-war Burma' in *Journal of Southeast Asian Studies*, vol. 13, no. 2 (Sept. 1982), p. 310-48.

Burma under British colonialism and the struggle for independence (1826-1948)

212 **Burma: the struggle for independence 1944-1948.**
Edited by Hugh Tinker. London: Her Majesty's Stationery Office, 1983-84. 2 vols. maps. (Constitutional Relations between Britain and Burma).

An invaluable source book documenting the unfolding drama by which in January 1948 Burma became the first country to leave the British Empire through negotiated independence. The two volumes of this massive (over 2,000 pages) documentary compilation have separate sub-titles indicating their scope: volume one, *From military occupation to civil government 1 January 1944 to 31 August 1946* (edited with the assistance of Andrew Griffin); and, volume two, *From general strike to independence 31 August 1946 to 4 January 1948* (edited with the assistance of Andrew Griffin and Stephen R. Ashton). The documents have been selected largely from the records of the Burma Office at the India Office Records (British Library, London), supplemented by some from the Public Record Office and from private sources. The documents (679 in volume one and 582 in volume two) are reproduced in chronological order and the editor has provided for each volume a lengthy historical introduction with cross-references to the documents, a chronological table of important events, a list of office holders concerned with Burma, a glossary and a helpful summary of contents of the documents. Among the additional material presented in the two volumes are extracts from the personal memoirs of British individuals involved in the events (those of G. Appleton, Arthur Bruce, F. S. V. Donnison, T. L. Hughes, Hubert Rance and John Wise in volume one; and of A. G. Bottomley, R. E. McGuire, P. G. E. Nash, Hubert Rance, D. R. Rees-Williams and W. I. J. Wallace in volume two); also included are biographical details of authors of documents and of individuals appearing in them and, in volume one, a note on the development of military forces in Burma and, in volume two, an analysis of the general election results. For a discussion by Tinker of his editorial approach and problems in compiling this work, see his article 'Burma: power transferred or exacted? Reflections on the constitutional process', in *British policy and the transfer of power in Asia: documentary perspectives*, edited by Ralph B. Smith, Anthony J. Stockwell (London: School of Oriental & African Studies, University of London, 1988, p. 19-29). (Also of relevance in the same work is a comparative study by Ralph B. Smith, 'Some contrasts between Burma and Malaya in British policy in South-East Asia, 1942-1946', p. 30-76).

213 **The foundations of local self-government in India, Pakistan and Burma.**
Hugh Tinker. London: Pall Mall Press; New York: Frederick A. Praeger, 1968. 2nd ed. 376p. maps. bibliog.

Originally published in 1954 (London: Athlone), the Burma section of this study (p. 214-44) is chiefly an examination of the British colonial dyarchy system of rule from 1923 to 1937 and of the introduction of rural self-government, with further references to Burma (education, health services, municipal services, etc.) throughout. A descriptive account of British Burma's legislative system, including dyarchy and local government reforms, and giving the background to the 1937 separation from India, is F. Burton Leach's *The future of Burma* (Rangoon: British Burma Press, 1937. 3rd rev. ed. 142p.).

214   **Twentieth century impressions of Burma: its history, people, commerce,
      industries and resources.**
      Edited by Arnold Wright, assisted by H. A. Cartwright,
      O. Breakspear.   London: Lloyd's Greater Britain Publishing
      Company, 1910. 416p.

This handsomely produced volume – one of a series on Britain's imperial possessions –
is a splendid source book on British Burma at the turn of the century, with article
contributed by many well-known figures of the day, biographical details of leading
businessmen, politicians, lawyers, etc., and over 350 black-and-white photographs of
contemporary scenes, individuals, and buildings (official, temples, business premises
private houses, schools, clubs, etc.). Its scope can be judged from the following
indication of its contents: History (with a list of chief commissioners, lieutenant
governors), constitution and law (by A. Agabeg), ethnology (by J. H. Hannay)
manners and customs (by May Oung), arts and handicrafts (by Arthur Browne
Roberts), Burmese archaeology (by Taw Sein Ko), religion (with sections on
Buddhism and on the various Christian missions), education, the press, transport
communications, finance (by M. F. Gauntlett), trade, port of Rangoon, fauna (by
G. H. Evans), teak (by E. J. Foucar), meteorology (by S. A. Smith), agriculture (by
A. McKerral), oilfields, cotton, coal mining (by A. E. Landon White) tin mining (by
J. A. Connor), geology (by J. H. de la Touche), medical administration, public works
police (by S. C. F. Peele), prisons (by E. P. Frenchman), military, sport, Rangoon
(municipality, Burma chamber of commerce, trade associations, tramway, lighting
clubs, etc.), Mandalay, Bassein, Akyab, Prome, Toungoo, the Shan States (by J. G
Scott). A feature of the work is the prominence it gives to business concerns with
photographs of premises, proprietors and their companies, and biographical details of
prominent businessmen and officials of all nationalities.

215   **A narrative of the mission to the court of Ava in 1855; together with the
      journal of Arthur Phayre envoy to the court of Ava, and additional
      illustrations by Colesworthy Grant and Linnaeus Tripe.**
      Henry Yule, introduction by Hugh Tinker.   Kuala Lumpur; London;
      New York: Oxford University Press, 1968. 391p. map. (Oxford in Asia
      Historical Reprints).

This is a handsomely produced reprint, with additional material, of a classic account of
mid-19th century Burma first published under the title *A narrative of the mission sen
by the Governor-General of India to the court of Ava in 1855, with notices of th
country, government and people* (London: Smith Elder, 1858). Henry Yule (1820-89
was a royal engineer and an under-secretary in the Public Works Department in India
when he was appointed secretary to Arthur Phayre's 1855 mission. Phayre's task was to
improve Anglo-Burmese relations in the wake of the Second Anglo-Burmese War of
1852 and to obtain a treaty recognizing the British annexation of Lower Burma. The
mission succeeded in improving goodwill, but did not persuade King Mindon to sign
formal treaty. Yule, in his capacity of secretary, reported fully in seven chapters all the
mission's proceedings and also, in six further chapters and thirteen appendixes
included a vast amount of information on all aspects of Burma and its inhabitants
Yule was a careful observer and tireless gatherer of information who also found time to
make the numerous pen-and-ink drawings which embellish his text. The volume is also
greatly enhanced by the inclusion of hand-coloured lithographs of drawings by
Colesworthy Grant (1813-80) and of photographs by Captain Linnaeus Tripe (1822
1902) who both also accompanied the mission. The original 1858 edition was in fact

reworking of the mission's official report printed two years earlier for submission to the Government of India as *Reports of the mission to Ava in 1855* (Calcutta, India: Baptist Mission Press, 1856). This consisted of a 'General report' by Henry Yule and a separately paginated 'Geological report' by Thomas Oldham. In Yule's 1858 (and 1968 reprint) *Narrative*, Oldham's report, entitled *Notes on the geological features of the banks of the River Irawadi, and of the country north of Amarapoora*, is printed as Appendix A. An important aspect of Yule's work is that he drew on various unpublished journals and papers (including some by Arthur Phayre, Henry Burney, Dr. G. T. Bayfield, Dr. D. Richardson, Capt. W. C. Macleod, Grant Allan), some of which were reproduced *in extenso* in the appendixes to the 1856 original report. Professor Tinker's introduction to the 1968 reprint edition discusses the original 1856 *Report* and its relationship to the 1858 published version, and also elaborates upon additional material included in the 1968 reprint, namely, extra photographs by Linnaeus Tripe and additional watercolours by Colesworthy Grant, and the text (p. xvii-xlvi) of Arthur Phayre's hitherto unpublished private journal. Very few of the more than 200 photographs taken by Tripe and of the 113 paintings and sketches made by Colesworthy Grant – which were all listed in the 1856 *Report* – were reproduced for publication. Grant's originals are in the India Office Library and are listed with a brief biography of Grant, in Mildred Archer, *British drawings in the India Office Library, vol. 2: official and professional artists* (London: Her Majesty's Stationery Office, 1969). Details of Tripe's Burma photographs and techniques can be found in Janet Dewan, Maia-Mari Sutnik, *Linnaeus Tripe: photographer of British India 1854-1870* (Toronto: Art Gallery of Ontario, 1986. 39p bibliog.). Tripe selected 120 of his Burma photographs which were printed in a limited edition of fifty sets – of which four sets are preserved in the India Office Library (of the British Library) – for the government of India in 1856-57.

Report on the Eastern frontier of British India: with a supplement on the British political relations with Ava.
See item no. 54.

The national liberation movement in Burma during the Japanese occupation period (1941-1945).
See item no. 256.

Last and first in Burma (1941-1948).
See item no. 262.

British military administration in the Far East, 1943-46.
See item no. 265.

The political impact of the Japanese occupation of Burma.
See item no. 270.

Aung San of Burma: a biographical portrait by his daughter.
See item no. 281.

My Burma: the autobiography of a president.
See item no. 284.

Burma and General Ne Win.
See item no. 291.

Saturday's son.
See item no. 294.

Henry Burney: a political biography.
See item no. 313.

The Shan States and the British annexation.
See item no. 431.

Bureaucratic transformation in Burma.
See item no. 532.

Economic history

216 **The Burma delta: economic development and social change on an Asian rice frontier, 1842-1941.**
Michael Adas.   Madison, Wisconsin: University of Wisconsin Press, 1974. 256p. 4 maps. bibliog.

An outstanding, detailed socioeconomic history of the dynamics of development in the Irrawaddy delta of Lower Burma, researched primarily from colonial land settlement reports. Adas develops and extends J. S. Furnivall's concept of the plural society – with separate groups of European, Indian, Chinese and indigenous Burmese – as a framework for analysis and examines, by decade and by district, such key factors as rapid population growth, immigration, the role of the Chettiars (Indian money lenders), rural indebtedness, land alienation, tenancy, and agrarian unrest (with special reference to the 1930-32 rebellion). There is also a discussion of major statistical sources in the appendix, and a detailed bibliography. Fuller statistical data can be found in Adas' original thesis (PhD, University of Wisconsin, Madison, Wisconsin 1971), *Agrarian development and the plural society in Lower Burma, 1852-1941* (available from Ann Arbor, Michigan: University Microfilms, order no. UM 71-20,653). See also his article, 'Immigrant Asians and the economic impact of European imperialism: the role of the South Indian Chettiars in British Burma', *Journal of Southeast Asian Studies*, vol. 33, pt. 3 (May 1974), p. 385-401.

217 **Irrigation in the heartland of Burma: foundations of the pre-colonial Burmese state.**
Michael Aung-Thwin.   DeKalb, Illinois: Northern Illinois University, Center for Southeast Asian Studies, 1990. 76p. 9 maps. (Northern Illinois University, Center for Southeast Asian Studies, Occasional Paper, no. 15).

This detailed statistical analysis takes a synchronic approach and argues that the productivity of Burma's ricelands was quite stable for centuries. Another study which examines quantification from source materials and factors encouraging the growth of cultivated acreage in the precolonial period is Victor B. Lieberman's article, 'Secular trends in Burmese economic history, c. 1350-1830, and their implications for state formation', *Modern Asian Studies*, vol. 25, pt. 1 (Feb. 1991), p. 1-31.

218 **Burmese entrepreneurship: creative response in the colonial economy.**
Aung Tun Thet.   Stuttgart, GFR: Steiner Verlag Wiesbaden
GmbH, 1989, 197p. bibliog. (Beiträge zur Südasienforschung,
Südasien-Institut, Universität Heidelberg, vol. 126).

This contribution to the literature of the economics of imperialism draws upon a wide
range of sources and argues that the development of indigenous Burmese entrepreneurship was arrested due to its 'decapitation' under British colonial rule. Several
case studies of this process are given (for example, for shipping, timber and spinning
industries), with data on Burmese businessmen at different periods from 1910 to 1961,
and an autobiographical account of a ceramics manufacturer, U Thaw (1893-1977).

219 **British quest for China trade by routes across Burma (1826-1876).**
Thaung Blackmore.   In: *Symposium on historical, archaeological and
linguistic studies on southern China, South-East Asia and the Hong
Kong region.* Edited by F. S. Drake. Hong Kong: Hong Kong
University Press, 1967, p. 180-90.

An account of British attempts in the 19th century to examine the commercial
possibilities of land routes across Burma and of establishing overland trade with China.
The British expeditions to survey different routes are described against the background
of mounting British commercial pressures and of shifts in British and Burmese policies.
Also relevant is Ralph C. Crozier's article, 'Antecedents of the Burma Road: British
plans for a Burma–China railway in the nineteenth century', *Journal of Southeast Asian
History*, vol. 3, no. 2 (Sept. 1962). p. 1-18.

220 **Calling to mind: being some account of the first hundred years (1870 to
1970) of Steel Brothers and Company Limited.**
Harold E. W. Braund.   Oxford; New York: Pergamon, 1975. 151p.
4 maps. bibliog.

This is not a dry company history, but a well-told story of a great commercial
enterprise, founded in Rangoon in 1870. Much of the Company's records, held at its
main offices in London and Rangoon, were destroyed in the Second World War, and
the author (an employee of Steel Brothers for over thirty years) has had to draw on
such source material as early written accounts and the Company's *House Magazine*, as
well as his own published memories, *Distinctly I remember* (q.v.). The first five
chapters trace Steels' involvement in rice, timber and oil and the Company's
diversification into cotton, rubber, cement, and other trading and production activities
in Burma. The Japanese invasion, Burma's independence and nationalization of
foreign concerns brought an end to Steels' operations in Burma, and the rest of the
book deals with Steels' interests in the UK, Middle East, India, Pakistan, Canada and
Australia.

221 **The rice industry of Burma.**
Cheng Siok-Hwa.   Kuala Lumpur: University of Malaya Press, 1968.
307p. maps. bibliog.

This study concentrates on the prewar period and highlights how little indigenous
Burmese benefited from the profits of the development of Burma's rice industry; with
extensive statistical appendixes (p. 237-75).

222　**A history of the Burmah Oil Company: vol. 1, 1886-1924; vol. 2, 1924-1966.**
　　　Thomas Anthony Buchanan Corley.　London: Heinemann, 1983, 1988. 2 vols. maps. bibliog.

The Burmah Oil Company, the oldest of Britain's oil enterprises, owes its existence to the faith and financial backing of David Sime Cargill who in the 1870s acquired the ailing Rangoon Oil Company and continued subsidizing its losses in the hope that political conditions and crude oil refining techniques would eventually improve and make operations profitable. The British annexation of Upper Burma on 1 January 1886 ended the Burmese royal monopoly on oil, and opened the way for full commercial exploitation of Burma's primitive oil industry. The Burmah Oil Company was registered in Edinburgh on 7 July 1886 in an attempt to attract funds and over the next few years the Company negotiated oil fields concessions, introduced mechanical drilling and modernized refining methods. This and the subsequent history of the Company and its expansion into Persia is told in great detail in volume one. The chronicle of events is leavened by an interesting chapter 'Working in the Company 1886-1924' which reconstructs what life was like for BOC employees in Burma. Volume one has 'Appendixes of principal characters', 'Financial data', and 'Production data'. Volume two covers Robert Irving Watson's long period as managing director of the London office, and describes the outbreak of the Second World War, the policy of denial to the enemy and the postwar rehabilitation programme. Burmah Oil's immediate postwar preoccupations were its claims for war damage compensation and the threat of expropriation once Burma's independence was granted. The civil war in Burma, the formation of a joint-venture company in 1954, Ne Win's military coup and the sale in 1963 of BOC interests in Burma to the People's Oil Industry are also described. The latter part of volume two covers BOC relations with British Petroleum and Shell, and BOC activities in India, Pakistan and Australia, 1945-66. Biographical notes, 'Crude oil production' and 'Refinery data 1924-61', and 'BOC financial data 1924-1966' conclude volume two.

223　**The British firms and the economy of Burma: with special reference to the rice and teak industries, 1917-1937.**
　　　Maria Serena Icasiano Diokno.　PhD dissertation, University of London, 1983. 297p. bibliog.

This thesis examines the structure of the rice and forestry industries and export economy of Burma and, in particular, the role of the Bullinger Pool rice cartel in the 1920s and of leading British firms and their subsidiary interests (in mining, shipping, merchandise, etc.).

224　**Colonial policy and practice: a comparative study of Burma and Netherlands India.**
　　　John Sydenham Furnivall.　Cambridge, England: Cambridge University Press, 1948. 568p. map. bibliog.; New York: New York University Press, 1956.

A classical comparative study which identifies the rule of law and economic freedom as the basic principle of British colonial policy in contrast to the Dutch policy of imposing restraints on economic forces by strengthening personal authority and conserving traditional custom. It recommends as a postwar reconstruction programme for Burma the control of economic forces in the interest of social welfare. Five separate chapters

p. 23-216) are devoted to Burma covering the periods 1826-70, 1870-1923, 1923-40 and treated thematically under the headings of 'Laissez-faire', 'Efficiency and social justice', and 'Political democracy'. A fuller, but to date unpublished, study by Furnivall on Burma is the mimeographed *A Study of the social and economic history of Burma* (Rangoon: Economic & Social Board, Office of the Prime Minister, 1957-59) and upon which the work, also mimeographed, by Aye Hlaing, *A study of economic development of Burma, 1870-1940* (Rangoon: Department of Economics, University of Rangoon 1964. 156p.) is in part based. See also the article by Aye Hlaing, Observations on some patterns of economic development, 1874-1914', *Burma Research Society Fiftieth Anniversary Publications*, no. 1 (Rangoon, 1961), p. 9-16. For further details and a bibliography of Furnivall, see F. N. Trager, *Furnivall of Burma* (q.v.).

25 An introduction to the political economy of Burma.
John Sydenham Furnivall, edited by John Russell Andrus.   Rangoon: Burma Book Club, 1938. 2nd rev. ed. 293p. map.

Originally written as a series of lectures for students at Rangoon University, this seminal work presents Furnivall's first analysis of the effects upon traditional Burmese society of the opening up of Burma under colonial rule to uncontrolled economic forces. It has chapters on the sources of Burma's wealth, crops and cultivation, the rural economy under Burmese rule, the main features of Burma's economic development, the reclamation of the delta, land owners, cultivators and labourers in Lower and Upper Burma, capital and debt, trade and industry, and the revenue of Burma. His account of the pre-colonial economy is based susbtantially on Burmese sources, especially the *sittan* (revenue inquest records), samples of which are given in Burmese with English translations in Appendix I (p. 271-87). Furnivall also published a rough translation of a series of these records as a three-part article entitled 'Some historical documents' in the *Journal of the Burma Research Society*, vol. 6, pt. 3 (Dec. 1916, p. 1-213; vol. 8, pt. 1 (April 1918), p. 40-52; vol. 9, pt. 1 (April 1919), p. 33-52. For a retranslation and comment on Furnivall's studies of Burmese historical documents, see Frank N. Trager and William J. Koenig, *Burmese sit-tans 1764-1826* (q.v.). Furnivall's book was first published in 1931 (Rangoon: Burma Book Club) and here is a postwar reprint (Rangoon: People's Literature Committee & House, 1957) of that original edition with a new forty-six page preface by Furnivall describing the problems facing independent Burma. A study that follows on and supplements Furnivall's *An introduction to the political economy of Burma* is that by J. Russell Andrus (with foreword by J. S. Furnivall), *Burmese economic life* (Stanford, California: University of California Press, 1947. 362p. 2 maps.) which surveys the economy of Burma for the period 1939-47, with chapters on agriculture, co-operatives, forestry, minerals, handicrafts, communications, public health, currency, banking, etc.

26 Arakan past–present–future: a résumé of two campaigns for its development.
John Ogilvy Hay.   Edinburgh, London: William Blackwood, 1892. 216p. map.

The author, a former resident and honorary magistrate of the town of Akyab in Arakan, strongly advocates the need to develop Arakan (annexed by the British in 1826), to build road and rail links with Chittagong, and to develop Akyab as a major port. His book is a compilation of his campaign and lobbying of the British Burma government on these matters in the period 1875-92 and consists of the texts of his correspondence with officials in Burma, India and London, and of his letters to the press.

227 Paddy Henderson, 1834-1961.
Dorothy Laird. Glasgow, London: George Outram, 1961. 230p.

A history of the Scottish shipping firm, P. Henderon & Company in the period from 1834 to 1961. Over half the book is devoted to the company's long association with Burma which began in the late 1850s when sailing ships returning from New Zealand called into Burma for homeward cargoes of teak and rice. With the opening of the Suez Canal in 1869 the company replaced their sailing ships with steamers and formed the British & Burma Steam Navigation Company. In the course of time P. Henderson & Company acted as Secretaries and provided the registered offices of both the British & Burma Steam Navigation Company and the mighty Irrawaddy Flotilla Company, many of whose directors were also partners of P. Henderson & Company. Lists of the ships and directors of all these inter-linked companies are provided in the appendixes.

228 Irrawaddy Flotilla.
Alister McCrae, Alan Prentice, foreword by Bernard Fergusson (Lord Ballantrae). Paisley, Scotland: James Paton, 1978. maps. bibliog.

A well-written history of the Irrawaddy Flotilla Company, founded in 1865, whose development and fortunes were linked to the growth of British commercial and political control over 19th-century Burma. After the British annexation of Upper Burma in 1886, the Irrawaddy Flotilla Company expanded to become at its peak in the 1920s the greatest inland water transport enterprise in the world. One chapter is devoted to the Company's role in helping the evacuation of the British army and civilians at the time of the Japanese invasion of Burma in 1942, and describes the wholesale scuttling of the fleet as a denial to the enemy. In the second part of the book, the authors have tried to bring the reader closer to their own and other experiences of running the steamers on Burma's waterways. A brief epilogue covers the years from 1942 to the nationalization of the Company in 1948. For technical data on the Irrawaddy Flotilla Company's fleet of steamers, motor vessels and other craft with a brief account of the history of the Company and of the characteristics of the Irrawaddy River, and sixty-seven black-and-white plates, see H. J. Chubb and C. L. D. Duckworth, *Irrawaddy Flotilla Company Limited 1865-1950* (London: National Maritime Museum, 1973, 177p. 2 maps. [Maritime Moographs and Reports no. 7]).

229 Scots in Burma: golden times in a golden land.
Alister McCrae. Edinburgh: Kiscadale, 1990. 110p. map. bibliog.

The first part of this book describes the 'trade makers', from the earliest European contact with Burma through to the highpoint of Victorian – predominently Scottish commercial enterprise in Burma. McCrae provides details on the foundation and trading practices of many of the great merchant houses which pioneered the exploitation of Burma's natural resources and dominated trade in the 19th and early 20th centuries. Among the companies profiled are Darwood & Co., Todd, Findlay Co., the Bombay Burmah Trading Corporation, Steel Brothers, Chas. R. Cowie Co., MacGregor & Co., and the Irrawaddy Flotilla Company, together with details the characters associated with these enterprises. McCrae's book elaborates upon an earlier research paper tracing the interlocking origins of many early enterprises Burma, *Pioneers in Burma* (Glasgow: Department of Economic History, University

;lasgow, 1986. 36p. map. [Occasional Papers in Economic & Social History, no. 2]).
he second part consists of a personal memoir by McCrae of his years in Burma
eginning in 1933 and his work for the Irrawaddy Flotilla Company (for a detailed
istory of which, see Alister McCrae and Alan Prentice's *Irrawaddy Flotilla* [q.v.]).
1cCrae's text is complemented by sixty-six black-and-white photographs, selected by
ohn Falconer, drawn from previously unpublished sources.

30 **History of Rangoon.**
Bertie Reginald Pearn.   Farnborough, England: Gregg International,
1971. 320p. 12 maps.

. facsimile reprint of the rare original edition published in 1939 by the American
aptist Mission Press, Rangoon. It provides a well-researched and to date unsurpassed
istory of the city from its origins as Dagon, through to its development in the 18th and
Ith centuries under the kings of the Kon-baung dynasty and to its considerable
rowth and expansion under the British in the period 1853-1938. The book contains
uch information on British individuals and companies associated with Burma, and
ie appendixes include much miscellaneous information (on shipping, the Armenian
id British cemeteries and on street names and the people they are named after).
ibliographical references are provided at the end of each chapter and the text is
ihanced by thirty-nine black-and-white plates. For colour illustrations of modern-day
angoon and detail and of new projects undertaken since the State Law and Order
estoration Council (SLORC) took power in September 1988, with a list of the
ormer foreign names' and the new 'Myanmar names' given to streets, parks, etc., see
ity of Yangon modernization record edited by Tin Maung Latt, translated by Tin Nwe
4aung (Yangon: Public Relations Information Division, for Yangon City Develop-
ent Committee, 1990. 67p.).

31 **The Bombay Burmah Trading Corporation Limited 1863-1963.**
A. C. Pointon.   Southampton, England: Millbrook, 1964. 142p.
map.

iis famous company had its origins in the firm of Wallace Brothers which in 1863
rmed the Bombay Burmah Trading Corporation to develop the business built up by
illiam Wallace (1818-88) in Burma. The Corporation's dispute with the King of
urma over the terms of its lease of forests and teak extraction rights was a factor
intributing to the outbreak of the Third Anglo-Burmese War in 1885. This official
impany history is concerned to show that the Corporation's differences with King
hibaw were 'the occasion, not the cause, of the war'. A brief chapter is devoted to
ephants and the progress of developing an anti-anthrax vaccine is charted. Also by
iinton is *Wallace Brothers* (Oxford: Oxford University Press, 1974. 120p.), a history
this family firm of East India merchants and its trading activities in Burma.

32 **The moral economy of the peasant: rebellion and subsistence in
Southeast Asia.**
James C. Scott.   New Haven, Connecticut: Yale University Press,
1976. 246p. bibliog.

iis study has stimulated much scholarly debate. Scott's main premise is that the
intral concern of traditional peasant communities is survival, and that what he calls
e 'subsistence ethic' governs their economic and political notions and determines
eir response to crises. Drawing on the history of agrarian society in Lower Burma
d Vietnam in the colonial period, Scott argues that the changes accompanying

75

colonial rule violated the peasants' 'moral economy' and led to revolt. The Hsaya Sa rebellion of 1930-32 in Burma is examined within this theoretical framework. Anothe comparative study which includes this rebellion as one of five case studies o millenarian movements is that by Michael Adas, *Prophets of rebellion: millenaria protest movements against the European colonial order* (Chapel Hill, Carolina University of North Carolina Press, 1979. 243p. bibliog.). See also Adas' articl discussing Scott's theories, 'Moral economy or contest state? Elite demands and th origins of peasant protest in Southeast Asia', *Journal of Social History*, vol. 13, no. (Summer 1980), p. 521-46.

233 **Burma's transport and foreign trade in relation to the economic development of the country 1885-1914.**
Shein. Rangoon: University of Rangoon, Department of Economics, 1964. 287p. bibliog.

This study was originally submitted as a PhD thesis to the University of Cambridge i 1959 under the title 'The role of transport and foreign trade in the economi development of Burma under British rule, 1885-1914'. It gives a detailed account of th growth of transport and foreign trade which are seen as two of the most importar determinants of economic development in Burma between 1885 and 1914. Th development of railways, roads, internal and overseas shipping is examined an documented, and patterns of trade and in particular the export of rice, teak an petroleum products is analysed.

234 **The forests of India.**
E. P. Stebbing. London: John Lane, The Bodley Head, 1922-26. vols. 1-3; Oxford: Oxford University Press, 1962. vol. 4; New Delhi: A. J. Reprints Agency, 1982-83. 4 vols. maps. bibliog.

These four volumes contain a wealth of information on the history of forestr operations in Burma, together with statistics and photographs. Volume one ha chapters on forest operations in Tenasserim from 1796 to 1850 (p. 125-90), and fror 1850 to 1857 (p. 231-43), on forest operations in Pegu 1850 to 1857 (p. 244-63) and o the introduction of forest conservancy in Burma in the period 1858 to 1864 and th work of Sir D. Brandis (p. 367-91). Volume two has chapters on the progress of fore conservancy in British Burma 1865 to 1870 (p. 181-214) and a brief account of th annexation of Upper Burma (p. 453-55). Volume three has chapters on fores administration in Burma and the Andaman Islands from 1871 to 1900 (p. 55-79), an from 1901 to 1925 (p. 261-305), on fire protection in Burma forests in the period 19C to 1925 (p. 392-99), on the progress of silviculture in the same period (p. 415-1 p. 450-52), on the progress of working plans in Burma (p. 506-15), the Burma Fore Department's record and output during the First World War (p. 534-41), moder methods of exploitation 1901 to 1925 (p. 631-35), and aerial forest surveys in Burm (p. 670-76). Volume four (edited by Harry Champion, F. C. Osmaston) has a chapte on forest administration in Burma from 1925 to 1947 (p. 437-72). Also of relevance A. H. Lloyd, *Engineering for forest rangers in tropical countries: with special referen to Burma* (Oxford: Clarendon, 1929. 228p. bibliog.), a practical guide coverir materials used in forest engineering, road and bridge construction, transport of timbe water supplies, use of explosives, elephants' pack gear, and water supplies.

235 **Money lending and contractual 'thet-kayits': a socio-economic pattern of the later Kon-baung period, 1819-1885.**
Toe Hla. PhD thesis, Northern Illinois University, DeKalb, Illinois, 1987. 386p. map. bibliog. Available from University Microfilms, Ann Arbor, Michigan, order no. UM 8806883.
Researched primarily from some 2,000 money-lending, land mortgage, bondage (debt slavery) and other forms of written agreements known in Burmese as *thet-kayit*, this invaluable study discusses 19th-century Burmese society, agriculture and trade and examines in detail the money-lenders and landowners (with profiles of leading Burmese families), the role played by the monastic order, the impact of British colonialism and King Mindon's monetary and agrarian reforms. It also discusses the pre-coinage monetary system of Burma as well as weights and the coinage introduced by King Mindon. With tables providing details of weights, land measures, land values, paddy and other crop prices, mortgages, taxation, cash contributions levied to pay the 1826 Yandabo Treaty indemnity, and of bondage agreements and debt slavery, etc. Translations of the original Burmese documents are given in the appendix.

The impact of colonialism on Burmese economic development.
See item no. 596.

The Anglo-Burmese Wars (1824-26; 1852; 1885)

236 **The eastern frontier of British India 1784-1826.**
Anil Chandra Banerjee. Calcutta, India: A. Mukhjerjee, 1964. 3rd ed. 516p. maps. bibliog.
This study of events leading to the First Anglo-Burmese War (1824-26) quotes extensively from original, unpublished sources. It covers disputes on the Arakan frontier, the question of Arakanese refugees, British commercial missions to Burma (1795-98), and the course of the 'long and mismanaged war', with a short account of events from 1826 to 1843 describing John Crawfurd's 1827 mission and the British Residency at the Burmese capital. Texts of the Treaty of Yandabo and of the Anglo-Burmese Commercial Treaty of 1826, and extracts from official documents are given in the appendixes.

237 **A narrative of the late military and political operations in the Burmese empire: with some account of the present condition of the country, its manners, customs and inhabitants.**
Henry G. Bell. Edinburgh: Constable, 1827. 87p.
A typical early British account of the First Anglo-Burmese War. It was reprinted as part of Bell's *An account of the Burman empire, compiled from the works of Colonel Symes, Major Canning, Captain Cox, Dr. Leyden, Dr. Buchanan, & c . . .: and, a narrative of the late military and political operations . . .* (Calcutta, India: D'Rozario, 1852. [203p.]) which consists of 'compendious selections' from earlier printed accounts.

238 **The Burma wars 1824-1886.**
George Bruce. London: Hart Davis, MacGibbon, 1973. 179p. map.
bibliog.

An account of the three Anglo-Burmese Wars which led to the establishment of British colonial rule in Burma. The first war, of 1824-26, is covered more thoroughly than the second (1852) and third (1885-86). The wars are viewed predominantly from the British perspective, but British mistakes and incompetence, especially in the First Anglo-Burmese War, are not glossed over.

239 **How wars are got up in India: the origins of the Burmese war.**
Richard Cobden. London: William & Frederick G. Cash, 1853. 59p.

The subject of the fiery tract by the celebrated free-trader and Anti-Corn Law agitator, Richard Cobden (1804-65), is the Second Anglo-Burmese War of 1852. Cobden, drawing on the parliamentary papers relating to the war, traces the escalation of a trading dispute into full-blown war and strongly censures Lord Dalhousie, Governor-General of India, asking '. . . ought not we to advertise in the *Times* for a Governor-General of India who can collect a debt of a thousand pounds, without annexing a territory which will be ruinous to our finances?' A spirited rejoinder to Cobden and a defence of Lord Dalhousie's annexation of Pegu in December 1852 was written by John Clark Marshman, *How wars arise in India: observations on Mr. Cobden's pamphlet, entitled 'The origins of the Burmese war'* (London: W. H. Allen, 1853. 71p.). Marshman predicts (correctly) that 'Whatever be the origins of the Burmese war, just or unjust, it is difficult to suppose that, with all Lord Dalhousie's reluctance, we can stop at Pegu . . . I wish to avoid inflicting any alarm on Mr. Cobden but he must make up his mind for the absorption, sooner or later, of the whole of the kingdom of Burmah'.

240 **British romantic views of the first Anglo-Burmese War (1824-1826).**
Richard M. Cooler. DeKalb, Illinois: Northern Illinois University, Department of Art, 1977. 13p. bibliog.

This exhibition catalogue describes and reproduces (in black-and-white) twenty-eight aquatints that were executed from drawings made by two officers who served in the First Anglo-Burmese War, Lieutenant Joseph Moore and Captain James Kershaw. Moore's work, *Eighteen views taken at or near Rangoon*, was first published in 1825-26 (London: T. Clay) and Kershaw's *Views in the Burman Empire*, in 1831 (London: Smith, Elder). Cooler's text links contemporary descriptions of the military action with the scenes depicted in the plates.

241 **A narrative of the first Burmese war 1824-26: with the various official reports and despatches describing the operations of the naval and military forces employed, and other documents bearing upon the origin, progress, and conclusion of the contest.**
G. W. DeRhé-Philipe. Calcutta, India: Superintendent, Government Printing, 1905. 405p.

This military account of the First Anglo-Burmese War has a brief description of each stage of the war, followed by voluminous extracts from official documents, campaign reports and officers' letters. Appendixes contain biographies of British military and naval officers and a list of all officers killed, wounded or captured by the enemy during the war. There is also a useful and detailed index.

242 **Memoir of the three campaigns of Major-General Sir Archibald Campbell's army in Ava.**
Henry Havelock.   Serampore, India [s.n.], 1828. 369p. map.
The author, a lieutenant in the 13th Light Infantry and deputy assistant adjutant general to the British forces engaged in the First Anglo-Burmese War, provides both a first-hand account and an overview of the war, in a style that uses 'barbarians' as synonymous with Burmans, which may be judged from his opening paragraph: 'The first war against the Burmans arose out of a singular, and audacious, but perfectly deliberate attempt on the part of the semi-barbarous court of Ava to deprive the British Government in India of a portion of its Eastern provinces'.

243 **Burmah: a series of one hundred photographs illustrating incidents connected with the British Expeditionary Force to that country from the embarkation at Madras, 1st Nov. 1885, to the capture of King Theebaw: with many views of Mandalay and surrounding country, native life and industries and most interesting descriptive notes.**
Willoughby Wallace Hooper.   London: J. A. Lugard; Calcutta, India: Thacker, Spink, 1887. 100p.
A comprehensive (fifty plates) photographic record of the military annexation of Burma and scenes in Upper Burma taken by the provost-martial of the British Expeditionary force of 1885-86. For details of the controversy caused by Hooper's photographs of executions, see John Falconer's article (which reproduces many of Hooper's photographs), 'Willoughby Wallace Hooper: "a craze about photography" ', *Photographic Collector*, vol. 4, no. 3 (1983), p. 253-86. Another contemporary album is Robert Blackall Graham's *Photographic illustrations of Mandalay and Upper Burmah* ([Birmingham, England]: [s.n.], 1887).

244 **Our Burmese wars and relations with Burma: being an abstract of military and political operations, 1824-25-26, and 1852-53, with various local, statistical, and commercial information, and a summary of events from 1826 to 1879, including a sketch of King Theebau's progress.**
William Ferguson Beatson Laurie.   London: W. H. Allen, 1880. 487p. maps.
Colonel Laurie served in the Second Anglo-Burmese War and published his personal narratives of the military campaign under the titles *The second Burmese war: a narrative of the operations at Rangoon in 1852* (London: Smith, Elder, 1853. 280p. maps.) and *Pegu: being a narrative of events during the second Burmese war from August 1852 to its conclusion in June 1853, with a succinct continuation down to February 1854* (London: Smith, Elder, 1854. 535p. maps.), based on his field notes and other participants' accounts, with plans and sketches by fellow officers. In this work he provides a long summary of the First Anglo-Burmese War and draws substantially on his earlier publications to describe the military operations of the Second Anglo-Burmese War. Various papers containing statistical and commercial information and a review of the first year of King Thibaw's reign are included. Laurie anticipates, and advocates, the British annexation of Upper Burma in two further bombastic works, *Ashé pyee, the superior country: or, the great attractions of Burma to British enterprise and commerce* (London: W. H. Allen, 1882. 283p.) and *Burma, the foremost country: a timely discourse to which is added John Bull's neighbour squaring up, or how the Frenchman sought to win an empire in the East, with notes on the probable effects of*

French success in Tonquin on British interests in Burma (London: W. H. Allen, 1884. 146p.).

245 Narrative of the naval operations in Ava, during the Burmese war in the years 1824, 1825 and 1826.
John Marshall.   London: Longman, Rees, Orme, Brown & Green, 1830. 126p.

Designed to do justice to the role of the Royal Navy in the First Anglo-Burmese War and to remedy omissions or inadequacies in J. J. Snodrass' *Narrative of the Burmese war* (q.v.); with extensive quotations from official despatches and memoranda, and a listing of naval personnel. Marshall also published a multi-volume *Royal naval biography: or memoirs of the services of all the flag officers, superannuated rear-admirals, retired captains, post-captains, and commanders . . . on the Admiralty list* (London: Longman, Rees, Orme, Brown & Green, 1823-35. 8 vols.) in which can be found details of naval officers involved in the First Anglo-Burmese War. Volume three, part one (1831) contains a biography of, among others, Frederick Marryat (p. 261-70) – later to achieve fame as a novelist – and also reprints as a 120-page appendix Marshall's *Narrative* under the title *Naval operations in Ava*. Marryat gave his own account of his experiences in Burma as a naval commander in the 'Diary on a Continent' section of his miscellany *Olla podrida* (London: Richard Bentley, 1840), while the study of Marryat (1792-1848) by Christopher Lloyd, *Captain Marryat and the old navy* (London, New York: Longmans, Green, 1939. 286p. bibliog.) has a chapter on Marryat and the first Anglo-Burmese War (p. 206-31).

246 Empires in collision: Anglo-Burmese relations in the mid-nineteenth century.
Oliver B. Pollak.   Westport, Connecticut; London: Greenwood, 1979. 214p. 2 maps. bibliog. (Contributions in Comparative Colonial Studies, no. 1).

This study centres on the Second Anglo-Burmese War of 1852 and its consequences during the reign of King Mindon (1853-78). The book's theme is the clash arising between two culturally disparate nations when the British 'imposed the standards of governmental efficiency, freedom of commerce and dynamic world view on a traditional society ill prepared to accommodate such novelties'.

247 Political incidents of the first Burmese war.
Thomas Campbell Robertson.   London: Richard Bentley, 1853. 252p. map.

Writing during the Second Anglo-Burmese War, the author reflects on the lessons of the First Anglo-Burmese War and his role as a political officer in Arakan and during the British advance on Ava. With observations on the 'Mugs' (more correctly Mugh or Magh) of Arakan and Chittagong, on routes through the Arakan Yoma to the Irrawaddy, and on the complicated peace negotiations with the Burmese in late 1825 to early 1826.

48 **British diplomacy and the annexation of Upper Burma.**
Damodar P. Singhal. New Delhi: South Asian Publishers, [c. 1981].
rev. ed. 158p. map. bibliog.

study of the diplomatic relations between British India and Burma and of incidents
ading to the Third Anglo-Burmese War of 1885. Documents reproduced in the
ppendixes include the Treaty of Yandabo (1826), Commercial Conventions between
rance and Burma (1873 and 1885), and between Germany and Burma (1885), the
dgement of the Hlutdaw in the Bombay Burmah case (1885) and the Treaty between
urma and British India (1867). The book is a revision of the author's *The annexation
* *Upper Burma* (Singapore: Eastern Universities Press, 1960. 129p.).

49 **Narrative of the Burmese War detailing the operations of Major-General**
Sir Archibald Campbell's army, from its landing at Rangoon in May
1824, to the conclusion of a treaty of peace at Yandaboo, in February
1826
John James Snodgrass. London: John Murray, 1827; New Delhi: BR
Publishing, 1985. 319p. map.

ne tone of Major Snodgrass' narrative of the First Anglo-Burmese War (1824-26) is
irly typical of British attitudes and accounts of this period. His concluding remarks
on the Burmese king are: 'Let him then vaunt and boast, and let us smile at his
irmless vanity and arrogant imbecility'. The appendix contains translations of
ptured Burmese military documents and the text of the Treaty of Yandabo.

50 **The pagoda war: Lord Dufferin and the fall of the Kingdom of Ava,**
1885-6.
Anthony Terence Quincey Stewart. London: Faber & Faber, 1972.
223p. 2 maps. bibliog.

ne first detailed study of the Third Anglo-Burmese War, a successful, but bitterly
ntroversial, military campaign that resulted in the deposition and exile of the
urmese monarchy, and the British annexation of Upper Burma. The volume is
ustrated with contemporary photographs of the campaign.

1 **A political history of the extraordinary events which led to the Burmese**
war: illustrated with a map of the British frontier.
William White. London: C. Hamilton, 1827. 169p. map.

critical account of the origins of the First Anglo-Burmese War with extensive
.otations from official documents and a plea that the powers of the directors of the
1st India Company be curbed. Captain White's theme is that 'The happy termination
the late disastrous contest with the Burmese Power . . . by no means supercedes
c] the necessity of a rigid enquiry into the circumstances which led to the sacrifice of
much human life, the desolation of province after province, with all the attendant
ls, and the expenditure of twelve millions of pounds stirling' [sic]. White details the
ıgstanding unrest in Arakan and the disputes between the British and Burmese
thorities about Arakanese refugees and border incursions and, unlike most other
ntemporary accounts, challenges the official British view that the Burmese were the
le aggressors.

252 **Documents illustrative of the Burmese war: with an introductory sketc**
of the events of the war, and an appendix.
Compiled and edited by Horace Hayman Wilson. Calcutta, India:
Government Gazette Press, 1827. [437p.].

A rare compilation of official documents relating to the First Anglo-Burmese V
(1824-26), arranged in three separately paginated sections: the first (96p.) gives
account of the war with cross-references to the original documents; the second (248
consists of the documents themselves; and the third consists of an appendix (93
giving topographical and statistical notices reproduced from the Calcutta Governm
Gazette and other sources. Wilson (1786-1860) was librarian of the East In
Company and director of the Royal Asiatic Society from 1837 to 1860. He a
produced a *Narrative of the Burmese war in 1824-26: as originally compiled fr
official documents* (London: Wm. H. Allen, 1852. 290p. map.) which up to p. 25'
substantially the same as the first section of his *Documents . . .* while the remain
pages give a brief account of British intercourse with Burma in the period 1826-4'

**The life of General Sir Harry N. D. Prendergast, R.E., V.C., G.C.B., ('
happy warrior).**
See item no. 335.

The coming of the great queen: a narrative of the acquisition of Burma.
See item no. 356.

The Second World War and the Japanese occupation

253 **Burma: the longest war 1941-45.**
Louis Allen. London; Melbourne, Australia: J. M. Dent, 1984;
London: J. M. Dent, 1986. 686p. 36 maps. bibliog.

A masterly account of a long and ferocious war, covering the onset of the wai
Burma, the retreat of the British army from Burma in 1942, the battles at Imphal
Kohima in 1944 – the greatest defeat suffered on land by the Japanese – the long-ra
penetration operations behind enemy lines, and the Japanese surrender. The strai
and politics of the Burmese nationalists, whose country was being fought over
fiercely, are also briefly discussed. The final chapter has sections on sex, race and
aesthetic response' and a sensitive discussion of English and Japanese novels of
war. What makes the book so remarkable is the author's balanced presentation of
campaign from both the allied and the Japanese side, using English and Japan
source material and personal narratives. It ranks as the definitive history of the wa
Burma. Included are an extensive bibliography (p. 663-77), appendixes discuss
casualty statistics, the debate on the Sittang bridge disaster, and listing British
Japanese units in Burma, 1944. The 1986 edition contains some corrections. Alsc
Allen is *Sittang the last battle: the end of the Japanese in Burma, July–August I*
(London: MacDonald, 1973. 267p. maps. bibliog.).

4 The Ledo road: General Joseph W. Stilwell's highway to China.
Leslie Anders.   Norman, Oklahoma: University of Oklahoma Press,
1965. 255p. 8 maps.

e story of the construction in 1943 by US Army Engineers commanded by Colonel
A. Pick of 'history's greatest military highway', the Ledo Road and of its
tribution to the allied military campaign in Northern Burma; with a brief epilogue
the postwar effect of the Ledo Road on the Kachin State. The road – 300 miles long
r malarial mountain terrain – went from the Indian railhead at Ledo over the Naga
s and through the remote Hukawng Valley to Mogaung.

5 Merrill's marauders.
Alan D. Baker.   London: Pan/Ballantine, 1972. 159p. maps. (The
Pan/Ballantine Illustrated History of World War II, Weapons Book).

well-illustrated account of the role of the American combat troops, officially
ignated 5307th Composite Unit (Provisional), trained for guerrilla operations
ind Japanese lines who fought a gruelling war in northern Burma in support of the
ance of General Stilwell's Chinese divisions and the recapture of Myitkyina on
ugust 1944.

**The national liberation movement in Burma during the Japanese
occupation period (1941-1945).**
Jan Bečka.   Prague: Oriental Institute, Czechoslovak Academy of
Sciences, 1983. 387p. bibliog. (Dissertationes Orientales, vol. 42).

re have been few detailed studies of the Japanese occupation of Burma. This
ount, based substantially on Burmese primary sources, describes and analyses
nges in the Burmese nationalist movement during the war years and also briefly
mines political repercussions in the postwar period.

**Netaji Subhas Chandra Bose in South-East Asia and India's liberation
war 1943-45.**
Moti Lal Bhargava.   New Delhi: Vishwavidya, 1984. 286p.

s study of the Indian National Army which fought on the Japanese side in the
ond World War has many references to Burma throughout and a chapter on the
le for Imphal (p. 74-90). The appendixes contain a 1944 American intelligence
ort (by the Office of Strategic Services) on Indian minorities in Southeast Asia and
background to the Indian independence movement (p. 193-240) which contains
rmation on Indians in Burma, relations between Indians and Burmans, and Indian
anizations in Burma. Also on Bose and the Indian National Army is Gerard Hugh
r's *The War of the springing tigers* (London: Osprey, 1975. 200p.). Another work
vant for its information on Japanese efforts to promote the activities of the Indian
ependence League and the Indian National Army in Burma, with a chapter on the
strous Imphal campaign, is Fujiwara Iwaichi, translated by Akashi Yoji, *F. Kikan:
anese army intelligence operations in Southeast Asia during World War II* (Hong
g, Singapore, Kuala Lumpur: Heinemann Asia, 1983. 338p. map. bibliog.).

258   **The Chindit war: the campaign in Burma, 1944.**
    Shelford Bidwell.   London: Hodden & Stoughton, 1979. 304p.
    11 maps. bibliog.

In 1944 some 20,000 troops trained for guerrilla warfare marched or were flown in
Burma behind the Japanese lines. Some 3,000, who came to be called the 'Marauder
were American under the command of General Joseph Stilwell, and the remaind
were 'Chindits', the brainchild of General Orde C. Wingate. This book focuses up
the contrasting methods of warfare waged by Stilwell and Wingate, the consequenc
of Wingate's death in March 1944, and, above all, relates how 'the dry work
operational planning staffs affected the fate of ordinary soldiers, whose hard task w
to realise the overall plan in a brutal war fought in a brutal environment'. The auth
provides a careful assessment of the personalities and tactics involved and vivi
portrays their effects at the fighting man's level.

259   **Wingate's phantom army.**
    Wilfred Graham Burchett, introduction by Michael Calvert.   London
    Frederick Muller, 1946. 195p. map.

A revised and updated version of the author's *Wingate adventure* (Melbour
Australia: F. W. Cheshire, 1944), the first account to be published of the operations
General Orde Wingate's long-range penetration forces (the Chindits) in Burn
Burchett, a wartime newspaper correspondent, writes with great immediacy and v
given access to unpublished military reports. Burchett's *Bombs over Bur*
(Melbourne, Australia: F. W. Cheshire, 1944. 260p.) is a vivid piece of war report
on the Japanese attack and the retreat to India, also published in an unillustra'
version under the title *Trek back from Burma* (Allahabad, India: Kitabistan, [194
330p.). For an assessment of Burchett and the background to his Burma despatches, '
Philip Knightley, 'Cracking the Jap: Burchett on World War Two' in *Burchett repor*
the other side of the world 1939-1983, edited by Ben Kiernan (London: Quartet, 198
p. 3-12.

260   **Burma, 1942-1945.**
    Raymond Callahan.   London: Davis-Poynter, 1978. 190p. map.
    bibliog. (The Politics and Strategy of the Second World War Series,
    edited by Noble Frankland, Christopher Dowling).

Essentially an overview of the Burma campaign during the Second World War and
place in the grand strategy of supreme command. See also the clear military survey :
chronology of the Burma campaign, with biographical notes on military command'
given in Geoffrey Matthews, *The re-conquest of Burma 1943-1945* (Aldersl
England: Gale & Polden, 1966. 104p. 10 maps. bibliog.). Also relevant are two e
accounts of the war, Frank Owen's *The campaign in Burma* (London: HMSO, 1'
175p. maps.) and Roy McKelvie's *The war in Burma* (London: Methuen, 1948. 3
9 maps.).

261   **Indian army triumphant in Burma (the Burmese campaign 1941-45).**
    Anil Chandra.   Delhi; Lucknow, India: Atma Ram, 1984. 234p.
    bibliog.

Researched principally from Indian archival sources, this study of the war in Bu
focuses on the great contribution of Indian Army officers and troops to the a
campaign and victory. The origins of the Indian National Army which fought on

apanese side are briefly discussed in an appendix. See also, James Gordon Elliott's *A roll of honour: the story of the Indian Army 1939-1945* (London: Cassell, 1963. 392p. maps. bibliog.) which has five chapters on the Burma campaign (p. 149-75, p. 268-52).

62 **Last and first in Burma (1941-1948).**
Maurice Collis.   London: Faber & Faber, 1956. 303p. 3 maps.
his narrative of 'how we lost Burma; and . . . of how the Burmese got it back' interweaves the military events of the war in Burma with political developments during ir Reginald Hugh Dorman-Smith's Governorship of Burma; with a chronology of principal events (p. 292-97).

63 **The army medical services campaigns: vol. 5, Burma.**
F. A. E. Crew.   London: Her Majesty's Stationery Office, 1966. 754p.
(History of the Second World War, United Kingdom Medical Series, edited by Arthur S. MacNalty).
his well-written medical history of the Burma campaign draws on war diaries, official ispatches, personal narratives and other sources. It follows the course of the war in urma, covering all engagements, and chronicles minutely the medical cover and rganization, casualties, diseases and treatment for every army corps at each stage of ie war, concluding with a general review of the work of the Army Medical Services in urma. The text is accompanied by thirty-seven appendixes, numerous illustrations, fty-four black-and-white plates and eighty-three statistical tables. For a study of merican Army medical work in the Burma campaign, see the study by James Herbert tone, *The United States Army Medical Service in combat in India and Burma, 1942 to)45* (PhD dissertation, Yale University, New Haven, Connecticut, 1947. 937p. bliog. Available from University Microfilms, Ann Arbor, Michigan, order no. M 65-4786).

54 **SOE in the Far East.**
Charles Cruickshank.   Oxford; New York: Oxford University Press, 1983. 285p. 6 maps. bibliog.
his official history of the secret wartime activities of the Special Operations Executive OE) in Asia contains a chapter on Burma (p. 163-90) as well as numerous references to Burma throughout. The intelligence and guerrilla operations of Force 136 help the advance of the Fourteenth Army are described in some detail. Also levant is J. G. Beevor, *SOE: recollections and reflections 1940-45* (London: Bodley ead, 1981. 269p.) which contains a clear outline of the complicated situation in urma (p. 220-22) and extracts from Mountbatten's report on South East Asia ommand's decision to support Force 136's proposal to make use of the Japanese-icked Burma Defence Army to rise against the Japanese (p. 249-52). Patrick owarth's *Undercover: the men and women of the Special Operations Executive* ondon: Routledge & Kegan Paul, 1980. 248p.) briefly describes SOE operations in urma and the work of Hugh Seagrim, Jimmy and Bill Nimmo, Eric McCrindle, nthony Irwin, John Gebhard, J. H. Williams, Harold Browne, R. G. Turrall and uncan Guthrie (p. 204-11). A blunt personal account by a Force 136 Captain is C. G. aylor's *The forgotten ones of 'South East Asia Command' and 'Force 136'* lfracombe, England: Arthur H. Stockwell, 1989. 88p.).

265 **British military administration in the Far East, 1943-46.**
Frank Siegfried Vernon Donnison. London: Her Majesty's Stationer
Office, 1956. 483p. 10 maps. (History of the Second World War,
United Kingdom Military Series).

Compiled chiefly from official, unpublished documents, this clear history of
complicated subject provides in part one (p. 3-52) an introductory narrative on t
Japanese invasion of Southeast Asia in 1941-42, and of the situation in Arakan and
the setting up of a British military administration; part two (p. 53-134) is solely
Burma and covers the creation of the Civil Affairs Service (Burma) and t
establishment of the Military Administration for Burma and its integration with t
rest of the military organization, linking administrative planning and developments
the progress of the military campaign and the reoccupation of Burma; part three cove
Malaya, Borneo and Hong Kong; part four (p. 217-330) looks at finance, rel
supplies, trade and industry, refugees and displaced persons, law and justice, labo
recruitment and propaganda, and has references to Burma throughout; part five de
with military government at the political level and has a chapter (p. 343-74)
nationalism in Burma, with a discussion of Aung San and other key figures, the Burr
National Army, the Kandy conferences and their outcome. Various milita
proclamations are reproduced in the appendixes.

266 **Dawns like thunder: the retreat from Burma.**
Alfred Draper. London: Leo Cooper, 1987. 298p. 2 maps. bibliog.

This book is neither an individual's account of wartime experiences, nor an offic
history. Based on solid research, it attempts to present what many soldiers, civilia
and officials involved in the defeat of Burma felt at the time. It provides a fre
appraisal of a tragic chain of events including the Sittang bridge disaster, and recor
the remarkable resilience and courage of the British, Indian and Gurkha soldiers, a
the many atrocities of the Japanese. It well explains why those who suffered so much
Burma felt they were 'the Forgotten Army'.

267 **The Johnnies.**
Geoffrey Charles Evans. London: Cassell, 1964. 231p. maps.

The story of the men of Z Force, largely recruited from members of the Burma For
Service and timber companies, who carried out twenty-six intelligence-gatheri
patrols behind enemy Japanese lines in Burma.

268 **The battle for Naw Seng's kingdom: General Stilwell's north Burma
campaign and its aftermath.**
Ian Fellowes-Gordon. London: Leo Cooper, 1971. 176p. map.

This account concentrates on General Joseph W. Stilwell's campaigns in Burma
1944-45 culminating in the allies' recapture of Myitkyina, and highlights the role of
Kachin Levies; with a brief note on the postwar Kachin Independence Ar
commanded by General Naw Seng.

9   Spitfires over the Arakan.
Norman Leslie Robert Franks.   London: William Kimber, 1988. 231p.

account of the role of Spitfires in the air war over Burma in 1943-44 incorporating
accounts and memories of former pilots, with illustrations of air crews and planes.
the same author is *Hurricanes over the Arakan* (Wellingborough, England: Patrick
phens, 1989. 223p. maps.) on operations in 1942-43, and *The air battle of Imphal*
ondon: William Kimber, 1985. 223p. map.). Also relevant are Gerry Beauchamp's
hawks over Burma (Earl Shilton, England: Midland Counties Publications
erophile], 1985. 311p.) which includes the war diary of Squadron Leader A. B.
nford (1919-68) and David J. Innes' *Beaufighters over Burma: no. 27 Squadron,*
F, 1942-45 (Poole, England: Blandford, 1985. 128p.). Oliver Moxon's trilogy, *Bitter
nsoon: the memoirs of a fighter pilot* (London: Robert Hale, 1955. 192p. map), *The
 monsoon* (London: Robert Hale, 1957. 174p.) and *After the monsoon* (London:
bert Hale, 1958. 160p.) provides a graphic account of air pilots operating in the
ttle for Imphal in 1944, while Kenneth Hemingway's *Wings over Burma* (London:
ality, 1944. 192p.) gives a vivid description of warfare in Burma as experienced
m the cockpit of a Hurricane. Also titled *Wings over Burma* are the reminiscences
J. Helsdon Thomas (Braunton, England: Merlin, 1991) describing the life of no. 67
hter Squadron in Burma as seen by a ground engineer. The story of the American
lunteer Group (AVG) of pilots which fought in Burma to delay the Japanese
vance and to protect the Burma Road and supplies to China from December 1941 to
y 1942 is given in Russell Whelan's *The flying tigers* (London: MacDonald, 1943.
5p.) and in William J. Koenig's *Over the hump: airlift to China* (London: Pan/
llantine, 1972. 158p. map. bibliog.).

0   The political impact of the Japanese occupation of Burma.
Dorothy Hess Guyot.   PhD dissertation, Yale University, New Haven,
Connecticut, 1966. 498p. bibliog. (Available from University
Microfilms, Ann Arbor, Michigan, order no. 67-71).

major study, based in part on research at the Defence Services Historical Research
titute in Rangoon, which contains much information on the birth of the Burma
dependence Army and its development into the Burma Army. The author examines
 nature of prewar politics, the destruction of British rule, the Burma Independence
my, the Japanese occupation and administration, political mobilization and
istance, and the dramatic impact of the war on Burmese politics. By the same
thor is 'Communal conflict in the Burma delta' in *Southeast Asian transitions:
proaches through social history* edited by Ruth T. McVey (New Haven, Connecticut;
ndon: Yale University Press, 1978, p. 191-234), analysing the communical warfare
tween Burmans and Karens in 1942 which Guyot sees as being the root of the Karen
bellion of 1949 and of the continuing Karen separationist movement. Also relevant is
drew Selth's *The anti-fascist resistance in Burma, 1942-1945: the racial dimension*
athan, Australia: James Cook University of North Queensland, Centre for
utheast Asian Studies, [1985]. 33p. bibliog.) reviewing the response of Burma's
nic minorities to the Japanese occupation and SOE's role in developing guerrilla
vements among the hill tribes.

271 **The war dead of the British Commonwealth and Empire: the register o**
the names of those who fell in the 1939-1945 War and have no known
grave: the Rangoon Memorial
Compiled by the Imperial War Graves Commission.   London: HMS(
1956-58. 25 parts. map. (Memorial Register 17).

An alphabetical register of the names of 27,000 'soldiers of many races united
service to the British Crown who gave their lives in Burma and Assam but to whom ▮
fortune of war denied the customary rites accorded to their comrades in death'. T
names are engraved at the Rangoon Memorial, Taukkyan War Cemetery, Burma. Tl
introduction to the register briefly describes the campaign in Burma, and gives
ground plan of the memorial and index of regiments and corps showing their positi
on the memorial. Further compilations are *The register of the names of those who fell*
the 1939-1945 War and are buried in cemeteries in Burma: Taukkyan War Cemete
Rangoon (London: HMSO, 1958. 7 vols.) listing over 6,000 servicemen and *T*
register of the names of those who fell in the 1939-45 War and are buried in cemeteries
Burma: Rangoon War Cemetery (London: HMSO, 1958. 2 vols. maps.) listi
approximately 1,400 servicemen (and one at the Rangoon Jewish Cemetery). T
Imperial War Graves Commission has also compiled and published registers of ▮
thousands of prisoners of war who died building the Burma–Siam railway.

272 **The Minami organ.**
Tatsuro Izumiya, translated by Tun Aung Chain.   Rangoon:
Universities' Press, for Translation and Publications Department,
Higher Education Department, 1981. 214p. map.

The Minami Organ was a clandestine group of the Imperial Japanese Army wh
organized an underground movement in Burma and smuggled a group of you
Burmese nationalists – the 'Thirty Comrades' – to Japan for military training, formi
the nucleus of the Burma Independence Army. The author, who served with ▮
Minami Organ from April 1941 to its dissolution in July 1942, gives an account of ▮
movement's origins, activities, conflict with the Imperial Japanese Army over ▮
question of Burma's independence, and its dissolution. Much information is provid
on Colonel Keiji Suzuki, head of the Minami Organ, and other Japanese personalit
as well as on Aung San and other leading Burmese figures. A list of seventy-
members of the Minami Organ is given in the appendix. Originally published
Japanese under the title *Sono na wa Minami Kikan* (Tokyo: Tokuma Shoten, 196

273 **The war against Japan.**
Stanley Woodburn Kirby.   London: HMSO, 1957-69. 5 vols. maps.
(History of the Second World War, United Kingdom Military Series,
edited by James Butler).

This official military history is an indispensable source, of which the following volum
are relevant for Burma: volume two, *India's most dangerous hour* covering the peri
from the Japanese invasion of Burma to late 1943; volume three, *The decisive batt*
covering South East Asia Command and operations in Arakan from November 1943
February 1944; and, volume four, *The reconquest of Burma*. Also relevant ▮
Official history of the Indian armed forces in the second world war, under the gene
editorship of Bisheshwar Prasad (Calcutta, India: Combined Inter-Services Histori
Section [India & Pakistan], 1944-59. 5 vols. maps. bibliog.), as follows: *The retr*
from Burma 1941-42 (edited by Bisheshwar Prasad); *The Arakan operations 1942*

History. The Second World War and the Japanese occupation

(by N. N. Madan), *The reconquest of Burma* (volume one by S. N. Prasad, K. D. Bhargava, P. N. Khera; volume two by P. N. Khera, S. N. Prasad). S. C. Gupta's *History of the Indian air forces 1933-45* (Delhi: Combined Inter-Services Historical Section India & Pakistan, 1961. 191p. maps.) contains details of the Burma campaign (p. 71-177).

274   **Japanese-trained armies in Southeast Asia: independence and volunteer forces in World War II.**
Joyce C. Lebra.   Hong Kong: Heinemann Education Books (Asia); New York: Columbia University Press, 1977. 226p. bibliog.
This study, based substantially on Japanese sources, contains chapters on Japan's sponsorship and training of the Burma Independence Army (p. 39-74) and on the eventual revolt of the independence armies against their Japanese masters (p. 146-66). The appendix contains, in English and Burmese, the Burma Independence Army's farewell letter to Colonel Suzuki on his recall to Tokyo in June 1942.

275   **'A hell of a licking': the retreat from Burma 1941-2.**
James Lunt.   London: Collins, 1986. 318p. 8 maps. bibliog.
The author was commissioned into the Army in 1937 and went to Burma in 1939 to serve with the Burma Rifles. He describes the general unpreparedness for war and the prevailing confusion as the Japanese began their attack and advance into Burma. The subsequent retreat of the British from Burma over a distance of nearly 1,000 miles and a period of five months was marked by a succession of military disasters and terrible suffering. Lunt's account strikes a fine balance between his own personal experiences as staff officer with the 2nd Burma Brigade during the retreat and a military overview and assessment of the personalities and tactics of commanders such as Wavell, Hutton, Smyth, Alexander and Stilwell. For the author, the humiliation of military retreat was made doubly bitter by his feeling that so many of the Burmese were glad to see the British go.

276   **Before the dawn: the story of two historic retreats.**
John Smyth.   London: Cassell, 1957. 220p. maps.
The British retreat from Burma in 1942 and, above all, the fateful decision to blow the Sittang bridge that cost General Smyth, Commander of the 17th Division, his military career are described on p. 109-210. Further reflections on this episode can be found in his *The only enemy: an autobiography* (London: Hutchinson, 1959. 352p.) in a chapter 'Battle for Burma' (p. 175-208).

277   **Burma in the anti-fascist war.**
Robert H. Taylor.   In: *Southeast Asia under Japanese occupation.* Edited by Alfred W. McCoy. New Haven, Connecticut: Yale University Southeast Asia Studies, 1980, p. 132-57. (Yale University Southeast Asia Studies Monograph Series no. 22).
This essay challenges standard assumptions about the nature of pre- and postwar Burmese politics and provides a fresh assessment of the 'Japanese interregnum' period in Burmese history. Taylor argues that new political forces emerged in this period which created the conditions for Burma's still unresolved civil war. He examines the creation of the Burma Independence Army by the Japanese, the motivation and

89

ideology of its leaders, the formation of the Anti-Fascist Organisation (AFO) in August 1944, and the Communists' role in organizing resistance to the Japanese.

278 **Marxism and resistance in Burma 1942-1945: Thein Pe Myint's Wartime traveler.**

Robert H. Taylor.   Athens, Ohio: Ohio University Press, 1984. 326p.

2 maps. bibliog. (Southeast Asia Translation Series, vol. 4).

This book is in two parts. The first (p. 1-94) gives a succinct exposition of the development of Marxism in Burmese politics, the origins of resistance in Japanese-occupied Burma, and the role of Force 136 and the Burmese Communists, and examines the shifting alliances of the period and the eventual Communist eclipse. The second part (p. 95-303) is a translation of an autobiographical account of the wartime years written by Thein Pe Myint (1914-78), a leading Burmese Marxist and novelist. Taylor's introduction and translation from the Burmese provide a different perspective on the underground movement from that found in most Western accounts. The story told in *Wartime traveler* – of Thein Pe Myint's decision to go underground and escape to India and of his propaganda activities and liaison work between the Burmese resistance and Force 136 – played a key part in the rescue of the Burma National Army and Aung San from the consequences of having accepted Japanese assistance. In Taylor's view, it changed Burmese history. Also relevant is Taylor's article, 'The Burmese communist movement and its Indian connection: formation and factionalism', *Journal of Southeast Asian Studies*, vol. 14, no. 1 (March 1983), p. 95-108. Other studies of Marxism, its role in the development of Burmese political thought, and of the postwar schisms in the Communist movement are John Seabury Thomas' 'Marxism in Burma' in *Marxism in Southeast Asia: a study of four countries*, edited by Frank N. Trager (Stanford, California: Stanford University Press; London: Oxford University Press, 1960, p. 14-57) and, John H. Badgley's 'Burmese communist schisms' in *Peasant rebellion and communist revolution in Asia*, edited by John Wilson Lewis (Stanford, California: Stanford University Press, 1974, p. 151-68).

279 **Burma: Japanese military administration, selected documents, 1941-1945.**

Edited with introduction by Frank N. Trager, translated by Won Zoon Yoon, assisted by Thomas T. Winant.   Philadelphia: University of Pennsylvania Press, 1971. 279p. bibliog.

This work consists of an introductory section, 'Historical notes on Japan's military occupation of Burma' (p. 1-24) by Trager giving a survey of the wartime setting with special reference to the Burma Independence Army and Aung San, followed by Won Zoon Yoon's translation of sixty-six Japanese documents (p. 25-236) covering Japanese plans for the conquest of Burma, military administration of Burma, the Burma Independence Army, the independence of Burma, educational system, the Shan States under the Japanese, and the construction of the Burma–Siam railway. The appendixes (p. 237-62) give lists of the Thirty Comrades – a group of young Burmese nationalists trained in Japan to lead an anti-British force – and of prominent Japanese in Burma, a glossary of terms and organizations in Burma, and charts of the Japanese military administration's organization. The selected bibliography (p. 269-79) includes Japanese works. A lot of information can also be found in the British compilation by the 'Burma Intelligence Bureau', *Burma during the Japanese occupation* (Simla, India: Government of India Press, 1943-44. 2 vols.). See also Won Zoon Yoon's dissertation, *Japan's occupation of Burma, 1941-1945* (PhD, New York University, Washington Square,

New York, 1971. 334p. Available from University Microfilms, Ann Arbor, Michigan, order no. UM 71-24 773) which, researched primarily from Japanese sources, is an important treatment of the subject and also of the Burmese nationalist movement. It is supplemented by his publication, *Japan's scheme for the liberation of Burma: the role of the Minami Kikan and the 'Thirty Comrades'* (Athens, Ohio: Ohio University Center for International Studies, Southeast Asia Program, 1973. 54p) [Papers in International Studies, Southeast Asia Series, no. 27]).

Troubled days of peace: Mountbatten and South East Asia Command 1945-46.
See item no. 188.

Epilogue in Burma 1945-48: the military dimension of British withdrawal.
See item no. 200.

Breakthrough in Burma: memoirs of a revolution 1939-1946.
See item no. 283.

U Hla Pe's narrative of the Japanese occupation of Burma.
See item no. 289.

Burma under Japanese rule: pictures and portraits.
See item no. 293.

Defeat into victory.
See item no. 395.

Autobiographies, Biographies and Memoirs

Burmese

280 **Visions of Shwedagon.**
Aung Aung Thaik. Bangkok: White Lotus, 1989. 269p.
The author, a Burmese artist, left Burma for America in 1972 and his book recalls his life, travels, friends and family in Burma; with black-and-white illustrations of his own pictures.

281 **Aung San of Burma: a biographical portrait by his daughter.**
Aung San Suu Kyi. Edinburgh: Kiscadale, 1991. 2nd ed. 66p.
A clear, concise and non-hagiographic biography which conveys both the facts and the essence of Aung San (1915-47), Burma's national hero and independence leader whose memory remains for the Burmese 'the guardian of their political conscience'. First published in 1984 (St. Lucia, Australia: University of Queensland Press. 42p.) under the title *Aung San*, the 1991 edition has an added 'photo essay' of black-and-white plates and an introduction by Roger Matthews describing Aung San Suu Kyi's entry into the forefront of Burmese politics from mid-1988 onwards.

282 **Burman in the back row: autobiography of a Burmese rebel.**
Aye Saung. Hong Kong: Asia 2000; Bangkok: White Lotus, 1989. 296p. 2 maps. (Burma Reader Series).
An account of the author's formative years in Burma under the rule of Ne Win, from 1962 to 1988. Aye Saung's autobiography chronicles his transition from rural schoolboy to Marxist student activist, describes his arrest, torture and four years' imprisonment, and his subsequent roving career on the run from the secret police, including a period with the rebel Shan State Army and ending with his crossing the border into Thailand to start a rebel movement in exile.

283 **Breakthrough in Burma: memoirs of a revolution, 1939-1946.**
Ba Maw, foreword by William S. Cornyn and Myint. New Haven,
Connecticut; London: Yale University Press, 1968. 460p. 3 maps.
Dr. Ba Maw (1893-1978) was one of Burma's most colourful politicians who rose to
prominence in 1932 as defence counsel for the peasant rebel leader, Hsaya San,
founded the *Sinyetha* (Poor Man's) Party in the 1930s and, following the 1935
Government of Burma Act which separated Burma from India, became Burma's Prime
Minister from 1937 to 1939 and, during the Japanese occupation of Burma, *Adipati* or
Head of State. Dr. Ba Maw's fluently written memoirs are devoted to the wartime
years. His account helps counteract the conventional British image of Ba Maw as an
unscrupulous collaborator with Japanese fascism by putting Burma's relationship with
the Japanese in the context of Burmese nationalist ambitions. Ba Maw emphasizes the
close ties between certain Burmese and the Japanese who helped organize the Burma
Independence Army. His book contains vivid portraits of such key figures in Burma's
history as General Aung San and U Nu. Appendixes to the book provide a glossary,
historical chronology and a Who's who. For a warm appreciation of Ba Maw, with
many details of his life and career, see Edward Law-Yone's 'Dr. Ba Maw of Burma' in
Essays on Burma edited by John P. Ferguson (q.v.).

284 **My Burma: the autobiography of a president.**
Ba U, foreword by J. S. Furnivall. New York: Taplinger, 1959. 106p.
These memoirs by the second president of Burma present a good picture of growing up
in colonial Burma, of life as a barrister and High Court judge during the nationalist
fervour of the 1920s and 1930s, of the Japanese occuaption of Burma and Burma's
struggle for independence. The memoirs cover only up to 1948.

285 **U Nu of Burma.**
Richard Butwell. Stanford, California: Stanford University Press,
1969. 2nd ed. 326p. bibliog.
First published in 1963 (Stanford, California: Stanford University Press. 306p.), this
informal biography of Nu, first prime minister of independent Burma, is based on
interviews with Nu and also on his written replies to questions and on other material
from Nu's contemporaries on the political stage. The 1969 edition is a reissue of the
1963 edition with an added chapter covering the first seven years (1962-69) of Ne Win's
Revolutionary Government. The extensive bibliography includes a selected listing of
Nu's own writings and speeches, with over eighty entries. Among Nu's literary works
are a novel, *Man, the wolf of man* (translated by Khin Zaw and serialized in the
Guardian, vol. 1, nos. 8-12 [June–Oct. 1954], vol. 2, nos. 1-3 [Nov. 1954–Jan. 1955]),
a play *The people win through*, translated by Khin Zaw and published in Rangoon
Society for the Extension of Democratic Ideals, 1952) and in an American edition
New York: Taplinger, 1957) with a biographical introduction by Edward Hunter. A
series of Nu's speeches were published in English translation and include the following
titles: *Towards peace and democracy* (Rangoon: Government Printing, 1949), *From
peace to stability* (Rangoon: Government Printing, 1951) and *Burma looks ahead*
Rangoon: Government Printing, 1952). His most important publications, however,
are *Burma under the Japanese* (q.v.) and his autobiography, *Saturday's son* (q.v.).

286 **Voices from the jungle: (Burmese youth in transition).**
Tokyo: Center for Christian Response to Asian Issues (CCRAI), 198(
88p. map.

This consists of personal statements, stories and poems by Burmese student refuge
who fled to border camps in Thailand following General Saw Maung's coup
18 September 1988 and the suppression of the pro-democracy movement in Burm
illustrated with photographs and student drawings.

287 **Daw Sein: les dix mille vies d'une femme birmane.** (Daw Sein: the ten
thousand lives of a Burmese woman.)
Claude Delachet Guillon.   Paris: Editions du Seuil, 1978. 174p.

An engaging account of a French teacher's meeting and friendship with a remarkat
character, eight-year-old Daw Sein, who introduces her to traditional Burme
massage and midwifery, spirit cults and festivals and, gradually, to the story of her l
and beliefs.

288 **The caged ones.**
Hla, translated by Sein Tu.   Bangkok: Tamarind Press, 1986. 144p.
(Asian Portraits).

Ludu U Hla (1910-82), one of Burma's best-known and most prolific modern autho
gathered these life stories of his fellow prisoners while in Rangoon Central Jail as
political prisoner from 1954-56. Illustrations are by Wa Thone. When first published
Burmese under the title *Lhaung-gyaing-dwin mha nhet-nge-mya* in 1958, it won
UNESCO award. By the same author is *The victim*, translated by Kathleen Forbes a
Than Tun, (Mandalay: Kyipwayay, 1976. 282p.), being another story of a fell
prisoner of Ludu U Hla, telling of his childhood, life under the Japanese occupatic
dacoity, sentence to life imprisonment in 1948 and of the inhumane prison conditic
of that period.

289 **U Hla Pe's narrative of the Japanese occupation of Burma.**
Hla Pe, recorded by Khin, foreword by Hugh Tinker.   Ithaca, New
York: Cornell University Southeast Asia Program, 1961. 96p. (Cornel
University Southeast Asia Program Data Paper no. 41).

The narrator held the post of director of press and publicity under the Ba M
government from 1942-45. His autobiographical account reveals much about t
conditions of life and Burmese attitudes during the Japanese occupation. Among oth
Burmese memoirs of the Japanese occupation period are Tun Pe's *Sun over Burn*
(Rangoon: Rasika Ranjani, 1949. 114p.) which tells of his (reluctant) editorship of t
official newspaper of the period *Bama khit* and Khin Myo Chit's *Three years under t
Japs* (Rangoon: The Author, 1945. 46p.), a strongly worded account of 'the re
conditions of a Fascist-occupied territory'.

90 **Aung San of Burma.**
Compiled and edited by Maung Maung, introduction by Harry J.
Benda. The Hague: Martinus Nijhoff, for Yale University Southeast
Asia Studies, 1962. 162p.

A tribute to Aung San (1915-47) in the form of documents selected and edited by
Dr. Maung Maung from Aung San's own speeches and writings, together with
memories and appreciative essays by Burmese and Western contemporaries of Aung
San, with a Who's who.

91 **Burma and General Ne Win.**
Maung Maung. Rangoon: Religious Affairs Department; London;
New York: Asia Publishing House, 1969. 332p. bibliog.

The theme of this book is 'the march forward of the nation' along the path of the
Burmese way to socialism under the inspired leadership of Ne Win (b. 1911) and its
aim is to serve as 'an aid to memory, to help us remember the past few decades of
Burma's political life through some of the main events and some of the people who
played their parts in those events'. It amounts to the only, to date, biography of Ne
Win and is cast in a distinctly eulogistic mould. It does, however, provide a fluent
narrative of the growth of the Burmese nationalist movement with many details from
Burmese sources. Dr. Maung Maung (b. 1925), a prolific author and former chief
justice of Burma, is a loyal and close associate of Ne Win of many years standing who
in the pro-democracy 1988 period briefly (19 August to 18 September) held the
position of president.

92 **To a soldier son.**
Maung Maung. Rangoon: Sarpay Beikman, 1974. 158p.

Dr. Maung Maung regards the Burma Army as his 'second home' and served in the
Burma Defence Army during the war. He wrote his reminiscences and memories of
this period and of the 1950s for his oldest son, a career officer in the Burma Army.

93 **Burma under Japanese rule: pictures and portraits.**
Nu, edited and translated with introduction by John Sydenham
Furnivall. London: Macmillan, 1954. 132p.

A personal narrative of Burmese life and politics during the Japanese occupation of
Burma with vivid portraits of U Nu's fellow nationalists and leading politicians.
Written between August and November 1945 during the first months of the British
reoccupation of Burma, the narrative ends with the Japanese surrender. The Who's
who at the end of the book was compiled by U Thant. For a discussion of how
Furnivall's translation and editing has tended to distort U Nu's original Burmese text
in order to fit more easily the anti-communist presuppositions of Western readers and
Furnivall's own political views', see Robert H. Taylor, *An undeveloped state: the study
of modern Burma's politics* (q.v.).

294 **Saturday's son.**
Nu, translated by Law Yone, edited by Kyaw Win.   New Haven:
Connecticut; London: Yale University Press, 1975. 358p. map.

This frank and confessional autobiography, written in the third person, by Nu (1909-),
first prime minister of independent Burma, gives an intimate account of his youth and
entry into student and national politics, and of his period as prime minister – 'an
amateur in office' – relating events only up to the 1962 military coup by Ne Win. His
memoirs do not include his subsequent years of imprisonment, while an account of his
period abroad as leader of forces opposed to Ne Win, his return to Burma and work on
translating Buddhist texts and his involvement in the pro-democracy movement in 1988
which led to his being placed under house arrest by SLORC has yet to be written. For
a stimulating and perceptive discussion of Nu's *Saturday's son*, see Robert H. Taylor's
review article, 'A modern Bodhisattva: how U Nu sees his life', *Politics* (Australia),
vol. 13, no. 1 (May 1978), p. 192-200.

295 **The world my country: the story of Daw Nyein Tha of Burma.**
Marjorie Procter.   London: Grosvenor, 1976. 142p.

The life and achievements of a remarkable Burmese Christian, Nyein Tha (1900-70)
whose family's conversion to Christianity dates from the time of Adoniram Judson in
Burma, and of her work in Burma and worldwide for the Moral Rearmament
Movement.

296 **The great Po Sein: a chronicle of the Burmese theater.**
Kenneth Sein, J. A. Withey.   Bloomington, Indiana; London: Indiana
University Press, 1965. 170p. bibliog.

An account of the life of the actor U Po Sein (1880-1952) and of the family theatrical
troupe, Sein Maha Thabin, and its place in Burmese theatrical history. Drawings are
by Ba Lone Lay.

297 **Memoirs of the four-foot colonel.**
Smith Dun, introduction by David I. Steinberg.   Ithaca, New York:
Cornell University Southeast Asia Program, 1980. 125p. map. (Cornell
University Southeast Asia Program Data Paper, no. 113).

The autobiography of a village Karen who fought with his battalion (2/20th Burma
Rifles) throughout the war, and became commander-in-chief of the Burma Army, but
had to resign during the Karen insurrections following Burma's independence. He
remained loyal to the Union of Burma, and went into 'self-imposed exile in the Kachin
State where there are few Karens and Burmese to cause any such clash'. General
Smith Dun (1906-79) includes his reflections on the Karen question, with numerous
quotations from earlier writers on the Karen people and from contemporaries caught
up in the Burman–Karen conflict.

298 **View from the UN.**
Thant.   Newton Abbot, England: David & Charles, 1974. 508p.

This is not specifically a book of memoirs or an autobiography, but an account of
U Thant's decade (1961-71) as secretary-general of the United Nations and of the
many world crises that marked his period of office. Thant does, however, take pains to
explain how his Burmese Buddhist religion and cultural background relates to his

concept of the role of a secretary-general and the UN. For a balanced account that conveys both Thant's personal qualities and his UN work, see that given by his press spokesman Ramses Nassif, *U Thant in New York 1961-1971: a portrait of the third UN Secretary-General* (London: C. Hurst, 1988. 140p.). For a full view of Thant's term of office see the papers and commentaries in *Public papers of the Secretaries-General of the United Nations*, vols. 6-8: *U Thant*, selected, edited and with commentary by Andrew W. Cordier, Max Harrelson (New York; London: Columbia University Press, 1976-77. 3 vols.). An enthusiastic biography of Thant, written while he was still secretary-general, is June Bingham's *U Thant of Burma: the search for peace* (London: Victor Gollancz, 1966. 256p. map. bibliog.). A useful portrait of Thant's work not only as secretary-general but as a government servant in Burma can be found in a memorial tribute to Thant (1909-74), 'Peacemaker from Pantanaw: a memorial tribute to U Thant' in *Asia* (*Supplement*), no. 3 (Spring 1977) (published by the Asia Society, New York, 1977. 75p.). This contains six essays (by Josef Silverstein, Fred Khouri, Lionel Landry, James Barrington, Edward Law Yone and Norman Cousins) and an extract from *View from the UN*. On the riots accompanying Thant's funeral in Burma, see Andrew Selth, *Death of a hero* (q.v.).

299 **The Shan of Burma: memoirs of a Shan exile.**
Tzang Yawnghwe (Eugene Thaik).   Singapore: Institute of Southeast Asian Studies, 1987. 275p. maps. bibliog. (Local History and Memoirs).

The author, a son of the Yawnghwe Prince Sao Shwe Thaike (who was the first president of the Union of Burma), narrates his early years and his involvement in the Shan nationalist movement and Shan State Army in the 1960s and 1970s. He presents a Shan perspective on Shan–Burman relations and politics, and on the opium trade and the resistance movement, drawing on personal experience as well as documentary sources. The final part of the book gives an extensive, but not always accurate, compendium of Who's who in Shan and Burmese history and politics.

300 **Profile of a Burma frontier man.**
Vum Ko Hau, foreword by Dr. Maung Maung.   Bandung, Indonesia: Kilatmadju, 1963. 502p.

These rambling autobiographical memoirs of a prominent Chin include his wartime experiences and the role of the Chin Freedom League, his participation in the Panglong Conference of 1947 and his recollections of General Aung San. The book also contains his father's memoirs, and translations of Chin folklore, songs and history. Correspondence with friends worldwide is reproduced and the author's views and research on such subjects as Burmese art and coinage are given. The book is illustrated with many black-and-white photographs of the author and his contemporaries.

Marxism and resistance in Burma 1942-1945: Thein Pe Myint's Wartime traveler.
See item no. 278.

Aung San Suu Kyi and Burma's unfinished renaissance.
See item no. 536.

Non-Burmese

301 **Back to Mandalay: an inside view of Burma.**
Gerry Abbott. Bromley, England: Impact, 1990. 221p. map. bibliog.
(Travellers' Tales).

The author was an English-language lecturer in Mandalay from 1986 to 1988. His well-written narrative of daily life and experiences there charts the growth of unrest and the outbreak of nationwide pro-democracy demonstrations and their suppression in 1988 – as seen from the limited and personal viewpoint of a foreign resident of Mandalay. His account is emotional, entertaining and saddening and, above all, strongly condemnatory of Ne Win and of 'the petulant vengeance, the xenophobia, the cosmetic tarting-up' which he sees as characteristic of Ne Win's style of rule that has reduced Burma to its present 'least developed status'. The appendix gives a translation of an account by Mandalay University students of the 'Sagaing massacre' in August 1988.

302 **A geologist in the service of the Raj.**
Cecil Thomas Barber. Henfield, England: The Author, 1978. 245p. map.

A personal memoir of years spent in the 1920s and early 1930s first as a field geologist and then as resident government geologist on the Yenangyaung, Singu and Indaw oilfields of Burma.

303 **Distinctly I remember: a personal story of Burma.**
Harold E. W. Braund. Mount Eliza, Australia: Wren, 1972. 296p. 6 maps.

These memories of an 'old Burma hand' vividly recapture the atmosphere of pre-war days in colonial Burma. Over half the book is devoted to the author's wartime experiences in guerrilla and intelligence operations with gallant Chin levies in Burma's remote Chin Hills.

304 **Burma as I saw it 1889-1917, with a chapter on recent events.**
Riou Grant Brown. London: Methuen, 1926. 234p. map.

Observations and opinions based on twenty-seven years in Burma as a magistrate and revenue officer. The author includes an account of Burmese legends and drama, with summaries of some popular plays and photographs of dramatic performances.

305 **Reminiscences of the court of Mandalay: extracts from the diary of General Horace A. Browne, 1859-1879.**
Horace Albert Browne. Woking, England: Oriental Institute, 1907. 196p.

Browne (1832-1914) spent twenty-three years in the administrative service of British (Lower) Burma, made several visits to the Upper Burman capital, Mandalay, and served as the last official British Resident there in 1879. His diary gives a vivid account and assessment of a varied cast of Europeans and Burmese at the Burmese court and in particular of King Thibaw's accession to the throne and the massacres that followed, with many details of diplomatic formalities and royal audiences. Browne's account concludes with his withdrawal of the British Residency – 'adieu to the mud and mire, moral and material, of Mandalay city'.

306 **Contacts with Burma, 1935-1949: a personal account.**
John F. Cady. Athens, Ohio: Ohio University, 1983. 117p. (Center for International Studies, Papers in International Studies, Southeast Asia Series no. 61).

These are the memoirs of a distinguished American scholar who played a leading role in the development of Southeast Asian studies in the United States. The period covered runs from Cady's first experience of Burma as a teacher at Judson College from 1935-38, to his work for the Office of Strategic Services (OSS) in 1943-45, his recruitment to the State Department and his fifteen-week assignment to the Rangoon consulate in 1946, concluding with his return to academia in 1949 following his disillusionment with attitudes in Washington in the Cold War era. Cady lists his secret 1944-46 research reports on Burma which have now been declassified, and gives references for some of the OSS documents in the National Archives, Washington, DC.

307 **Letters from Mandalay: a series of letters for the most part written from the royal city of Mandalay during the troublous years of 1878-79, together with letters written before the last Burmese campaign of 1885-88.**
James Alfred Colbeck, edited by George H. Colbeck.
Knaresborough, England: Alfred W. Lowe, 1892. 113p.

Colbeck (d. 1888), a missionary for the Society for the Propagation of the Gospel, lived in Mandalay in 1878-79 and returned there as chaplain to the British Expeditionary Force on the outbreak of the Third Anglo-Burmese War in 1885. His letters are informal, immediate and vivid and among the events he describes are the funeral of King Mindon, the rescue of Prince Nyaung-yan and other royal relatives fleeing King Thibaw's massacres, the British occupation of Mandalay and the fate of the royal library at Mandalay palace.

308 **The journey outward: an autobiography.**
Maurice Collis. London: Faber & Faber, 1952. 292p. map.

In this, the first volume of an autobiographical trilogy, Collis (1889-1973) – an untypical colonial official in Burma from 1912 to 1934 and from 1935 a prolific author – tells of his early life in Ireland and England, and of his joining the Indian Civil Service (ICS) and posting to Burma in 1912, his early experiences there and in Palestine and Egypt during the First World War (with a regiment of Burmese and Karen soldiers). Collis' second volume, *Into hidden Burma: an autobiography* (London: Faber & Faber, 1953. 268p. map.) relates his experiences in Burma from 1919 to 1934, and gives details of his time in Mergui which inspired his first book, *Siamese White* (London: Faber & Faber, 1936. 230p.; London: Faber & Faber, 1965. rev. ed. 312p. maps. bibliog.), about a late 17th-century English merchant adventurer in Mergui (at that time under Siamese rule), and an historical drama exploring White's character, *White of Mergen: a play* (London: Faber & Faber, 1955. 99p.). Collis has written in more detail of his 1930 judicial decisions which put him at odds with Burma's colonial administration in *Trials in Burma* (q.v.). Collis' autobiograpical trilogy is completed by *The journey up: reminiscences 1934-68* (London: Faber & Faber, 1970. 222p.).

309 Trials in Burma.

Maurice Collis. London: Faber & Faber, 1938. 294p.

Arguably Collis' most famous book on Burma, this collection of personal reminiscences of his work as a deputy commissioner and as a district magistrate has great immediacy. Collis' principled commitment to Burma (rather than to the British colonial establishment and its racial defensiveness) is revealed in his judgements in a series of law (including sedition) cases in Burma. Collis gives a dramatic description of the events of 1930-31 which included the anti-Indian riots in Rangoon, the Rangoon Jail mutiny and the Hsaya San rebellion, as well as of episodes from his early years in Burma. Collis concluded that the colonial government 'must know when and how to put Burmese interests first, and so prove to the Burmese that they are in our hearts as well as in our minds'.

310 Chindwin to Criccieth: the life of Godfrey Drage.

Charles Drage. Caernarvon, Wales: Gwenlyn Evans, 1956. 158p.

This biography of a soldier and colonial administrator includes a lively section (p. 24-93), written in the first person, on Drage's career in the Shan States in the 1890s and early 1900s. It gives a good picture of life in a remote area, with anecdotes of two famous superintendents of the Shan States, Hildebrand and Scott, and of Shan *Sawbwas* (chiefs), and tales of the Wild Wa and Palaung tribes. Illustrations are by a Shan artist.

311 I lived in Burma.

Emil Charles Victor Foucar. London: Dennis Dobson, 1956. 272p. map.

Born in Burma in the 1890s to a family with a long established timber extraction and milling business, the author spent from 1903 to 1922 in England, returning to Burma to begin practice as a barrister, first in Moulmein and then in Rangoon, and becoming a member of Burma's Legislative Council. Foucar stayed in Burma until the Japanese invasion and then lived there again from the end of the Second World War until 1951. His personal reminiscences give a vivid picture of life in British Burma of the coming of war to Burma ad the retreat to India, and his reaction to the Aung San–Attlee talks on the independence of Burma: 'we British understood that we had lost the country for which so much blood had been shed'. Under the pseudonym of Ray Carr, Foucar also published a spate of mystery, romance and historical novels set in Burma, beginning with *Love in Burma: a tale of the silken East* (q.v.).

312 The changing of kings: memories of Burma 1934-1949.

Leslie Glass, foreword by Jan Morris. London: Peter Owen, 1985. 241p. map.

These engaging memoirs span the author's years as a young member of the élite Indian Civil Service (ICS) in prewar Burma, his wartime work as head of the Burmese section of the Far Eastern Bureau, and his return to Burma as oriental secretary in the first British Embassy in independent Burma. Sir Leslie (1911-88), who modestly describes his book as 'an album of verbal snapshots', has succeeded in vividly portraying his experiences and many colourful contemporaries, as well as his affection for Burma and its people.

313 **Henry Burney: a political biography.**
Daniel George Edward Hall.   London; New York; Kuala Lumpur:
Oxford University Press, 1974. 330p. 2 maps. bibliog.

Henry Burney (1792-1845) was one of the East India Company's most noteworthy
servants. Hall's study of this remarkable diplomat and scholar provides a detailed
examination of the British interest and role in Southeast Asia and focuses upon
Burney's two diplomatic missions – to Thailand in 1825-26 and to Burma as British
Resident at the Court of Ava (1830-37). It provides useful insights into the different
reactions of the Thai and Burmese rulers to Western pressures and draws on some
sources not available to Professor Desai for his *History of the British Residency in
Burma, 1826-1840* (q.v.). For a catalogue and translation of the Burmese folding book
manuscripts collected by Burney as a record of his meetings and negotiations with
Burmese officials, with a supplement on additional Burney papers by Evans Lewin,
Patricia M. Herbert, and David Wyatt, see Thaung Blackmore, *Catalogue of the
Burney parabaiks in the India Office Library* (London: The British Library, 1985. 120p.
bibliog. [Oriental Documents VII]).

314 **The forgotten land.**
Gordon Hunt.   London: Geoffrey Bles, 1967. 223p.

In 1928 the author at the age of twenty-one started his forestry career in Burma.
Posted to the enormous forests surrounding the remote Indawgyi valley beyond
Myitkyina, Hunt found his true home. His book is full of stories of jungle life,
elephants and remarkable characters. The story of Hunt's escape in May 1942 from the
Japanese by trekking over 800 miles from Bhamo in Northern Burma to Kunming in
China is told in his *One more river* (London: Collins, 1965. 255p. map.).

315 **Not forgetting the elephants.**
Charles Braimer Jones.   Lewes, England: The Book Guild, 1983, 118p.
map.

An autobiographical account of life as a forestry official of the Bombay Burmah
Trading Company in the 1930s, and of war service with Force 136 organizing guerrilla
forces behind the Japanese lines in Eastern Burma.

316 **Inside a Soviet embassy: experiences of a Russian diplomat in Burma.**
Aleksandr Kaznacheev, edited by Simon Wolin.   London: Robert
Hale, 1963. 187.

This narrative of a Russian diplomat in Burma from 1957-59 who defected to the West
provides vivid details of the intelligence work of Soviet embassy staff during the Cold
War period and at a time of deteriorating Sino-Soviet relations.

317 **Life in the Burmese jungle.**
A. A. Lawson.   Lewes, England: The Book Guild, 1983. 195p.
2 maps.

An account of life as a Burma forests assistant from 1928-48 that straightforwardly
conveys a great deal of jungle and elephant lore. It gives a good picture of the work of
teak extraction and of some aspects of colonial society. The author has a dry sense of
humour which he can bring to bear even on such subjects as elephant enemas and anti-
rabies injections.

318 **A corner of heaven: my Burmese reminiscences.**
Chin Yang Lee.   London: W. H. Allen, 1960. 207p.

Happy and humorous memories of the author's years 1940-42, as secretary to the
Sawbwa (hereditary ruler) of the Shan State of Mangshih on the border with Yunnan,
and of the Sawbwa's modernization plans. Published in the USA under the title *The
Sawbwa and his secretary* (New York: Farrar, Straus & Cudahy, 1959). Lee is better
known as the author of the popular *Flower drum song* (London: Victor Gollancz, 1957.
239p.) on which the popular Rodgers and Hammerstein musical of the same name was
based.

319 **Tales of Burma.**
Alister McCrae.   Paisley, Scotland: James Paton, 1981. 168p. map.

A collection of stories and reminiscences written by 'old Burma hands' who lived and
worked in Burma during the last years of British rule. Alister McCrae (who joined the
Irrawaddy Flotilla Company in 1933) has contributed three stories to this collection as
well as biographical notes on his fellow contributors, namely, Harold Braund, Ritchie
Gardiner, Christopher Lorimer, Hamish Mackay, Hugh Nisbet, Alan Prentice, Noel
Stevenson and 'Tawtha'.

320 **Forty years in Burma.**
John Ebenezer Marks, edited by Rev. W. C. B. Purser.   London:
Hutchinson, 1917. 307p. map.

These memoirs (selected and with an introduction by Rev. W. C. B. Purser) of the
Rev. Dr. Marks (1832-1915), Anglican missionary and educationalist, cover his first
years in Burma from 1860 and the founding of St. John's College of Rangoon, his
residence at Mandalay from 1869-74, relations with King Mindon and the king's
support for a SPG 'Royal School', his work in Rangoon and Moulmein, furloughs in
Britain, and his last return visit to Burma in 1900. A selection of Marks' letters from
Mandalay are given in the appendix. The book is illustrated with good photographs of
Marks and his church and school contemporaries, and with topographical photographs,
principally by D. A. Ahuja of Rangoon. An additional perspective on Marks can be
obtained from the selection of reports and letters, many signed by Marks, concerning
the Mandalay palace massacres of 21 September 1884 which were published under the
title *Mandalay massacres: Upper Burma during the reign of Theebaw*, edited by David
M. Gray, with preface by W. H. Wootton (Rangoon: Rangoon Gazette Press, 1884.
44p.).

321 **Four years in Burmah.**
W. H. Marshall.   London: Charles J. Skeet, 1860. 2 vols.

The author worked in India for nine years as a journalist and law pleader before sailing
to Burma in 1854 where he spent four years in law practice in Moulmein and Rangoon,
and became, briefly, co-proprietor and editor of the *Rangoon Chronicle* newspaper.
His observations, being those of an early resident of British Burma, have some interest
and cover many aspects of life at that time, including a long description of Burmese
boat races.

322 **Heaven-born in Burma. Vol. 1, The daily round; Vol. 2, Flight of the heaven-born; Vol. 3, Swan-song of the heaven-born.**
Maurice Maybury.   Castle Cary, England: Folio Hadspen, 1984-86.
3 vols. maps.

This trilogy gives a detailed and fascinating picture of the daily life and diverse tasks performed by a member of the 'heaven-born' – the government officials of colonial Burma. The author's account covers his first posting at the age of twenty-five in 1940 to Kawkareik subdivision, east of Moulmein, the Japanese invasion and British exodus, the restoration of peace and the short-lived return of the British leading up to Burma's independence in 1948. The author hopes that his story will help 'to show that we were neither disliked by the people we ruled nor the tools of imperial oppression and exploitation . . .'.

323 **Scott of the Shan Hills: orders and impressions.**
Geraldine Edith Mitton (Lady Scott).   London: John Murray, 1936.
348p.

This biography of Sir James George Scott (1851-1935), best known for his first and greatest book, *The Burman, his life and notions* (q.v.), is compiled and edited by Lady Scott from Scott's diaries, correspondence and official reports and provides an informative and interesting account of his life and remarkable career. Scott's association with the Shan Hills began in 1886 when he was appointed assistant political officer to the Shan States with the difficult and dangerous task of persuading the Shan chiefs to accept British rule. Scott was a keen photographer and the book contains many photographs of hill tribes, as well as of Scott and his colleagues. A bibliography of Scott's publications is also given, but omits two novels written under the pseudonym Shway Dinga which can most probably be attributed to Scott, *Wholly without morals: a romance of Indo-Burman life and racing* (London: Duckworth, 1911. 318p.) and *The repentance of destiny: a romance of Anglo-Burmese life* (London: Duckworth, 1913. 286p.).

324 **The life and murder of Henry Morshead: a true story from the days of the Raj.**
Ian Morshead, introduction by Mark Tulley.   Cambridge, England:
Oleander, 1982. 207p. 3 maps. bibliog.

This is not just a biography, but an account of a personal quest by the author to come to terms with the unsolved mystery of his father's murder in the Burmese jungle in 1931. Lt. Col. Henry Morshead at the time of his death was based in Maymyo as director, Burma Circle, of the Survey of India. Fifty years after his father's death, his son travelled to India and Burma where he had spent his early childhood, Hauntingly written, the narrative gains the pace and suspense of a detective story as the author returns to Maymyo, meets people with memories of his father, and tries to piece together what really happened.

325   **The square egg: and other sketches, with three plays and illustrations,
       with a biography by his sister.**
       Hector Hugh Munro ('Saki').   London: John Lane The Bodley Head,
       1924. 318p.

The writer Munro, better known under his pseudonym of Saki, was born in Burma and
spent thirteen months in the Military Police in 1893-94. Unlike George Orwell, he did
not produce from these experiences a great novel of Burma, but his letters home from
Burma are an early revelation of the literary gifts and humour for which he became
famous. Excerpts from these letters are given in the biographical sketch by his sister,
Ethel M. Munro, included in *The square egg* (p. 3-120), which also contains a short
story by Saki set in Burma 'Comments of Moung Ka' (p. 161-65). For a biography of
Munro (1870-1916), see *Saki: a life of Hector Hugh Munro* by A. J. Langguth (Oxford:
Oxford University Press, 1982. 366p.).

326   **The image of war or service on the Chin hills.**
       Arthur George Edward Newland, introductory note by J. D.
       Macnabb.   Calcutta, India: Thacker, Spink. 1894. 91p.

This account of British military expeditions in the Chin Hills in the late 1880s and early
1890s with its 270 photographs including 36 full plate pictures provides a valuable
contemporary pictorial record. The text, written with informal immediacy, and the
photographs capture scenes of camp life, British officers and Indian troops, Chin
leaders and villagers and aspects of Chin life. The introduction by Macnabb, political
officer in the Chin Hills, is less cheery than the main text and provides a survey of
expeditions to the Lushai and the Chin tribes who live in a 'land that produces nothing
but the savages who inhabit it. A thorn in the sides of all who have to do with it, it has
no future and appears capable of no development'. See also James Kiers Watson,
edited by Bertie Reginald Pearn, *Military operations in Burma, 1890-1892: letters from
Lieutenant J. K. Watson, K.R.R.C.* (Ithaca, New York: Cornell University, Southeast
Asia Program, 1967. 72p. [Cornell University Southeast Asian Program Data Papers,
no. 65]) for vivid descriptions of military action, primarily in the Chin Hills in the
1890s, by a junior officer of the King's Royal Rifle Corps.

327   **Experiences of a jungle-wallah.**
       Hugh Nisbet ('Nibs').   St. Albans, England: Fisher, Knight, 1936.
       96p.

The author arrived in Burma in 1879 and spent thirty-seven years there working for the
Bombay Burmah Trading Corporation. His account covers experiences with dacoits,
military expeditions to the Karenni and Shan States, as well as reminiscences of work
in the teak forests.

328   **Forgotten land: a rediscovery of Burma.**
       Harriet O'Brien.   London: Michael Joseph, 1991. 249p. map.

A personal account of a return visit to Burma which in 1988 at the height of the pro-
democracy movement seemed on the brink of change, and where the author, daughter
of a former British ambassador to Burma, spent much of her adolescence. In scope it
ranges from Burma's past history to an account of meeting refugee students in the
Thai–Burma border camps in 1990. Throughout the book, the author blends personal
observations and reminiscences to provide an overall general introduction to
contemporary Burma.

329 **Myamma: a retrospect of life and travels in Lower Burma.**
Charles Thomas Paske, edited by Frederick George Aflalo. London:
W. H. Allen, 1893. 265p.
The author, an army surgeon, came to Burma during the Second Anglo-Burmese War
(1852) and his reminiscences cover the period 1852-58.

330 **Burma retrospect and other sketches.**
Cecil John Richards. Winchester, England: Cathedral, 1951. 152p.
Nostalgic reminiscences and stories of Burma by a retired ICS district officer,
dedicated 'to the people of Burma to whom I owe so much'. Also by Richards are
Wind over Fowlmere and other stories (Winchester, England: Wykeham, 1953. 217p.),
No buses running (Winchester, England: Wykeham, 1956. 232p.) and *Born under
Pisces and other stories* (Alresford, England: C. J. Richards, 1976. 81p.) – short stories
and reminiscences with a blending of English and Burmese backgrounds – as well as a
collection of poems, *Rainbow land and other Burma verses* (Winchester, England:
Herbert Curnow, 1948. 36p.). Richards retired to England in 1948 after twenty-five
years in Burma, but made a return visit in 1958 which he describes in his travelogue,
Dusty pilgrimage: by motor coach across Europe and Asia and other wanderings
(Ilfracombe, England: Arthur H. Stockwell, 1961), p. 65-90.

331 **Reverie of a qu'hai and other stories.**
John Keith Stanford. Edinburgh, London: William Blackwood &
Sons, 1951. 324p.
The author, an ICS officer in Burma from 1919-38, gives in part one (p. 1-162) a
humorous account of an administrator's life in Burma with stories of up-country club
life, crime, and court cases. Stanford also wrote lighthearted sketches of hunting and
shooting, some set in Burma, published under the title *Mixed bagmen* (London:
Herbert Jenkins, 1949. 157p.), a novella *Last chukker* (London: Faber & Faber, 1951.
76p.) with a memorable description of a polo match in Burma, and a well-written
account of a scientific expedition in Burma, *Far ridges* (q.v.).

332 **Quiet skies on Salween.**
Ellen Thorp. London: Jonathan Cape, 1945. 175p.
Happy memories of a childhood in the Shan States. The author's father was principal
from 1902-18 of a school opened by the government in Taunggyi for the sons and
relatives of the Shan chiefs. The author, under the name of Morwenna Thorp, also
wrote a novel of star-crossed love, set partly and authentically in Burma, *The gilded
Buddha* (London: Robert Hale, 1972. 239p.).

333 **Boh San Pe and other glimpses of life in Burma.**
Louis Upton Graham Tripp. Bombay, India: The Author, 1944.
141p.
Tales of colonial life in Burma in the 1930s, with a Somerset Maugham flavour.

334 **Peacock dreams.**
Bill Tydd, foreword by Sir William Gladstone. London: British
Association for Cemeteries in South Asia (BACSA), 1986. 193p. map.
Among the subjects covered in these memoirs of an officer in the Burma Police from
1929 to 1942 are anti-dacoit operations, the Tharrawaddy rebellion of 1930, and the
1938 riots in Rangoon.

335 **The life of General Sir Harry N. D. Prendergast, R.E., V.C., G.C.B.,**
(the happy warrior).
Henry Meredith Vibart. London: Eveleigh Nash, 1914. 445p. 3 maps.
This biography of Harry North Dalrymple Prendergast (1834-1913) includes a detailed
account (p. 195-313) of Prendergast's career in Burma (1883-86) and of his command
of the British Expeditionary Force to Upper Burma from November 1885 to March
1886, with extracts from Prendergast's letters and from official despatches. Colonel
Vibart strongly defends Prendergast from criticisms of his command and corrects
inaccuracies in the official military history of the Third Anglo-Burmese War.
Appendix II (p. 431-34) contains a list of 100 pictures illustrating the war that were
published in the *Illustrated London News* from 31 October 1885 to 1 May 1886.

336 **Burmese interlude.**
C. V. Warren. London: Skeffington & Son, 1937. 288p. map.
Well-told tales of a British timber company (Swan Bros.) forestry officer's five years in
the Burmese jungle, including his experiences during the Hsaya San rebellion of 1930-
32.

337 **The Burma of 'AJ': memoirs of AJS White.**
Arthur John Stanley White, introduction by F. S. V. Donnison.
London: British Association for Cemeteries in South Asia (BACSA),
1991. 244p. map.
White (1896-1991) was a member of the Indian Civil Service in Burma from 1922 to
1937 and he describes his postings in the districts as subdivisional officer, settlement
officer and deputy commissioner (to Thayetmyo District during the Hsaya San
rebellion) and at the centre of government, the Rangoon Secretariat, and as an official
member of the Legislative Council. His memoirs provide a good picture of life in
British Burma between the wars, with immediacy supplied by many extracts from his
letters home, and with frank vignettes of his British colonial and Burmese
contemporaries.

338 **A civil servant in Burma.**
Herbert Thirkell White. London: Edward Arnold, 1913. 314p.
Gentle memories of thirty years' service from 1878 to 1910 in the administration of
Burma. Sir Herbert Thirkell White (1855-1931) rose to become chief judge (1902-05)
and lieutenant-governor (1905-10) of Burma. His career – the epitome of a 'genuine
Anglo-Burmese administrator' – is discussed in the article by Edith Lamm Piness, 'The
British administrator in Burma: a new view', *Journal of Southeast Asian Studies*
vol. 14, no. 2 (Sept. 1983), p. 372-78), while her dissertation, *Moulmein to Mandalay:
sketches of Anglo-Burmese administrators* (PhD, Claremont Graduate School,
Claremont, California 1977. 302p. Available from University Microfilms, Ann Arbor,

Michigan, order no. UM 77-16930) examines the careers of White, and of A. D. Maingy (Administrator of Tenasserim, 1825-34), and Albert Fytche (Chief Commisioner 1867-71 and author of *Burma past and present* [q.v.]).

39 Elephant Bill.
James Howard Williams, foreword by Field-Marshall Sir William Slim.   London: Rupert Hart-Davis, 1965. 245p. 4 maps. (The Adventure Library).

First published in 1950 (London: Rupert Hart-Davis. 320p.), the first part of this autobiography tells of Williams' life in Burma from 1920 when he joined the Bombay Burmah Trading Corporation and learnt the management of elephants, jungle lore and teak extraction. The second part describes the role played by Williams' elephants in the evacuation of civilians to India following the Japanese invasion of Burma and of his command of an 'Elephant Brigade' in the Fourteenth Army. Williams' *Bandoola* (London: Rupert Hart-Davis, 1953. 251p.) gives the true story of a remarkable elephant. Other works by Williams are *The spotted deer* (London: Rupert Hart-Davis, 1957. 161p.) – humorous stories of training a new forestry assistant in the aftermath of the Burma rebellion (1930-32) and of a timber survey in the Andaman islands assisted by a group of Burmese convicts – and *In quest of a mermaid* (London: Rupert Hart-Davis, 1960. 199p.) relating episodes from his twenty-six years in the teak forests and jungles of Burma. *The footprints of Elephant Bill* by Susan Williams London: William Kimber, 1962. 224p. tells how she first met Williams in the Burmese jungle and of their life together.

40 Six months in British Burmah: or, India beyond the Ganges in 1857.
Christopher Tatchell Winter.   London: Richard Bentley, 1858. 288p.

A description, principally of Moulmein and Tavoy, with sketches by the author, and notes on Burmese literature, and the fauna, flora and natural resources of the Tenasserim provinces. An account of the First Anglo-Burmese War by which the British obtained Tenasserim is given on p. 197-282.

Burma past and present: with personal reminiscences of the country.
See item no. 192.

True Love and Bartholomew: rebels on the Burmese border.
See item no. 418.

Christian missionaries

341 **To the golden shore: the life of Adoniram Judson.**
Courtney Anderson. Boston, Massachusetts: Little Brown, 1956;
Grand Rapids, Michigan: Zondervan, 1972. 530p.

This biography of Adoniram Judson (1788-1850), first American missionary to Burma although it has no new facts to add, scores more highly than 19th-century biographies of Judson in its fluid narrative of the life and times of a remarkable man. Major 19th-century biographies of Judson are Francis Wayland's, *A memoir of the life and labours of the Rev. Adoniram Judson, D.D.* (London: James Nisbet, 1853. 2 vols.), Hannah O'Brien Chaplin Conant's *The earnest man: or the character and labors of Adoniram Judson* (Boston, Massachusetts: Phillips, Sampsun, 1856. 498p.), and Edward Judson's *Adoniram Judson, DD: his life and labours* (London: Hodder & Stoughton, 1883 601p. maps.). A brief but informative biography that avoids the pious eulogies that characterize so many missionary biographies is Bertie Reginald Pearn's *Judson of Burma* (London: Edinburgh House Press, 1962. 96p.).

342 **Pioneer trails, trials and triumphs: personal memoirs of life and work as a pioneer missionary among the Chin tribes of Burma.**
Laura Hardin Carson. New York: Baptist Board of Education, Department of Missionary Education, 1927. 255p.

The author went to Burma as an American Baptist missionary in 1883 and in 188? established with her husband the first Chin mission at Thayetmyo, followed in 1899 by missions in Haka and the more remote areas of the Chin Hills. Among the many other minor accounts by American missionaries are Henry Park Cochrane's *Among the Burmans: a record of fifteen years of work and its fruitage* (New York; London Fleming H. Revell, 1904. 281p.) which is strongly critical of Buddhism and couched mostly in the form of advice to future missionaries, and Olive Jennie Bixby's *My child life in Burmah: or recollections and incidents* (Boston, Massachusetts: W. G. Corthell 1880. 172p.) recalling the 1850s and 1860s in Toungoo.

343 **Beyond his calling: the life of Chester Leroy Klein (1893-1942).**
Harold E. Klein, Thomas O. Klein. New York: Carlton, 1983. 241p.
map. bibliog.

The subject of this detailed biography spent twenty-two years as an American Baptist Missionary to the Karens of Burma, and died in Assam just after completing the trek from Burma following the Japanese invasion.

344 **I always wore my topi: the Burma letters of Ethel Mabuce 1916-1921.**
Ethel Lindy Mabuce, edited by Lucille Griffith. Alabama: University of Alabama Press, 1974. 336p.

These letters of an American Methodist missionary to Burma give a good idea of missionary's life and outlook at the time.

345　**Civilizing mountain men: or sketches of mission work among the Karens.**
Ellen Huntley Bullard Mason.　London: James Nisbet, 1862. 384p.

A lively and anecdotal account of an American missionary's work, first as the wife of the Rev. E. Bullard (d. 1847) in Moulmein and then as the wife of Francis Mason (to whom she was married by Adoniram Judson in 1847), with the greater part of the book devoted to her work founding self-supporting girls' schools for the education of Karens at Toungoo. The book has a colour frontispiece engraving of the Karen National Institute for Girls at Toungoo. Mrs. Mason, who was described as 'dangerously eccentric' – for a blunter contemporary epithet, see below – published further works under the name of Eleanor Mason including an account of her late husband written in the form of a letter to their children and entitled *Last days of the Rev. Francis Mason, D.D.* (Rangoon: Whittam, 1874. 61p.). Glimpses of a seething Baptist missionary row about Mrs. Mason and her schools' status and funding can be found in some peculiar tracts published by Eleanor Mason: *Dr. and Mrs. Mason's land leases in Toungoo* (Rangoon: Whittam, 1874. [20p.]) and *The Toungoo God-language conspiracy* (Rangoon: Albion, 1878-79. 134p.) in which Mrs. Mason attempts to state her own case and to defend herself from charges of insanity by reprinting letters and remarks from missionaries and others, both for and against her – to cite just one: 'It is suggested that we punish Bro. Mason still harder for not restraining his abominable wife who seems to be a witch of the first degree'. Another publication by Mrs. Mason solicited funds for Indian famine relief, *A song of the famine: dedicated to the young folks of the Anglo-Indian community of Burma* (Rangoon: Albion, 1874. [34p.]) and concluded with a song 'The sailors' home in Rangoon' to be sung to the tune of Yankee Doodle!

346　**The story of a working man's life: with sketches of travel in Europe, Asia, Africa, and America, as related by himself.**
Francis Mason, introduction by William R. Williams.　New York: Oakley, Mason, 1870. 462p.

This missionary autobiography contains an account of Mason's first years in Burma (p. 233-305) from 1831 to 1854 with many details of his missionary, translation, printing, educational and scientific work in Tavoy and Moulmein, principally among the Karens and the Mons; with a further section on his and Mrs. Mason's work in Toungoo from 1857 with notes and observations on the Karenni (Red Karens), the condition of the people in British Burma and on the press (p. 389-437). In addition to his ambitious scientific compilation *Burma, its people and productions* (q.v.), his translations of the Bible into Karen and his *A dictionary of the Karen language* (Tavoy, Burma: [s.n.], [s.d.]. 324p.) and *Synopsis of a grammar of the Karen language, embracing both dialects, Sgau and Pgho, or Sho* (Tavoy, Burma: Mission Press, 1846. 458p.). Mason produced an account of the first Karen convert, *The Karens: or a memoir of Ko Thah-Byu, the first Karen convert* (Toungoo, Burma: Institute Press, 1868), *A Burmese handbook of medicine* (in Burmese) (Toungoo, Burma: Karen Mission Press, 1868. 76p.), a memoir of his first wife, *A cenotaph to a woman of the Burman mission: or views in the missionary path of Helen M. Mason* (New York: Colby, 1851. 187p.), and several articles on Mon and Pali in the *Journal of the American Oriental Society*. Further details of the Masons' educational work in Burma can be found in the book by his second wife, Ellen H. B. Mason, *Civilizing mountain men* (q.v.).

347 **Exodus to a hidden valley.**

Eugene Morse. London: Collins, 1975. 224p. map.

The remarkable story of the Morse family, missionaries to the Lisu and Rawang tribes, who when served with an expulsion order by the Burmese government in December 1965, trekked from Putao into a remote valley to live in a Lisu village on Burma's border with India.

348 **An ambassador in bonds: the story of William Henry Jackson, priest, of the Mission to the Blind of Burma.**

Mary C. Purser. London: Society for the Propagation of the Gospel in Foreign Parts, 1933. 2nd ed. 83p.

This memoir of Father Jackson (1889-1931), inventor of a Braille type for Burmese script, was written by his sister.

349 **Burma surgeon.**

Gordon Stifler Seagrave. London: Victor Gollancz, 1944. 159p. map.

An American medical missionary's remarkable story of his work from 1922 in the Shan States where he built a hospital at Namkham, and of the outbreak of war when he formed a Mobile Surgical Unit with the US army commanded by General Stilwell in the remote China–Burma–India theatre of war. Seagrave's *Burma surgeon returns* (London: Victor Gollancz, 1946. 205p. maps.) continues with events from 1943 to 1945, while his *My hospital in the hills* (London: Robert Hale, 1957. 253p. map.) takes up the story with Seagrave's return to Namkham in 1945, the outbreak of insurgencies following Burma's independence, and his arrest and trial on a charge of high treason, his acquittal and return to Namkham Hospital. Seagrave also gives details of his family's unbroken 120 years' connection with Burma through his missionary forebears, the Vintons and Haswells. Among the many achievements of Seagrave (1897-1965) was his training of Karen, Kachin and Shan nurses and medical staff. One of the best and frankest portraits of Seagrave is to be found in an account by an American medical family who worked with Seagrave at Namkham for the last two years of his life, *The devil in god's old man* by Sue Mayes Newhall (New York: W. W. Norton, 1969. 253p.) – who comments on the Burma government's nationalization of Seagrave's hospital following his death: 'I do not believe in ghosts but sometimes I wish I did . . . A shaggy, grey-haired old specter is ranting and raving in several languages. During the sixty-eight years that he lived in the body of Gordon S. Seagrave, he was never quiet or at peace with himself. Now all that he worked for and dreamed about had been reduced to an ill-functioning instrument of the Burmese government, and he still can't rest'. An account of working with Dr. Seagrave's Mobile Surgical Unit for the Chinese 6th Army during the war is contained in Stanley W. Short's *On Burma's eastern frontiers* (London: Marshall, Morgan & Scott, 1945. 144p.) which also describes the life of the Shorts (members of the Bible Churchmen's Missionary Society) from 1940-42 in a village in the Southern Shan States where they opened a dispensary and hospital. *Bamboo hospital: the story of a missionary family in Burma* by Katherine L. Read, with Robert O. Ballou (London: Peter Davies, 1961. 216p.) tells the story of Read's parents, Albert and Cora Henderson, and their work as American Baptist medical missionaries in the Shan States from 1893 to 1937.

350 **Personal recollections of British Burma and its church mission work in 1878-79.**
Jonathan Holt Titcomb. London: Wells Gardner, Darton, for the Society for the Propagation of the Gospel in Foreign Parts, 1880. 103p. map.

Titcomb (1819-87) went to Burma in 1878 as the first bishop of the newly created bishopric of Rangoon. He was an energetic evangelist with a great enthusiasm for Burma throughout which he travelled extensively. His memoirs are illustrated with engravings of Burmese scenes. Further details of Titcomb's life and career can be found in Allen T. Edwards, *A consecrated life: memoir of the Right Rev. Bishop Titcomb, D.D.* (London: Robert Banks, 1887. 132p.).

351 **For God alone: the life of George West, Bishop of Rangoon.**
John Tyndale-Biscoe. Oxford: Amate, 1984. 113p.

The subject of this biography, George Algernon West (1893-1980), spent over twenty years in Burma (from 1921 to 1948) – apart from the war years – rising to become bishop of Rangoon. The book testifies to one man's mission and faith and his achievements in breaking down barriers between different denominations, religions and races. West wrote sketches of his early missionary life among the Karens in three books, *Jungle folk*, written with D. C. Atwool, (London: Society for the Propagation of the Gospel, 1933. 83p.), *Jungle friends* (London: Society for the Propagation of the Gospel, and Society for the Propagation of Christian Knowledge, 1937. 63p. map.), and – an account of the Karen Christians of Kappali during the Japanese occupation – *Jungle witnesses* (London: Society for the Propagation of the Gospel, 1948. 53p. map.). West's reminiscences with the theme of personal change and commitment to the Christian cause, *The world that works* (London: Blandford Press, 1945. 111p.) also contain tales of his experiences as a missionary and as bishop of Rangoon.

352 **Four years in Upper Burma.**
W. R. Winston. London: C. H. Kelly, 1982. 266p. map.

An account of Wesleyan Methodist mission work in Upper Burma from 1887 and of the founding of a Home for Lepers in Mandalay.

Military

The Anglo-Burmese Wars

353 **Travels from India to England, comprehending a visit to the Burman Empire and a journey through Persia, Asia Minor, European Turkey, etc. in the years 1825-26.**
James Edward Alexander. London: Parbury, Allen, 1827. 301p. 2 maps.
Part one (p. 1-75) contains the author's first-hand account of participation in the First Anglo-Burmese War (1824-26). The appendix contains a chronology of the events of the war (p. 263-68).

354 **The recent operations of the British forces at Rangoon and Martaban.**
Thomas Turner Baker. London: Thomas Hatchard, 1852. 78p.
The author was chaplain on HMS Fox, commanded by Commodore Lambert who led the British naval squadron's attack on Rangoon in 1852. Baker provides an eye-witness and unobjective account of events leading to the outbreak of the Second Anglo-Burmese War and of the hostilities from January to March 1852. Baker died of cholera in Burma in April 1852 and the book has an added chapter based on official reports and despatches covering the events of April 1852. With a hand-coloured lithographed frontispiece of an official Burmese deputation, and three ink drawings of Rangoon and the British attack. See also the anonymous ('by an officer') publication, *Six months a Martaban during the Burmese war: and an essay on the political causes which led to the establishment of British power in India* (London: Partridge, Oakey & Co., [1854] 131p.) which gives (p. 1-77) in diary form from April–December 1852, the views of a British officer stationed in Martaban on the progress of the war and its effect on the local inhabitants.

355 **Narrative of the captivity of an officer who fell into the hands of the Burmahs during the late war.**
Richard Bennett. Madras: Male Asylum Press, 1827. 145p.
This rare publication was published anonymously and tells of Lt. Bennett's capture in November 1825, his imprisonment at the Burmese capital, his fellow prisoners, his jailors, and the progress of peace negotiations.

356 **The coming of the great queen: a narrative of the acquisition of Burma.**
Edmond Charles Browne. London: Harrison & Sons, 1888. 451p. 3 maps.
The author, a major in the Royal Scots Fusiliers, gives an eye-witness account of the British military expedition against Upper Burma in 1885 and the deposition of King Thibaw. Also provided is a brief history of Burma, an account of dacoits and of Burmese women, and sections on ethnic groups of Burma. The book's tone and theme can be judged from the following extract: 'The incubus of the sham power which sat enthroned at Mandalay, with its rotten, crumbling government, its corrupt ministers and its oppressive and retrograde laws, has been removed; and a strong and stable government has replaced it'.

357 **Reminiscences of the Burmese war in 1824-5-6.**
F. B. Doveton. London: Allen, 1852. 375p.

A personal narrative, originally published in the *Asiatic Journal*, by an ensign in the Madras European Regiment telling of participation in the First Anglo-Burmese War, with five lithographs from original sketches by the author.

358 **Burmah: letters and papers written in 1852-53.**
Henry Thomas Godwin. London: Thomas Bosworth, [1854]. 79p.

General Godwin (1784-1853) commanded the 41st Madras Infantry in the First Anglo-Burmese War (1824-26) and was criticized for quartering his troops at Rangoon rather than advancing at once on the Burmese capital, Ava. His letters, written as commander-in-chief of the British Expeditionary Forces in the Second Anglo-Burmese War (1852-53), contain references to the problems and criticisms he encountered in both campaigns. The letters were published posthumously.

359 **A personal narrative of two years' imprisonment in Burmah.**
Henry Gouger. London: John Murray, 1862. 2nd ed. 345p.

The author was a private merchant in Bengal when in 1822 he sailed to Burma to investigate prospects for selling British cottons and other goods to Burma. He describes his audience with King Bagyidaw, the two months he spent at the capital Ava, and his return there a year later. The greater part of his book, however, covers his imprisonment, following the outbreak of the First Anglo-Burmese War in 1824, in the fearsome Let-ma-yun ('hand shrink not') prison, with vivid details of its horrors and of his fellow prisoners who included the missionaries Adoniram Judson and Dr. Jonathan Price and the merchants Rodgers and Laird. First published in 1860 (London: John Murray), the second edition has an additional final chapter on Anglo-Burmese relations since 1826, and a preface by A. Gouger (who saw the new edition through the press following the death of Henry Gouger) explaining how his brother came to write his narrative and to have such good recall.

360 **Memoir of the early operations of the Burmese War: addressed to the editor of the United Service Journal.**
H. Lister Maw. London: Smith, Elder, 1832. 106p.

A navy lieutenant's defence of the role of the British forces in the First Anglo-Burmese War of 1824-26.

361 **Two years in Ava: from May 1824 to May 1826, by an officer on the staff of the quarter-master-general's department.**
Thomas Abercrombie Trant. London: John Murray, 1827. 455p.
maps.

An interesting account of the progress of the First Anglo-Burmese War giving not only details of military action, but a picture of a country at war and of the effect on the local population. With much descriptive matter on local life, particularly as observed during several months encamped at Prome. Among the material recorded by Trant is a description of the first Burmese delegation sent to negotiate with General Campbell (p. 297-300), impressions of Pagan (p. 379-85), the musical notation of Burmese war-boat songs (p. 218-20), and a plan of the Burmese fort at Danubyu. Trant's account was published anonymously.

The Second World War

362 **The reluctant major.**
David Atkins. Pulborough, England: Toat, 1986. 110p. maps.
Unpretentious and humorous memoirs of running Indian Army transport and suppli
to Kohima and Imphal on the Burma front in 1942, and of building the Tiddim Tra
from Imphal through malarial ranges to Tiddim in the Northern Chin Hills. Atkins te
the story of turning the Tiddim Track from a three-foot-wide mule track into an arn
supply route and of the desperate battle for Imphal in 1944 in a sequel, *The forgotte
major* (*in the siege of Imphal*) (Pulborough: Toat, 1989. 145p. maps.).

363 **The hump: the greatest untold story of the war.**
Jack Barnard. London: Souvenir, 1960. 192p. map.
The author was a forestry assistant working for Steel Brothers until the Japane
invasion of Burma in 1942. His book tells of his joining the Kachin Levies (und
Colonel H. N. C. Stevenson of the Burma Frontier Service), training in guerri
warfare, sabotage work behind the Japanese lines, and an epic trek out of Burma wi
the retreating Chinese 96th Division over the mountainous barrier of the Hur
(Gompa La) into Yunnan. Barnard was then seconded to 101 OSS and in Februa
1943 was dropped by parachute 250 miles behind the Japanese lines, subsequent
receiving the Military Cross.

364 **Surgeon in the jungle war.**
John A. Baty. London: William Kimber, 1979. 196p.
An army surgeon's account of his wartime experiences with No. 7 Indian Mob
Surgical Unit in Burma.

365 **Burma post: a personal story of air mails and other activities in the
Burma campaign, 1944-45.**
Richard Baxter. Worthing, England: Churchman, 1989. 150p. map.
The author was called up for the Army Post Office at the outbreak of war and sent,
1944, to organize postal services of 4th Corps (part of the Fourteenth Army).
describes frankly the problems of organizing mail services by air drops and oth
means to an army which was advancing rapidly in Burma and the services' importan
as a morale booster in wartime. He summarizes his time in Burma as 'a journey to
bizarre, sometimes beautiful, sometimes horrifying, always interesting wonderland
now look back on it as a journey through a looking glass'.

366 **Burma drop.**
John Beamish. London: Elek, 1958. 222p. map.
Born in Burma and with first-hand knowledge of its jungles acquired while working f
the Bombay Burmah Trading Corporation, the author made an ideal recruit to t
secret Force 136 after the Japanese invasion of Burma. Beamish made three parachu
jumps behind enemy lines on intelligence and sabotage work – for which he w
awarded the military cross for gallantry – and his book provides a gripping account
war in the jungles of Burma.

67   Report my signals.
Antony Brett-James.   London: Hennel Locke, in association with George G. Harrap, 1948. 352p.

hese well-written war memoirs pay tribute to the 'unknown Indian Other Ranks' and clude a long section (p. 85-267) on service with the Ninth Brigade in Arakan, the attle for Imphal, and the Chin Hills.

68   Prisoners of hope.
Michael Calvert.   London: Leo Cooper, 1971. rev. ed. 320p. 7 maps.

irst published in 1952 (London: Jonathan Cape), the 1971 edition contains a ostscript by the author designed to 'set the record straight' as 'many foolish and norant things have been written in the intervening years'. Calvert provides a detailed rst-hand account of the operations carried out by the 77th Infantry Brigade under his ommand in Burma in 1944 as part of Wingate's Special force of Chindits. He believes rongly that 'neither Wingate nor the Chindits have been given their military due for eir sacrifices and tactical and strategic successes'. The appendixes contain military ocuments and statistics and Japanese military commanders' views on aspects of the ampaign. Calvert's autobiographical memoirs, *Fighting mad* (London: Jarrolds, 1964. 24p. map) contain much on his wartime experiences, while his *Chindits: long range netration* (London: Pan/Ballantine, 1974. 159p. maps) and *Slim* (London: Pan/allantine, 1973. 159p. maps. bibliog.) are useful, well-illustrated basic studies.

69   Chindit column.
Charles Carfrae.   London: William Kimber, 1985. 194p.

nother wartime memoir of service with the Chindits, made unusual by the fact that olonel Carfrae's troops were from the Nigerian Regiment, Royal West African ontier Service, whose service in Burma is not well-known.

70   Desperate journey.
Francis Clifford.   London: Hodder & Stoughton, 1979. 192p.

eparated in 1942 from the rest of the retreating British Army, Captain Arthur hompson led a dwindling band of fellow British Officers and Karen and Indian ldiers of the 1st Battalion Burma Rifles on a harrowing trek out of Burma via Fort ertz through nearly 1,000 miles of Japanese-occupied territory. This account was ritten in 1944 before Thompson became better known as the suspense novelist ancis Clifford, but was only published after his death in 1975.

71   A child at arms.
Patrick Davis.   London: Hutchinson, 1970. 258p. map.

eflective memories of a young officer's wartime service with the 4/8th Gurkha Rifles the Burma campaign.

72   Chindit indiscretion.
John Howard Denny.   London: Christopher Johnson, 1956. 256p.; London: Hamilton, 1959. 187p. maps.

ne story of a fantastic chain of incidents that led to a young Chindit officer from ingate's forces being accepted by the Japanese and the Indian National Army as one their agents in Burma, and of the dangerous game of double bluff that ensued.

373 **Behind Japanese lines: with the OSS in Burma.**
Richard Dunlop. Chicago: Rand McNally, 1979. 448p. maps. bibliog

The fullest account yet published of the guerrilla war fought in Burma by members of
America's Office of Strategic Services Detachment 101 and their Kachin allies. The
narrative style is immediate and well matches the mixture of grim, tragic, brave and
noble events it portrays.

374 **Amiable assassins: the story of the Kachin guerrillas of north Burma.**
Ian Fellowes-Gordon. London: Robert Hale, 1957. 159p.

A British officer's account of service with the Kachin Levies in Burma from 1942 to
1945.

375 **Beyond the Chindwin: being an account of the adventures of Number
Five Column of the Wingate expedition into Burma.**
Bernard Fergusson. London: Collins, 1945; London: Collins, 1962.
256p. 7 maps.

A memorable non-sensational account of Wingate's first overland expedition into
Burma in 1943 written by the Column's commander 'to rescue my own impression
from the morass of tall stories which have been in circulation'. Of the original 318
members of the Column only 95 returned. Also by Fergusson is *The wild green earth*
(London: Collins, 1946. 228p.; London: Collins, Fontana, 1956. 254p. 5 maps.) which
describes 16th Brigade's role in the second Chindit expedition of 1944. Unlike the
other airlifted Chindit groups, Fergusson's Brigade went overland from Ledo (in
Assam) into Burma with the objective of establishing a stronghold cutting off the
Japanese. Fergusson gives a picture of how events were seen at the time from the
ground and also includes, in part two of the book, reflections and advice on jungle
warfare, distilled from bitter experience. In *Return to Burma* (London: Collins, 1962.
256p. maps.), Fergusson revisits wartime scenes and relates his search, fifteen years
after the war, for the people who had helped his Chindit missions. Fergusson's
autobiographical account of his military career, *The trumpet in the hall, 1930-19.*
(London: Collins, 1970. 286p. maps.) has a long section (p. 142-91) on the Chindit
campaigns and a particularly good assessment of Wingate. Also by Fergusson is *The
watery maze: the story of Combined Operations* (London: Collins, 1961. 445p. maps.
biblog.) which has a chapter (p. 362-83) describing landings along the Arakan coast in
1945 and Operation Dracula to retake Rangoon.

376 **The long trek.**
John Francis Friend. London: Frederick Muller, 1957. 187p.

The long trek is an epic story of endurance. The author was the only survivor of
Special Service Detachment 2 (SSD 2) operation in Burma and of a nine-month 2,000
miles' trek through Japanese-occupied territory.

377 **Quiet jungle angry sea: my escapes from the Japanese.**
Denis Gavin. Oxford: Lennard, 1989. 196p.

The author, who joined the East Surrey Regiment in 1938, recalls his remarkable
escapes from the Japanese: first from Singapore to Sumatra and then by sailing boat to
Moulmein where he was captured in February 1942. He spent the next three years as a
prisoner of war in Moulmein and Rangoon jails, and escaped again on 28 April 1945
and found his way with Karen help to the advancing British lines. Gavin writes vividly

f his comrades – of his eleven fellow escapees, seven lived to see the end of the war –
nd of the hardships of the prisoner of war camps.

78 **Out of the Burma night: being the story of a fantastic journey through
the wilderness of the Hukawng Valley and the forest clad mountains of
the Naga tribes peoples at the time of the Japanese invasion of Burma.**
R. H. Gribble. Calcutta, India: Thacker, Spink, 1944. 154p. 2 maps.

A Burma Frontier Service officer's account of a routine expedition in the Hukawng
Valley in northwest Burma from December 1941 to March 1942, and of the coming of
var to those remote parts, followed by his diary from 1 May 1942 to 11 June 1942
overing 'the nightmare trek to Ledo' helping evacuate thousands of refugees through
he Hukawng Valley to safety in Assam.

79 **With Wingate in Burma: being the story of the adventures of Sergeant
Tony Aubrey of the King's (Liverpool) Regiment during the 1943
Wingate expedition with Burma.**
David Halley. Glasgow; Edinburgh, London: William Hodge, 1945.
189p. map.

A down-to-earth account of a 'small part of the show' written before it was known 'just
vhat the Expedition did achieve, and what effects it has had on the campaign in Burma
s a whole'. There is a second edition (Glasgow; Edinburgh, London: William Hodge,
946. 196p.) which adds an epilogue setting the scene for Wingate's second expedition
f 1944.

80 **Monsoon victory.**
Gerald Hanley. London: Collins, 1946; London: White Lion, 1974.
189p.

he story of the advance of the Fourteenth Army in 1944 in pursuit of the Japanese
lown the Kabaw Valley to the Chindwin and on to the capture of Kalewa. Less a
nilitary history than a tribute to the men of the 11th East African Infantry Division in
vhich the author portrays the horrors and heroism of war from his personal
xperiences.

81 **A sapper in the forgotten army.**
John Henslow. Peterfield, England: The Author, 1986. 261p. 4 maps.

he author joined the army straight from school in August, 1941. By April 1943 he was
n officer in Queen Victoria's Own Madras Sappers and Miners at Bangalore from
vhere he obtained a posting to the distant war front in Burma. He fought at the Battle
If Kohima and was in overall command of the company responsible for the longest
ssault crossing undertaken in the war – of the Irrawaddy River at Nyaungu.
Entertaining and forthright in his opinions, and sometimes scathing in his criticisms of
igh command, Henslow provides a vivid picture of a fighting man's war in the 14th
Army.

382 **The rats of Rangoon.**
Lionel Hudson. London; Melbourne, Australia; Johannesburg: Leo
Cooper, 1987. 220p.

An Australian airforce officer's account of life as a prisoner of war in Rangoon jail an
of how, after the Japanese withdrawal from Rangoon, the POWs defended themselve
until the allied forces occupied the city. Much of the account is reconstructed from th
scraps of paper that formed the secret diary kept by the author from February to Apr
1945. Other accounts of the grim conditions of Rangoon jail as a prisoner of th
Japanese can be found in John Tim Finnerty's *All hell on the Irrawaddy* (Bogn
Regis, England: Anchor, 1985. 286p.) which gives substantially the same account as i
his *All quiet on the Irrawaddy* (Bognor Regis, England: New Horizon, 1979. 225p.
Kenneth Pirie Mackenzie's *Operation Rangoon jail* (London: Christopher Johnsor
1954. 201p.) giving a medical officer's account of the difficulties of doctoring 'men wh
should have lived'; and Philip Godfrey Stibbe's *Return via Rangoon* (London: Newma
Wolsey, 1947. 223p. map.) which is dedicated to Maung Tun of the Burma Rifles wh
was tortured and shot by the Japanese for refusing to disclose Stibbe's jungle hidir
place.

383 **Burmese outpost.**
Anthony Irwin. London: Collins, 1945. 160p.

A British officer's account of guerrilla operations with V Force, working with loc
Muslims and tribal groups against the Japanese in Arakan, with a description of 7t
Indian Division's fighting in the Battle of the Box.

384 **Chindit.**
Richard Rhodes James, foreword by Bernard Fergusson. London:
John Murray, 1980. 214p. map. bibliog.

There have been many books about the Chindits and their famous and unorthodo
creator, General Orde Wingate, who masterminded the flying in of men, mules an
supplies behind enemy lines in Japanese-occupied Burma. This book is a person:
account of the 1944 operation by a cipher officer in the column commanded by Joh
Masters, 111 Brigade – and it is interesting to compare his account with Masters', i
The road past Mandalay (q.v.). Rhodes James' account of the doomed operation wi
its terrible casualties and minimal military profit is controlled and objective, but at th
same time has an immediacy that fulfils the author's hope 'that some of the mud is st
clinging to its pages'.

385 **The marine from Mandalay.**
James Leasor. London: Leo Cooper, 1988. 146p. bibliog.

The true story of Royal Marine William Doyle's long, solitary march – barefoo
unarmed and wounded – from Mandalay to India in 1942.

386 **Retreat from Burma: an intelligence officer's personal story.**
Tony Mains. London: W. Foulsham, 1973. 151p. maps.

An account of the evacuation of Rangoon and of the British Army's retreat fror
Burma in 1942. With appendixes on civil, military and police organizations in India an
Burma, and a list of Army 'Dramatis Personae'.

87 The road past Mandalay: a personal narrative.
John Masters.   London: Michael Joseph, 1961. 344p. maps.

his second volume of the author's autobiographical memoirs covers his experiences as
1 Indian Army officer in wartime India and Burma. A strong narrative of 111
Chindit) Brigade in Burma which reveals the strains of a harrowing campaign.

88 Grandfather Longlegs: the life and gallant death of Major H. P. Seagrim.
Ian Morrison.   London: Faber & Faber, 1947. 239p. 2 maps.

Iajor Hugh Paul Seagrim (1909-44) of the Burma Rifles stayed behind in the Karen
ills inside Japanese-held territory after the collapse of the civil administration and
treat of the British forces, and organised loyal Karens into a resistance and
telligence network. In March 1944 in an attempt to save Karen villagers from brutal
apanese reprisals for sheltering him, Seagrim surrendered, was sentenced to death
1d, in September 1944, executed together with seven of his followers. Morrison's
loving account, written soon after the events its describes, vividly conveys Seagrim's
nswerving Christian faith and example, and the Karen people whose love he so
spired.

89 The jungle in arms.
Balfour Oatts.   London: William Kimber, 1962. 207p. map.

Burma Frontier Force officer's account of the prewar expedition in the Naga Hills
1d of wartime service on the Northwest Frontier in command of the Western Chin
evies. With vignettes of fellow officers such as Harold Braund and Noel Stevenson,
1d an unsympathetic portrayal of Aung San – 'a traitor' – and Burmese nationalists.

90 Out of the blue: a pilot with the Chindits.
Terence O'Brien.   London: Collins, 1984. 272p. map.

xperiences of an Australian RAF pilot carrying out airdrops as part of Wingate's
hindit operations in the remote mountainous region between northern Burma and
'unnan. The account is written with a lot of humour and forthright criticism of some
igh command decisions.

91 Behind the Burma Road.
William R. Peers, Dean Brelis.   Boston, Massachusetts: Little Brown,
1963. 246p; London: Robert Hale, 1964. 194p. maps.

eers commanded Detachment 101's OSS guerrilla operations in the Kachin Hills from
)ecember 1943 to July 1945, and Brelis served under him as a field agent. Their book
rovides a detailed and lively first-hand account of the command problems of a
omplex guerrilla operation and of the experiences of men in the field. The book ends
ith the following tribute to the Kachins: 'They were the fighters who raised the flag of
eedom in Burma. As guerrillas, they never lost a battle. It was the Kachins who
rote the splendid accomplishments of 101'.

392 **Helen of Burma: the autobiography of a wartime nurse.**
Helen Rodriguez.   London: William Collins, 1983; London: Corgi
Books, 1988. 187p.

The author, daughter of a Scottish nurse and a Portuguese surgeon, was born an
brought up in Taunggyi, Burma. She was a matron at Taunggyi's civil hospital whe
the invading Japanese bombed and occupied the town, and – refusing the chance t
leave with the retreating British army – she stayed on to nurse throughout the Japanes
occupation, surviving internment and torture.

393 **Special force: a Chindit's story.**
Jesse Shaw.   Gloucester, England: Allan Sutton, 1986. 271p.

A lively and humorous autobiography of a cockney soldier whose beloved Wes
African regiment served with the Chindits in Burma. His experiences of the secon
Wingate expedition related in this book were also published in an earlier version unde
the name of John Shaw, including an introduction by Bernard Fergusson, with the titl
The march out: the end of the Chindit adventure (London: Rupert Hart-Davis, 1953
206p.).

394 **Green shadows: a Gurkha story.**
Denis Sheil-Small, foreword by General Sir Walter Walker.   London:
William Kimber, 1982. 198p. maps.

A vivid account of the author's personal experiences in the Burma campaign whic
well conveys the 'smell of battle' and the bravery of the men of the 4/8th Gurkha Rifle
(part of the 7th Indian Division).

395 **Defeat into victory.**
William Joseph Slim.   London: Cassell, 1956; London: Papermac,
1986. 576p. 21 maps.

This elegant and frank personal narrative by Field Marshall Viscount Slim (1899-1970)
Commander of the Fourteenth Army in Burma, constitutes the major English memoi
of the campaign. Slim's classic account provides a commander's overview of a comple
war on many fronts, told with feeling for the ordinary soldier. It includes an account c
Slim's crucial meeting with General Aung San (p. 515-20) following which h
concluded 'I could do business with Aung San'. Assessments of Slim's command in th
Burma campaign (and good operational and route maps) can be found in Geoffre
Charles Evans, *Slim as military commander* (London: B. T. Batsford; Princeton, Ne
Jersey: D. Van Nostrand, 1969. 239p. maps. bibliog.) and in Ronald Lewin, *Slim th
standard bearer: a biography of Field–Marshall The Viscount Slim, KG, GCB, GCMC
GCVO, DSO, MC* (London: Leo Cooper, 1976. 350p. maps. bibliog.).

396 **The Stilwell papers.**
Joseph Warren Stilwell, arranged and edited by Theodore H. White,
with an introduction by J. F. C. Fuller.   London: MacDonald, 1949.
327p. map.

These terse passages from the campaign diaries of General Stilwell (1883-1946)
supplemented by his letters to his wife and by longer essays and military analyses
convey vividly the pressures upon Stilwell of acting as chief of staff to Chiang Kai-she
and as commander of US forces in the China–Burma–India theatre of war. The

caused a sensation when published and have been an invaluable source of lively quotation for historians. For a vivid picture of Stilwell's campaign in Burma, see Barbara W. Tuchman, *Stilwell and the American experience in China, 1911-45* (London: Macmillan, 1971, p. 328-445). A first-hand narrative of the retreat of Stilwell's Chinese troops from Burma is given by Jack Belden, *Retreat with Stilwell* (London: Cassell; New York: Alfred A. Knopf, 1943. 368p.) who concludes: 'Of all the high officials who came out of Burma, there was only one [Stilwell] who had the guts and honesty to tell the world the simple truth . . . we were licked'.

397 **Orde Wingate.**
Christopher Sykes.   London: Collins, 1959. 575p. maps.
The major biography of Orde Charles Wingate (1903-44) whose remarkable military career took him to Palestine where he, a trained Arabist, became an ardent Zionist, to Ethiopia and, finally, to Burma (p. 360-546) where he achieved military immortality as the creator of the Chindits, and was killed in a plane crash three weeks after the start of the second Wingate expedition in March 1944. Sykes provides some comments and correctives to Oswald Mosley's biography of Wingate, *Gideon goes to war* (London: Arthur Barker, 1955. 256p.) and to various military accounts of the Burma operation. See also Derek Tulloch's *Wingate in peace and war* (London: MacDonald, 1972. 300p. maps. bibliog.) which concentrates on the Chindit operations and vigorously defends Wingate's reputation. Also useful is the article by Peter W. Mead, 'Orde Wingate and the official historians', *Journal of Contemporary History*, vol. 14, no. 1 (Jan. 1979), p. 55-82. For an enthusiastic portrayal of Wingate, written before the term 'Chindits' was in common usage and before the outcome of the war was known, see Charles James Rolo's *Wingate's raiders: an account of the incredible adventures that raised the curtain on the battle for Burma* (London: George G. Harrap, 1945. rev. ed. 199p. maps.).

Spitfires over the Arakan.
See item no. 269.

'A hell of a licking': the retreat from Burma 1941-2.
See item no. 275.

Before the dawn: the story of two historic retreats.
See item no. 276.

The Burma–Siam Railway

398 **A life for every sleeper: a pictorial record of the Burma–Thailand railway.**
Hugh V. Clark.   Sydney; London: Allen & Unwin, 1986. 114p. maps.
The author presents, from documents, photographs and maps preserved in the records of the Australian War Memorial and from his own experiences as an Australian prisoner of war working on the Burma–Siam railway in 1943-44, a clear account of the stages of the railway's construction and of the work done by British, American, Australian and Dutch prisoners of war and by Asian conscript labourers. Of these,

some 13,000 allied prisoners of war and over 70,000 Asians are estimated to have died constructing the railway. The account is illustrated with excellent photographs of the period, including some taken by a Japanese engineer, and supplemented in a final chapter by photographs taken in 1978 and 1985. For a detailed account of the railway's construction and its historical context, illustrated with contemporary sketches of POW life in the camps of the Burma–Siam railway, see Clifford Kinvig, *Death railway* (London: Pan/Ballantine, 1973. 160p. maps. bibliog. [The Pan/Ballantine Illustrated History of World War II, Campaign Book]). Kinvig concludes: 'The railway could well serve as the supreme monument to futility: it cost the lives of approximately 393 men . . . for every mile of its useless track'.

399   **One for every sleeper: the Japanese death railway through Thailand.**
Jeffery English.   London: Robert Hale, 1989. 205p. map.

A stark narrative of working on the Burma–Siam railway, by a survivor who has managed to forgive but not forget. Among the many other personal narratives of experiences on the Burma–Siam railway are Basil Peacock's *Prisoner on the Kwai* (Portway, England: Cedric Chivers, 1973. 2nd ed. 291p. map.); Ray Parkin's *Into the smother: a journal of the Burma–Siam railway* (London: Hogarth Press, 1963. 291p. map.) which includes an appendix by E. E. Dunlop, 'Medical experiences in Japanese captivity' (p. 271-91); Stanley John Harper Durnford's *Branch line to Burma* (London: Macdonald, 1958. 207p. map; London: New English Library, 1966. 160p.); Ernest Gordon's *Miracle on the River Kwai* (London: Collins, 1963. 254p.); and – the earliest first-hand account – John Coast's *Railroad of death* (London: Commodore, 1946. 256p.; London: Brown Watson, 1958. 315p.).

400   **The Burma–Thailand railway of death.**
E. R. 'Bon' Hall.   Armadale, Australia: Graphic, 1981. 295p. map.
bibliog.

This is an account by an Australian prisoner of war of his harrowing experiences working on both the Burma and the Thailand sides of the Burma–Siam railway. The author also recounts his rehabilitation difficulties after the war, and the psychological and physical damage caused by his experiences.

401   **The flame of freedom: Corporal Ras Pagani's escape from the railway of death.**
Robert Hammond.   London: Leo Cooper, 1988. 183p. 2 maps.
bibliog.

The subject of this account escaped from the infamous Burma–Siam railway and, after walking barefoot for over 200 miles, made contact with Major Hugh Seagrim, Commander of the Karen Levies and joined the Karen guerrilla operations against the Japanese. Pagani was recaptured by the Japanese and suffered weeks of torture and the haunting memory of seeing Seagrim, the man who had inspired him and so many others, being driven to his execution in Kemmendine Cemetery. Another story of extreme hardships and heroism is told in James Bradley's *Towards the setting sun: an escape from the Thailand–Burma railway, 1943* (London; Chichester, England: Phillimore, 1982. 139p.). Bradley was one of four survivors of a group of eight officers who escaped and reached the Tavoy coast, only to be betrayed by a Burman, recaptured and tried by the Japanese Army in June 1944.

402   The Burma–Siam railway: the secret diary of Dr. Robert Hardie 1942-
45.
Robert Stevenson Hardie.   London: Imperial War Museum, 1983;
London: Quadrant, 1984. 183p. maps.

Dr. Hardie (1904-73) managed to keep his diary and sketches hidden from his
Japanese guards throughout his captivity. He records, in a prose made all the more
effective for its objective restraint, the squalor and torment, diseases and deaths of the
prisoners of war working on the Burma–Siam railway and the unequal struggle of a
small band of allied medical officers to alleviate suffering in appalling conditions. A
biographical index is appended. Published posthumously, with a personal note by his
widow, Elspeth Hardie. Another account by a medical officer is that by Sir Edward
Dunlop, a lieutenant colonel in the Royal Australian Medical Corps, as recorded in his
The war diaries of weary Dunlop: Java and the Burma–Thailand railway 1942-1945
(Wheathamstead, England: Lennard, 1987. 400p.), while *Last man out: surviving the
Burma railroad* by H. Robert Charles (Marlborough, England: Crowood, 1989. 201p.
map. bibliog.) is a testimony to the work of a Dutch Colonial Army doctor, Henri
Hekking, among a group of American prisoners of war at Thanbyuzayat.

403   **And the dawn comes up like thunder.**
Leo Rawlings.   [Harpenden, England]: Rawlings, Chapman, 1972.
160p. map.

A fierce record in words and pictures of life as a prisoner of war on the Burma–Siam
railway and at Changi Jail, Singapore, and the story of the author's painful postwar
realization that 'even when one survived the horror of the camps, the effects came
home with us, later to venture into the open and mock us for imagining we'd escaped'.
Illustrated with 119 plates of the author's ingeniously executed paintings and drawings,
this work, kept hidden from the Japanese guards, documents life and death in the
prisoner of war camps.

404   **To the River Kwai: two journeys – 1943, 1979.**
John Stewart.   London: Bloomsbury, 1988. 175p. map.

Taken prisoner in Singapore in 1942, the author learnt Japanese and was sent to work
as an interpreter at the infamous Sonkurai camp on the Burma–Siam railway where he
kept a diary of his experiences. His narrative intersperses events from 1943 with an
account of his return to the River Kwai in 1979 when he travelled beyond Sonkurai to
the Three Pagodas Pass and crossed into Burma with soldiers of the Mon rebel army.
The author raises many questions about the nature of suffering, survival and the
Japanese. The book also contains Stewart's observations on the making of the famous
film *The Bridge on the River Kwai* in 1958 and on Pierre Boulle's novel on which it was
based.

Population and Minorities

General

405 **Burma 1983 population census.**
Rangoon: Census Division, Immigration and Manpower Department,
Socialist Republic of the Union of Burma, 1986. [360p.]. maps.
This official publication is in two parts: a report and analysis of the 1983 census, and
census tables giving detailed data, state and divisional breakdowns, etc. The 1983
census (the latest conducted) gives the total population of Burma as 35,307,913 (which,
growing at a rate of 2.2 per cent per annum, makes a 1991 population of over 40
millions). An associated set of publications has been issued by the Census Division
giving detailed breakdowns for Rangoon City, Rangoon Division, Mandalay Division,
Magwe Division, etc. For a brief study of the 1973 and 1983 censuses, see the article by
S. Gunasekharan and Mya Than, 'Population change in Burma: a comparison of the
1973 and 1983 censuses', *Sojourn*, vol. 3, no. 2 (Aug. 1988), p. 171-86. Also relevant
are the survey articles by M. Ismael K. Maung, 'Population trends in Burma',
Southeast Asian Affairs (1979), p. 95-102, and 'Cultural pluralism and urban fertility
differentials in postwar Burma', *Asian Profile* (Hong Kong), vol. 6, no. 5 (Oct. 1978),
p. 423-53. A survey of Burma censuses in the period 1872 to 1983 can be found in
Eliane Domschke and Doreen S. Goyer, *The handbook of national population
censuses: Africa and Asia* (New York; Westpoint, Connecticut; London: Greenwood,
1986, p. 586-94).

406 **Races of Burma.**
Colin Metcalf Dallas Enriquez.   Delhi: Manager of Publications, 1933;
New York: AMS, 1981. 98p. bibliog.
This succinct introduction to the peoples of Burma is written from the point-of-view of
a military recruiting officer and contains many asides on Burmese military history.
Originally pubished in 1924 (Calcutta, India: Government of India Central Publication
Department), this revised edition appeared in the series 'Handbooks for the Indian
Army'. It contains good photos illustrating different racial groups, and a photo

purportedly of the armour of the Burmese general Maha Bandula who was killed in the First Anglo–Burmese War.

407 **Ethnic groups of mainland Southeast Asia.**
Frank M. LeBar, Gerald C. Hickey, John K. Musgrave. New Haven, Connecticut: Human Relations Area Files, 1964. 288p. 2 maps. bibliog.
This useful reference work is based on extensive fieldwork and a wide range of ethnographic studies on the approximately 1,200 ethnic groups of mainland Southeast Asia. The text treats these under four main headings: Sino-Tibetan, Austroasiatic, Tai–Kadai, and Malayo–Polynesian. Each of these headings is subdivided in turn, and individual racial and tribal peoples listed. Each entry provides, for the most part, data on location, linguistic pattern and demography, settlement pattern and housing, economy, kin groups, marriage and family, socio-political organization and religion. The population statistics are by now out-of-date. Helpful features are a listing of synonyms after each entry, and an indispensable index of names and a country-name concordance. The accompanying (in pocket) colour maps of the region are keyed to the arrangement of the groups in the text, and linguistic affiliation within major divisions and subdivisions is indicated by a number and colour key.

408 **Southeast Asian tribes, minorities, and nations.**
Edited by Peter Kunstadter. Princeton, New Jersey: Princeton University Press, 1967. 2 vols. bibliog.
A disparate set of papers prepared for a conference on the subject of tribes, minorities and central governments in Southeast Asia, held at Princeton University in May 1965. Burma is represented in the first volume by a brief editorial introduction (p. 75-91) and two papers: 'Ethnic categories in Burma and the theory of social systems' by F. K. Lehman, (p. 93-124); and 'Towards a basis for understanding the minorities in Burma: the Kachin example' by Maran La Raw (p. 125-46). Kunstadter's introduction includes some tables attempting a linguistic classification and statistics on population and linguistic affiliations of the ethnic groups of Burma.

409 **The tribes of Burma.**
Cecil Champain Lowis. Rangoon: Superintendent, Government Printing, 1910; Government Printing, 1919. 109p. map. bibliog. (Ethnographical Survey of India: Burma, no. 4).
A description of the ethnic minorities and tribal groups of Burma (excluding the Arakanese, Mon and Shans), with population statistics from the 1901 census, and useful bibliographical notes (p. 51-106). Lowis (1864-1948) was superintendent of the Ethnographical Survey of Burma and a prolific novelist writing approximately fourteen novels set in Burma, commencing with *The treasury–officer's wooing* (q.v.) in 1899.

410 **Burma and beyond.**
James George Scott. London: Grayson & Grayson, 1932. 349p. map.
Conceived as a companion volume to his *The Burman* (q.v.), Scott draws on his own observations and those of contemporary colonial officials to sketch the beliefs, customs and daily life of Burma's minority ethnic groups – the Shans, Karens, Chins, Kachins, Padaung, Wa, etc. The book is illustrated with Scott's own photographs and contains a final chapter by G. E. Mitton (Lady Scott) on the Burmans.

Indigenous ethnic minorities

411 The Selungs of the Mergui archipelago.
John Anderson. In: *Contributions to the fauna of Mergui and its archipelago*. Compiled by John Anderson. London: Taylor & Francis, 1889, p. 375-421.

A summary of research on the sea gypsies of the Mergui archipelago, off the coast of Tenasserim, with a Selung vocabulary. Anderson's account was published as part two in volume one of his two-volume compilation on the marine zoology of the Mergui archipelago in which collections made for the Indian Museum, Calcutta, during an expedition to the Mergui Archipelago in 1881-82 are described and illustrated by a team of scientists. A brief study which includes a vocabulary of over 200 Selung (or Salon) words, with their English, Thai and Malay equivalents is that by William James Sherlock Carrapiett, *The Salons* (Rangoon: Superintendent, Government Printing, 1909. 27p. [Ethnographical Survey of India: Burma. no. 2]).

412 Les lautu: contribution à l'étude de l'organisation sociale d'une ethnie chin de Haute–Birmanie. (The Laotu: contribution to the study of the social organization of a Chin group in Upper Burma.)
André Bareigts. Paris: SELAF, 1981. 312p. 6 maps. bibliog. (Langues et Civilisations de l'Asie du Sud-Est et du Monde Insulindien 11).

An anthropological and ethnographic study, based on fieldwork conducted 1959-66, of the Laotu, one of the dozens of Chin groups inhabiting the mountains of western Burma. The appendix contains Laotu language texts.

413 Karennis: les combattants de la spirale d'or. (The Karenni: combatants of the golden spiral.)
Patrick Bernard, Michel Huteau. Paris: L'Harmattan, 1988. 127p. map.

A handsome, colour-illustrated, emotive photo-reportage of 'the daily struggle to survive' of the people of Karenni (or, in official Burmese designation, Kayah) State and of the Karenni insurgency movement. Includes many photographs of the 'giraffe necked' Padaung women including some who are refugees in Thailand and objects of 'tourist voyeurism'.

414 The Chin hills: a history of the people, our dealings with them, their customs and manners, and a gazetteer of their country.
Bertram Sausmarez Carey, H. N. Tuck. Rangoon: Superintendent, Government Printing, 1896; Delhi: Cultural Publishing House, 1983. 2 vols. map.

Carey (1864-1919) and his colleague Tuck served as political officers in the Chin Hills. Their book is divided into four parts: the first provides a general introduction and then covers in detail British negotiations with the Chins and British military expeditions – in which the authors participated – in the 1880s and 1890s, with chapters on the different tribes inhabiting the hills; part two covers Chin customs, laws, economy, weapons and warfare; part three consists of a gazetteer of Chin villages; and part four contains road reports and routes. Among the illustrative matter are ethnographic photos, a plan of a Haka Chin house, and Chin family trees.

15 The Shans.
Wilbur Willis Cochrane. Rangoon: Superintendent, Government Printing, 1915; New York: AMS, 1981. 227p.

An American missionary's pioneering history of the Shans in Burma with chapters on Shan language and religion.

16 Amongst the Shans.
Archibald Ross Colquhoun. London: Field & Tuer; Simpkin, Marshall; New York: Scribner & Welford, 1885. 392p.

The main text of Colquhoun's book is preceded by a separately paginated fifty-five page introduction 'The cradle of the Shan States' by Terrien de Lacouperie, while supplementary chapters (p. 327-71) contain a 'Historical sketch of the Shans' by Holt S. Hallett, who also illustrated the book. Colquhoun was an engineer in the India Public Works and he and Hallett made separate expeditions to survey routes for a railway connection between British Burma, Southwest China, the Shan States and Thailand. Press and official opinions on Colquhoun's proposed routes are reprinted in the appendix. Hallett contributed nearly fifty illustrations to the book which are primarily of Lao scenes, but also include depictions of Shan agricultural, domestic and spinning implements. A large part of the book concerns Chiangmai in Thailand, but Colquhoun does include descriptions of various hill people of Burma. Colquhoun also published earlier a two-volume work, *Across Chrysê: being the narrative of a journey of exploration through the South China border lands from Canton to Mandalay* (London: Sampson Low, Marston, Searle, & Rivington, 1883) which has detailed route maps, but little on Burma apart from the usual optimistic speculations about overland trade with China and remarks on possible railway routes to China. Colquhoun further elaborated upon the trading potential of Burma and railway connections in his *Burma and the Burmans: or 'the best unopened market in the world'*. (London: Field & Tuer, Leadenhall, 1885. 58p. map.).

17 A Burmese arcady: an account of a long and intimate sojourn among the mountain dwellers of the Burmese hinterland and of their engaging characteristics and customs, etc.
Colin Metcalf Dallas Enriquez. London: Seeley, Service, 1923. 282p. map.

An affectionate portrait of the Kachins among whom the author, a major in the Kachin Rifles, spent most of his life. Some account is given also of the Lisu people. Enriquez commanded a company of Kachins, 85th Burma Rifles, in Mesopotamia in 1917-19 and compiled a military vocabulary, *Kachin military terms* (Rangoon: Superintendent, Government Printing, 1919. 92p.) giving over 1,500 words, phrases, sentences – arranged English to Jinghpaw (an indigenous term for Kachin) – and samples of Kachin soldiers' letters home. Enriquez wrote many other books on Burma, including a short history of Pagan, *Pagan: being the first connected account in English of the 11th century capital of Burma, with the history of a few of its most important pagodas* (Rangoon: Hanthawaddy, 1914. 46p.), a series of travelogues, beginning with *A Burmese enchantment* (q.v.), and a chatty general introduction to 'the charm of Burma', *Beautiful Burma* (Rangoon: Myanmahita Magazine, 1935. 148p.).

418 **True Love and Bartholomew: rebels on the Burmese border.**
Jonathan Falla, foreword by Nigel Barley. Cambridge, England:
Cambridge University Press, 1991. 400p. map. bibliog.

The author spent a year (1986-87) living in the Burmese jungle with the Karen rebels who have been fighting the Burmese government for autonomy since 1949. Falla, a trained nurse, was engaged in a research project to survey demography and disease patterns, economics and pharmaceutical drug supplies in rebel territory and to investigate the viability of a village health-care scheme, but such matters are not the primary focus of this book which, in the author's words, 'is, rather, a portrait of what appeared to me to be a very singular thing – a completely illegal and unrecognised nation state defended by only a few thousand armed men, which has yet been the home of thousands of families since well before I was born'. Falla draws extensively on past literature about the Karen people while providing, above all, a closely observed and intense account of contemporary village life in the Karen Free State (Kawthoolei) based on the lives of individual Karens (including the book's eponymous True Love and Bartholomew).

419 **The Kachins: religion and customs.**
C. Gilhodes. Calcutta, India: Catholic Orphan Press; London: Kegan Paul, Trench, Trübner, 1922. 304p.

The author, a Catholic missionary of the Paris Foreign Missions among the Laphai tribe of the Kachins, has produced a careful anthropological record of Kachin life and oral literature and accounts, admirably free of any interjections from the Christian or Western point of view. The book is in seven parts: folklore (a narration of Kachin oral stories of their and the world's origins); mythology and religion (on Kachin spirits, ritual, the supreme beings, ancestor and spirit worship); culture (including the nature of man, the Kachin country, dress, food, dwellings, fire); birth and childhood; marriage, death and obsequies; diseases and their remedies.

420 **The Talaings.**
Robert Halliday. Rangoon: Superintendent, Government Printing, 1917. 164p.

A pioneering anthropological account of Mon culture – Talaing being an old designation of the Mon people – by a Scottish missionary stationed in Tenasserim. Halliday makes comparisons between the Mon of Burma and of Thailand, drawing on his extensive knowledge of Mon dialects and folklore and on his visits to Mon settlements in Thailand. His book, well-illustrated with photographs of Mon life, has seven short sections: introductory (on history, etc.); domestic life (houses, agriculture, fishing, pottery, weaving, medicine, music, etc.); social customs (birth, marriage, funeral ceremonies, education); religion (Buddhism, monastic life, festivals); belief in the unseen (spirit cults, witchcraft, astrology); language; literature.

421 **The Kachins: their customs and traditions.**
Ola Hanson. Rangoon: American Baptist Mission Press, 1913; New York: AMS, 1982. 225p.

Hanson (1864-1929), served as an American Baptist missionary in the southern Kachin area from 1890-1920. His book is a solid ethnographic study with chapters on the origins of the Kachins, Kachin dialects, customs, government and law, industries, weapons and warfare, social life, mythology, religion, birth, marriage and funeral ceremonies, etc. It admirably fulfils the author's modest aim of providing 'a practical working knowledge of Kachin ways, habits and customs'. For a biography of Hanson giving details of his Kachin language and translation work and personal recollections, see Gustaf A. Sword, *Light in the jungle: life story of Dr. Ola Hanson of Burma* (Chicago: Baptist Conference Press, 1954. 189p.).

422 **Ethnic adaptation and identity: the Karen on the Thai frontier with Burma.**
Edited by Charles F. Keyes. Philadelphia: Institute for the Study of Human Issues, 1979. 278p. 2 maps. bibliog.

Based on fieldwork, the contributions in this book by the editor and fellow anthropologists Peter Hinton, Shigeru Iijima, Peter Kunstadter, F. K. Lehman, David H. Marlowe and Theodore Stern explore the origins and identity of the Karen group of tribes living in a region spanning Thailand's border with Burma. The Sgaw, Pwo and Kayah (or Red) Karen are distinguished and aspects of their ethnic identity, relation to other groups, and adaptation to change explored.

423 **Political systems of highland Burma: a study of Kachin social structures.**
Edmund Ronald Leach. London: G. Bell, 1954; London: Athlone, 1981. 324p. maps. bibliog.

This study, now in its fifth reprint, has become a classic anthropological analysis of the Kachin and Shan population of Northeast Burma. Leach addresses himself to the question of how far Kachin culture and social structure can be considered uniform, redefines myth and ritual, and postulates that seeking for power is the basis of social choice.

424 **The structure of Chin society: a tribal people of Burma adapted to a non-western civilization.**
Frederick K. Lehman. Urbana, Illinois: University of Illinois Press, 1963. 244p. maps. bibliog. (Illinois Studies in Anthropology, no. 3).

An anthropological analysis of Chin society based on field work in the Chin Hills of Burma in 1957-58. Lehman discusses Chin society and culture in terms of its adaptation to local resources and of its response to Burman civilization, with chapters on Chin history, land use and agricuture, land tenure and inheritance, Southern Chin social systems, Northern Chin social systems, economics, conceptual structures in Chin religion, Chin attitudes and psychological orientations, social and cultural changes. See also Lehman's 'Internal inflationary pressures in the prestige economy of the feast of merit complex: the Chin and Kachin cases from Upper Burma', in *Ritual, power, and economy: upland–lowland contrasts in mainland Southeast Asia*, edited by Susan D. Russell (DeKalb, Illinois: Northern Illinois University, Center for Southeast Asian Studies, 1989, p. 89-102).

425 **Peoples of the golden triangle: six tribes in Thailand.**
Paul Lewis, Elaine Lewis. London: Thames & Hudson, 1984. 300p. maps. bibliog.

A splendid full-colour illustrated study of six tribal groups – the Karen, Hmong, Mien, Lahu, Akha and Lisu – their way of life, costumes and artifacts. Although the tribes featured in this book were observed and photographed in Thailand in the border areas with Burma and Laos, the book also has much relevance for the study of the Karen, Lahu, Akha and Lisu people of Burma. The authors spent from 1947 to 1966 in Kengtung State, Burma, as American Baptist missionaries, and Paul Lewis has also published an extensive source book on the Akha, *Ethnographic notes on the Akhas of Burma* (New Haven, Connecticut: Hraflex, 1969-70. 4 vols. [Descriptive Ethnography Series]) and an *Akha–English dictionary* (q.v.).

426   **The Karens of the golden Chersonese.**
      Alexander Ruxton McMahon.   London: Harrison, 1876. 423p. map.

A pioneering general account of the Karen people which draws on the author's own experiences in administering Toungoo, in Tenasserim, as well as on earlier accounts and observations to present a synthesis of information. With eight tinted lithographs from the author's original drawings. Also by McMahon (1829-99) is *Far Cathay and farther India* (London: Hurst & Blackett, 1893. 340p.), which concentrates on overland trade possibilities with China, the border problem and border tribes, with chapters on different ethnic groups of Burma.

427   **The Karen people of Burma: a study in anthropology and ethnology.**
      Harry Ignatius Marshall.   Columbus, Ohio: Ohio State University Press, 1922; New York: AMS, 1980. 329p. bibliog.

This detailed, illustrated description of the Sgaw Karens derives from the author's years of observation and study while serving as a missionary to the Karens in the Irrawaddy Delta. There are short chapters on virtually all aspects of Karen life (language, dress and ornaments, houses, food, agriculture, spinning and weaving, bronze drums, weapons, musical instruments, magic, etc.), although the author has excluded detailed study of Karen folklore. A glossary of Karen words is appended. Marshall's study was originally published as volume 26, no. 13 of *The Ohio State University Bulletin* in 1922.

428   **The home of an eastern clan: a study of the Palaung of the Shan States.**
      Mary Lewis (Mrs. Leslie) Milne.   Oxford: Clarendon, 1924. 428p.

A closely observed study of the social life and customs of the Palaung of Tawngpeng in the Northern Shan States, with sections on history, family life and birth, childhood, marriage, death, medicine and charms, religion, cosmogony, proverbs, riddles and folk literature. Mary Lewis (Harper) Milne (1860-1952) was clearly a resourceful lady who studied in remote parts of the Northern Shan States in the period 1907-08 and 1911 and took her own photographs for this book, resorting on one occasion to painting an 'obliging Palaung' with egg white to make his intricate neck-to-heel tattoos show up. Amongst the oral material recorded here are children's rhymes, proverbs and folk tales; with an appendix on different marriage customs (which with some tribal groups includes organized elopement). Mrs. Milne also produced the first grammar and dictionary of the Palaung language. A short ethnographic survey of the Palaung hill tribes, with a brief English–Pale–Palaung vocabulary is Cecil Champain Lowis' *A note on the Palaungs of Hsipaw and Tawngpeng* (Rangoon: Superintendent, Government Printing, 1906. 43p. map. [Ethnographical Survey of India: Burma, no. 1]).

429   **Shans at home: with two chapters on Shan history and literature by the Rev. Wilbur Willis Cochrane.**
Mary Lewis (Mrs. Leslie) Milne.   London: John Murray, 1910; New York: Paragon, 1970. 289p. map.
Based on fifteen months' residence among the Shans of Namkham, in the State of North Hsen-wi near the frontier with Yunnan, this study of the Shans emphasizes family life and customs and is illustrated with the author's own photographs. Amongst the wealth of detail provided are designs for woven bed coverlets and translations of folk tales. The chapters contributed by Cochrane are chapters one (p. 1-30) and seventeen (p. 208-20).

430   **The Tarons of Burma: the results of a scientific expedition.**
Mya Tu, Ko Ko, Aung Than Batu, Kywe Thein, C. J. R. Francis, Than Tun Aung Hlaing.   Rangoon: Burma Medical Research Institute, 1966. 199p. map. (Burma Medical Research Institute, Special Report Series, no. 1).
This report of a 1962 expedition to survey the Tarons, a pygmy tribe living in the Adung Long river valley in northernmost Burma, covers their social, cultural and physical anthropology, nutrition and diet, haematological and other physical and medical data; with many supporting tables and illustrations.

431   **The Shan states and the British annexation.**
Saimong Mangrai.   Ithaca, New York: Cornell University Southeast Asia Program, 1965. 319p. bibliog. (Cornell University Southeast Asia Program Data Papers, no. 57).
A major study of the Shan people, their relations with the Burmese, the arrival of the British, and British military expeditions of the 1880s. With lengthy extracts from early British accounts of expeditions among the Shans, Karenni and Wa, as well as from other sources and a brief account of the post-1886 status of the Shan and Karenni States. The appendixes give tables of Shan rulers, translations of historical texts and of official documents. Also relevant is Robert H. Taylor's contribution 'British policy and the Shan States' in *Changes in Northern Thailand and the Shan States 1886-1940*, edited by Prakai Nontawasee (Singapore: Southeast Asian Studies Program, Comparative Research Award Report no. 1, 1988, p. 13-62). Also by Saimong Mangrai is an accomplished translation of two manuscript chronicles of the Eastern Shan State of Kengtung, *The Padaeng chronicle and the Jengtung state chronicle translated* (Ann Arbor, Michigan: University of Michigan, Center for South and Southeast Asian Studies, 1981. 301p. map. bibliog.), which includes an introduction to the Khun people, their script, dating systems, and Buddhism, together with script and calendrical charts. Also relevant is his article, 'Cula sakaraja and the sixty cyclical year names', *Journal of the Siam Society*, vol. 69, pts. 1-2 (1981), p. 4-12. An account of the introduction of Buddhism to the Shan states and the story of the images associated with the famous Phaung-taw-u pagoda festival on Inle Lake is given in Saimong Mangrai's article 'The Phaungtaw-u festival' *Journal of the Siam Society*, vol. 68, pt. 2 (July 1980), p. 70-81. Sao Saimong Mangrai (1913-87), a relative of the *Sawbwa* (hereditary chief) of Kengtung, had a distinguished career in education and government service, including a period as principal education officer, Southern Shan States, suffered a period of imprisonment in the 1960s under Ne Win's military régime, and was married to Mi Mi Khaing, author of *Burmese family* (q.v.).

131

432 **Burma and the Karens.**
San Crombie Po. London: Elliot Stock, 1928. 94p.
This well-illustrated account of the place of the Karens in Burma has portraits and biographies of many eminent Karens, and advocates separate self-government for the Karens.

433 **The loyal Karens of Burma.**
Donald Mackenzie Smeaton. London: Kegan Paul, Trench, 1887. 264p.
An introduction to the Karens who are described as 'the staunchest and bravest defenders of British rule' with sections on Karen language, literature, customs and religion. Smeaton (1848-1910) gives extensive quotations in the introductory chapter (p. 1-65) from the letters of the American medical missionary, Dr. Vinton, written in 1886 describing the turbulent times following the British annexation, and with the theme and fear 'that, after profiting by the loyalty, devotion, and bravery of the Karens, the British Government will again forget them . . .'.

434 **Economics of the central Chin tribes.**
Henry Noel Cochrane Stevenson, foreword by Reginald Hugh Dorman-Smith, Governor of Burma. Bombay: Times of India Press, [1943]. 200p. 3 maps; Farnborough, England: Gregg, 1968.
A Burma Frontier Service officer's anthropological dissertation based on research during 1934-36 carried out while assistant superintendent at Falam, and covering, within an economic theoretical framework, many aspects of Chin culture; with twenty-two black-and-white plates and a glossary of Chin words.

435 **Zo history, with an introduction to Zo culture, economy, religion and their status as an ethnic minority in India, Burma, and Bangladesh.**
Vumson. Aizawl, India: The Author, 1987. 334p. map. bibliog.
This history of the Chin frontier peoples concentrates on the Chin in Burma, and provides a Chin perspective on relations with the Burmese government, especially in the post-1962 period.

436 **Far frontiers: people and events in North-Eastern India 1857-1947.**
John Whitehead. London: BACSA, 1989. 204p. 3 maps. bibliog.
A collection of seven narratives freely drawn from anthropological, historical and personal accounts of India's northeastern frontier with Burma in the period 1857 to 1947. The theme is the relationship between this remote area's tribal peoples (Lushai, Naga, Lakher, Chin, etc.) and the British administrators, soldiers, scholars and missionaries who came into contact with them. The author, who served as wartime training officer to the Chin Hills Battalion and remained in Burma until 1948, includes his own personal memories of the Chins.

A thousand miles on an elephant in the Shan States.
See item no. 48.

Lords of the sunset: a tour in the Shan States.
See item no. 62.

Land of jade: a journey through insurgent Burma.
See item no. 71.

Where Burma meets China: life and travels in the Burma–China border lands.
See item no. 73.

Gazetteer of Upper Burma and the Shan States.
See item no. 111.

Memoirs of the four-foot colonel.
See item no. 297.

Profile of a Burma frontier man.
See item no. 300.

The dictionary of Lahu.
See item no. 464.

A practical handbook of the language of the Lais as spoken by the Hakas and other allied tribes of the Chin Hills (commonly the Baungshe dialect).
See item no. 466.

The Muslims of Burma: a study of a minority group.
See items no. 497.

A century of growth: the Kachin Baptist Church of Burma.
See item no. 509.

Burma: extrajudicial execution and torture of members of ethnic minorities.
See item no. 522.

La Birmanie ou la quête de l'unité: le problème de la cohesion nationale dans la Birmanie contemporaine et sa perspective historique. (Burma or the quest for unity: the problem of national cohesion in contemporary Burma and its historical perspective.)
See item no. 529.

The Shans and the Shan States of Burma.
See item no. 539.

Burma in search of peace.
See item no. 541.

Burmese politics: the dilemma of national unity.
See item no. 553.

Burma: insurgency and the politics of ethnicity.
See item no. 558.

Constitutional and political bases of minority insurrections in Burma.
See item no. 559.

Hand book on the Haka Chin customs.
See item no. 584.

Bulletin du Cédok.
See item no. 805.

A guide to Mon studies.
See item no. 831.

Indians, Chinese and Eurasians

437 **The Indian minority in Burma: the rise and decline of an immigrant commuity.**
Nalini Ranian Chakravarti. London: Oxford University Press, 1971.
214p. map. bibliog.

This straightforward, solid account of the role of the Indian minority in Burma concentrates on an analysis of their economic position and political problems during the 1900-41 period. An epilogue covering the period 1942-68 shows the continuing decline in the Indian population in Burma and highlights 'the drastic measures taken by Burma to displace Indians'. Two earlier detailed studies of Indian labour conditions are A. Narayana Rao's *Contract labour in Burma* (Triplicane, India: Current Thought, 1930. 194p.) and E. J. L. Andrew's *Indian labour in Rangoon* (Calcutta, India: Oxford University Press, 1933. 300p. map.). Also relevant is the study by Philip Siegelman, *Colonial development and the Chettyar: a study in the ecology of modern Burma 1850-1941* (PhD thesis, University of Minnesota, Minneapolis, Minnesota, 1962. 325p. bibliog. [Available from University Microfilms, Ann Arbor, Michigan, order no. UM 64-7301]). The immediate postwar position of Indians in Burma and questions of Indian labour, repatriation and citizenship are covered in one chapter devoted to Burma (p. 68-86) in Moti Lal Bhargava's *Indian National Congress: its affiliates in South and East Asia* (New Delhi: Reliance, 1986. 192p. bibliog.).

438 **The Eurasian population in Burma.**
John Clement Koop. New Haven, Connecticut: Yale University
Southeast Asia Studies, 1960. 66p. bibliog. (Cultural Report Series,
no. 6).

A study of the size, problems and place of Eurasians in Burma with statistical data for the period up to 1949. It combines two previous studies by Dr. Koop originally published in Rangoon in small editions: *Preliminary survey of the social and economic condition of the Eurasian people in Rangoon: Gedhawk* (1948) and a survey sponsored by the Anglo-Burman Union, *A demographic study of the Eurasian population in Rangoon in 1949* (1952).

439   **The Chinese in Southeast Asia.**
      Victor Purcell.   London; Kuala Lumpur; Hong Kong: Oxford
      University Press, under the auspices of the Royal Institute for
      International Affairs, 1965. rev. ed. 623p. 3 maps. bibliog.
This book, first published in 1951, is the standard introduction to the history of the
overseas Chinese in Southeast Asia. The section on the Chinese in Burma (p. 41-79)
briefly covers demographic features, the economic position of the Chinese in Burma,
border issues, and relations with China in the period 1949-63. The useful bibliography
includes Chinese and Japanese publications.

440   **Minority problems in Southeast Asia.**
      Virginia Thompson, Richard Adloff.   Stanford, California: Stanford
      University Press, issued under the auspices of International Secretariat,
      Institute of Pacific Relations, 1955. 295p. bibliog.
This introductory survey has sections on the Chinese in Burma (p. 54-55), the Indians
(p. 69-93), the Eurasians (p. 146), the Arakanese (p. 151-58), and Chinese minorities
(p. 258-67), with emphasis on political aspects of the minorities' situation. See also the
more recent general work examining the role of religion in ethnic conflict and the
formation of state policy towards minorities, *Ethnic conflict in Buddhist societies: Sri
Lanka, Thailand and Burma*, edited by K. M. de Silva, Pensri Duke, Ellen S.
Goldberg, Nathan Katz (London: Pinter; Boulder, Colorado, Westview, 1988. 220p.)
which contains two contributions on Burma: 'Minorities in Burmese history' by Ronald
D. Renard (p. 77-91) and 'Religious minorities in Burma in the contemporary period'
by Trevor O. Ling (p. 172-86).

The Muslims of Burma: a study of a minority group.
See item no. 497.

Languages

General

441 Language policy and planning in Burma.
Anna J. Allott. In: *Papers in South-East Asian Linguistics No. 9: language policy, language planning and sociolinguistics in South-East Asia*. Edited by David Bradley. Canberra: Dept. of Linguistics, Research School of Pacific Studies, Australian National University, 1985. p. 131-54. (Pacific Linguistics Series A, no. 67).

This article provides a useful introduction to the Burmese language, and traces its position under British rule and its development as the national language in the post-independence period. Some information on the position of English from 1948 and on education for the minority peoples is also given. The author concludes that Burma has made substantial progress in developing Burmese as the national language by such means as devising terminology and a standard spelling, and producing dictionaries and teaching materials.

442 South-East Asian linguistics: essays in honour of Eugénie J. A. Henderson.
Edited by Jeremy H. C. S. Davidson. London: School of Oriental & African Studies, University of London, 1989. 235p. (Collected Papers in Oriental & African Studies).

This contains three papers relevant to Burma: 'Uncles and aunts: Burmese kinship and gender' by David Bradley (p. 147-62); 'The bulging monosyllable, or the mora the merrier: echo-vowel adverbialization in Lahu' by James A. Matisoff (p. 163-98); and 'The Yaw dialects of Burmese' by John Okell (p. 199-218). The linguistics publications of Eugénie Henderson (1914-89) which include *Tiddim Chin: a descriptive analysis of two texts* (London: Oxford University Press, 1965. 172p.) are listed on p. 5-9.

443   **Linguistic survey of India.**
Edited by George Abraham Grierson.   Calcutta, India:
Superintendent, Government Printing, 1903-28. 13 vols. maps.
Of this monumental work the first three volumes are relevant to Burma. Volume one
contains an introduction reviewing pioneering language surveys (which, in the Burma
context, includes work by Felix Carey, Francis Buchanan and John Leyden) and
comparative vocabularies; volume two covers Mon-Khmer and the Thai language
family; and volume three, in three parts, the Tibeto–Burman languages (but, since a
separate language survey for Burma was planned – although in the event never carried
out – this is mainly on the Chin, Kachin and Naga languages).

444   **Hobson–Jobson: a glossary of colloquial Anglo–Indian words and
phrases.**
Henry Yule, Arthur C. Burnell.   London: John Murray, 1903. 2nd ed;
London: Routledge & Kegan Paul, 1985. 1021p.
This delightful source-book of Anglo-Indian language and life in 19th-century colonial
India, has many entries relevant to Burma, including the etymology of Burmese place
names, with citations illustrating different uses. *Hobson–Jobson* was first published in
1886, and the 1985 reprint of the 1903 edition (which was edited by William Crooke)
has a new foreword by Anthony Burgess.

Phases of pre-Pagan Burma: languages and history.
See item no. 140.

Southeast Asian history and historiography: essays presented to D. G. E. Hall.
See item no. 147.

Burma: literature, historiography, scholarship, language, life, and Buddhism.
See item no. 649.

South-East Asia languages and literatures: a select guide.
See item no. 837.

Bibliography and index of mainland Southeast Asian languages and linguistics.
See item no. 839.

Burmese

445   **The university English–Burmese dictionary.**
Ba Han.   Rangoon: Hanthawaddy, 1966. 2 vols.
A major compilation (of 2,292p.) updating and replacing the pioneering English–
Burmese dictionary of the 19th-century American missionary, Adoniram Judson, and
virtually all subsequent dictionaries. For technical vocabulary there is a dictionary
arranged in order of English terms with their Burmese equivalents, published under
the bilingual title *Pyin-nya yat waw-hara-mya/Scientific and technical terms* (Rangoon:
Ministry of Education, 1971-74. 8 parts; reprinted in one volume, 1980). There is also

a 'Dictionary of economic terms' compiled by the Economic Research Group and published as a supplement in Tun Nyein, *The students' English–Burmese dictionary* (Rangoon: Paw U Sa-pei, 1971. 3rd ed. 991p. [+127p. supplement by Tun Aung Gyaw and 74p. economic terms supplement]).

446 **Dictionnaire birman–français.** (Burmese–French dictionary.)
Compiled by Denise Bernot. Paris: Centre de Documentation sur l'Asie du Sud-est et le Monde Insulindien, 1978-. 14 vols.

The compilation of this excellent Burmese–French dictionary is still in progress by a team of researchers led by Mme. Bernot of the Ecole des Langues Orientales, Paris with one more volume expected in 1991 to complete the dictionary. The clear entries are enhanced by line drawings used to clarify terms and definitions, especially relating to architecture, weaving, botany, biology and costume. Contains over 40,000 entries.

447 **Manuel de birman: langue de Myanmar.** (Manual of Burmese: language of Myanmar.)
Denise Bernot, Marie-Helene Cardinaud, Marie Yin Yin Myint. Paris: L'Asiathèque, 1990. 246p. (Langes de l'Asie – INALCO).

A well-structured language course with tape cassette introducing the student to both spoken and written Burmese, with grammatical notes following each exercise an French–Burmese and Burmese–French vocabularies at the end.

448 **Beginning Burmese.**
William S. Cornyn, D. Haigh Roop. New Haven, Connecticut; London: Yale University Press, 1968. 501p. (Yale Linguistic Series).

A good general introductory course, with exercises and vocabularies, which constitute a revision and updating of Cornyn's *Spoken Burmese: basic course* (United States Armed Forces Institute, 1946; Ithaca, New York: Spoken Lanuage Services, 1970 2 vols.). Among Cornyn's other works for students of the Burmese language are *Burmese chrestomathy* (Washington, DC: American Council of Learned Societies 1957. 393p.) and, with John K. Musgrave, *Burmese glossary* (Washington, DC American Council of Learned Societies, 1958. 209p.).

449 **Burmese phrasebook.**
David Bradley. South Yarra, Australia: Lonely Planet, 1988. 121p. map. (Language Survival Kits).

A pocket-sized phrasebook for travellers in Burma with phrases reproduced both phonetically and in Burmese script in the optimistic expectation that 'communication the more remote areas will cease to be a problem'.

450 **Wörterbuch Burmesisch–Deutsch.** (Burmese–German dictionary.)
Annemarie Esche. Leipzig, GDR: Verlag Enzyklopädie, 1976. 546p.

Approximately 17,000 entries with Burmese words in script and phonetic transcription Also relevant are Annemarie Esche and Eberhardt Richter, *Burmesisches Übungsbuch* ('Burmese exercise book.') (Leipzig, GDR: Verlag Enzyklopädie, 1988. 443p.) an Eberhardt Richter, *Lehrbuch des modernen Burmesisch: Umgangsprache* ('Textbook of modern colloquial Burmese'.) (Leipzig: Verlag Enzyklopädie, 1983. 405p.).

51   Judson's Burmese–English dictionary.
Adoniram Judson, revised and enlarged by Robert C. Stevenson, F. H.
Eveleth.   Rangoon: Baptist Board of Publications, 1986. 1120p.

Judson's original pioneering dictionary was first published in 1852 although its
antecedents go back to 1826, and it was revised and enlarged in 1893 and 1918. The
preface to the 'centenary edition' of 1953 (and reprinted in the 1966 and 1986 editions)
describes the dictionary's history, while the article by E. P. Quigly, 'Some early
references to the first Burmese–English dictionary of 1826', *Journal of the Burma
Research Society*, vol. 40, pt. 2a (May 1958), p. 348-53, is also relevant. There is also
by Adoniram Judson, revised and enlarged (from the original 1849 edition) by E. O.
Stevens, Francis Mason and F. H. Eveleth, *Judson's English and Burmese dictionary*
Rangoon: Baptist Board of Publications, 1966. 10th ed. 928p.), and *A grammar of the
Burmese language* (Rangoon: Baptist Board of Publications, 1951. rev. ed. 66p.).

52   First steps in Burmese.
John Okell.   London: School of Oriental and African Studies,
University of London, 1989. 130p.

A well-structured and practical foundation course in colloquial Burmese for learners
with no previous knowledge of Burmese. It introduces the student to essential
grammatical structures and a limited range of useful vocabulary. The material is
presented in small doses – fifty-two 'steps' in all – and the accompanying five language
tapes run for a total of six hours. The tape exercises are given in the text in both
Burmese script and in transcription.

**53   Nissaya Burmese: a case of systematic adaptation to a foreign grammar
and syntax.**
John Okell.   *Journal of the Burma Research Society*, vol. 50, pt. 1
(June 1967), p. 95-123.

An examination of *nissaya* – works in which each word or phrase of a Pali text is
followed by its Burmese translation – and the prestige and dissemination of the *nissaya*
style in Burmese. Also relevant is Tin Lwin, 'Pali–Burmese nissaya', *Journal of the
Burmese Research Society*, vol. 46, pt. 1 (June 1963), p. 43-52.

54   A reference grammar of colloquial Burmese.
John Okell.   London: Oxford University Press, 1969. 2 vols. bibliog.

This comprehensive grammar of colloquial Burmese offers a system of classification of
the various elements of the language, with examples of their usage and meaning. Also
by Okell is *A guide to the romanization of Burmese* (London: Royal Asiatic Society,
1971. 69p. [James G. Furlong Fund, vol. 27]).

55   An introduction to the Burmese writing system.
D. Haigh Roop.   New Haven, Connecticut; London: Yale University
Press, 1972. 122p. (Yale Linguistic Series).

A step-by-step introduction to learning the Burmese script, with reading and writing
exercises.

456 **Burmese.**
Julian K. Wheatley. In: *The major languages of East and South-East Asia.* Edited by Bernard Comrie. London: Routledge, 1990, p. 106-26. bibliog.

An outline of the development of the Burmese language, its phonology, writing system, morphology and syntax. This was previously published in a larger compilation, *The world's major languages,* edited by Bernard Comrie (London; Sydney: Croom Helm, 1987, p. 834-54).

Minority languages

457 **A Shan and English dictionary.**
Josiah Nelson Cushing. Rangoon: American Baptist Mission Press, 1914. 2nd ed.; Farnborough, England; Gregg International, 1971. 708p.

The standard dictionary for Shan, first published in 1881. Also by Cushing is *Grammar of the Shan language* (Rangoon: American Baptist Mission Press, 1887. 2nd ed. 118p.) and *Elementary handbook of the Shan language* (Rangoon: American Baptist Mission Press, 1906. 2nd ed.; Farnborough, England: Gregg International, 1971. 272p.).

458 **A grammar of the Sgaw Karen.**
David Gilmore. Rangoon: American Baptist Mission Press, F. D. Phinney, 1898. 51p.

This concise grammar is designed as an introduction to the Karen language and builds on the work of other early missionary scholars, most notably that of Francis Mason and Jonathan Wade. Much rarer is the more extensive work by Francis Mason, *Synopsis of a grammar of the Karen language* (q.v.) and that by Jonathan Wade, *Karen vernacular grammar* (Moulmein, Burma: American Mission Press, 1861. 256p.). Wade also compiled the first (and incomplete) *Karen dictionary* (Tavoy, Burma: American Baptist Mission, 1843-44) and *A dictionary of the Sgau Karen language* (Rangoon: American Baptist Mission, 1896. 1,341p.), and, with Mrs. J. P. Binney (1863), revised and abridged by George E. Blackwell, *The Anglo-Karen dictionary* (Rangoon: American Baptist Mission, 1954.). Another early missionary compilation (1846) is Cephas Bennett's, *An Anglo–Karen vocabulary: monosyllables, for the use of Karen schools* (Rangoon: American Mission Press, 1875. 2nd ed. 148p.). The most recent Karen language studies are those of Robert B. Jones, principally his *Karen linguistic studies* (Berkeley, California: University of California Press, 1961. 283p. [University of California Publications in Linguistics]).

459   **A Mon–English dictionary.**
Robert Halliday.   Bangkok: Siam Society, 1922; Rangoon: Mon
Cultural Section, Ministry of Union Culture, Government of the
Union of Burma, 1955. 512p.

Entries in Mon script and romanization. With a thirty-page preface giving notes on
Mon grammar, and the names of the months, days of the week, and signs of the
zodiac.

460   **A dictionary of the Kachin language.**
Ola Hanson.   Rangoon: American Baptist Mission Press, 1906. 751p.;
Rangoon: Baptist Board of Publications, 1966. 739p.

The only authoritative Kachin–English dictionary, with a brief introduction to the
language, dialects and literature of the Kachin. Also by Hanson is a grammar, *A handbook of the Kachin or Jinghpaw language: including grammar, phrase-book,
English–Kachin and Kachin–English vocabularies* (Rangoon: American Baptist
Mission Press, 1917. 258p.) which is a much revised and enlarged edition of the
author's pioneering *A grammar of the Kachin language* (Rangoon: American Baptist
Mission Press, 1896. 104p.). See also Henry Felix Hertz, *A practical handbook of the
Kachin or Chingpaw language: containing the grammatical principles and peculiarities
of the language, colloquial exercises and a vocabulary, with an appendix on Kachin
customs, laws and religion* (Rangoon: Government Printing & Stationery, 1935, rev.
ed. 163p.). There is also a rare recent dictionary compiled by Manam Hpang, with
over 15,000 entries and an appendix of botanical, biological, medical and other terms,
English–Kachin–Burmese dictionary ([Burma]: [s.n.], 1977. 644p.).

461   **Grammatical notes and vocabulary of the Peguan language: to which are
added a few pages of phrases, etc.**
James M. Haswell.   Rangoon: American Baptist Mission Press, 1901.
2nd ed. 357p.

This is an expanded edition of the Rev. Haswell's original study (Rangoon: American
Mission Press, 1874. 160p.), which provided the first comprehensive account of the
Mon language. It contains a grammar, phrases (in Mon script, transliteration and
English), extracts from Mon literature (in Mon and English translation) a
Mon–English–Burmese vocabulary, and an appendix of geographical names.

462   **Akha–English dictionary.**
Paul Lewis.   Ithaca, New York: Cornell University Southeast Asia
Program, 1968. 363p. (Cornell University Southeast Asia Program
Data Paper, no. 70).

A dictionary of the standard (Puli) dialect of Akha as spoken in Central and Central-
eastern Kengtung State, Burma, based on data collected while working as a missionary
with the Burma Baptist Convention.

463 **Synopsis of a grammar of the Karen language embracing both dialects, Sgau and Pgho, or Sho.**
Francis Mason. Tavoy, Burma: Karen Mission Press, 1846. 458p.
A pioneering grammar of Sgaw and Pwo Karen, with indexes of words (p. 301-444), and a sample subject index on conchology (p. 447-53) with entries in Karen, Burmese and English. The work reflects Mason's interests paying particular attention to natural history terminology. Also given (in a duplicate pagination sequence of p. 299-314) is the Pwo Karen text of a 'Buddhist romance' called 'The clandestine marriage' included by Mason as an exercise in the usage of language rather than as a piece of literature.

464 **The dictionary of Lahu.**
James A. Matisoff. Berkeley, California; London: University of California Press, 1988. 1,436p. map. bibliog. (University of California Publications in Linguistics, vol. 3).
This massive Lahu–English dictionary was twenty years in the making and also contains a useful introduction to the Lahu people and their language; with an extensive bibliography and a list of Lahu language publications (p. 1,415-36), and eighty black-and-white plates illustrating Lahu life and objects. Also by Matisoff is *The grammar of Lahu* (Berkeley, California: University of California Press, 1973. 673p.; Berkeley, California: University of California Press, 1982. 693p. rev. ed. [University of California Publications in Linguistics, vol. 75]).

465 **A dictionary of English–Palaung and Palaung–English.**
Mary Lewis (Mrs. Leslie) Milne. Rangoon: Superintendent, Government Printing, 1931. [673p.].
Arranged in two separately paginated sequences (p. 1-383, p. 1-290), this pioneering work remains the only dictionary of the language of the Palaung of Tawnpeng, Northern Shan States. An appendix lists relationship terms, Palaung measures, and dialect words for Rumai, Kumkaw, Kwanhai and Wa, collected in various villages. Also by Milne is *An elementary Palaung grammar* (Oxford: Clarendon, 1921. 187p.) and an anthropological study, *The home of an eastern clan* (q.v.).

466 **A practical handbook of the language of the Lais as spoken by the Hakas and other allied tribes of the Chin Hills (commonly the Baungshe dialect).**
Anthony George Edward Newland. Rangoon: Superintendent, Government Printing, 1897. 687p.
This study is divided into four parts: grammar (p. 1-46), Chin sentences (p. 47-136), English–Chin dictionary (p. 137-312), Chin words, phrases and idioms (p. 313-687). With many notes on Chin customs and other aspects of Chin life, incorporating Newland's observations derived from three years' residence in the Chin Hills. Other words on the Chin language are Bernard Houghton's *Essay on the language of the Southern Chins and its affinities* (Rangoon: Superintendent, Government Printing, 1892. 131p.) which includes Chin–English and English–Chin vocabularies, and appendixes giving some Chin myths and anthropological details; Frank Montagu Rundall's *Manual of the Siyin dialect spoken in the Northern Chin Hills* (Rangoon: Superintendent, Government Printing, 1901. 47p.), which is designed to be of practical use and includes many medical terms and words 'such as are not used in refined

society'; and L. B. Naylor's *A practical handbook of the Chin language* (*Siyin dialect*) (Rangoon: Government Printing & Stationery, 1925. 122p.).

467   **A dictionary of modern spoken Mon.**
Harry Leonard Shorto.   London: Oxford University Press, 1962. 280p.
Entries are in romanization only, apart from an index of literary forms. Also by Shorto is *A dictionary of the Mon inscriptions from the sixth to the sixteenth centuries: incorporating materials collected by the late C. O. Blagden* (London: Oxford University Press, 1971. 406p. bibliog. [London Oriental Series, vol. 24]).

468   **A grammatical sketch of Eastern Kayah (Red Karen).**
David Benedict Solnit.   PhD thesis, University of California, Berkeley, California, 1986. (Available from University Microfilms, Ann Arbor, Michigan, order no. UM 8718164).
This 376-page thesis studies the major language of the Kayah State of Burma spoken by the Karenni. Includes a bibliography.

Historical and cultural studies in Burma.
See item no. 155.

A guide to Mon studies.
See item no. 831.

Religion

Buddhism and spirit cults

469 **The world of Buddhism.**
Edited by Heinz Bechert, Richard Gombrich. London: Thames &
Hudson, 1984. 308p. maps. bibliog.
Several distinguished international scholars have contributed to this book which
examines the origins, teachings and spread of Buddhism in Asia. It is profusely
illustrated, and has exceptionally fine and well-chosen photographs (eighty-two in
colour), many depicting Burmese Buddhist scenes, objects and manuscripts. There are
references to Burma throughout the book as well as a separate chapter on Burma
(p. 147-58) written by Heinz Bechert.

470 **The life or legend of Gaudama, the Buddha of the Burmese: with**
   annotations, the ways to Neibban, and notice on the phongyies or
   Burmese monks.
Paul Ambrose Bigandet. London: Kegan Paul, Trench, Trübner,
1911. 4th ed. 2 vols. in 1 (267p+326p.); Delhi: Bharatiya, 1979. 2 vols.
A careful presentation of the life of the Buddha according to the Burmese tradition
and of monastic practice and precept. Bigandet's work has undergone some changes
since its first publication under the title *The life or legend of Gaudama the Budha of the
Burmese: with annotations, notice on the phongyies or Budhist religious and ways to
Niban* (Rangoon: Pegu Press, Thos. Stowe Ranney, 1858. 327p.) The second edition
(Rangoon: American Mission Press, C. Bennett, 1866. 538p.) was much enlarged by
expanded notes and additional translations from manuscript sources providing fuller
information on episodes in the Buddha's life. The third edition (London: Trübner,
1880. 2 vols.) was a 'faithful reprint' of the 1866 edition, as was the fourth edition of
1911, with a slight title change. The main part of the book consists of a translation into
English of the *Ma-la-lin-gara wut-htu*, a Burmese translation of a Pali life of the
Buddha, with extensive notes by Bigandet and supplemented, from the second edition
onwards, by a translation of the Pali text *Tathagathaudana*, giving additional material

144

on the Buddha's life; the remainder of Bigandet's book comprises abstracts of some Jataka (stories of the previous lives of the Buddha), a long section on the Buddhist monastic order in Burma, and a summary of Buddhist metaphysics. Bigandet (1813-94), a French Catholic missionary, first came to Burma in 1837 and worked at Tavoy and Mergui until 1842, and after spending from 1842 to 1856 in Penang, returned to Burma in 1856. He established a number of schools, orphanages and convents, formed a close scholarly association with Sir Arthur Phayre (to whom he dedicated the second edition of his book), and became vice-president of the Rangoon Educational Syndicate - an unusual position for a Catholic Bishop under a British colonial government. Portions of Bigandet's *Life of the Buddha* first appeared in the *Journal of the Indian Archipelago and Eastern Asia* in 1852-55 (vols. 6-9). Bigandet was a much revered figure in British Burma and, following his death, a compilation of obituaries, memoirs, tributes and excerpts from the press was published under the title *In memoriam Right Reverend Dr. P. A. Bigandet, KCCI, FCU, Bishop of Ramatha and Vicar Apostolic of Southern Burma* (Bassein, Burma: St. Peter's Institute Press, 1894. 75p.).

471 **Burmese religion and the Burmese religious revival.**
John Frank Brohm. PhD thesis, Cornell University, Ithaca, New York, 1957. 507p. bibliog. (Available from University Microfilms, Ann Arbor, Michigan, order no. UM 20831).
Based on field work in a Burmese village in 1952-53, this anthropological study provides valuable documentation of religious life at the village level, with photographs. Burmese Buddhist practices in cosmopolitan areas are also studied. Also relevant is Brohm's article, 'Buddhism and animism in a Burmese village', *Journal of Asian Studies*, vol. 22 (Feb. 1963), p. 155-67. A critique of this study and also of Melford Spiro's *Burmese supernaturalism* (q.v.) and *Buddhism and society* (q.v.) can be found in the historiographical review of the history and sociology of Buddhism by Terence P. Day, *Great tradition and little tradition in Theravada Buddhist studies* (Lewiston, New York: Edward Mellen Press, 1988, p. 85-112. [Studies in Asian Thought and Religion, vol. 7]).

472 **On the religion and literature of the Burmas.**
Francis Buchanan. *Asiatick Researches*, vol. 6 (1799), p. 163-308.
Dr. Buchanan accompanied Michael Symes' 1795 mission to Burma, and, besides being a keen botanist - some of his plant drawings are reproduced in Michael Symes' *An account of an embassy to the kingdom of Ava sent by the Governor-General of India in the year 1795* [q.v.]) - proved himself a keen observer of Burmese matters. His article is a little-known early attempt to describe Burmese cosmography, religion and literature. Buchanan drew on three Latin treatises procured from Father Vincentius Sangermano in Burma and translated them 'intermixing them throughout with such observations, as my personal acquaintance with the subject, and my reading, have enabled me to collect'. Buchanan thus gave Sangermano's work some currency before the publication in 1833 of Sangermano's *A description of the Burmese empire* (q.v.) and also provides some details on Sangermano's sources of information saying that the treatise on Buddhism was originally written by 'a king's confessor with the intention of converting the Christians'. The other treatises were on the ordination of Buddhist monks (a translation of the *Kammavaca* text) and on Burmese Buddhist cosmography, together with illustrations of the zodiac and constellations (drawn by Joannes Moses, customs collector of Hanthawaddy and 'the most intelligent man with whom we conversed').

473 **A life of the Buddha from a Burmese manuscript.**
Edited by Michael Edwardes. London: Folio Society, 1959. 188p.
A revised and freer version (with drawings by T. J. Widdaker) of the translation of
Burmese text made a hundred years previously by the American Baptist missiona
Cephas Bennett, 'Life of Gaudama, a translation from the Burmese book entitled M
la-len-ga-ra Wottoo', *Journal of the American Oriental Society*, vol. 3 (1851), p. 1-16

474 **The symbolic dimensions of the Burmese Sangha.**
John P. Ferguson. PhD thesis, Cornell University, Ithaca, New York
1976. 298p. bibliog. (Available from University Microfilms, Ann
Arbor, Michigan, order no. UM 76-5935).
An anthropological study of the Burmese monkhood as a national religious symbo
Ferguson investigates the interrelationship of monastic and royal lineages and identifi
four basic patterns of 'symbolic bonded dimensions' preserved throughout Sang
history. Also by Ferguson is a contribution to a volume on the cross-cultural study
feminine deities, 'The great goddess today in Burma and Thailand: an exploration
her symbolic relevance to monastic and female roles', in *Mother worship: theme a*
variations edited by James J. Preston (Chapel Hill, North Carolina: University
North Carolina Press, 1982, p. 283-303) in which Ferguson discusses the popular ear
goddess figure known in Burma as Wei-thon-daya. See also the article by Ferguson a
E. Michael Mendelson, 'Masters of the Buddhist occult: the Burmese weikzas' i
Essays on Burma (q.v.) edited by John P. Ferguson. Another study by John
Ferguson is 'The quest for legitimation by Burmese monks and kings: the case of t
Shwegyin sect (19th-20th centuries)' in *Religion and legitimation of power in Thailan*
Laos and Burma edited by Bardwell L. Smith (Chambersburg, Pennsylvania: Anim
1978, p. 66-86).

475 **Folk elements in Burmese Buddhism.**
Htin Aung. London; Bombay; New York; Oxford University Press,
1962; Rangoon: Buddha Sasana Council Press, 1975; Westport,
Connecticut: Greenwood, 1978. 140p. bibliog.
An examination of folklore, alchemy, cults and *nat* (spirit) worship, and of the ne
year festival (*thingyan*), and the festival of lights. Originally presented as a series
lectures on pre-Buddhist cults of Burma, Htin Aung's study records much of the o
and traditional lore of Burma and explores its influence on Burmese Buddhism.

476 **The initiation of novicehood and the ordination of monkhood in the
Burmese Buddhist culture.**
Htun Hmat Win. Rangoon: Department of Religious Affairs, 1986.
172p.
This account is mostly useful for its details of the Buddhist texts (*Kammavaca*) used
Buddhist ordination ceremonies, and as a general introduction to the subject.

477 **Living Buddhist masters.**
Jack Kornfield. Santa Cruz, California: Unity, 1977. 322p.
This presentation of Buddhist teachings upon the practice of meditation inclue
chapters on the following Burmese teachers: Mahasi Sayadaw (p. 51-82), Sun
Sayadaw (p. 83-116), Taungpulu Sayadaw (p. 185-92), Mohnyin Sayadaw (p. 193-20

Mogok Sayadaw (p. 209-34), and U Ba Khin (p. 235-56), as well as a general introduction to meditation in Burma, Thailand and Laos, and an account of different methods. As Burmese meditation techniques have increasingly attracted Western followers, various publications have been issued in English in recent years, some by the Department of Religious Affairs, for example: Mahasi Sayadaw, *The satipatthana vipassana meditation* (Rangoon: Department of Religious Affairs, 1979), and Kyaw Min, *Introducing Buddhist Abhidhamma meditation and concentration* (Rangoon: Department of Religious Affairs, 1979). The Mahasi Sasana Yeiktha (Buddhist meditation centre) in Rangoon also publishes many texts including that of lectures by the Mahasi Sayadaw on his world missionary tours, while in the United Kingdom the Sayagyi U Ba Khin Memorial Trust has a publication series which includes *The anecdotes of Sayagyi U Ba Khin*, compiled by Chit Tin (Calne, England: Sayagyi U Ba Khin Memorial Trust, 1982). A relevant German study is Gerhard Meier, *Heutige Formen von Satipatthana-Meditationen* ('Present day forms of Satipatthana meditation') (Hamburg, GFR: 1978. 233p.), while the most detailed and recent study of Burmese meditation to date is the thesis (PhD, University of London, 1990) by Gustaaf Houtman, *Traditions of Buddhist practice in Burma*. This investigates concepts and hierarchy in Burmese Buddhism and meditation practices, with teachers' life plans, biographies, sect affiliations, lineages and a list of Mahasi centres worldwide in the period 1930-80 provided in the appendixes. For personal accounts of meditation experiences, see W. L. King, *A thousand lives away* (q.v.).

78 A thousand lives away: Buddhism in contemporary Burma.
Winston L. King.   Cambridge, Massachusetts: Harvard University Press, 1964. 238p.

Despite its title, this is primarily a study in comparative religion and draws many interesting parallels and contrasts between Christian and Buddhist beliefs and experiences. It contains a chapter on meditation and an appendix chronicling the author's ten-day course at the International Meditation Centre in Rangoon. Also by King is *Theravada meditation: the Buddhist transformation of yoga* (University Park, Pennsylvania: Pennsylvania State University Press, 1980. 172p.) which contains a chapter on contemporary Burmese forms of meditation. A fuller personal description of learning Vipassana ('insight') meditation at the Maha Bodhi Meditation Centre in Mandalay, with a description of some other Burmese centres can be found in Marie Beuzeville Byles' *Journey into Burmese silence* (London: George Allen & Unwin, 1962. 220p. bibliog.), while E. H. Shattock's *An experiment in mindfulness* (London: Rider, 1970. 2nd ed. 158p.) gives an admiral's straightforward account of learning to meditate in Burma.

79   The advent of Buddhism in Burma.
Gordon H. Luce.   In: *Buddhist studies in honour of I. B. Horner*. Edited by L. Cousins, A. Kunst, K. R. Norman. Dordrecht, Holland; Boston, Massachusetts: D. Reidel Publishing, 1974, p. 119-38.

A clear survey of early Buddhism in Burma up to the Pagan era, drawing on archaeological and inscriptional evidence.

147

480 **Sangha and state in Burma: a study of monastic sectarianism and leadership.**
E. Michael Mendelson, edited by John P. Ferguson. Ithaca, New York: London: Cornell University Press, 1975. 400p. map. bibliog.

This complex and detailed study of Burmese political and religious interaction is based on anthropological field work and documentary research in Burma in the late 1950. The book has been ably compiled and edited by Ferguson – who has written a thesis o a related subject, *The symbolic dimensions of the Burmese Sangha* (q.v.) – from th author's unfinished manuscript and notes. It is particularly useful for its level of deta on the Buddhist Order (*Sangha*) during the reign of King Mindon (1853-78) ar observations on the role of monks in nationalist politics and in independent Burma (fr the pre-1962 period). Mendelson in various articles has also examined the relationsh of Buddhism and *nat* (spirit) cults in Burma, as follows: 'Observations on a tour in th region of Mount Popa, Central Burma', *France-Asie*, vol. 179 (1963), p. 786-807; 'Th uses of religious scepticism in modern Burma', *Diogenes*, vol. 41 (1963), p. 94-116; ' messianic Buddhist association in Upper Burma', *Bulletin of the School of Oriental African Studies*, vol. 24 (1961), p. 560-80; 'The king of the weaving mountain', *Journ of the Royal Central Asian Society*, vol. 48 (1961), p. 229-37. Also relevant in th context are some studies by H. L. Shorto including his 'The 32 myos in the mediev Mon kingdom', *Bulletin of the School of Oriental & African Studies*, vol. 26, pt. (1963), p. 572-91.

481 **Anthropological studies in Theravada Buddhism.**
Manning Nash, Gananath Obeyesekere, Michael M. Ames, Jasper Ingersoll, David E. Pfanner, June C. Nash, Michael Moerman, May Ebihara, Nur Yalman. New Haven, Connecticut: Yale University Southeast Asia Studies, 1966. 223p. (Yale University Southeast Asia Studies, Cultural Report Series, no. 13).

This volume of papers contains three which focus on religious practices at the rur level in Burma, as follows: 'The Buddhist monk in rural Burmese society', by David I Pfanner (p. 77-96); 'Ritual and ceremonial cycle in Upper Burma', by Manning Na (p. 97-116); and, 'Living with Nats: an analysis of animism in Burma', by June C. Na (p. 117-36).

482 **An introduction to the study of Theravāda Buddhism in Burma: a stud in Indo-Burmese historical and cultural relations from the earliest time to the British conquest.**
Niharranjan Ray. Calcutta, India: Calcutta University Press, 1946. 306p. bibliog.

A historical study of the coming of Buddhism to Burma and its establishment ar florescence there, based on inscriptions, Burmese and Mon chronicles and Pali tex Particularly useful for its emphasis on monastic Pali scholarship, controversies ar reforms in the *Sangha* (Buddhist Order) and exchange of missions with Ceylon.

148

483 **Sanskrit Buddhism in Burma.**
Niharranjan Ray.   Calcutta, India: University of Calcutta, 1936;
Rangoon: Buddha Sasana Council Press, [1970]. 116p. bibliog.
An examination of Mahāyāna and Tantric Buddhist elements in early Burmese
Buddhism, based on iconographic and archaeological evidence and Sanskrit inscrip-
tions. With fifteen pages of black-and-white plates of images and wall paintings from
temples at Pagan. This study was written as the author's doctoral dissertation at the
University of Leiden in 1936.

484 **Modern Buddhism in Burma: being an epitome of information received
from missionaries, officials and others.**
Edited by William Charles Bernard Purser, Kenneth James Saunders.
Rangoon: Christian Literature Society, Burma Branch, 1914. 103p.
Contains a selection of replies received from over thirty correspondents to sixty-three
questions posed on the nature of Burmese Buddhism. Intended primarily as a guide to
Buddhism for Christian missionaries, it manages to contain some interesting
observations and information.

485 **Paradox and nirvana: a study of religious ultimates with special
reference to Burmese Buddhism.**
Robert Lawson Slater.   Chicago, Illinois: University of Chicago Press,
1951. 145p. bibliog.
The starting point for this study was the author's inquiry into 'what it was that
constituted Buddhism a living religion, able to inspire the loyalty of the Burmese
people through so many centuries' which in turn led him gradually to the conclusion
that 'paradoxical expression is intimately associated with vitality in religion'.

486 **Religion and politics in Burma.**
Donald Eugene Smith.   Princeton, New Jersey: Princeton University
Press, 1965. 350p.
An exploration of the interaction of religion and politics in Burma from the pre-
colonial period to the early 1960s. Burmese attempts to relate Buddhism to the
ideologies of nationalism, democracy and socialism are examined and particular
emphasis placed on U Nu's administration and the debates and decisions leading to the
establishment of Buddhism as the state religion in 1961.

487 **Buddhism and society: a great tradition and its Burmese vicissitudes.**
Melford E. Spiro.   Berkeley, California; Los Angeles, California;
London: University of California Press, 1980. 2nd ed. 510p. bibliog.
A detailed anthropological study of Buddhism as expressed in its Burmese context.
Spiro's interest and focus is the interaction between the great tradition of Theravada
Buddhism and the Burmese people's perceptions and practice of Buddhism. The
author is concerned to identify the antecedent social, cultural and psychological
conditions that might account for the persistence of Buddhism from generation to
generation and to interpret the discrepancies between textual doctrines and religious
beliefs and practices. The text of the second edition is unchanged from that of the first
(1970) edition, and expanded only by the addition of a new preface which gives an

149

excellent summary of Theravada Buddhist doctrines and, in response to some critic of the first edition, an explanation of the author's aims. For a recent anthropologica study of lay practices and beliefs in the Mandalay region, see Juliane Sybille Schober *Paths to enlightenment: Theravada Buddhism in Upper Burma* (PhD dissertation University of Illinois at Urbana-Champaign, 1989. 381p. bibliog. Available from University Microfilms, Ann Arbor, Michigan, order no. UM 9011007).

488 **Burmese supernaturalism: a study in the explanation and reduction of suffering.**
Melford E. Spiro.   Philadelphia: Institute for the Study of Human Issues, 1978. 2nd ed. 300p. bibliog.

A comprehensive study of Burmese supernatural beliefs in ghosts, demons, witche and, above all, the spirits whom the Burmese call *nat.* with detailed discussions of case of possession and rituals of exorcism. Spiro sees the function of supernaturalism a providing a more satisfying explanation of suffering than Buddhism offers, and h explores the social and psychological consequences of this, and the relationshi between the *nat* cults and Buddhism. The 1978 'expanded edition' is the same as th original edition (Englewood Cliffs, New Jersey: Prentice-Hall, 1967), except for a added thirty-six page preface in which Spiro discusses some of the book's underlyin theoretical issues, and recent scholarly debate and publications, including Charles F Keyes' *The golden peninsula: culture and adaptation in mainland Southeast Asia* (Nev York: Macmillan; London: Collier, 1977. 370p. 4 maps.). A more recent study, base on research in Burma in 1984 and 1986 and concentrating on *nat* ceremonies, witl good colour photographs, is Bénédicte Brac de la Perrière, *Les rituels de possession er Birmanie: du culte d'état aux cérémonies privées* ('Rituals of possession in Burma: fron state cult to private ceremonies') (Paris: Editions Recherche sur les Civilisations, 1989 227p.).

489 **Animism in Kengtung State.**
James Haxton Telford.   Rangoon: Zabu Meitswe Pitaka Press, 1937. [151p.]

Based on the author's divinity thesis research (PhD, University of Edinburgh, 1933), i the Eastern Shan State, this study examines the place of animism in the life an ceremonies of the people of Kengtung State from birth to death. Reprinted from a article in the *Journal of the Burma Research Society*, vol. 27, pt. 2 (August 1937) p. 87-238.

490 **The thirty-seven nats: a phase of spirit worship prevailing in Burma.**
Richard Carnac Temple.   London: W. Griggs, 1906. 71p.

A magnificent art folio volume on the Burmese spirits known as *nats* and their place i Burmese life and beliefs. The main text (p. 1-71) is preceded by a nineteen-page ful colour reproduction of the pages of a Burmese *parabaik* (folding book manuscript illustrating the thirty-seven *nats*. The text describes supernatural beliefs and spiri worship in Burma, and also includes a discussion of Burmese cosmology witl illustrations from an original 19th-century manuscript. Temple establishes an 'authenti list' of the thirty-seven *nats*, and also describes and illustrates variant cycles of *nats* The stories, legends and cults associated with each *nat* are related. Temple include black-and-white photographs of his own collection of wooden *nat* images (now in th Ashmolean Museum, Oxford), and, in eleven supplementary pages, black-and-whit line drawings of the *nats*, matching the set of full page colour illustrations. The text i mbellished throughout by superb colour and gilded designs. A supplementary work y Temple is 'A native account of the thirty-seven nats: being a translation of a rare urmese manuscript', *Indian Antiquary*, vol. 35 (1906), p. 217-27, which, according to 'emple, he 'overlooked' when preparing his *The thirty-seven nats*, and gives an lentification of each *nat* and its place in Burmese history and a description of the dress nd ceremonies for each *nat* cult. Temple (1850-1931) served in the Indian Army and, ollowing the Third Anglo-Burmese War of 1885-86, held a variety of civilian and ilitary posts in Burma as cantonment magistrate, Mandalay, assistant-commissioner 1887) and deputy-commissioner (1888), president of Rangoon Municipality and Port ommission (1891), before becoming chief commissioner of the Andaman and Nicobar slands in 1894. He became proprietor and editor of the monthly journal *Indian ntiquary* and in its pages published a long-running series of articles on Burmese oinage – 'Currency and coinage among the Burmese'. *Indian Antiquary*, vols. 26 1897), 27 (1898), 42 (1913), 48 (1919), 57 (1928), 60 (1931) – and on many other urma topics. He had a keen interest in Burmese art and archaeology in general and lso published 'Notes on antiquities in Ramannadesa (the Talaing country of Burma)', *ndian Antiquary* vol. 22 (Dec. 1893), p. 327-66 [+ 24p. of plates including a series of lazed plaques from Pegu] which was reprinted as a monograph (Bombay, India: ducation Society's Steam Press, 1894. 40p. [+ 24p. of plates]). A reprint of Temple's *he thirty-seven nats*, with an introduction by Patricia M. Herbert and a bibliography f Temple's writings on Burma, is forthcoming (London: Kiscadale, 1992).

91 **Essays on the history and Buddhism of Burma.**
Than Tun, edited by Paul Strachan. Whiting Bay, Scotland:
Kiscadale, 1988. 185p. bibliog.

eprinted in this book are ten major essays by the eminent Burmese historian,)r. Than Tun, originally published between 1959 and 1980 (mostly in the *Journal of ie Burma Research Society*), as follows: 'History of Burma 1000–1300' (p. 3-21); Religion in Burma 1000–1300' (p. 23-45); 'Social life in Burma 1044-1287' (p. 47-57); Religious buildings in Burma 1000-1300' (p. 59-67); 'The legal system in Burma 1000-300' (p. 69-83); 'Mahakassapa and his tradition' (p. 85-101); 'History of Burma 1300-400' (p. 103-15); 'Administration under King Thalun 1629–48' (p. 117-31); 'Occultism Burma' (p. 133-49); 'A history of the Shwegyin sect of Burma' (p. 151-79). A ibliography of Than Tun's publications appears on p. 181-84.

92 **History of Buddhism in Burma, AD 1000-1300.**
Than Tun. *Journal of the Burma Research Society*, vol. 61, pts. 1-2
(Dec. 1978), p. 1-265.

his substantial study is a revised and enlarged version of the author's thesis, *The uddhist church in Burma during the Pagan period (1044-1287)* (PhD thesis, University f London, 1956). Dr. Than Tun's history is based on epigraphic evidence and hallenges many versions of events given in the Burmese chronicles. The first three hapters deal with the political history of the Pagan monarchy. A further seven hapters examine in detail the nature of Buddhism in the Pagan period, its structure, nonastic organization, and religious buildings. The votive tablets of Burma are iscussed and illustrated in an appendix. A detailed bibliography, index and glossary re also provided. On votive tablets, see further the illustrated study (Burmese text) by 1ya, *Shei-haung ok-hkwet yok-pwa hsin-du-daw-mya. Votive tablets of Burma* Rangoon: Rangoon University Press, 1961. 2 vols.).

151

493 **The Sangha and Sasana in socialist Burma.**
Tin Maung Maung Than. *Sojourn*, vol. 3, no. 1 (Feb. 1988), p. 26-61.
The development of the role of the *Sangha* (Buddhist Order) in Burma as a centralized
institution is traced with special emphasis on the post-1962 period and with an analysis
of the 1980 state-purification of the *Sangha*. Also relevant is the article by Heinz
Bechert, 'The recent attempt at a reform of the Buddhist Sangha in Burma and its
implications', *Internationales Asienforum: International Quarterly for Asian Studies*,
vol. 20 (1989), p. 303-24.

494 **Buddhism: art and faith.**
Edited by Wladimir Zwalf. London: British Museum Publications,
1985. 300p. 3 maps. bibliog.
This catalogue of a joint British Museum–British Library exhibition held in London
from July 1985 to January 1986 as well as illustrating (in black-and-white and numerous
colour plates) the more than 400 items exhibited provides a lucid explanation of the
Buddhist faith and its art. It has chapters on early cult monuments, the Buddha legend,
the scriptures and their transmission, and the Buddha image, followed by chapters on
the art of each country associated with Buddhism from Afghanistan to Japan. The
chapter on Burma (p. 157-74) outlines the introduction and spread of Buddhism in
Burma, and illustrates and describes twenty-seven Burmese art objects and
manuscripts. Further information on Burma and illustrations are given in the chapter
on the transmission of Buddhist texts, while the introduction contains an account of
Buddhism in contemporary Burma.

Burma and Japan: basic studies on their cultural and social structure.
See item no. 6.

Special Burma Studies Issue.
See item no. 7.

Essays on Burma.
See item no. 10.

The soul of a people.
See item no. 13.

Historical and cultural studies in Burma.
See item no. 155.

Sri Lanka and South-East Asia.
See item no. 178.

Buddhist backgrounds of the Burmese revolution.
See item no. 545.

Burma: literature, historiography, scholarship, language, life, and Buddhism.
See item no. 649.

Burmese monk's tales.
See item no. 654.

Islam

95 The coming of Islam to Burma down to 1700 AD.
Ba Shin. *Bulletin of the Burma Historical Commission*, vol. 3 (1963), p. 1-19.

The author draws on European sources, Burmese inscriptions and chronicles and the evidence of coinage and language to present a pioneering account of the influence of Islam in Burma, with special emphasis upon Arakan. A list of Arabic and Persian loan words is given. Ba Shin's paper was originally presented at the Asian History Congress, New Delhi, in December 1961.

96 The acculturation of the Burmese Muslims.
Khin Khin Su. Rangoon: [The Author], 1960. 135p. bibliog.

This thesis (MA, Rangoon University, 1960) examines the history and place of Muslims in Burmese society.

97 The Muslims of Burma: a study of a minority group.
Moshe Yegar. Wiesbaden, GFR: Otto Harrassowitz, 1972. 151p. map. bibliog. (Schriftenreihe des Südasien–Instituts der Universität Heidelberg).

This trailblazing and, to date, unsurpassed study of the Muslim community in Burma covers from the 11th century to 1962. The author, an Israeli diplomat, conducted his research in Burma in 1960-62 and was able to interview informants and to draw on many source materials unavailable outside Burma. The bibliography constitutes a valuable reference source for this material. The book has chapters on the beginnings of Muslim settlement in Burma and in Arakan, on Muslims under British colonial rule, on Muslims in independent Burma, and on Muslim community life. It gives details of Muslim societies and organizations, and considers the position of Burmese Muslims, Indian Muslims and Arakanese Muslims, the interactions of the various groups with each other and with state authority and the Burmese Buddhist majority. The appendixes contain statistical data, legislation on Islamic subjects, documents of the General Council of Burman Moslem Associations, and details of the Muslim press in Burma. Also by Yegar is 'The Muslims in Burma' in *The crescent in the East: Islam in Asia Major*, edited by Raphael Israeli (London: Curzon, 1982, p. 102-39) which reviews Burma's Muslim population from the 19th century to the 1970s, with a discussion of the difference between the Indian Muslims of Burma and the Burmese Muslims.

Christianity

498 **The early Catholic missionaries in Burma: a study of the manuscripts and the first casting and printing of Burmese alphabets, outline grammar, and catechism in 1776, from Latin, Italian, Portuguese and French sources.**
Vivian Ba. *Guardian*, vol. 9 (Aug. 1962), p. 17-20; (Sept. 1962), p. 17-20; (Oct. 1962), p. 21-24; (Nov. 1962), p. 29-32; (Dec. 1962), p. 20-24.

This well-researched series of articles focuses on early printing and the books printed by the Press of the Propaganda de Fide in Rome from 1776 onwards, beginning with the *Alphabetum Barmanum*, and also provides many details of Catholic missionary and educational work in Burma. Also by Ba is 'Odyssey of the first Burmese type', *Journal of the Burma Research Society*, vol. 45, pt. 2 (1962), p. 209-13. Other relevant articles by Ba include 'One centenary recalls another', *Journal of the Burma Research Society*, vol. 46, pt. 1 (June 1963), p. 65-79 on a little-known Italian history of missionary activity in Burma by Luigi Gallo published in 1862, and '110th anniversary of Gallo's manuscript 1859-1969', *Journal of the Burma Research Society*, vol. 54, pts. 1-2 (Dec. 1971), p. 115-17 with details of an 18th-century Barnabite botanical work and map. A rare source is Paul Ambrose Bigandet, *An outline of the history of the Catholic Burmese Mission from the year 1720 to 1887* (Rangoon: [s.n.], 1887), while A. Darne, *Aux rives de l'Iraouaddy* ('On the banks of the Irrawaddy') (Hong Kong: Imprimerie de la Société des Missions-Etrangères de Paris, 1931. 196p. map.) also gives a brief history of Catholic missions in Burma (p. 181-95), plus many observations on Burmese Buddhism. Details of other missionary and printing activities can be found in B. R. Pearn's article 'Felix Carey and the English Baptist Mission in Burma' (q.v.).

499 **Mission for life: the story of the family of Adoniram Judson, the dramatic events of the first American foreign mission, and of the course of evangelical religion in the nineteenth century.**
Joan Jacobs Brumberg. New York: Free Press; London: Collier Macmillan, 1980. 302p. bibliog.

This refreshingly non-hagiographical study of the first American Baptist missionary to Burma. Adoniram Judson (1788-1850), his wives and descendants, is set against the wider background of the evangelical movement in 19th-century America and emphasizes the importance of women in the movement. Its bibliography is conveniently divided into a listing of 'works by the Judsons' and 'primary and secondary sources dealing specifically with the Judsons'. Genealogical charts are given on the end papers.

500 **Sketches from the Karen hills.**
Alonzo Bunker. New York, London: Fleming H. Revell, 1910. 215p.

Episodes from forty years' American Baptist missionary work from 1866 to 1906 among the Karenni and the Karens of Toungoo, with an account of the foundation of the Loikaw Mission. By the same author is *Soo Thah: a tale of the making of the Karen nation* (London; Edinburgh: Oliphant, Anderson & Ferrier, 1902. 280p.), a narrative about a Karen convert to Christianity.

501 **Self-support illustrated in the history of the Bassein Karen Mission from 1840 to 1880.**
Chaplin Howard Carpenter.   Boston, Massachusetts: Rand, Avery, Franklin Press, 1883. 426p.
This history of American missionary work among the Karens of Bassein District is compiled, with copious quotations, from original reports and letters – especially those of the Rev. E. L. Abbott (1809-54) and J. S. Beecher (1820-66) – and has illustrations of Karen Christians, churches and schools.

502 **Mission in Burma: the Columban Fathers' forty-three years in Kachin country.**
Edward Fischer.   New York: Seabury, 1980. 164p. map.
A well-told story of the heartaches, satisfactions and humour that the priests of the Columban Fathers' Mission experienced while living among the Kachins and Shans of Upper Burma from 1936 to 1979.

503 **A history of American Baptist missions in Asia, Africa, Europe and North America.**
William Gammell.   Boston, Massachusetts: Gould, Kendall & Lincoln, 1849. 359p. maps.
An official history compiled from documents and reports of the American Baptist Mission as well as from the journals of individual missionaries. It provides a useful chronological narrative of American Baptist missionary enterprise in Burma (p. 1-186).

504 **A brief history of the planting and growth of the church in Burma.**
Kawl Thang Vuta.   D. Miss. thesis. Fuller Theological Seminary, 1983. 363p. (Available from University Microfilms, Ann Arbor Michigan, order no. UM 8322605).
This dissertation surveys the introduction of Christianity to Burma, missionary medical and educational work in the 19th and 20th centuries and the problems facing the church in Burma today.

505 **Christian progress in Burma.**
Alexander McLeish.   London: World Dominion Press 1929. 100p. maps.
This work surveys the work of different Christian missionary societies in Burma, with statistical information in the appendixes and an account of translations of the Bible into the languages of Burma. A map showing the location of Burma mission stations is provided.

506 **Felix Carey and the English Baptist Mission in Burma.**
Bertie Reginald Pearn.   *Journal of the Burma Research Society*, vol. 30, pt. 1 (1938), p. 1-91.
This article documents the eccentric career of Felix Carey (d. 1822) and early Baptist printing in Burmese at Serampore, India and in Burma. Also relevant is Pearn's Burmese printed books before Judson', *Journal of the Burma Research Society*,

vol. 30, pt. 1 (1940), p. 384-85. For a useful survey of early printing, see Dennis E Rhodes, *The spread of printing: India, Pakistan, Ceylon, Burma and Thailand* (Amsterdam: Vangendt; London: Routledge & Kegan Paul, 1969) whose Burma chapter (p. 79-89) contains details in particular of early printing at the Karen Mission Press (of Karen dictionaries and vocabularies by Jonathan Wade and Cephas Bennett) Frank Dennis Phinney, *The American Baptist Mission Press: historical, descriptive 1816-1916* (Rangoon: American Baptist Mission Press, 1916. 80p.) gives details of the equipment, publications and missionaries associated with this Press, with photos of the presses and staff.

507 **Christian missions in Burma.**
William Charles Bertrand Purser, preface by Arthur M. Knight.
London: Society for the Propagation of the Gospel in Foreign Parts,
1911. 246p. map. bibliog.

An account primarily of Anglican missions in Burma with a brief notice of Baptist missions, and of ministering to different racial communities, with a discussion of Buddhism. Includes details and photos of individual missionaries and churchmen and women. Brief details of the Rangoon Diocesan Association and of Anglican school and orphanages in Burma are listed in the appendix.

508 **Full fifty years: the BCMS story.**
Stanley Farrant Russell. London: Patmos, 1972. 89p.

This publication commemorating fifty years of the Bible Churchmen's Missionary Society contains a chapter on Burma (p. 14-20) with details of the missionaries who worked there in the period 1924 to 1966. The author spent seventeen years as a medical missionary in Burma, and tells of the wartime evacuation of BCMS missionaries in *Muddy exodus: a story of the evacuation of Burma, May 1942* (London Epworth, 1943, 64p.). An earlier account of BCMS work among the Kachins in Upper Burma in the 1920s and 1930s is provided by Arthur Theodore Houghton, *Dense jungle green: the first twelve years of the B.C.M.S. Burma Mission* (London: Bible Churchmen's Missionary Society, 1937. 255p. map. bibliog.) and by his *Tailum Jan Christian widow in the wild mountains of Upper Burma* (London: Morgan, Marshall & Scott, 1930. 114p. map.). An interesting thesis focusing on the Bible Churchmen' Missionary Society work in Arakan is that by Ann N. Nason, *The adoption and diffusion of Christianity amongst the Khumi-Chin people of the Upper Kaladan river area of Arakan, North-West Burma from 1900 to 1966* (with an appendix up-date to 1988) (MA thesis, University of Warwick, Coventry, England, 1988. 170p.).

509 **A century of growth: the Kachin Baptist Church of Burma.**
Herman G. Tegenfeldt. South Pasadena, California: William Carey
Library, 1974. 512p. 8 maps. bibliog.

The author and his family served as American Baptist missionaries in Burma, primarily among the Kachins, for twenty-five years until 1966 (when foreign missionaries were ordered by the Burmese government to leave). His book provides a definitive history of the Kachin Baptist Church and is divided into three parts: part one gives background to the Kachins (covering language, history, social structure, religion customs, folklore, etc.); part two presents a history of the Church and its growth, with details of the first missionaries (E. Kincaird, A. Taylor Rose, Francis Mason, C. H Carpenter, Josiah N. Cushing); part three analyses growth factors, missionary motivations, attitudes, goals and methods, and Kachin leadership.

510 **Burma through missionary eyes: views of the Burmese in the nineteenth century.**
Helen G. Trager.   New York: Frederick A. Praeger; London: Asia Publishing, 1966. 239p. map. bibliog.

This book discusses the nature and implications of Christian missionary writings on Burma from the late 18th century to the mid-19th century. The author believes that the predominantly negative portrayal of the Burmese in missionary writings can be accounted for by the missionaries' lack of success in making converts, by their poor opinion of Buddhism, and by the difficulties of life in an isolated, alien, and often hostile environment. The study concentrates on American missionaries in Burma, beginning in 1813 with the American Baptist Mission of Adoniram and Ann Judson. There is also, however, useful information on the arrival of Christianity in Burma and on the work of the first Catholic missions. A plan of the royal city of Ava is given on the book's endpapers. Appendix IV contains a note on Gaetanao M. Mantegazza (1745-94), a Barnabite missionary whose manuscript account of Burma predates the better-known account by Father Sangermano, *A description of the Burmese empire* (q.v.) and represents the first detailed account of Burma based on direct observation. Although Sangermano's account was first published in English translation in Rome in 1833, Mantegazza's was unknown until it was edited by Renzo Carmignani and published under the title *La Birmania: relazione inedita del 1784 del missionario Barnabita G. M. Mantegazza* ('Burma: an unpublished account of 1784 by the Barnabite missionary G. M. Mantegazza') (Rome: Ed. A. S., 1950. 208p. maps. bibliog.). In this Carmignani provides an introduction to missionary enterprise in Burma and to Mantegazza's life (p. 11-79), followed by Mantegazza's original French text (p. 83-196), *Relation des royaumes d'Ava et Pegou* ('Account of the kingdoms of Ava and Pegu'), with a map of Burma by Mantegazza and title pages of Propaganda de Fide imprints of the 1780s, and three appendixes in Italian containing letters and observations by fellow Italian missionaries Giovanni Maria Percoto and Guiseppe d'Amato.

511 **The land of the gold pagoda: the story of the Burma Mission of the Methodist Missionary Society.**
F. Deauville Walker.   London: Cargate Press, [1935]. 152p.

Traces missionary and educational work in Burma from its beginnings in 1887, with a listing of Methodist missionaries in Burma. Also relevant is *Methodism in Burma* (Halifax, England: Halifax Methodist Circuit, 1986. 24p.) which gives a brief history of Methodist missionary work in Burma and extracts from the memoirs of Dorothy Emma Mackley (1910-85), a missionary in Burma from 1940-42 and from 1949-59. (Copies may be obtained from Halifax Methodist Circuit, c/o Russell House, 19 Raw Lane, Illingworth, Halifax HX2 8JD).

To the golden shore: the life of Adoniram Judson.
See item no. 341.

Bibliotheca Catholica Birmana.
See item no. 838.

Judaism

512 **The last Burmese Jews.**
Ruth Fredman Cernea. *B'nai B'rith International Jewish Monthly*
(Washington, DC), vol. 102, no. 10 (June/July 1988), p. 26-30.

This article surveys the history of the Jewish community in Burma and the Rangoon synagogue, built in 1857, and describes the tiny remaining Jewish community in Burma.

Society, Health and Medicine

513 **Drugs, the US, and Khun Sa.**
Francis W. Belanger.   Bangkok: Editions Duong Kamal, 1987. 146p.
map. bibliog.
This study of the world-wide narcotics problem focuses on the Golden Triangle, with
much material on Burma – the largest producer of illicit opium – and on the role of the
Shan warlord Khun Sa and others in the heroin trade; with statistics on drug
production in Burma. An earlier study which gives an account of opium production
and traffic in the Golden Triangle and of the Shan States Army is that by Alfred W.
McCoy, *The politics of heroin in Southeast Asia* (New York; London: Harper & Row,
1972. 464p.), but it is now rather dated. See also Bertil Lintner's *The Shans and the
Shan States of Burma* (q.v.).

514 **Narcotics report 1988.**
Central Committee for Drug Abuse Control, Union of Burma.
Rangoon: CCDAC, Ministry of Home & Religious Affairs, 1989. 114p.
An illustrated government report describing the work of the Central Committee for
Drug Abuse Control (CCDAC), law enforcement activities, crop substitution and
livestock introduction programmes, social and vocational rehabilitation of drug addicts,
preventive drug education and mass media campaigns; with Burma drug abuse data
and extracts from the Burma press deploring the US decision to terminate aid. For a
general study with brief entries on Burma under the headings of drug abuse, treatment
and rehabilitation, and legal enforcement measures, see *Drug abuse in East Asia* by
C. P. Spencer and V. Navaratnam (Kuala Lumpur: Oxford University Press, 1981.
227p. bibliog.).

515 **Handbook of biological data on Burma.**
Khin Maung Lwin, Mya Tu. Rangoon: Burma Medical Research
Institute, 1967. 291p. (Special Report Series, no. 3).

A compilation of basic biological data on man in Burma, divided into the following
sections: environment, population, morphology, nutrition, metabolism, blood, car-
diovascular, digestive, urinary, health, and vital statistics. Another report, compiled by
the Technical Committee of the Burma Medical Research Council, and giving data on
Burmese fitness, stature and growth rates and nutrition is *Physical fitness of the
Burmese* (Rangoon: Burma Medical Research Institute, 1968. 71p. bibliog. [Special
Report Series, no. 5.]).

516 **The practice of medicine among the Burmese, translated from original
manuscripts, with an historical sketch of the progress of medicine from
the earliest times.**
Keith Norman MacDonald. Edinburgh: MacLachlan & Stewart, 1879;
New York: AMS, 1979. 268p.

The first part of this book (p. 1-71) contains a brief introduction to Burma followed by
the first detailed description to be published in English of the Burmese system of
medicine, compiled and translated from Burmese manuscript sources. MacDonald
(b. 1834) was a medical officer stationed at Prome and he provides comments based on
his own personal observations, such as that the Burmese have long practised
innoculation against smallpox. The second part of the book, unrelated to Burma,
(p. 72-260) gives a descripton of the principles and progress of Western medicine.

517 **Little change in rural Burma: a case study of a Burmese village (1960-
80).**
Mya Than. *Sojourn*, vol. 2, no. 1 (Feb. 1987), p. 55-88.

An attempt to trace the extent to which social and economic changes have occurred in
a Lower Burman village over two decades. Another case study using data from field
studies made in 1956, 1969 and 1978 is Mya Than's 'A Burmese village revisited' in
Seven probes in rural Southeast Asia: socio-economic and anthropological, edited by
Barend Jan Terwiel (Gaya, India: Centre for South East Asian Studies, 1979, p. 1-15).
For an earlier village study, see Charles S. Brant, *Tadagale: a Burmese village in 1950*
(Ithaca, New York: Cornell University, 1954. 41p. [Cornell University Southeast Asia
Program Data Paper, no. 13]).

518 **Urbanization and economic development in Burma.**
Naing Oo. *Sojourn*, vol. 4, no. 2 (Aug. 1989), p. 233-60.

An investigation of levels, trends and causes of urbanization, the relative contributions
of various components of urban growth, the availability of urban services, and urban
poverty. The author is not optimistic, given Burma's 'dire economy and failure to take
account of urbanization' in its national development policies, about the urban future of
Burma.

519 **The golden road to modernity: village life in contemporary Burma.**
Manning Nash. New York; London: John Wiley, 1965; Chicago;
London: University of Chicago Press, 1973. 333p. maps. bibliog.
A major anthropological study based on field work in two villages of Upper Burma.
Nash presents a wealth of data on social and political organization and religious beliefs
and practices and compares a mixed dry crop farming community with an irrigated rice
growing community. Nash's concern is the process of social change and the problems
encountered at village level when land reform and development programmes are
formulated by an urban élite without consulting the rural majority. Writing in the early
1960s, he is optimistic about Burma's future, but cautions: 'If Burma does not succeed
in developing a modern economic, political, and social structure, it will be a failure of
human effort, a matter of social and cultural variables, a case of organizational and
ideological inadequacy'. Also by Nash is *Unfinished agenda: the dynamics of
modernization in developing nations* (Boulder, Colorado; London: Westview, 1984.
148p.) which analyses social change since decolonization and has extensive references
to Burma throughout.

520 **Kinship and marriage in Burma: a cultural and psychodynamic analysis.**
Melford E. Spiro. Berkeley, California; Los Angeles, California;
London: University of California Press, 1977. 313p. bibliog.
A detailed description and analysis of kinship, family and marriage, based on research
and interviews conducted in Upper Burma and Thailand. It deals with cultural
concepts of kinship and kin relations, the village context of Burmese family relations,
kinship and forms of marriage, and interpersonal and sexual aspects of marriage.
Spiro's study emphasizes the psychological dimensions of his subject and provides the
first major exposition of Burmese kinship.

521 **Collaboration in health development in South East Asia 1948-1988.**
New Delhi: World Health Organization, Regional Office for South-
East Asia, 1988. 548p. map. bibliog. (SEARO Regional Publications,
no. 19).
This solidly researched (primarily by Dr. Mya Tu) work, commemorating the fortieth
anniversary of the World Health Organization (WHO), traces chronologically the
development and expansion of WHO's work in the regions member states (namely,
Thailand, India, Burma, Sri Lanka, Indonesia, Nepal, Mongolia, Maldives, Bangladesh,
North Korea, Bhutan). It contains much information and statistical data on health
infrastructure, resources and programmes, and diseases in Burma.

The world of Burmese women.
See item no. 21.

The Burman: his life and notions.
See item no. 27.

The army medical services campaigns: vol. 5, Burma.
See item no. 263.

Burma surgeon.
See item no. 349.

Burma, nationalism and ideology: an analysis of society, culture and politics.
See item no. 550.

Intellectuals and the national vision: the Burmese case.
See item no. 645.

Who's who in medicine in Burma.
See item no. 827.

Annotated bibliography of medical literature on Burma (1866-1976).
See item no. 841.

Politics and Government

522 Burma: extrajudicial execution and torture of members of ethnic minorities.

London: Amnesty International, 1988. 71p. map.

The accounts given in this report (AI Index: ASA/16/05/88), compiled from interviews with refugees in Thailand, document a pattern of extrajudicial execution and torture of unarmed minority (Karen, Kachin and Mon) villagers since 1984 carried out by members of Burma's armed forces engaged on counter-insurgency operations. A supplementary report (AI Index: ASA 16/10/88), *Burma: extrajudicial execution, torture and political imprisonment of members of the Shan and other ethnic minorities* (London: Amnesty International, 1988. 25p.) and supplementary *Bulletins* issued by Amnesty International are based primarily on interviews with Shan refugees. Further (1991) Amnesty International reports include *Myanmar (Burma): continuing killings and ill-treatment of minority peoples* (AI Index: ASA 16/05/91) and *Thailand: concerns about treatment of Burmese refugees* (AI Index: ASA 39/15/91).

523 Myanmar 'in the national interest': prisoners of conscience, torture, summary trials under martial law.

London: Amnesty International, 1990. 55p. map.

This report (AI Index: ASA 16/10/90) documents human rights' violations in Burma in the period of pro-democracy demonstrations in 1988 and in the period following the military coup of 18 September 1988, and examines martial law, and arrest, detention and judicial procedures under martial law, with profiles of prisoners and details of torture methods and individual cases. Also published simultaneously by Amnesty International is a seventeen-page illustrated document *Myanmar: Amnesty International briefing* which gives a profile of Burma and of the events during 1988-90. An earlier report by Amnesty International is *Myanmar (Burma): prisoners of conscience, a chronicle of developments since September 1988* (London: Amnesty International, 1989. 77p. [Reference no. AI Index: ASA 16/28/89]). This reviews the background to the establishment of rule in Burma by the military junta, the State Law and Order Restoration Council (SLORC) in September 1988, and chronicles martial law

163

proclamations, the position of political parties and student groups, demonstrations and arrests since that date, with a listing of over one hundred prisoners of conscience who are 'being held solely for the exercise of their rights to hold opinions and to express them freely without having used or advocated violence'. The US State Department's annual *Human Rights Report* for 1990 also strongly condemns Burma's 'deplorable human rights situation'. The *Amnesty International Report* (London: Amnesty International, 1980-) also provides an annual review of the situation in Burma.

524 **Human rights in Burma (Myanmar).**
New York: Asia Watch, 1990. 58p.

This report examines the political events of 1988 and their aftermath, with sections on human rights in Burma, portering as practised by the Burma Army (the enforced enlistment of local people to act as porters), violations against civilians in rural areas, violations by the guerrillas, and US policy and Burmese refugees in Thailand. Asia Watch also issues regular updates on the Burma situation in their series 'News from Asia Watch'. Copies may be obtained from Asia Watch, 485 Fifth Avenue, New York NY10017, USA.

525 **The roots of the revolution: a brief history of the Defence Services of the Union of Burma and the ideals for which they stand.**
Ba Than. Rangoon: Director of Information, 1962. 86p. maps. bibliog.

A brief, illustrated history of the Burma Army up to the military coup of 2 March 1962, with the emphasis on wartime patriotism and postwar idealism. Written by a retired colonel of the 4th Burma Rifles, it was first published in Burma's *The Guardian* newspaper on 27 March 1962.

526 **Politics among Burmans: a study of intermediary leaders.**
John H. Badgley. Athens, Ohio: Ohio University Center for International Studies, 1970. 115p. (Southeast Asia Series, no. 15).

The field research for this empirical study of intermediary leadership was conducted just before Ne Win's military coup in 1962. The author examines changes from community to state consciousness and argues that Burma's 'revolution' has failed to tap the ability of local leaders. A more wide-ranging study by Badgley which examines significant political traditions under the kings and during British rule, the polity and parties (Anti-Fascist People's Freedom League and the Communists), politics and administration, politicians and the military is *Progress and polity in Burma* (PhD thesis, University of California, Berkeley, California, 1962. [Available from Inter-library Loan Service, Photoduplication Section, The General Library, University of California, Berkeley, CA 94720]).

527 **Burma's golden triangle: on the trail of the opium warlords.**
André Boucaud, Louis Boucaud; translated from the French by Diana-Lee Simon, revised and edited by Lesley D. Clark. Hong Kong: Asia 2000; Bangkok: Pacific Rim, 1988. 187p. 6 maps. bibliog. (Burma Reader Series).

First published in French under the title *Birmanie: sur la piste des seigneurs de la guerre* (Paris: L'Harmattan, 1985), this English language edition contains some updated material. The authors have travelled extensively into the remote and dangerous

Golden Triangle, centre of opium cultivation, and report on their meetings with separatist armies, mercenary bands and opium warlords. They trace the history of Burma's ethnic separatist struggles and unravel its cultural and political complexities, concluding: 'A political compromise is needed to solve this long struggle. Putting an end to the civil war which destroys both the people and the economy is the only way to eradicate the opium trade'.

528   **Army's accumulation of economic power in Burma 1940-1990.**
       Burma Review, no. 20 (Oct. 1990), p. 17-22.
This text of a paper, authorship unindicated (apparently by U Thaung) presented at the Burma Seminar held in Washington, DC in October 1990, chronicles the Burma Army's involvement in business and economic affairs, describing the activities of the Defence Service Institute founded in 1951 and its takeover of private sector enterprises during the period of Ne Win's caretaker government (1958-60), and the setting up of the Burma Economic Development Corporation. The socialist economic policies pursued by the Revolutionary Council after Ne Win's military coup of 1962 and the military government's nationalization of private and foreign enterprises (including DSI and BEDC) are analysed and the building of the Burmese Way to Socialism 'to eliminate the exploitation of man by man' is characterized as 'a new system of exploitation of man by the army'. The change under SLORC from Burmese socialism to an avowedly open market economic system, the State-Owned Economic Enterprise Law of March 1989 and the establishment in February 1990 of the Union of Myanmar Holding Company Limited are also examined and the increase in the military's 'self-endowed economic power' charted. In the same issue of *Burma Review* are excerpts from other papers delivered at the Burma Seminar including Josef Silverstein's 'Burma's six domestic challenges in the 1990s' (p. 14-16); Court Robinson's 'Burmese refugees in Thailand' (p. 23-25); and, Thant Myint-U's 'Prospects for change in Burma' (p. 26-27, p. 31).

529   **La Birmanie ou la quête de l'unité: le problème de la cohesion nationale**
       dans la Birmanie contemporaine et sa perspective historique. (Burma or
       the quest for unity: the problem of national cohesion in contemporary
       Burma and its historical perspective.)
       Pierre Fistié.   Paris: Ecole Française d'Extrême-Orient, 1985. 459p.
       2 maps. bibliog. (Publications de l'Ecole Française d'Extrême-Orient,
       vol. 139).
The author's theme is that Burma's present-day quest for unity can only be understood in the context not only of Burma's colonial past but above all of pre-existing ancient problems. Introductory chapters describe Burma's ethnic heterogeneity and problems, followed by chapters analysing the 1947 constitution, the prelude to the 1962 military takeover, the economy under the Ne Win régime, military and political attempts to end the ethnic rebellions, and, finally, a chapter on the Burma Communist Party, the communist rebels and on relations between Rangoon and Peking. The author sees no short term solution to Burma's ethnic conflicts and concludes 'the causes of the divisions which exist at the heart of Burma can, in the final analysis, be considered as the main reason for its political choices'. It provides a more up-to-date coverage than Josef Silverstein's *Burmese politics: the dilemma of national unity* (q.v.).

530 **Die Kommunistische Partei Birmas: von den Anfangen bis zur**
Gegenwart. (The Communist Party of Burma from its beginnings to the
present day.)
Klaus Fleischmann. Hamburg, GFR: Institut für Asienkunde,
1989. 431p. bibliog. (Mitteilungen des Instituts für Asienkunde
Hamburg, no. 171).
A detailed study of the Communist Party of Burma, with copious quotations in English
from a wide range of sources. The appendixes contain details of the Party's
organization and structure, names of central and regional committee members, and
brief biographies of leading Burmese communists. There is also a companion volume
in English entitled *Documents on communism in Burma 1945-1977*, edited by Klaus
Fleischmann (Hamburg: Institut für Asienkunde, 1989. 278p. bibliog. [Mitteilungen
des Instituts für Asienkunde Hamburg, no. 172]). Fleischmann provides a useful
historical introduction to each set of key documents, as well as remarks and notes on
the source and text of each individual document.

531 **The governance of modern Burma.**
John Sydenham Furnivall. New York: Institute of Pacific Relations,
International Secretariat, 1960. 2nd ed. 154p.
First published in 1958, this edition is enlarged by an introductory 'Appreciation' of
J. S. Furnivall (1878-1960) by F. N. Trager and by a 'Supplement' (p. 133-54) by John
Seabury Thompson on the 1958-60 Caretaker Government of Ne Win. Furnivall was
an Indian Civil Service administrator in Burma from 1902-31, and returned to Burma
for the period 1948-59 as Adviser on National Planning to the government of the
Union of Burma. His *Governance* gives an historical account of the pre-independence
years, followed by an analysis of the machinery of central, regional and local
government. Furnivall's thesis was that the 'forms of government inherited from
British rule were as little suited to the new functions of government of independent
Burma as were the forms originally inherited from Burmese rule' and his study
addressed the problems of the adaptation of form to function. His study contains a
frankly written 'post mortem' on the collapse of the AFPFL (Anti-Fascist People's
Freedom League) government in 1958.

532 **Bureaucratic transformation in Burma.**
James F. Guyot. In: *Asian bureaucratic systems emergent from the*
British imperial tradition. Edited by Ralph Braibanti. Durham, North
Carolina: Duke University Press, 1966. p. 354-443.
Based on field work in Burma in 1961 and 1962, this study examines the changes in
Burma's bureaucracy since independence and also provides a valuable analysis of the
bureaucratic structure developed by the British in Burma. A useful study of the
colonial period system of administration is that by Frank Siegfried Vernon Donnison,
Public administration in Burma: a study of development during the British connexion
(London: Royal Institute of International Affairs, 1953. 119p. bibliog.). Khin Maung
Kyi's *Patterns of accommodation to bureaucratic authority in a transitional culture: a*
sociological analysis of Burmese bureaucrats with respect to their orientations towards
authority (PhD thesis, Cornell University, Ithaca, New York, 1966. 283p. bibliog.
Available from University Microfilms, Ann Arbor, Michigan, order no. UM 66-10274)
analyses the post-colonial period Burma Civil Service and the perceptions of its
members.

533 **Myanmar in 1989: Tatmadaw V.**
James F. Guyot, John H. Badgley. *Asian Survey*, vol. 30, no. 2 (Feb. 1990), p. 187-95.

A clear survey of Burma under the rule of the State Law and Order Restoration Council (SLORC) junta, reviewing martial law and politics, and economic measures (privatizations, joint ventures) and foreign policy innovations. The authors see continuities between the political actions of SLORC and those of the Revolutionary Government in the period 1962-74 when all dissent was effective crushed. They point to evidence of a quickening pace of change and to the narrowing of the SLORC régime's options brought about by the curtailment of new foreign aid programmes. A survey article a year later by James F. Guyot, 'Myanmar in 1990: the unconsummated election' *Asian Survey*, vol. 31, no. 2 (Feb. 1991), p. 205-11, examines SLORC's response to the elections of 27 May 1990 which the 'NLD clearly won and SLORC clearly lost', with a table giving the election results and percentage of seats and votes won by each party.

534 **Post-election Myanmar: a popular mandate withheld.**
Washington, DC: International Human Rights Law Group, 1990. 18p.

This report, prepared by the International Human Rights Law Group (a non-governmental and nonpartisan independent organization of lawyers), assesses the legitimacy of SLORC to rule Burma and of its Declaration 1/90 (issued by SLORC on 27 July 1990) from which SLORC claims it derives its authority. SLORC continues to hold onto power against the will of the citizens of Burma as expressed in the elections of May 1990 for a Pyei-thu Hlut-taw (People's Assembly) when over eighty per cent of the seats were won by representatives of the National League for Democracy. The report concludes that the SLORC government is unconstitutional and illegitimate under both international and national law and that the People's Assembly alone can be regarded as the lawful and legitimate government of Burma. It further states that the question of whether or not a new constitution is to be drafted is a decision to be made by the People's Assembly and calls upon the United Nations and individual governments to urge SLORC to transfer power to the elected civilian government of Burma. Copies are available from the International Human Rights Law Group, 1601 Connecticut Avenue NW, Suite 700, Washington, DC 20009. Another recent publication, this time emanating from the Lawyers Committee for Human Rights, is *Summary injustice: military tribunals in Burma (Myanmar)* (New York: Lawyers Committee for Human Rights, 1991. 63p. map.) which examines the proceedings of the military tribunals established by SLORC in 1989 and their contravention of fair trial procedures as mandated by international law. Copies may be obtained from Lawyers Committee for Human Rights, 330 Seventh Avenue, 10th Floor, New York, NY 10001, USA.

535 **Military rule in Burma since 1962: a kaleidoscope of views.**
Edited by Frederick K. Lehman. Singapore: Maruzen Asia, issued under the auspices of the Institute of Southeast Asian Studies, 1981. 81p.

A collection of six short papers on political and economic aspects of Burma in the period 1962-80 as follows 'Foreign policy of Burma since 1962: negative neutralism for group survival' by Maung Maung Gyi (p. 9-28); 'Burmese economics: the conflict of ideology and pragmatism' by David I. Steinberg (p. 29-50); 'Minority problems in Burma since 1962' by Josef Silverstein (p. 51-58); 'Tradition in the service of

167

revolution: the political symbolism of taw-lhan-ye-khit' by Jon Wiant (p. 59-72); 'Comments on the recent situation in Burma' by Edward W. Martin (p. 73-78); 'Some reflections on contemporary Burma' by Charles F. Keyes (p. 79-81).

536 **Aung San Suu Kyi and Burma's unfinished renaissance.**
Bertil Lintner. London: Peacock, 1990. 33p. bibliog.

A brief portrait of Aung San Suu Kyi (1945-), daughter of Burma's independence hero General Aung San, and of her emergence in 1988 as leader of Burma's pro-democracy movement, with an account of political events in Burma 1988-90. Aung San Suu Kyi, who has been under house arrest in Rangoon since July 1989, won the 1990 Sakharov Prize (the European Parliament's human rights and freedom of thought award) and was awarded the 1991 Nobel Peace Prize. A compilation and translation of her speeches and writings entitled *Freedom from fear*, edited by her husband Michael Aris, is forthcoming (Harmondsworth, England: Penguin, 1991).

537 **Outrage: Burma's struggle for democracy.**
Bertil Lintner. London: White Lotus UK; Bangkok: White Lotus, 1990. rev. ed. 208p.

A revised updated edition of the work which quickly sold out when first published in 1989 (Hong Kong: Review Publishing). It gives the fullest account to date of the dramatic events of 1988 when mass pro-democracy demonstrations against the rule of Ne Win and his Burma Socialist Programme Party ended in the demonstrators' brutal suppression and a resumption of power by the Burma Army. Compiled by Bertil Lintner, the Bangkok-based correspondent of the *Far Eastern Economic Review*, from first-hand observation and corroborated by other sources and eye-witness accounts, with photographs of the demonstrations and of key personalities, a chronology of events in Burma from 10 August 1987 to 13 March 1990, and profiles of the main dramatis personae. *Outrage* was denounced in Burma's state-controlled *Working People's Daily* newspaper of 14 September 1989 as 'a pot-pourri of maliciously selected misrepresentations, misinterpretations, fabrications and rumour-sourced disinformation about the Myanmar Naing-Ngan put together into book form by past master of malice, foreign journalist Bertil Lintner'.

538 **The rise and fall of the Communist Party of Burma (CPB).**
Bertil Lintner. Ithaca, New York: Southeast Asia Program, Cornell University, 1990. 111p. 14 maps. (Southeast Asia Program Series, no. 6).

A lucid and up-to-date study of the Communist Party of Burma, with photographs of CPB leaders and brief biographies (p. 55-70) deriving from the author's several months' research in the CPB base areas and interviews with many of its leaders. Lintner traces the history of the CPB from its origins, and describes its shift to an underground insurgent organization, ideological and leadership splits, links with Chinese Communism, political and military strategies, its diverse ethnic membership and, finally, the CPB's disintegration in April 1989 when a 'mutiny' by rank-and-file members forced its ageing Burman Maoist leaders to flee into China. Lintner concludes with a brief description of the smaller groups that the former CPB had fragmented into by the end of 1989, and with a trenchant examination of the response of the Burmese military government (SLORC) to the changed scenario. Three appendixes to the book chart the organization of the CPB, the CPB's base areas and guerrilla zones, and ethnic insurgent groups and warlord armies in Burma.

539   **The Shans and the Shan States of Burma.**
Bertil Lintner.   *Contemporary Southeast Asia*, vol. 5, no. 4 (March 1984), p. 403-50.
This article attempts to clarify and analyse the complex and murky world of the opium trade and politics in the Shan States. It examines the role of the Kuomintang (KMT) forces, the CIA and the United States government, the Burma Communist Party, various Shan leaders, factions and armies, and the Burmese government. The author argues that the US government and the Burmese government (of Ne Win) have both chosen the wrong strategy in dealing with the 'Golden Triangle' opium trade. Appendixes to the article reproduce the texts of the 1947 Panglong Agreement, chapter ten of the 1948 constitution of the Union of Burma (providing for the right of secession), and the 1973 and 1975 proposals to terminate the opium trade made by the Shan States Army and its allies to the US government. A 'Who's who in the Shan States' is also provided. A further and fuller updating study on this subject by Lintner is *Cross-border drug trade in the Golden Triangle* (*S.E. Asia*) (Durham, England: Boundaries Research Press, for International Boundaries Research Unit, Department of Geography, University of Durham, 1991. 65p. maps. bibliog. [International Boundaries Research Unit, Territory Briefing, no. 1]). This contains an excellent bibliography (p. 49-53) and appendixes giving international boundary agreements, and in addition to documenting the 'revitalization' of the drugs trade covers recent political, economic and foreign relations developments in Burma.

540   **Burmese political values: the socio-political roots of authoritarianism.**
Maung Maung Gyi.   New York: Praeger, 1983. 274p. bibliog.
The author see authoritarianism as the dominant Burmese political value and seeks to explain why parliamentary democracy failed to strike firm roots in Burma. The text is enlivened by translations of Burmese sayings and quotes from Burmese politicians. Maung Maung Gyi (1920-88) was a former professor and dean of Mandalay University, who following Ne Win's military coup of 1962, became an exile and joined the faculty of Bates College, Maine, USA.

541   **Burma in search of peace.**
Edited by Edith T. Mirante.   *Cultural Survival Quarterly*, vol. 13, no. 4 (1989), p. 2-42.
This issue of *Cultural Survival Quarterly*, a journal designed to inform and stimulate action on behalf of tribal peoples and ethnic minorities, is mainly devoted to Burma, under the guest editorship of Mirante, with fifteen short articles on the problems of Burma since the military takeover of September 1988. The articles are as follows: 'Has the world forgotten Burma?' by Josef Silverstein (p. 2); 'Burma or Myanmar?' by Edith T. Mirante (p. 3); 'Burma and World War II' by Martin Smith (p. 4-6); 'War without end' by Marip Hkawn (p. 7-9); 'The tradition of democracy in the Shan States' by Sao Ying Sita (p. 10-12); 'The Panglong agreements' [edited text] (p. 13-14); 'The Karenni and Pa-oh: revolution in Burma' by Mika Rolly (p. 15-17); 'Indigenous people mired in "foreign mud"' by Edith T. Mirante (p. 18-20); 'The rise and fall of Burma's Communist insurgency' by Bertil Lintner (p. 21-24); 'Autobiography of a Burmese rebel' by Aye Saung (p. 25-26); 'Burma's Muslim borderland: sold down the river' by Martin Smith (p. 24-29); 'Karen education: children on the front line' by Naw Rebecca (p. 30-31); 'The Kawthoolei women's organization' by Pippa Curwen (p. 32-33); 'Mon women speak out for peace' by Mi Chan, and Mi Chan Mon (p. 34-35); 'Few winners in Burma's teak war' by Robert Hirsel (p. 36-37); 'Loikaw: a town under siege'

[anonymous author] (p. 38-39). With miscellaneous news, suggested readings and a list of associations concerned with Burma.

542 **The crisis in Burma: back from the heart of darkness?**
Moksha Yitri. *Asian Survey*, vol. 29, no. 6 (June 1989), p. 543-58.

This article is written under a pseudonym by a Burmese citizen of Rangoon in the hope of providing a better understanding in the outside world of events in Burma. The author gives a clear, plain-speaking account of the state of Burma and events in 1988, as viewed from the inside and begins: 'Practically all the violent, destructive and depressing events in the turbulent four decades of independent Burma seem to have been compressed and replayed in 1988'. Ne Win's style of rule and the military régime's failure to establish and nurture a healthy economy and society are discussed in some detail. The author is strongly condemnatory of the Tatmadaw (Burma Army) – 'a predatory and distorted product of the BSPP years' – and sees the savage killings of pro-democracy demonstrators as 'standard behaviour' by the army with urban citizens being subject this time around to the same treatment, only on a larger scale in 1988, as has been commonplace for decades in ethnic minority zones where the army is operational. The author warns that 'no amount of clever manipulation by the regime can hold back the deeply felt antipathy against the soldiers, and the Tatmadaw will have to live with this as history'.

543 **The Burma road from the Union of Burma to Myanmar.**
Mya Maung. *Asian Survey*, vol. 30, no. 6 (June 1990), p. 602-24.

The author contends that despite Burma's change of name, the nature and functioning of the Burmese polity have not changed substantially and that under military rule traditional barriers to modernization and democratization have become stronger. He contrasts the 1948-58 period with that from 1962-88 which resulted in a 'stagnated country' and Burma's application to the United Nations for 'least developed nation' status in 1987. Mya Maung examines Ne Win's personality and style of dictatorship and states that 'using the Sino-Soviet model of a communist-cadre political system as a disguise, the regime cleverly resurrected the ancient body politic with a centralised government from which the will and the wish of the dictator radiated through the administrative hierarchy of state councils, township councils, and village councils of the BSPP'. The factors setting in motion the political protests of 1988 – shortage of goods at government shops, corruption, a widening gap in living standards between the élite and the public, soaring inflation – are described and the events of March to September 1988 charted. The draconian measures taken in the name of the 'rule of law' by the State Law and Order Restoration Council, the general elections of May 1990 and SLORC's failure to relinquish power are also described.

544 **Politics, personality and nation building: Burma's search for identity.**
Lucian W. Pye. New Haven, Connecticut: Yale University Press, 1962. 307p.

This book on the 'relationship of political culture to nation building' presents generalizations about the 'national character' and the country's modernization prospects couched in the language of social science models and psychology. It draws extensively on published sources and on a small number of field interviews (conducted in the 1950s) to produce observations based on personality types about Burmese attitudes and orientations towards the political process. In a more recent general study

Asian power and politics: the cultural dimensions of authority (Cambridge, Massachusetts; London: Harvard University Press, 1985. 414p.), Pye includes references to Burma and a section contrasting the responses of Burma and Thailand to the West.

545 **Buddhist backgrounds of the Burmese revolution.**
Emmanuel Sarkisyanz, preface by Paul Mus. The Hague: Martinus Nijhoff, 1965. 248p.
A detailed study of Burmese political thought and intellectual history, drawing on a wide range of Burmese sources. The early chapters describe aspects of Burmese Buddhist kingship and cosmology, followed by an account of the allegedly deleterious effects of British colonial rule, and by a discussion of independent Burma focusing on Nu's period of government. Sarkisyanz's study is of most value for its investigation of the new role of religion in defining a nationalist economic approach to Burman life by linking Buddhism and socialism, a theme which he also explores in his 'Buddhist backgrounds of Burmese socialism' in *Religion and legitimation of power in Thailand, Laos and Burma* edited by Bardwell L. Smith (Chambersburg, Pennsylvania: Anima, 1978).

546 **The split story: an account of recent political upheaval in Burma with emphasis on AFPFL.**
Sein Win. Rangoon: The Guardian, 1959. 92p.
Written by the chief editor of Burma's *Guardian* newspaper (now defunct) and originally serialized therein from January to February 1959, this account chronicles the events, intrigues and personal feuds that culminated in the final split in the Anti-Fascist People's Freedom League (AFPFL) in April 1958 and led to Nu's invitation to Ne Win to form a 'caretaker government' in September 1958. It is a partisan view of the Kyaw Nyein-Ba Swe faction. For a useful analysis of the AFPFL split, see John H. Badgley, 'Burma's political crisis', *Pacific Affairs*, vol. 31 (1958), p. 336-51.

547 **Death of a hero: the U Thant disturbances in Burma, December 1974.**
Andrew Selth. Nathan, Australia: Centre for the Study of Australian–Asian Relations, Griffith University, 1989. 32p. bibliog. (Australia–Asia Papers, no. 49).
An account of the abduction of the body of U Thant (1909-74), former UN secretary-general, in Rangoon 1974, and the riots triggered by student resentment of the lack of recognition for Thant by Ne Win and his government. The author points to some 'striking parallels' between the disturbances of 1974 and the mass anti-government demonstrations of 1988 and their suppression.

548 **A rich country gone wrong.**
Stan Sessor. *New Yorker*, 9 Oct. 1989, p. 55-95.
An above average reportage of Burma under the rule of Ne Win, with an account of the pro-democracy movement in Burma in 1988 and its suppression, with bleak predictions for Burma's future under the present military régime.

549   **The military in Thailand, Burma, and Indonesia.**
Takashi Shiraishi.   In: *Asian political institutionalization*. Edited by
Robert A. Scalapino, Seizaburo Sato, Jusuf Wanandi. Berkeley,
California: Institute of East Asian Studies, University of California,
1986, p. 157-80. (Research Papers and Policy Studies, 15).
This comparative study of the role of the military and its expansion beyond national
security to include political, governmental and economic concerns emphasizes the
political and economic stagnation of Burma under military rule. A more theoretical
comparative study of the conditions which lead to the intervention of the military in
non-military matters is Moshe Lissak's *Military roles in modernization: civil–military
relations in Thailand and Burma* (Beverly Hills, California; London: Sage, 1976.
255p.).

550   **Burma, nationalism and ideology: an analysis of society, culture and
politics.**
Shwe Lu Maung.   Dhaka, Bangladesh: [Dhaka] University Press,
1989. 117p. maps.
The chief value of this study which is dedicated to 'opponents of the military regime' is
its internal Burmese interpretation, making many points and using material not to be
found in Western studies. It analyses the means by which Ne Win and the military have
maintained power since 1962, and Burma's failure to develop into a modern nation.

551   **Aung San Suu Kyi: is she Burma's woman of destiny?**
Josef Silverstein.   *Asian Survey*, vol. 30, no. 10 (Nov. 1990), p. 1007-
19.
A useful profile of Aung San Suu Kyi, Burma's pro-democracy leader currently under
house arrest whose party, the National League for Democracy, won over eighty per
cent of the seats in the general elections of May 1990 (but whose electoral mandate has
since been denied by the SLORC army junta). Silverstein attempts to analyse Aung
San Suu Kyi's political beliefs (on the basis of her speeches and the National League
for Democracy's manifesto) and speculates on her capacity to solve Burma's problems
should she ever attain political office.

552   **Burma: military rule and the politics of stagnation.**
Josef Silverstein.   Ithaca, New York; London: Cornell University
Press, 1977. 224p. map. bibliog.
The title well reveals the book's theme, and the author concentrates on the period of
military rule from 1962 to 1974 and of 'constitutional dictatorship' thereafter. An
account of the constitutional period from 1948 to 1962 is also provided, together with
chapters on Burma's economy and its problems, and on Burma's foreign policy and
foreign relations. The author concludes by identifying two fundamental problems –
national unity and the gap between the élite and the masses – that are yet to be
resolved.

553 **Burmese politics: the dilemma of national unity.**
Josef Silverstein.   New Brunswick, New Jersey: Rutgers University
Press, 1980. 263p. map. bibliog.

The author sees the issue of national unity as fundamental to an understanding of
modern Burmese politics and focuses upon constitutional issues. The background and
political history of the major ethnic groups and their interaction under both Burmese
and British colonial rule is reviewed. Independent Burma's problems in building a
modern state incorporating unity in national diversity are also explored. Silverstein's
analysis concentrates upon the Panglong Agreement of 1947 and Burma's first
constitution (1947). The author sees the failure to resolve the resulting 'politics of
contradiction' as ultimately providing 'the pretext in 1962 for the seizure of power and
the displacement of the constitutional system by dictatorship'. Only perfunctory
treatment is given to the post-1962 period and to the 1974 constitution. A German
study of the colonial period background to minority politics is that by Roland Bless,
foreword by Emmanuel Sarkisyanz, *Divide et impera?: Britische Minderheitenpolitik in
Burma 1917-1948* ('Divide and rule?: British minority politics in Burma 1917-1948'
Stuttgart, Germany: Steiner, 1990. 376p. map. bibliog.).

554 **Burmese student politics in a changing society.**
Josef Silverstein.   *Daedalus*, vol. 97 (Winter 1968), p. 274-92.

A survey and analysis of the student movement in historical perspective. Also relevant
and focusing on student opposition after the 1962 military coup of General Ne Win and
on the army's destruction of the students' union in July 1962 is the article by Josef
Silverstein and Julian Wohl, 'University students and politics in Burma', *Pacific
Affairs*, vol. 37, no. 1 (Spring 1964), p. 50-65. For student involvement in the riots of
December 1974 over the funeral of U Thant, see Andrew Selth, *Death of a hero* (q.v.)
and for the role of students in the 1988 pro-democracy movement, see Bertil Lintner,
Outrage (q.v.) and Martin Smith, *Burma: insurgency and the politics of ethnicity* (q.v.).

555 **The future of Burma in perspective: a symposium.**
Edited, with an introduction by Josef Silverstein.   Athens, Ohio: Ohio
University Center for International Studies, Southeast Asia Program,
1974. 92p. (Papers in International Studies, Southeast Asia Series,
no. 35).

A collection of papers by American and Burmese scholars on Burma in the isolationist
period 1962-74, as follows: 'The historical background of the new constitution' by Mya
Sein (p. 1-9); 'Military management of the Burmese economy: problems and prospects'
by Mya Maung (p. 10-23); 'The crucial third dialectic of Burma's neutralism under
U Ne Win' by Maung Maung Gyi (p. 24-42); 'The Ne Win–BSPP style of Bama-lo' by
John Badgley, Jon A. Wiant (p. 43-64); 'Democratic and authoritarian rule in a not so
newly independent country' by Frank N. Trager (p. 65-79); and, 'From soldiers to
civilians: the new constitution of Burma' by Josef Silverstein (p. 80-92).

Politics and Government

556 Independent Burma at forty years: six assessments.

Edited by Josef Silverstein. Ithaca, New York: Cornell University
Southeast Asia Program, 1989. 112p. (Southeast Asia Program Series,
no. 4).

A collection of papers in which Burma specialists of different academic disciplines
examine Burma's forty years of independence and offer interpretations of the recent
past: 'From a political to an administrative state, 1948-1988: whatever happened to
democracy?' by Josef Silverstein (p. 7-18); '1948 and Burma's myth of independence'
by Michael Aung-Thwin (p. 19-34); 'Neither silver nor gold: the 40th anniversary of
the Burmese economy by David I. Steinberg (p. 35-50); 'Changes and continuities in
Burmese Buddhism' by Sarah M. Bekker (p. 51-62); 'Burmese ideology: a comment'
by John H. Badgley (p. 63-80); 'The Burman military: holding the country together?'
by Chao Tzang Yawnghwe (p. 81-102). The papers were originally presented at the
Association for Asian Studies' 1988 annual conference, and a few revisions to take into
account the subsequent political upheavals in Burma have been made for publication,
while David I. Steinberg contributes an updating paper, 'Afterwards: forty plus one'
(p. 103-10) which briefly chronicles the political events and changes of 1988 and early
1989. For a further updating review of events in Burma in 1988-89 and of the
international response, see the article by Josef Silverstein, 'Civil war and rebellion in
Burma', *Journal of Southeast Asian Studies*, vol. 21, no. 1 (March 1990), p. 114-34.

557 The Burmese Communist Party in the 1980s.

Charles B. Smith. Singapore, Institute of Southeast Asian Studies,
Regional Strategic Studies Programme, 1984. 126p.

This study provides a brief introduction to the origins and growth of Marxism and the
Communist Party in Burma. Much of the book (p. 31-126) consists of translations from
Party policy statements broadcast in 1979 by the BCP radio station, together with
Smith's brief analysis of these documents. Fuller, and more up-to-date studies of the
subject are those by Klaus Fleischman, *Die Kommunistische Partei Birmas* (q.v.),
Bertil Lintner, *The rise and fall of the Communist Party of Burma* (*CPB*) (q.v.), and
Martin Smith, *Burma: insurgency and the politics of ethnicity* (q.v.).

558 Burma: insurgency and the politics of ethnicity.

Martin Smith. London: Zed, 1991. 412p. 2 maps.

An outstanding major study of the complexities of modern Burma's long-running
guerrilla wars between the government, the Communist Party of Burma, the Karen
National Union and myriad other ethnic and regional movements, based on extensive
original research and interviews with many of the leading participants. Smith charts the
rise of modern political parties in the British colonial and Japanese occupation period
and the roots of the conflict, insurrections in the parliamentary era, the Ne Win era
and the upheavals of the 1980s and examines the roles of China, America and the
West, the opium trade factor, the aftermath of the virtual collapse of the Communist
Party of Burma in 1989, the general elections of May 1990, and the continuing rule of
Burma by the military régime known as SLORC. This forms an essential source for
understanding modern Burmese history and politics and the unresolved question of
Burma's national unity. There is no bibliography *per se*, but references in extensive
footnotes, useful profiles of leaders, and a detailed index.

559 **Constitutional and political bases of minority insurrections in Burma.**
David I. Steinberg. In: *Armed separatism in Southeast Asia*. Edited by
Lim Joo-Jock, Vani Shanmugaratnam. Singapore: Institute of
Southeast Asian Studies, 1984, p. 49-80. (Issues in Southeast Asian
Security).

An examination of the question of ethnicity and ethnic perceptions in Burma, the
historical background to inter-ethnic relations, minorities and the 1947 and 1974
constitutions, and the financing and future of ethnic rebellions. Steinberg sees little
chance of a solution to the ethnic minority insurrections and concludes: 'The tragedy of
Burmese development is that a nation with such rich potential for growth and progress
should find its efforts to achieve a better life for its inhabitants stifled by attitudes that
are now so engrained that there seems to be little hope for an early resolution'. Two
appendixes list Burma's linguistic groups and ethnically related rebel groups. See also
the article by Robert H. Taylor, 'Perceptions of ethnicity in the politics of Burma'.
Southeast Asian Journal of Social Science vol. 10, no. 1 (1982), p. 7-22.

560 **The future of Burma: crisis and choice in Myanmar.**
David I. Steinberg. Lanham, Maryland; New York; London:
University Press of America and The Asia Society, 1990. 98p. map.
bibliog. (Asian Agenda Reports, 14).

A useful and succinct description and analysis of Burma in the period 1988 to 1990
focusing on the political upheavals of 1988 and the rule of the State Law and Order
Restoration Council since 18 September 1988, with prognostications for Burma post-
1990. Brief details of key figures are given, and a list of members of SLORC.

561 **Burma.**
Robert H. Taylor. In: *Military–civilian relations in South-East Asia*.
Edited by Zakaria Haji Ahmad, Harold Crouch. Singapore; Oxford;
New York: Oxford University Press, 1985, p. 13-49.

This informative essay summarizes the history and colonial antecedents of the Burma
Army and analyses its role in politics from its formation in 1942 to the early 1980s.
From being a key element in the 1940s' nationalist politics and backing civilian
politicians in the 1950s, the army moved to take over power in 1962 and to establish a
one-party state. Among other studies by Taylor are his contribution 'Burma' – giving a
brief introduction to Burmese political history and political parties – in *Political parties
of Asia and the Pacific* edited by Haruhiro Fukui (Westport, Connecticut; London:
Greenwood Press, 1985, p. 99-154) and 'Burma: political leadership, security
perceptions and policies' in *Leadership perceptions and national security: the Southeast
Asian experience* edited by Mohammed Ayoob and Chai-Anan Samudavanija
(Singapore: Regional Strategic Studies Programme, Institute of Southeast Asian
Studies, 1989), p. 205-23.

Politics and Government

562 **The state in Burma.**
Robert H. Taylor. London: C. Hurst; Honolulu: University of
Hawaii Press; Hyderabad, Pakistan: Orient Longman, 1987. 395p.
2 maps. bibliog.

This represents the first study of modern Burma to be written by a Western political
scientist who has extensively used Burmese language as well as English source
materials and who has been able to conduct recent research in Burma. The author'
stated purpose is to put in historical perspective Burma's political development since
1962 when the military took power under General Ne Win and began the process of
converting Burma into a one-party socialist state. The state's development is examined
in the pre-colonial, colonial and post-independence periods and the changes in idea
that have shaped the relationship of the state with society are analysed. Taylor's book
has a solid historical grounding and provides much useful information and statistical
data concerning the functions of the state, organization and membership of the Burma
Socialist Programme Party, and the economy. The author's theoretical framework and
emphasis on the concept of the state provides a rationale for the post-1962 policies in
Burma, but precludes any portrayal of the actual state of the country under the rule of
Ne Win. The realities of life in Burma after twenty-six years of military socialist rule
are not conveyed and there is no mention at all of the pervasive Military Intelligence
Service. Since the book's publication, the events of 1988 onwards in Burma have
provided an answer to Taylor's concluding observation that 'it is difficult to know to
what extent the state has been able to legitimize itself in the eyes of the bulk of the
population and thus ensure its dominance and perpetuation'. Taylor deals with events
since 1988 in two more updating articles: firstly, 'Burma's ambiguous breakthrough
Journal of Democracy, vol. 1, no. 4 (Fall 1990), p. 52-71, which seeks to explain the
army's failure to relinquish power since the 1990 election in terms of Burma's political
history and structure and, secondly, 'Change in Burma: political demands and military
power', *Asian Affairs*, vol. 22, pt. 2 (June 1991), p. 131-41, which discusses the
political turmoil of 1988 and its ramifications for the distribution of political power in
Burma. For an idea of the moral and political effect of fear in modern Burma, it is
necessary to read the article by Aung San Suu Kyi, 'The glass splinters: remaining free
from fear in modern Burma', *Times Literary Supplement*, no. 4606 (12 July 1991), p.
(and also published in such other journals as the *Far Eastern Economic Review* and
Burma Affairs Bulletin to mark the award to Aung San Suu Kyi by the European
Parliament of the 1990 Sakharov Prize for Freedom of Thought).

563 **An undeveloped state: the study of modern Burma's politics.**
Robert H. Taylor. In: *Sociology of 'developing societies': Southeast
Asia*. Edited by John G. Taylor, Andrew Turton. London: Macmillan,
1988, p. 33-47.

This critique of 20th-century political studies of Burma also gives a historiographical
survey of Western writings in general on Burma. It was originally published as
separate monograph (Melbourne, Australia: Monash University Centre of Southeast
Asian Studies, 1983. 45p. [Working Papers, no. 28]).

564 **Burma: the military and national development.**
Jon A. Wiant, David I. Steinberg. In: *Soldiers and stability in Southeast Asia*. Edited by J. Soedjati Djiwandono, Yong Mun Cheong. Singapore: Institute of Southeast Asian Studies, 1988, p. 293-321.
This useful and clear analysis of the role of the Burma Army attempts to place Burma's revolutionary period within a broad pattern of Burmese history and culture. The authors conclude that 'the developmental failure of Burma cannot be attributed, except indirectly, to the military regime. Far more responsible has been the attitudes and predilections of its leader, Ne Win, and the Burman political and cultural tradition'.

565 **Insurgency in the Shan State.**
Jon A. Wiant. In: *Armed separatism in Southeast Asia*. Edited by Lim Joo-Jock, Vani Shanmugaratnam. Singapore: Institute of Southeast Asian Studies, 1984, p. 81-107.
An enquiry into the factors which have influenced the growth of Shan State insurgencies with an examination of the groups involved and a 'genealogy of the Shan State Army' from 1958 to 1983. Wiant considers the Burmese government 'lacks the military force to impose control on the opium production areas and, at the same time, is unable to institute the development programmes which would provide an alternative to the opium economy'.

Burma: a country study.
See item. no. 3.

Burma: a socialist nation of Southeast Asia.
See item no. 28.

Land of jade: a journey through insurgent Burma.
See item no. 71.

Marxism and resistance in Burma 1942-1945: Thein Pe Myint's *Wartime Traveler*.
See item no. 278.

Burman in the back row: autobiography of a Burmese rebel.
See item no. 282.

U Nu of Burma.
See item no. 285.

Voices from the jungle: (Burmese youth in transition).
See item no. 286.

Burma and General Ne Win.
See item no. 291.

The Shan of Burma: memoirs of a Shan exile.
See item no. 299.

Back to Mandalay: an inside view of Burma.
See item no. 301.

Politics and Government

True Love and Bartholomew: rebels on the Burmese border.
See item no. 418.

Religion and politics in Burma.
See item no. 486.

Burma and Indonesia: comparative political economy and foreign policy.
See item no. 567.

Burma Affairs Bulletin.
See item no. 807.

Far Eastern Economic Review.
See item no. 813.

Myanmar Press Release.
See item no. 818.

Asia Yearbook.
See item no. 821.

Southeast Asian Affairs.
See item no. 823.

Foreign Relations and Defence

166 The foreign policy of Burma.
John H. Badgley. In: *The political economy of foreign policy in Southeast Asia.* Edited by David Wurfel, Bruce Burton. London: Macmillan, 1990, p. 204-18.
This thoughtful analysis concentrates on the Ne Win era (1962-88) and concludes that 'foreign policy has been a reflection of domestic constraints in Burma, far more than a reaction to foreign pressures' while pointing out that 'morale and economic conditions are sufficiently depressed by recent domestic policy errors to require major changes'.

167 Burma and Indonesia: comparative political economy and foreign policy.
Kalyani Bandyopadhyaya. New Delhi; Madras: South Asian Publishers, 1983. 250p. bibliog.
This comparative study is divided into two parts: the first examines politico-economic systems, and the second foreign policy. The author argues that 'military rule cannot be a viable substitute for democratic government from the point of view of modernization and nation-building' and that both countries' military régimes 'have failed, almost completely, to achieve political and economic modernization or any kind of stability or growth'.

168 Arakan: Konfliktregion zwischen Birma and Bangladesh. (Arakan: conflict region between Burma and Bangladesh.)
Klaus Fleischmann. Hamburg, GFR: Institüt für Asienkunde, 1981. 222p. 2 maps. bibliog. (Mitteilungen des Instituts für Asienkunde, no. 121).
An examination of the historical background to the flight of approximately 200,000 Muslims from Arakan to Bangladesh in 1978, and of the subsequent repatriation programme and its consequences for Burmese and Bangladeshi relations and policies.

569 **Why nations realign: foreign policy restructuring in the postwar world.**
Kalevi Jaakko Holsti. London: George Allen & Unwin, 1982. 225p.
This volume of essays contains Holsti's case study on Burma 'From diversification to
isolation: Burma, 1963-67' (p. 105-33) which analyses Burma's turn towards isolationism
in the mid-1960s as a response to extreme foreign penetration and domestic turmoil.

570 **Burma's foreign policy: a study in neutralism.**
William Crane Johnstone. Cambridge, Massachusetts: Harvard
University Press, 1963. 339p.
An analysis of Burma's foreign policy since independence that evaluates fourteen years
of 'positive neutrality' as a success in the eyes of Burmans, and, reflecting US Cold
War period preoccupations, mistakenly predicts that Burma's foreign policy would lead
'toward the fatal entrapment of dependency upon the Communist bloc'. The
appendixes contain a list of Burma Research Project papers, Sino-Burma Treaties, an
assessment of U Nu by Law Yone entitled 'A hard look at Mr. Tender', and the
Revolutionary Council's 1962 Manifesto 'The Burmese way to Socialism'.

571 **An epilogue on Burma–American relations: a Burmese perspective.**
Kanbawza Win. *Asian Perspective*, vol. 10, no. 2 (Fall–Winter 1986),
p. 311-31.
The author, a former Burmese government official, reviews Burmese–American
relations in the period from the 1940s to the mid-1980s, emphasizing the Burmese
interpretation of events, and concludes that 'it is a pity that the Americans chose to
have minimal relation and aid to Burma, the only country in Southeast Asia that has
been fighting the communist tooth and nail for the last decades or so'.

572 **Different strokes: divergent reactions to Rangoon's instability.**
Bertil Lintner. *Far Eastern Economic Review*, 23 February 1989,
p. 12-13.
An examination of the different approaches to their relations with Burma adopted by
Burma's immediate neighbours – India, China and Thailand – in the aftermath of the
suppression of the pro-democracy movement in Burma. Also by Lintner is 'Tugging
the tiger's tail: India concerned at growing Sino-Burmese ties', *Far Eastern Economic
Review*, 16 November 1989, p. 19-20. The article by Nigel Holloway, 'Muted harping:
Japan recognises military regime in Rangoon', *Far Eastern Economic Review*,
16 March 1989, p. 20-21, reports on Japanese relations with Burma.

573 **Soviet relations with South-East Asia: an historical survey.**
Robert Argent Longmire. London; New York: Kegan Paul
International, 1989. 176p. bibliog.
This study charts the development of Soviet policy towards Southeast Asia – a region
in which the interests of four great powers, the USA, USSR, China and Japan, meet
and overlap – and seeks to determine if there is any pattern or consistency to the
policy. Russia's relations with Burma from the 19th century onwards are surveyed and
described, with an account of the Burmese communist movement and of the
implications of Burma's neutralist stance and of her relations with China.

74 China in Burma's foreign policy.
Ralph Pettman.   Canberra: Australian National University Press,
1973. 56p. (Contemporary China Papers, no. 7).
This short study traces Burma's relations with China since 1948, and concludes that
Burma's policy of careful neutrality has won China's respect. Also relevant is the
article by Robert A. Holmes, 'Burma's foreign policy toward China since 1962', *Pacific
Affairs*, vol. 45, no. 2 (Summer 1972), p. 240-54. A useful study is Daphne Whittam's
The Sino–Burmese boundary treaty', *Pacific Affairs*, vol. 34, no. 2 (Summer 1961),
. 174-83. Robert W. Martin's *Southeast Asia and China: the end of containment*
Boulder, Colorado: Westview, 1977. 114p. map) draws on the author's experiences
nd observations while serving as US ambassador to Burma in the 1970s and examines
eking-oriented insurgencies in Southeast Asia, the overseas Chinese, economic factors
nd implications of Chinese internal developments for US foreign policy. A historical
reatment of Sino–Burmese relations (excluding frontier questions), largely based upon
Chinese sources, is that by Edward Harper Parker, *Burma with special reference to her
elations with China* (Rangoon: Rangoon Gazette Press, 1893. 103p.).

**75 Burma and India 1948-1962: a study in the foreign policies of Burma
and India and Burma's policy towards India.**
Uma Shankar Singh.   New Delhi: Oxford & IBH, 1979. 256p. bibliog.
This study concentrates on Burma's role in the non-alignment movement in the period
rom 1948 to 1962. Among Singh's other studies on Burma and India are 'Burma's
conomic relations with India, 1948-62', *International Studies* (New Delhi), vol. 17,
o. 1 (Jan.–March 1978), p. 99-111; and, 'Burma's foreign policy in the seventies',
ndia Quarterly, vol. 34, no. 3 (July–Sept. 1978), p. 347-64. Also relevant is the thesis
PhD, University of Pennsylvania, Philadelphia, 1959) by Richard Joseph Kozicki, *India
nd Burma, 1937-57: a study in international relations* (Ann Arbor, Michigan:
Jniversity Microfilms, 1977. 475p. bibliog.) which discusses economic and financial
elations and Burma's neutralist policy. A more up-to-date article is that by K. P.
Misra, 'Burma's farewell to the nonaligned movement', *Asian Affairs*, vol 12, pt. 1
Feb. 1981), p. 49-56, which discusses the factors leading to Burma's decision to
rithdraw from the non-aligned movement, as announced at the sixth conference of
eads of state of non-aligned countries held in Havana in September 1979.

**76 Chinas Grenzen mit Birma und mit der Sowjetunion: Völkerrechtliche
Theorie und Praxis der Volksrepublik China.** (China's borders with
Burma and with the Soviet Union: international legal theory and
practice in the People's Republic of China.)
Michael Strupp.   Hamburg, GFR: Institut für Asienkunde, 1987. 2nd
rev. ed. 559p. maps. bibliog. (Mitteilungen des Instituts für Asienkunde
Hamburg, no. 155).
he first part of the book covers Burma (p. 55-164) and examines the background to
he China–Burma boundary demarcation dispute and Sino–Burmese relations since
961 and up to the signing in Rangoon in June 1986 of a Sino–Burmese Draft Protocol
n the First Joint Inspection (and Re-Demarcation) of the Sino–Burmese border. A
ummary of the book in English appears on p. 531-38.

577 **Burma: defence expenditure and threat perception.**
Robert H. Taylor. In: *Defence spending in Southeast Asia*. Edited by Chin Kin Wah. Singapore: Institute of Southeast Asian Studies, 1987, p. 252-80. (Issues in Southeast Asian Security).

An analysis of Burma's defence expenditure and the perceptions upon which it i predicated, and of the implications of defence expenditure for economic development with statistical tables of military expenditure 1948-84.

578 **Foreign and domestic consequences of the KMT intervention in Burma.**
Robert H. Taylor. Ithaca, New York: Cornell University Southeast Asia Program, 1973. 77p. bibliog. (Cornell University Southeast Asia Program Data Papers, no. 93).

A succinct study of the invasion of Burma by Chinese nationalist (Kuomintang) troop of Chiang Kai-shek in 1950, the international repercussions, and Burmese military an diplomatic efforts to force their withdrawal. Taylor considers that the Kuomintang' support to the Shan and Karen rebels was a contributing factor to General Ne Win' military coup in 1962. The Burmese government published an official accoun *Kuomintang aggression against Burma* (Rangoon: Ministry of Information, Govern ment of Union of Burma, 1953. 221p.) describing Kuomintang actions in Burma fror 1949 to 1953 and proceedings at the UN General Assembly, while an individu contemporary Burmese account is provided by Maung Maung, *Grim war against th KMT* (Rangoon: Nu Yin Press, 1953. 86p.). American support for the Kuomintan troops in Burma is briefly discussed in Oliver Edmund Chubb, *The United States an the Sino-Soviet bloc in Southeast Asia* (Washington, DC: Brookings Institution, 196. 173p.), p. 84-88. See also the study by Kenneth Ray Young, *Nationalist Chinese troop in Burma: obstacles in Burma's foreign relations 1949-61* (PhD thesis, New Yor University, 1970. 254p. bibliog. Available from University Microfilms, Ann Arbo Michigan, order no. UM 71-2356).

579 **Common vision: Burma's regional outlook.**
Than Han. Washington, DC: Institute for the Study of Diplomacy, Georgetown University, 1988. 78p. (Occasional Paper, Georgetown University, Institute for the Study of Diplomacy, School of Foreign Service).

The author, a senior Burmese diplomat, attempts to throw light on how Burm identifies itself with and relates to its Southeast Asian neighbours. Her study examine changing regional relationships since the end of the Second World War and pa; particular attention to the impact of the Indochina wars, and the ramifications in th region of the triangular power relationship between China, the United States an Russia.

580 **Burma's national security and defence posture.**
Tin Maung Maung Than. *Contemporary Southeast Asia*, vol 11, no. (June 1989), p. 40-60.

An examination of the challenge to Burma's security posed by armed separatist ar communist insurgencies since 1948 and of the Burma Army's response and initiative It provides a useful analysis of the structure and strength of the Army, with statistic bles (compiled from such sources as the International Institute for Strategic Studies' *ilitary Balance*).

1 **Burma's role in the United Nations 1948-1955.**
Frank N. Trager, Patricia Wohlgemuth, Lu-Yu Kiang.   New York: International Secretariat, Institute of Pacific Relations, 1956. 100p.

brief examination of Burma's delegations and UN Committee memberships, her rtners in the UN, and position on peace and security, colonial questions and onomic development. With extensive appendixes (p. 27-100) listing Burmese legates and their speeches at the UN, documents submitted, and Burmese voting cord. The bibliography (Appendix IV, p. 59-100) lists UN documents relating to ırma.

ırma: insurgency and the politics of ethnicity.
e item no. 558.

Law and Constitution

582 **Burmese Buddhist law.**
E Maung. Rangoon: Daw Than Tint, Mya Sapay, 1970. 224p.
A standard work, with rulings, primarily on marriage, divorce and inheritance. Th
author published an earlier and slightly fuller work under the same title (Rangoon
New Light of Burma Press, 1937. 304p.) and states in his preface to the 1970 edition:
find that some of the views expressed by me in the present work are inconsistent wit
those I have stated in the earlier work. For the discrepancies I can only repeat th
plea, I once made at the Bar . . ., that every man is entitled to grow in wisdom wit
the passage of years'. Also by E Maung is an article discussing the legal problem
caused by the Japanese occupation of Burma, 'Enemy legislation and judgements i
Burma', *Journal of Comparative Legislation and International Law*, vol. 30 (1948
p. 11-17.

583 **The Jardine Prize: an essay on the sources and development of Burmese
law from the era of the first introduction of the Indian law to the time o
the British occupation of Pegu (with text and translation of King
Wagaru's Manu Dhammathatham).**
Emil Forchhammer. Rangoon: Government Press, 1885. 109p.
A seminal work on the history of Burmese legal literature which adopts a three-fol
chronological division based on the degree of 'Burmanization' of legal texts from
supposed Indian model. Forchhammer, a Swiss linguist, was Professor of Pali ;
Rangoon and Government Archaeologist and won the 1,000 rupees prize offered b
Sir John Jardine, Judicial Commissioner for British Burma, for an essay on the origi
of Burmese law. An extensive discussion and critique of Forchhammer's 'essay' and
Burmese legal historiography in general can be found in Ryuji Okudaira, *The Burme*
dhammathat (q.v.). Also relevant are John Sydenham Furnivall's 'Manu in Burma
Journal of the Burma Research Society, vol. 30, pt. 2 (1940), p. 351-70 and Kyin Swi
'The origin and development of the dhammathats', *Journal of the Burma Researc*
Society, vol. 49, pt. 2 (1966), p. 173-205.

584 **Hand book on the Haka Chin customs.**
W. R. Head. Rangoon: Superintendent, Government Printing, 1917; Rangoon: [s.n.], 1966. 49p.
Collected by the author during thirteen years' experience as an administrator in the Chin Hills, this is a compilation of customs and customary law grouped under the following subjects: marriage, divorce, inheritance, funeral rites, feasts, taxes and propitiations, miscellaneous, and diseases.

585 **A concise legal history of South-East Asia.**
Michael Barry Hooker. Oxford: Clarendon, 1978. 289p. bibliog.
A good survey with information on Burma within sections dealing with the Indian legal world (p. 17-25) and the English legal world (p. 143-52). An earlier study by Hooker, *Legal pluralism: an introduction to colonial and neo-colonial laws* (Oxford: Clarendon, 1975) contains a section 'Burmese Buddhist Law' (p. 83-93) examining the principles governing the laws of British Burma and Burmese Buddhist law since independence. Hooker's *Islamic law in South-East Asia* (Singapore; Oxford: Oxford University Press, 1984) has a chapter on Burma (p. 44-83) examining Anglo-Muhammadan law in Burma, principles of Burmese Muslim law and the situation in post-independence Burma. An examination of judicial policy and legal decisions in relation to Chinese matters is given in Hooker's article, 'The "Chinese Confucian" and the "Chinese Buddhist" in British Burma 1881-1947', *Journal of Southeast Asian Studies*, vol. 21, no. 2 (Sept. 1990), p. 384-401.

586 **Burmese law tales: the legal element in Burmese folk-lore.**
Htin Aung. London: Oxford University Press, 1962. 157p. bibliog.
This book consists of sixty-five law tales not included in Dr. Htin Aung's 1948 publication, *Burmese folk tales* (q.v.). The author provides a long introduction on the development of Burmese law and legal literature, and identifies the legal point involved in each tale.

587 **Burma in the family of nations.**
Maung Maung. Amsterdam: Djambatan, 1956. 236p. bibliog.
This wide-ranging legal study, written as a doctoral thesis at the University of Utrecht, examines Burma's foreign relations, treaty and diplomatic practice and constitutional developments from the time of the kings to the 1950s. With short chapters on royal Burma, Anglo–Burmese relations, law and administration under the British, constitutional changes, war and the Japanese occupation, independence, the 1947 constitution, Burma since independence and Burma 'in the family of nations'. Included are sixteen appendixes reproducing treaties and related documents ranging from the Treaty of Yandabo of 1826 to the Reparations and Economic Co-operation Agreement between Burma and Japan of 1954.

588 **Burma's constitution.**
Maung Maung, foreword by John S. Furnivall. The Hague: Martinus Nijhoff, 1961. rev. ed. 340p.
A detailed study of the drafting and adoption of Burma's first constitution in 1947 and of amendments to it, together with an examination of the constitution's individual clauses, and examples and legal citations of the application of the constitution in independent Burma for the period 1948 to 1960. The appendixes contain the texts of

the constitution of Burma (August 1943) under the Japanese occupation, the draft constitution approved by the AFPFL Convention (May 1947), the Constitution of the Union of Burma (p. 258-308), the 1951 and 1961 Constitution Amendment Acts, the 1960 Burma–China Boundary Treaty, and other related documents; with a chronology of events to 4 January 1961. First published in 1959 (The Hague: Martinus Nijhoff), the revised 1961 edition has an added chapter on the break up of the AFPFL and on Ne Win's military 'Caretaker Government' (1958-60). Maung Maung's preface to this edition, written after U Nu's 1960 re-election, expresses the hope that: 'Peace and stability, law and order, the rule of law, a strong civil service, an independent and fearless judiciary, a strong Parliament – the big beating heart of democracy – all this must be restored or reinforced or created altogether anew'. Thirty years on, this reads like a forlorn epitaph for a Burma that might have been. Furnivall's foreword is more prescient, making observations on and several criticisms of trends in judicial interpretation and practices in Burma.

589 Law and custom in Burma and the Burmese family.

Maung Maung. The Hague: Martinus Nijhoff, 1963. 155p. bibliog.

A study of Burmese customary law and the impact of British law with sections on the family, marriage, children, property and on Buddhism and the state and on the legal profession in Burma.

590 Burma's constitution and elections of 1974.

Albert D. Moscotti. Singapore: Institute of Southeast Asian Studies, 1977. 184p. (Research Notes and Discussion Series, no. 5).

A collection of documents, compiled from the Burmese official press and other sources on the lengthy process of drafting a new state constitution for Burma 1971-74, and of the elections of 1974 for a 'Pyithu Hluttaw' (People's Assembly), with text of the 1974 Constitution of the Socialist Republic of the Union of Burma (p. 73-130), a chronology of events, and list of members of the People's Assembly elected January–February 1974.

591 The Burmese dhammathat.

Ryuji Okudaira. In: *The laws of South-East Asia: vol. 1, The pre-modern texts.* Edited by Michael Barry Hooker. Singapore: Butterworth, 1986. p. 23-142.

A masterly and detailed survey of Burmese legal texts (*dhammathat*) covering their sources and content, with a historiography of European and Burmese research, translations and commentaries on law texts, including the 19th-century work of Richardson, Sparks, Jardine, Forchhammer, and Kin Wun Mingyi U Gaung, and also modern Burmese scholarship. There is an extensive bibliography of over 140 items.

592 Burma's national unity problem and the 1974 constitution.

Robert H. Taylor. *Contemporary Southeast Asia*, vol. 3, no. 3 (Dec. 1979), p. 232-48.

This article analyses the 1974 constitution of the Socialist Republic of the Union of Burma (in force until 1988), giving particular attention to the ruling élite's efforts to create a system of regional and local government able to cope with Burma's long-standing problems of minority disaffection and national unity. It also briefly compares the 1947 constitution drafted by the nationalist leaders of the Anti-Fascist People's

Freedom League with the 1974 constitution written by the Burma Socialist Programme Party (BSPP). The author argues that the contrasting assumptions and principles in the two constitutions reveal the evolving concepts of state and social relations held by Burma's political élite.

Burma and Japan: basic studies on their cultural and social history.
See item no. 6.

Special Burma Studies Issue.
See item no. 7.

A description of the Burmese empire: compiled chiefly from Burmese documents.
See item no. 25.

Burma.
See item no. 835.

Post-election Myanmar: a popular mandate withheld.
See item no. 534.

Constitutional and political bases of minority insurrections in Burma.
See item no. 559.

Economy

593 **Technical co-operation and comparative models of development: lessons drawn from the UNDP experience in Egypt and Burma.**
Hassan M. Amin. Brighton, England: Institute of Development Studies at the University of Sussex, 1977. 37p. (Discussion Papers).
This paper attempts to establish criteria for technical co-operation based on the typology of development and the nature of government administration in the recipient country. A brief description of the general economic situation and government institutions in Egypt and Burma is followed by a discussion of the role of the United Nations Development Programme (UNDP) in the co-ordination of assistance, UNDP technical co-operation strategy, the country programming experience, the types, size and forms of assistance and, lastly, implementation of projects.

594 **Burma today: economic development and political control since 1962.**
Sekhar Bandyopadhyay. Calcutta, India: Papyrus, 1987. 119p. map.
All assessments of the situation in Burma are limited by the paucity of available data. This work provides a broad overview of economic and political developments in Burma since 1962. In the author's words: 'What has been achieved is a more equitable distribution of the burden of poverty, rather than prosperity for all, which was originally the goal of General Ne Win's socialist revolution'.

595 **The rice economy of Asia.**
Randolph Barker, Robert W. Herdt, with Beth Rose. Washington, DC: Resources for the Future, 1985. 324p. map. bibliog.
An examination of trends and changes in the Asian rice economy since the Second World War, covering historical, institutional and agronomic factors, research management, marketing, consumption, trade factors and government policies. The data and statistics presented are useful in the Burma context for assessing developments in Burma's rice economy in comparison with other Asian countries. It also acts as a successor to the prewar survey by V. D. Wickizer and M. K. Bennett

The rice economy of monsoon Asia (Palo Alto, California: Stanford University Press, 1941. 358p.).

596   **The impact of colonialism on Burmese economic development.**
Allen H. Fenichel, W. G. Huff.   Montreal: Centre for Developing-Area Studies, McGill University, 1971. 68p. bibliog. (Occasional Paper Series, no. 7).

A useful, succinct introduction to Burmese economic history with twenty-nine tables accompanied by a note on sources. The authors conclude that the result of the British *laissez-faire* policy in colonial Burma was 'to relegate the Burmese to the position of landless agrarian labourer almost totally excluded from any role in the process of modernization'.

597   **An inward-looking economy in transition: economic development in Burma since the 1960s.**
Hal Hill, Sisira Jayasuriya.   Singapore: Institute of Southeast Asian Studies, 1986. 74p. bibliog. (Occasional Paper, no. 80).

This analysis of economic development in Burma since 1962 places special emphasis on the period from the mid-1970s, and provides twenty-nine tables of statistical data. It looks at Burmese development in regional perspective and examines planning and ideology. Foreign trade and the balance of payments are outlined and the principal economic sectors, focusing especially on agriculture and industry, are analysed. A salutary note on data limitations is given in the appendix.

598   **Burma and Pakistan: a comparative study of development.**
Mya Maung.   New York: Praeger, 1971. 164p.

An interpretative piece of work exploring the relationship between socioeconomic factors and choices in development policy for Burma and Pakistan.

599   **Cultural value and economic change in Burma.**
Mya Maung.   *Asian Survey*, vol. 4, no. 3 (March 1964), p. 757-84.

An examination of the influence of cultural and religious values on economic development, a subject analysed in more detail in Mya Maung's thesis, *The genesis of economic development in Burma: the plural society* (PhD thesis, Catholic University of America, Washington, DC, 1961. 228p. Available from University Microfilms, Ann Arbor, Michigan, order no. UM 62-2015). A critique of Mya Maung's article is provided by Trevor Ling's 'Buddhist values and the Burmese economy' in *Buddhist studies in honour of I. B. Horner*, edited by L. Cousins, A. Kunst, K. R. Norman (Dordrecht, The Netherlands; Boston, Massachusetts: D. Reidel, 1974, p. 103-18) which seeks to distinguish specifically Buddhist values from Burmese cultural values. Further articles by Mya Maung on aspects of modern Burma's economy are 'Socialism and economic development of Burma', *Asian Survey*, vol. 4, no. 12 (Dec. 1964), p. 1182-90; 'Agricultural co-operation in Burma: a study on the value-orientation and effects of socio-economic action', *Social and Economic Studies*, vol. 14 (1965), p. 321-38; and, 'The Burmese way to socialism beyond the welfare state', *Asian Survey*, vol. 10, no. 6 (June 1970), p. 533-51. A sociological exploration of the problems of economic development in Burma is provided by Sein Maung, *Socio-cultural values and economic backwardness: a case study of Burma* (PhD thesis, New York University,

1964. 279p. Available from University Microfilms, Ann Arbor, Michigan, orde
no. UM 65-1648).

600 **Myanmar dilemmas and options: the challenge of economic transition in
the 1990s.**
Edited by Mya Than, Joseph L. H. Tan.   Singapore: ASEAN
Economic Research Unit, Institute of Southeast Asian Studies, 1990.
288p. bibliog.

This collection of papers by economists addresses the chronic economic situation c
Burma and offers practical prescriptions for the country's economic recovery an
development in the 1990s. Major issues concerning the role of the state and economi
management, new directions in resource, agricultural and industrial development an
the challenges arising from the opening up of the economy to the stimuli of externa
trade and capital movements are discussed in detail. The papers are as follows
'Optimism for Myanmar's economic transition in the 1990s?' by Mya Than, Josepl
L. H. Tan (p. 1-17); 'The Myanmar economy at the crossroads: options an
constraints' by Tun Wai (p. 18-52); 'Monetary and fiscal policies for development ii
Myanmar' by Myat Thein (p. 53-88); 'Agricultural policy reforms and agricultura
development in Myanmar' by Mya Than, Nobuyoshi Nishizawa (p. 89-116); 'A
economic analysis of Burmese rice-price policies' by Tin Soe, Brian S. Fisher (p. 117
66); 'Industrial development and industrial policy in Myanmar: turning challenges int
changes' by Wilfred Lutkenhorst (p. 167-85); 'The Union of Burma foreign investmen
law: prospects of mobilizing foreign capital for development?' by Mya Than (p. 186
218); 'Burma and Asian–Pacific dynamism: problems and prospects of export
orientated growth in the 1990s' by Richard W. A. Vokes (p. 219-47); 'United Nation
technical aid and development in Burma' by Soe Saing (p. 248-66); and, 'Remodellin
Myanmar' by John H. Badgley (p. 267-88).

601 **United Nations technical aid in Burma: a short survey.**
Soe Saing.   Singapore: Institute of Southeast Asian Studies, 1990.
115p.

Gives information on Burma and its classification as 'least developed status' in 1987
with details of the operation of United Nations technical assistance and developmen
aid in Burma. Details of current UNDP projects in Burma can be found in the annua
UNDP in Myanmar (pre-1989 issues entitled *UNDP in Burma*) (Rangoon: UNIC
1986-).

602 **Burma's road towards development: growth and ideology under militar
rule.**
David I. Steinberg.   Boulder, Colorado: Westview, 1981. 233p.
2 maps. bibliog. (Westview Special Studies on South and Southeast
Asia).

The author's stated purpose was to make Burma, virtually a closed country since 1962
better known to development specialists and to provide up-to-date (for the time
information on political and economic developments. His book provides a thoughtfu
analysis of Burmese policies and useful factual information.

603 **Burma's third Four-Year Plan: half-way to socialism and industrialization.**

David I. Steinberg. *Contemporary Southeast Asia*, vol. 5, no. 1 (June 1983), p. 1-26.

This article outlines the reforms initiated in Burma since the 1971 Congress of the Burma Socialist Programme Party and assesses their effect on the economy. The author concludes that the third Four Year Plan (1978/79-1981/82) has been the most successful so far especially in the field of agriculture, but considers that the industrialization targets of Burma's Twenty Year Plan (1974-94) are unattainable.

604 **International rivalries in Burma: the rise of economic competition.**

David I. Steinberg. *Asian Affairs*, vol. 30, no. 6 (June 1990), p. 587-601.

A clear analysis of the changed economic situation inaugurated by the dissolution of the Burma Socialist Programme Party and the new Foreign Investment Law of 30 November 1989 which has opened up Burma to the private sector – both internal and foreign – and has made Burma a focus for international economic rivalry at a time when most foreign aid has been terminated. Steinberg reviews Burma's economic situation and policies from 1962 to 1988, and describes the economic crisis of 1987 and the expansion of foreign interests in Burma, trade with China and Thailand both before and after SLORC's assumption of power, and relations with other countries. Steinberg considers Burma has become 'a country in which to watch economic rivalries played out, and more generally to further study the capacity and the political economies of states trying to adopt technology, trade, and investment selectively, while maintaining an idealized image of their pristine pasts'. He signals the important role of Japan in the event of a significant resumption of foreign assistance to Burma. See also Steinberg's article 'Japanese economic assistance to Burma: aid in the "Tarenagashi" manner?' in *Crossroads*, vol. 5, no. 2 (1990), p. 51-107, which gives a detailed analysis of the different forms of Japanese aid to Burma, including war reparations, in the period 1950 to 1990, with thirteen statistical tables.

605 **Building a welfare state in Burma, 1948-1956.**

Frank N. Trager. New York: Institute of Pacific Relations, 1958. 118p.

A revised and enlarged version of a 1954 paper by Trager published under the title, *Towards a welfare state in Burma: economic reconstruction and development, 1948-1954* New York: International Secretariat, Institute of Pacific Relations, 1954. 60p. Secretariat Paper, no. 6]). It examines the problems facing Burma at independence and the series of economic, political and social plans to build a 'Pyei-daw-tha' – a country of peace and prosperity. The government of Burma's official development programme was published under the title, *Pyidawtha the new Burma: a report from the government to the people of the Union of Burma on our long-term programme for economic and social development* (Rangoon: Economic & Social Board, Government of the Union of Burma, 1954. 128p. map.). See also the in-depth study by Louis J. Walinsky, *Economic development in Burma* (q.v.).

606 **Economic development in Burma 1951-60.**
Louis J. Walinsky. New York: Twentieth Century Fund, 1962. 680p.
maps.

An important study of independent Burma's first decade of economic development covering the formulation and implementation of Burma's 'Pyidawtha' programme, by a senior economic advisor and member of a team of American economic consultants to the government of Burma in the 1950s. The book is divided into six parts: part one on the pre-independence background; part two on the formulation of development plans and programmes in the post-independence period; part three is a chronological account of changes, emphases and problems 1952-60; part four on the implementation and impact of the programmes in the public and private sectors; part five an analysis of the problems affecting implementation; part six assesses the significance for Burma and for Western aid policy and practice of such programmes. The text is accompanied by key documents in the appendixes, and eighty-nine statistical tables throughout. The report of the American company employed by the government of Burma, Knappen, Tippetts, Abbett Engineering Company (in association with Pierce Management and Robert R. Nathan Associates) was published under the title *Comprehensive report: economic and engineering development of Burma, prepared for the government of the Union of Burma* (Aylesbury, England: Hazell, Watson & Viney, 1953. 2 vols. maps.) and contains much useful information on the resources of Burma. For a case study of this Knappen, Tippetts, Abbett report and an analysis of the structure of thought characteristic of Western-style development planning, see the dissertation by John Thomas Davenport, *Philosophical considerations of western technical thought: technical assistance in Burma* (PhD thesis, Colorado State University, Fort Collins, Colorado, 1981. 368p. bibliog. Available from University Microfilms, Ann Arbor, Michigan, order no. UM 8119697). For a summary account by an economist who changed his opinions after his experiences in Burma, see Everett E. Hagen, *The economic development of Burma* (Washington, DC: National Planning Association, Center for Development, 1956. 88p.).

Burma: a country study.
See item no. 3.

Economic resources of the Union of Burma.
See item no. 97.

Military rule in Burma since 1962: a kaleidoscope of views.
See item no. 535.

Burma: defence expenditure and threat perception.
See item no. 577.

Industrialization in Burma in historical perspective.
See item no. 610.

Foreign loans and aid in the economic development of Burma.
See item no. 612.

Country Report: Thailand, Burma.
See item no. 812.

Industry, Trade and Finance

607 **State and oil in Burma: an introductory survey.**
Raja Segaran Arumugam. Singapore: Institute of Southeast Asian Studies, 1977. 37p. (Research Notes and Discussions Series, no. 3).
There is a dearth of literature on the oil industry of Burma. This paper outlines the growth of the oil industry in the British colonial period, the policies of the Burmese government after independence and the nationalization of the oil industry in 1963, and examines the progress, problems and policy changes relating to the state oil industry from 1963 to 1976. Some statistical data is provided in tables at the end.

608 **An outline of Burma's oil industry.**
Ba Kyaw ('MBK'). Rangoon: Myawaddy, 1982. 124p. map. bibliog.
This brief survey of oil in Burma covers from early indigenous extraction methods to oil field explorations and developments of 1981. Originally published as a series of articles in the *The Working People's Daily* (and therefore full of references to the guidance of Chairman Ne Win), the English text of the book occupies p. 1-54, and is followed by a translation into Burmese. See also, Khin Maung Gyi, *Memoirs of oil industry in Burma 1905-1980* (Rangoon: 1989. 100p.) which gives historical background and some technological details.

609 **The complete guide to countertrade and offset in South East Asia, China and the Far East.**
Jonathan Bell. London: COI Publications (Countertrade & Offset Intelligence), 1988. 399p. bibliog.
Countertrade is defined as payment for goods and services by barter or other mechanisms not involving the exchange of money. This investigation of the multiplicity of reciprocal trade contains a chapter on Burma (p. 53-60) giving a countertrade overview, government policy and guidelines, and describing briefly Burmese development and countertrade, and the countertrade products, with examples of recent (1985-87) countertrade transactions with Bangladesh, Malaysia, West Germany, Japan, France, and Yugoslavia.

610 **Industrialization in Burma in historical perspective.**
Hal Hill. *Journal of Southeast Asian Studies*, vol. 15, pt. 1 (March 1984), p. 134-49.

This articles focuses on the manufacturing sector of the Burmese economy and describes developments before 1962 and analyses industrial policies and progress from 1962 to 1980. The author finds that the manufacturing sector has changed little in the last forty years (when it was first surveyed in an article by O. H. K. Spate, 'The beginnings of industrialization in Burma', *Economic Geography* vol. 17, no. 1 [1941], p. 75-92). Hill concludes that Burma has been relatively successful in its policy objectives of self-reliance with full domestic ownership of productive and natural resources, and of a reduced share of foreign trade in net output, but that Burma has fallen short of its other objectives.

611 **Taxation in the Asian–Pacific region: a country by country survey.**
Jap Kim Siong. Singapore: Asian–Pacific Tax & Investment Research Centre, 1988. 3rd rev. ed. 364p.

The Burma section (p. 47-54) of this compilation covers the collection and classification of taxes and levies, and outlines income tax, supertax, profits tax, sales tax, etc., with references to relevant legislation.

612 **Foreign loans and aid in the economic development of Burma 1974/75 to 1985/86.**
Khin Maung Nyunt. Bangkok: Institute of Asian Studies, Chulalongkorn University, 1989. 155p. bibliog.

A survey of the development of external assistance to Burma, describing the forms of financial flow, the structures and their impact on Burma's economic development.

613 **Market research of principal exports and imports of Burma with special reference to Thailand (1970/71 to 1985/86).**
Khin Maung Nyunt. Bangkok: Institute of Asian Studies, Chulalongkorn University, 1988. 133p. bibliog.

A study of the growth of Burma's foreign trade with the theme of Burma's need to achieve better economic growth through expansion of foreign trade. The organization of the foreign trade sector and changes in its functions and structure are examined. There is a statistical appendix and further statistical data are included throughout.

614 **Burma gems, jade and pearl emporium.**
Rangoon: Ministry of Mines, Myanma Gems Corporation, Government of Socialist Republic of the Union of Burma, 1984. 97p.

A colour-illustrated guide to the annual gems emporium held in Rangoon at the Inya Lake Hotel for invited foreign gem traders since 1964. See also the article by Cho Tun, 'Burma gems emporium' *Guardian*, vol. 33, no. 12 (Dec. 1986), p. 6-8 which contains a table listing proceeds in US dollars from the emporium for the period 1964-86.

615 **An overall view of the rubber industry of Burma.**
Tin Htoo. *Journal of the Burma Research Society*, vol. 45, pt. 1 (June 1962), p. 91-107.

This article examines the development and expansion of rubber cultivation from its beginnings at Mergui in 1876 to the early 1960s, with statistical details. By the same author is 'A district by district account of the rubber industry of Burma', *Journal of the Burma Research Society*, vol. 45, pt. 2 (Dec. 1962), p. 181-208, and, 'Rubber industry in Mergui District', *Journal of the Burma Research Society*, vol. 42, pt. 2 (Dec. 1959), p. 153-70. See also the article by Phin Keong Voon, 'The rubber industry of Burma, 1876-1964', *Journal of Southeast Asian Studies*, vol. 5, pt. 2 (Sept. 1973), p. 216-28.

616 **Burma's energy use: perils and promises.**
Tin Maung Maung Than. *Southeast Asian Affairs* (1985), p. 68-95.

A useful survey of Burma's commercial and domestic energy use, the formation of a new Ministry of Energy, and the development of on-shore and off-shore gas fields and other energy exploration projects. For a disquieting up-to-date picture of the electrical power sector, see the report, 'Burmese electricity: where angels fear to tread', *Power in Asia* (3 June 1991), p. 5-7.

617 **Burma's currency and credit.**
Tun Wai, foreword by Hla Myint.   Bombay, India: Orient Longmans, 1962. rev. ed. 238p. bibliog.

This study originated as a doctoral thesis (Yale University, 1949) and was first published in 1953 (Bombay: Orient Longmans). The author has rewritten and updated the postwar section of the book for this edition, but has left the prewar section 'practically unchanged'. The book covers the development of banking in Burma and its organization, the postwar separation of the Burmese banking system from that of India, money lending operations, the supply of capital, and the working of the currency and credit system.

618 **Role of foreign capital in Southeast Asian countries.**
Tun Wai.   Singapore: Institute of Southeast Asian Studies, 1989. 35p.

An analysis of the policy issues and of the costs and benefits to selected Asian countries from using foreign capital. It provides some statistical data for Burma and a brief examination of the Burmese authorities' reluctance (pre-1988) to allow direct foreign investment.

619 **Guide to foreign investment in Myanmar.**
Rangoon: Union of Myanmar Foreign Investment Commission, 1989-90. 2 vols. maps.

This two-part official publication contains up-to-date information and seeks to encourage foreign investment in Burma, permitted since the government's change of economic policy in 1988 and liberalization of trade. Part two, published in 1990, is a more detailed and updated version of the text contained in part one. It provides a basic introduction to the country and its natural resources, followed by chapters on foreign investment policy and procedures, export and import procedures, tax structure, financial structure (banks and insurance), labour, economic infrastructure (transport and communications, fuel, electricity etc.), and giving general information (public holidays, hotels, weights and measures, the media, etc.), with twelve appendixes listing permitted economic activities, state-owned economic enterprises, fields open to foreign investment and joint venture operations, draft foreign investment contracts, addresses of Burmese embassies abroad, state-owned economic enterprises, chambers of commerce, lawyers and accountants, Five Star Line agencies, etc. There is a colour map which uses the romanized forms of place names that were introduced in 1989 (Yangon for Rangoon, Ayeyarwady for Irrawaddy, Bago for Pegu, Mawlamyine for Moulmein, Dawei for Tavoy, Myeik for Mergui, etc.). Among other recent Burmese government publications relating to trade are *Trade directory of Myanmar* (Rangoon: Union of Myanmar Ministry of Trade, 1989. 157p.) and *Export list of Myanmar* (Rangoon: Union of Myanmar Ministry of Trade, 1990. 105p.). Also useful is the UK publication, *Hints to exporters visiting Burma* (Stratford-on-Avon, England: Department of Trade & Industry Export Publications, 1990. rev. ed. 47p.), a successor to an earlier British Board of Trade publication, regularly updated. In this context also, the *SEATAG Bulletin* (London: British Overseas Trade Board, South East Asia Trade Advisory Group, 1979-. quarterly), while primarily focused on ASEAN countries, carries British embassy reports on the commercial situation, news of trade seminars and promotions and provides free export advice and a brief 'data bank' on individual countries, including Burma. For a report on the effects of economic liberalization, see the joint articles by Jonathan Friedland and Bertil Lintner, 'A policy of pillage' and 'Licensed to drill' in *Far Eastern Economic Review*, (8 August 1991), p. 56-61. Lastly, many of the newsletters published by Burmese exile groups monitor current foreign and other commercial activities in Burma, including forestry, oil exploration and other deals. For details of such publications, see *Burma Affairs Bulletin* (q.v.).

Economic resources of the Union of Burma.
See item no. 97.

The oil fields of Burma.
See item no. 102.

Myanmar dilemmas and options: the challenge of economic transition in the 1990s.
See item no. 600.

Agriculture, Forestry and Fisheries

620 **Some aspects of seasonal agricultural loans in Burma and agroeconomic problems in Burma.**
Aye Hlaing.   Rangoon: Department of Economics, Statistics and Commerce, University of Rangoon, 1958. 37p. (Economics Research Project, Papers nos. 14 and 21).
A useful study of the problems of rural indebtedness and its social and economic implications. Also relevant is Aye Hlaing's *Commercial policy and economic development: some notes on the Burmese experience* (Rangoon: Department of Economics, Statistics and Commerce, University of Rangoon, 1961. 53p. [Economics Research Project, Paper no. 15]).

621 **Agricultural economy in Burma.**
Bernard Ottwell Binns.   Rangoon: Superintendent, Government Printing, 1946. 192p.
Primarily an examination of the problems of land tenure and of agricultural credit in Burma. With sections on irrigation, co-operatives, soil erosion, veterinary matters, and seventy-two pages of appendixes giving details of proposals and draft legislation for the solution of Burma's agrarian problems, and statistical data including cultivators' balance sheets.

622 **Fisheries in Burma.**
Khin.   Rangoon: Superintendent, Government Printing & Stationery, 1948. 180p. bibliog.
An official report on the rich fishery resources of Burma, with chapters on food fishes, inland fisheries and methods of working them, marine fisheries, pisciculture, marketing of fish and fish products, fisheries in relation to agricultural and other interests, and fishery legislation and administration. With forty plates, and a list of important food fishes of Burma and a glossary of Burmese terms in the appendixes.

623 Modernization of Burmese agriculture: problems and prospects.

Khin Maung Kyi. *Southeast Asian Affairs* (1982), p. 15-31.

A review of the pre-1974 situation and of policy changes and new measures since 1974 designed to achieve a 'breakthrough' in rice production, pointing out the need for the relaxation of rigid controls. See also the article by Harvey Demaine, 'Current problems of agricultural development planning in Burma', *Southeast Asian Affairs* (1979), p. 95-103.

624 Burma and the CGIAR centers: a study of their agricultural research.

Kyaw Zin. Washington, DC: World Bank, [1986]. 105p. bibliog. (CGIAR Study Paper 0257-3148, no. 19).

An illustrated review of the work of the Consultative Group on International Agricultural Research (CGIAR) in, and relating to, Burma's agricultural development.

625 Aquaculture in Southeast Asia: a historical overview.

Shao-Wen Ling, edited by Laura Mumaw. Seattle, Washington; London: University of Washington Press, 1977. 108p. bibliog.

This practical illustrated guide to aquaculture history and practices in Southeast Asia contains some scattered data on species cultivated in Burma. Two research papers exploring the potential for the development of aquaculture in Burma are Nyan Taw's *Potential for possible utilization of aquatic and geo-hydrological resources for aquaculture development in Burma* (Rangoon: Planning & Research Division, People's Pearl & Fishery Corporation, [1987]) and *Potential sites for the development of fish/ prawn culture in Burma* (Rangoon: People's Pearl & Fishery Corporation, 1986).

626 Le palmier à sucre (Borassus flabellifer) en Birmanie centrale. (The toddy palm [Borassus flabellifer] in central Burma.)

Guy Lubeigt. Paris: Publications du Département de Géographie de l'Université de Paris–Sorbonne, 1979. 197p. maps. bibliog. (Publications du Département de Géographie de l'Université de Paris–Sorbonne, no. 8).

An illustrated field study of the place of the sugar (toddy) palm in the agricultural economy of Burma, giving details of its cultivation and exploitation and of the lives of cultivators and tappers in the central dry zone; with sections on its uses including liquor, culinary and medical applications, and on its place in literature and popular traditions. Lubeigt has also produced a shorter study on jute cultivation, '*L'introduction d'une nouvelle culture dans un état socialiste: le cas de jute en Birmanie.* (The introduction of a new crop in a socialist state: the case of jute in Burma.), in *Types de cultures commerciales paysannes en Asie du sud-est et dans le monde insulindien* ('Types of peasant cash crops in mainland and island Southeast Asia') (Paris: Centre d'Etudes de Géographie Tropicale, Centre Nationale de la Recherche Scientifique, 1975, p. 235-74. [Travaux et Documents de Géographie Régionale, no. 20]).

627   **Growth pattern of Burmese agriculture: a productivity approach.**
Mya Than.   Singapore: Institute of Southeast Asian Studies, 1988.
43p. bibliog. (ISEAS Occasional Paper, no. 81).
This paper examines Burma's agricultural development from the mid-1970s using
productivity analysis as a measure of development. The author also attempts to
develop policy criteria that could be used to help pull Burmese agriculture out of its
present stagnation.

628   **The physical environment and agriculture of Burma: a study based on
field survey data and on pertinent records, materials and reports.**
M. Y. Nuttonson.   Washington, DC: American Institute of Crop
Ecology, 1963. 142p.
An examination of the agriculture of Burma in relation to its ecological background,
with an examination of crops and their production and distribution; with a glossary of
crop terms, and forty-nine tables of meteorological data for different towns and
regions.

629   **Thai loggers 'rape' Burma teak forest.**
James Pringle.   *The Times*, 26 May 1990.
Following the Thai government's ban on teak extraction in 1988 in its own country
where logging has reduced Thailand's forest cover to just eighteen per cent and had
serious ecological consequences, the Thai government was able to obtain generous
logging (and gems and fishing) concessions from the SLORC régime, at that time in
urgent need of funds. The indiscriminate teak extraction methods of Thai logging
companies in Burma are described, together with the implications of the deal for
Burma's minority ethnic groups and student refugees along the Thailand–Burma
border. Publications such as *Country Report: Thailand, Burma* (q.v.) and *Asia
Yearbook* (q.v.) and *The Far East and Australasia* (q.v.) survey developments in
forestry and other commercial activities. The specialist journal *Asian Timber* (London:
Ernest Benn, 1982-. bimonthly) can also be of relevance.

630   **The Union of Burma.**
H. V. Richter.   In: *Agricultural development in Asia*. Edited by R. T.
Shand. Canberra: Australian National University Press; London:
George Allen & Unwin, 1969, p. 140-80.
This survey of agricultural development in the colonial period and after independence
identifies trends in agricultural production and describes government planning and
agrarian reform in the period from 1947 to the early 1960s, with comments on Burma's
potential for future growth. By the same author is 'The impact of socialism on
economic activity in Burma', in *Opportunity and response: case studies in economic
development*, edited by T. Scarlett Epstein and David H. Penney (London: C. Hurst,
1972), p. 216-39.

631   **Farm household economy under paddy delivery system in contemporary Burma.**
Teruko Saito.   *Economic Development and Cultural Change*
(Chicago), vol. 19, no. 4 (Dec. 1981), p. 367-97.
An account of the paddy procurement system implemented in Burma after the nationalization of internal and external trade in rice and other major products, based on field work in a village in southern Burma. Saito argues that the combination of the land tenure system and the paddy procurement system provides the means by which the state controls the economic life of the peasantry. See also Saito's study, 'Development of high yielding rice program in Burma' in *Historical and cultural studies in Burma*, edited by Yoshiaki Ishizawa (q.v.), p. 133-68.

Some common Burmese timbers: and other relevant information.
See item no. 116.

The forests of India.
See item no. 234.

Myanmar dilemmas and options: the challenge of economic transition in the 1990s.
See item no. 600.

Southeast Asian Affairs.
See item no. 823.

Transport and Communications

632 Highways and major bridges of Burma.

Ba Thann Win.   Rangoon: The Author, 1976. 179p. maps.

A description of Burma's major roads and bridges, constructed in the period 1962 to 1976, with photographs, plans and brief technical details. Many of Burma's bridges and roads were destroyed or damaged during the Second World War and the book includes both new bridges and the reconstruction of old ones such as the famed Ava bridge. Altogether nine highways and twenty-one bridges are featured. The Burmah Oil Company's *The motor roads of Burma* (Rangoon: Rangoon Gazette, 1948. 4th rev. ed. 121p.) covers the immediate postwar condition of Burma's roads, with details of routes, petrol and food supplies, rest houses, etc. and period piece descriptions of 'picturesque motoring' in Burma.

633 South-East Asian transport: issues in development.

Thomas R. Leinbach, Chia Lin Sien.   Singapore; Oxford; New York: Oxford University Press, 1989. 265p. bibliog. (East Asian Social Science Monographs).

This study attempts to bring together the scattered information on transportation in Southeast Asia and to provide a comparative analysis of national transport systems. It concentrates on the countries comprising the Association of Southeast Asian Nations (ASEAN), and has little on Burma apart from data on the growth of its national fleet between 1970 and 1985 (p. 102-104).

634 The building of the Burma Road.

Tan Pei-Ying.   New York; London: McGraw-Hill Book Company, 1945. 200p. map.

An account of the Herculean task of building the Burma Road from Kunming to Lashio in the period 1937 to 1938, and of then having to destroy the Salween bridge and fifteen miles of road to try to stop the Japanese advance. Written by the managing director of the Yunnan–Burma Highway Engineering Administration, with good photographs of the road under construction. A fictionalized and sentimental account of the road's construction is Chiang Yee's *The men of the Burma Road* (London: Methuen, 1942. 88p.), while wartime assessments of the strategic role of the Burma Road can be found in Alan Houghton Brodrick, *Beyond the Burma Road* (London, New York: Hutchinson, 1944. 112p. map.) and in Herbert Girton Deignan, *Burma: gateway to China* (Washington, DC: Smithsonian Institution, 1943. 21p. map. bibliog.).

Burma Road: the story of the world's most romantic highway.
See item no. 78.

Burma's transport and foreign trade in relation to the economic development of the country 1885-1914.
See item no. 233.

The Ledo road: General Joseph W. Stilwell's highway to China.
See item no. 254.

Labour Relations

635 **The trade union situation in Burma: report of a mission from the International Labour Office.**
Geneva: International Labour Office, 1962. 74p. map.
This informative report of a four-week ILO mission to Burma in November 1961 provides an introduction to the country and its economy, followed by an account of the trade union movement in Burma and its role in industrial relations. Its optimistic conclusion that 'the situation seems favourable for the growth of a well-organised and influential trade movement' was not realised after the 1962 military coup of General Ne Win.

636 **Labour and labour movement in Burma.**
Myo Htun Lynn. Rangoon: Department of Economics, University of Rangoon, 1961. 168p.
A study of labour conditions and trade unions in Burma: with a list of registered trade unions and their finances (as of 1953) in the appendixes.

637 **Labor problems in Southeast Asia.**
Virginia Thompson. New Haven, Connecticut: Yale University Press; London: Oxford University Press, 1947. 283p.
Contains a chapter on Burma (p. 17-61) discussing the prewar labour situation covering types of labour, immigrant labour, legislation and working conditions, organized labour, as well as immediate postwar developments.

The Indian minority in Burma: the rise and decline of an immigrant community.
See item no. 437.

Education

638 **Educational progress in Southeast Asia.**
John Sydenham Furnivall. New York: Institute of Pacific Relations, International Secretariat, 1943. 186p. (IPR Inquiry Series).

A concise historical account of indigenous educational systems and the development of new systems under Western influence and rule, with references to Burma throughout and separate brief sections on Burma in the period 1800-1940 (p. 25-29, 52-64). The work was published with a supplement by Bruno Lasker, *Training for native self-rule* (p. 135-73).

639 **A survey of the history of education in Burma before the British conquest and after.**
Kaung. *Journal of the Burma Research Society*, vol. 46, pt. 2 (Dec. 1963), p. 1-124.

A pioneering account (written as an MA thesis, University of London, 1929) that still ranks as the major study of the educational system of traditional and colonial Burma. Burmese monastic and secular schools, the early history of Christian missionary education, and the system under British rule are described. Parts of this study were published earlier in two articles entitled 'The beginning of Christian missionary education in Burma, 1600-1824', *Journal of the Burma Research Society*, vol. 20, pt. 2 (Dec. 1930), p. 59-75, and '1824-1853: Roman Catholic and Baptist mission schools', *Journal of the Burma Research Society*, vol. 21, pt. 1 (June 1931), p. 1-12. See also Vivian Ba's article, 'The beginnings of western education in Burma: the Catholic effort', *Journal of the Burma Research Society*, vol. 47, pt. 2 (Dec. 1964), p. 287-324. The thesis (MPhil, University of London, 1976) by L. E. Bagshawe, *A literature of school books: a study of the Burmese books approved for use in schools by the Education Department in 1885, and of their place in the developing educational system in British Burma* concentrates on the problems of grafting a Western-style secular education onto an existing indigenous monastic system, and has much information on 19th-century printing activities in Burma. Kaung also drew attention to the first books printed in Burmese, a subject which was taken further in a series of articles by Vivian Ba, 'The early Catholic missionaries in Burma' (q.v.).

640 **The development of university education in Burma.**
Nyi Nyi. *Journal of the Burma Research Society*, vol. 47, pt. 1 (June 1964), p. 11-76.

This article describes the history of higher education, the founding of the University of Rangoon, the student strikes of 1920 and 1936, and the postwar expansion and development of university education. On the 1920 strike in particular, see Lu Pe Win, *History of the 1920 university boycott* (Rangoon: Student Press, 1970. 46p.). The fiftieth anniversary of the founding of Rangoon University was commemorated in 1970 by various other publications including the two volume *Yan-gon Tet-gatho hnit nga-ze 1920-1970* which, although predominently in Burmese, also contains some articles and reminiscences in English on the history of the university. The thesis (PhD, Cornell University, Ithaca, New York, 1961) by William Keith Gamble, *An analysis of agricultural education, training and personnel requirements as a basis for national development in Burma* (available from University Microfilms, Ann Arbor, Michigan: order no. UM 61-6668) examines the needs of twelve major Burmese government agencies engaged in agricultural development.

641 **The Burmese experience in university education by correspondence.**
Tun Lwin. *Bulletin of the UNESCO Regional Office of Education in Asia and Oceania*, vol. 19 (June 1978), p. 150-63.

A report on the system of correspondence courses and regional colleges set up after a number of student disturbances at Rangoon University in the period 1974-76 and the university's (temporary) closure by the military authorities.

642 **The World of Learning.**
London: Europa Publications, 1950-. annual.

This provides a useful listing of learned societies, research institutes, libraries, museums, universities and colleges, with names of directors, librarians, addresses, details of library holdings and academic staff and student numbers, etc. The 1991 edition's listing under Myanmar is given on p. 963-64. Another directory which gives more detailed information on universities and technical colleges etc. is the *International Handbook of Universities and other Institutions of Higher Education*, edited by D. J. Aitken (Paris, London; New York: International Association of Universities, 1962-. biennial).

Selected bibliography on education in Southeast Asia.
See item no. 845.

Literature

Burmese

643 Burmese literature.
Anna Allott. In: *Far Eastern literatures in the twentieth century, a guide: based on the encyclopaedia of world literature in the twentieth century*. Edited by Leonard S. Klein. Harpenden, Hertfordshire: Oldcastle, 1988, p. 1-9.

A brief introduction to modern Burmese writers and literature, with more detailed profiles of Thahkin Ko-daw Hmaing (1876-1964), Thaw-da Hswei (1919-), and Thein Pe Myint (1914-78). Also by Allott is another contribution with the same title 'Burmese literature' in *A guide to Eastern literatures*, edited by David Marshall Lang (London: Weidenfeld & Nicolson, 1971), p. 387-401, giving a listing of Burmese writers and their works from all periods.

644 The short story in Burma with special reference to its social and political significance.
Anna J. Allott. In: *The short story in South East Asia: aspects of a genre*. Edited by Jeremy H. C. S. Davidson, Helen Cordell. London: School of Oriental and African Studies, 1982. p. 101-138.

This article traces the development of the short story in Burma and illustrates with many quotations how the genre both reflects and is affected by social and political changes. Several writers are briefly profiled, among them, Thein Hpei Myint, Dagon Ta-ya, Gya-ne-gyaw Ma Ma Lei, Hkin Hnin Yu and the prolific Thaw-da Hswei who has written over 500 short stories.

645 **Intellectuals and the national vision: the Burmese case.**
John H. Badgley. In: *Essays on literature and society in Southeast Asia: political and sociological perspectives.* Edited by Tham Seong Chee. Singapore: Singapore University Press, 1981, p. 36-55.

A thoughtful analysis of the themes and attitudes found in thirty-two selected Burmese works written between 1936 and 1962. The books surveyed include novels, biographies, histories, travelogues and political commentaries. Badgley identifies four main themes – ideology, ethics, education and romance – and examines in particular the attitudes of intellectuals towards rural people, within the larger context of the political process of bridging the gap between the village and the capital in a society where there has been no 'tradition of involvement with the peasant'. Among the writers whose novels are examined are Ma Ma Lay, Shwe U Daung, Maha Swe, Yangon Ba Swe and Maung Tin. Based on research carried out in Burma in 1961-62, and first published in *Asian Survey*, vol. 9, no. 8 (Sept. 1969).

646 **The Maniyadanabon of Shin Sandalinka.**
Translated from the Burmese by Lionel Ewart Bagshawe. Ithaca, New York: Cornell University, Southeast Asia Program, 1981. 132p. (Cornell University Southeast Asia Program Data Paper, no. 115).

An accomplished translation of a collection of precedents 'precious as jewels' compiled in 1781 by the monk, Shin Sandalinka, from the submissions and decisions of the wise minister Min Yaza who was advisor to the kings of Ava in the late 13th and early 14th centuries. The work illustrates statecraft as understood in pre-colonial Burma and is full of reflections on kingship, on the qualities of a king, of the importance of right attitudes and pleasant speech, of the restraints on a king, of the virtues and disposition to be expected from ministers and counsellors, etc. The preface to the translation provides information on the original Burmese work and on early printed editions; with a list of Burmanized Pali names and their original Pali form.

647 **The Pali literature of Burma.**
Mabel Haynes Bode. London: Royal Asiatic Society, 1966. 119p. (Prize Publications Fund, vol. 2).

Originally published by the Society in 1909, this is an indispensable, but not infallible, historical survey of the subject which highlights the contribution of Burmese scholars in the field of Pali and Buddhist studies. There is also a photo reprint edition (Rangoon: Burma Research Society, 1965) with an added two-page review of Bode's book by Charles Duroiselle, originally published in the *Journal of the Burma Research Society*, vol. 1, no. (June 1911), p. 119-22. A useful supplementary work is the article by Shwe Zan Aung, 'Abhidhamma literature in Burma', *Journal of the Pali Text Society* (1910-12), p. 112-32. Also relevant is Victor B. Lieberman's 'A new look at the Sasanavamsa', *Bulletin of the School of Oriental & African Studies*, vol. 39, pt. 1 (1976), p. 137-49.

648 **Ancient proverbs and maxims from Burmese sources: or the Niti
literature of Burma.**
James Gray. London: Trübner, 1886. 179p.; Rangoon: Buddha
Sasana Council, [s.d.].
The Niti texts – or codes of conduct texts – occupied an important place in traditiona
Burmese education and as a source of political and ethical wisdom. Gray's pioneering
translation helped make this literature known and available. There have been othe
translations, especially of the most popular text the *Lokaniti* – from Richard Temple':
'The Lokaniti: translated from the Burmese paraphrase', *Journal of the Royal Asiati*
Society of Bengal, vol. 47, pt. 1 (1878), p. 239-57, to a more recent one by Sein Tu
The Lokaniti (Mandalay: Tetnaylin, 1962. 382p.). The critical edition of the texts b
Heinz Bechert and Heinz Braun, *Pali Niti texts of Burma: Dhammaniti, Lokaniti*
Maharahaniti, Rajaniti, a critical edition and study (London: Pali Text Society, 1981
231p. bibliog.) has a useful eighty-four page introduction reviewing earlier scholarship
and extant texts, translations and commentaries. On the philosophical content of the
texts, see Khin Win Kyi's thesis (PhD, Washington University, Saint Louis, Missouri
1986 [Available from University Microfilms, Ann Arbor, Michigan, order no. UM
8703497]), *Burmese philosophy as reflected in Caturangabala's 'Lokaniti'* (Ann Arbor
Michigan: University Microfilms International, 1987. 442p.).

649 **Burma: literature, historiography, scholarship, language, life, and
Buddhism.**
Hla Pe, foreword by Professor Stuart Simmonds Singapore: Institute
of Southeast Asian Studies, 1985. 214p. bibliog.
This is a selection of lectures and talks delivered on various occasions in the 1960s and
1970s by Professor Hla Pe, who retired from the School of Oriental and Africa
Studies, University of London, in 1980. Hla Pe began his long academic career in 194!
when he was appointed Lecturer in Burmese at the School, rising to become Professo
of Burmese in 1966. His teaching and fund of knowledge have benefitted generation
of students and the material in this volume provides insights into Burmese literature
culture and beliefs through the author's own personal life and career. A bibliograph
of Hla Pe's wide range of publications on Burmese language and literature is included.

650 **Burmese poetry (1300-1971).**
Hla Pe. *Journal of the Burma Research Society*, vol. 54, pts. 1-2 (Dec
1971), p. 59-114.
A disquisition on classical and modern Burmese poetry, with many extracts and detai
of content and form. Also by Hla Pe is 'The hkit-thit Burmese poetry: la nouvell
poésie birmane', *Cahiers de l'Asie du Sud-Est*, no. 25 (1989), p. 147-92 – being th
English text of lectures delivered in May 1988 at the Institut National des Langues e
Civilisations Orientales (INALCO) in Paris, and focusing on the postwar poets wit
bio-bibliographical details and a discussion of fifteen poets.

651 **Burmese proverbs.**
Hla Pe. London: John Murray, 1962. 114p. bibliog.
This charming collection of 496 Burmese proverbs reflects different aspects of Burmes
life. The proverbs are arranged under five headings: human characteristics, huma
behaviour, human relationships, the world, and man. Professor Hla Pe provide
helpful explanatory notes and an introduction to each section, and his translation o

the original rhymed Burmese proverbs into idiomatic English prose captures both the spirit and the sense of the original.

652 **Burmese drama: a study, with translations, of Burmese plays.**
Htin Aung. Calcutta, India: Oxford University Press, 1937; Westport, Connecticut: Greenwood, 1978. 266p.

This to date unsurpassed study of Burmese drama has chapters on the origins of Burmese drama, on the rise of court drama and the Rama play, on the plays of U Kyin U (c. 1773-c. 1838) and U Pon-nya (c. 1812-c. 1886), on drama of the late-19th century, and on actors, dramatic practice and the puppet theatre. Twelve appendixes contain extracts from Burmese plays.

653 **Burmese folk-tales.**
Htin Aung. London; Calcutta, India: Oxford University Press, 1954. 249p.

A collection of seventy Burmese folk tales translated into English and grouped into four classes (animal tales, romantic tales, wonder tales and humorous tales), with an introduction and explanatory notes by Dr. Htin Aung. These folk tales, the first published collection from Burma, were recorded from the oral traditions of villagers between 1933 and 1937. Other collections by Htin Aung are *Thirty Burmese tales* (London: Oxford University Press, 1952. 116p. and *Folk tales of Burma* (New Delhi: Sterling, 1976. 112p.) which contains twenty-seven folk tales, including some from the hill peoples of Burma. Also by Htin Aung, with Helen G. Trager, and illustrated by Paw Oo Thet is a collection for children entitled *A kingdom lost for a drop of honey: and other Burmese folktales* (New York: Parents' Press Magazine, 1968. 95p.). Other folk tale collections in English include *Prince of rubies and other tales from Burma* by Ludu U) Hla, translated by Than Tun and Kathleen Forbes (Mandalay, Burma: Kyipwayway, 1980. 309p.); *The city of the dagger and other tales from Burma* by H. H. Keely and Christine Price (London: Frederick Warne, 1972. 208p. map.), with elegant woodcut illustrations; *Favourite stories from Burma* by Margaret Siek, illustrations by Paw Oo Thet (Hong Kong; Singapore; Kuala Lumpur: Heinemann Asia, 1975. 59p.) and *More favourite stories from Burma* by Margaret Siek (Hong Kong; Singapore: Kuala Lumpur: Heinemann Asia, 1978. 62p.). Ludu U Hla has published in Burmese many collections of folk tales of the different ethnic peoples of Burma, some of which have been translated into German and Russian.

654 **Burmese monk's tales.**
Htin Aung. New York; London: Columbia University Press, 1966. 181p. bibliog.

A collection of fifty-nine tales by a famous and learned Burmese monk, the Thin-gaza Isaya-daw (1815-86), and of twelve tales by other Burmese monks, translated and introduced by Htin Aung and based on a Burmese compilation of monks' tales by Isaya Thein first published in 1911. Htin Aung's introduction characterizes the tales as a new literary form – merry, satirical stories dealing with the problems besetting monks and laity at a time of great social, political and economic change. Htin Aung also provides in his introduction a brief account of Burma as a Buddhist country and of the different monastic movements and religious controversy in 19th-century Burma.

655 **Epistles written on the eve of the Anglo–Burmese war.**
Translated and introduced by Htin Aung.   The Hague: Martinus
Nijhoff, 1968. 48p.

A translation of seventeen *myit-taza* (letters of loving kindness) composed by a famou
Burmese monk, Kyi-gan Shin-gyi (1757-c. 1824), on behalf of villagers and monk
writing to their families and to royal officials. Besides their intrinsic literary worth, th
letters – particularly those written from Rangoon and Lower Burma – convey vividl
daily life at a time of great social and economic flux and of impending war with th
British.

656 **Burmese poems through the ages: a selection.**
Translated by Friedrich V. Lustig (Ashin Ananda).   Rangoon: Sabe-u
1986. 173p.

A selection of forty-five poems from all periods printed with the original Burmese tex
and English translation on facing pages. Other collections translated by Lustig ar
Burmese classical poems (Rangoon: Rangoon Gazette, 1966. [80p.]) and *A glimpse o
contemporary Burmese poetry: a selection* (Rangoon: Rangoon Gazette, 1968. [96p.])
Lustig (1912-) was born in Estonia and has lived in Burma since 1949 as a Buddhis
monk (Ashin Ananda) and is titled Buddhist Archbishop of Latvia. He has als
published his own poetry under the titles *Fluttering leaves* and *Winking candles an
blazing trails*.

657 **Anawrahta of Burma.**
Khin Myo Chit, foreword by Chief Justice Dr. Maung Maung,
illustrations by U Ba Kyi.   Rangoon: Sarpay Beikman, 1970. 244p.

An historical novel about the life and conquests of King Aniruddha (Anawrahta) wh
ruled Pagan from 1044 to 1077.

658 **Not out of hate: a novel of Burma.**
Ma Ma Lay, translated from the Burmese by Margaret Aung-Thwin,
edited by William Frederick, with introduction by Anna Allott.
Athens, Ohio: Ohio University Press, 1991. 222p. map. bibliog.
(Monographs in International Studies, Southeast Asia Series, no. 88).

This novel by one of Burma's most talented and outspoken women writers, Gya-n
gyaw Ma Ma Lay (1917-82), offers many insights into the conflict between Western an
Burmese culture in Burmese society in the pre-Second World War period, and tells th
story of the tragic marriage of a young woman and her Anglicized 'modern' husband
It is the first full-length Burmese novel – published as *Mon-ywei mahu* (Rangoo
Shumawa, 1955) – to be translated into English. It contains an 'Afterword' by Robe
E. Vore (p. 197-220) that makes comparisons between *Not out of hate* and Georg
Orwell's *Burmese days* (q.v.).

659 **Tales of Burma.**
Maung Maung Pye, illustrated by Thet Win.   Calcutta, India; London
Macmillan, 1952. 114p.

Presented here are nineteen legends and historical tales of Burma. Also by Maun
Maung Pye is a collection of personal anecdotes and stories of Burmese life, *Burmes
sunshine: sunbeams of wit and humour* (Rangoon: Khittaya, 1956. 152p.).

560 Burmese folk-songs.
Collected and translated from the Burmese by Myint Thein, foreword by Htin Aung. Calcutta, India: P. Lal/Writers Workshop, 1987. 2nd ed. 59p.

A charming collection of fifty folk songs, translated during a period of political detention (from 1962 to 1968) by a distinguished chief justice (1956-62) of Burma 'to relieve myself of the tedium that accompanies such restraint'. It was first published in 1970 (Oxford: Asoka Society. 63p.). Also by Myint Thein (1899-) is a collection of fifty poems, *When at nights I strive to sleep: a book of verse* (Oxford: Asoka Society, 1971. 75p.) and *Burmese proverbs explained in verse* ([Rangoon]: [s.n.], 1984. 125p.).

561 Konmara pya zat: an example of popular Burmese drama in the XIX century, volume 1.
Pok Ni, introduction and translation by Hla Pe. London: Luzac, 1952. 162p. bibliog.

A revised version of Hla Pe's 1944 PhD thesis for the University of London. The work is in two parts: the first gives a brief history of popular Burmese drama with an account of rhyme schemes and content, and discusses in detail the work of U Pok Ni (1849-93); the second part consists of a translation of Pok Ni's play, *Konmara pya zat*. A projected second volume providing a commentary on the play never appeared.

562 Literary heritage of South-East Asia.
Himansu Bhusan Sarkar. Calcutta, India: Firma KLM, 1980. 280p. bibliog.

The author's theme is the influence of ancient India on the culture and civilization of Southeast Asia. A chapter, entitled 'The ancient literature of Burma' (p. 132-58), describes the Pali and Sanskrit texts composed and/or studied in Burma.

563 One thousand hearts and other modern Burmese short stories.
Rangoon: Sarpay Beikman, 1973. 166p.

Eighteen short stories by leading Burmese writers have been translated into English for this book, published with the assistance of UNESCO. Brief biographies of the authors are provided.

564 Selected short stories of Thein Pe Myint.
Thein Pe Myint, translated from the Burmese, with introduction and commentary by Patricia M. Milne. Ithaca, New York: Cornell University Southeast Asia Program, 1973. 105p. bibliog. (Cornell University Southeast Asia Program Data Papers, no. 91).

A translation of eight short stories written between 1934 and 1951 by the noted author and journalist, Thein Pe Myint (1914-78), with an introduction discussing Thein Pe Myint's life and work, and a bibliography of his extensive writings (p. 14-17). There is also a reprint edition (Rangoon: Sarpay Yeiktha, 1975. 268p.). Information on Thein Pe Myint's place in Burmese politics and on his political writings can be found in Robert H. Taylor, *Marxism and resistance in Burma 1942-1945: Thein Pe Myint's Wartime Traveler* (q.v.).

665 **The role of literature in nation building in Burma.**
Tin Htway. In: *Southeast Asia in the modern world*. Edited by
Bernhard Grossmann. Wiesbaden, GFR: Otto Harrassowitz, 1972, p. 3
60. (Schriften des Instituts für Asienkunde in Hamburg, vol. 33).
Describes and comments on the emergence and development of Burmese political
literature from the early 20th century to the eve of the Second World War, with a
bibliography of Burmese and English sources. The essay was published as an article in
the *Journal of the Burma Research Society*, vol. 55, pts. 1-2 (Dec. 1972), p. 19-46.

666 **Modern Burmese poetry.**
Translated by Win Pe. Rangoon: Mya-wadi sa-zin, 1978. 280p.
An anthology of eighty-nine poems by forty-two 20th-century Burmese poets. Printed
with original Burmese text and English translation on facing pages.

**Essays offered to G. H. Luce by his colleagues and friends in honour of hi
seventy-fifth birthday.**
See item no. 2.

Burma and Japan: basic studies on their cultural and social structure.
See item no. 6.

Essays on Burma.
See item no. 10.

Perspective of Burma: an Atlantic Monthly supplement.
See item no. 15.

Colourful Burma.
See item no. 16.

**Through Burma to western China: being notes of a journey in 1863 t
establish the practicability of a trade-route between the Irrawaddi and th
Yang-tse-kiang.**
See item no. 58.

Burma past and present: with personal reminiscences of the country.
See item no. 192.

The caged ones.
See item no. 288.

On the religion and literature of the Burmas.
See item no. 472.

Burmese law tales: the legal element in Burmese folk-lore.
See item no. 586.

Ramayana in Burmese literature and arts.
See item no. 777.

South-East Asia languages and literatures: a select guide.
See item no. 837.

Southeast Asian literature in translation: a preliminary bibliography.
See item no. 840.

Western novels of Burma

667 The purple plain.
Herbert Ernest Bates. London: Michael Joseph. 1947. 224p.
A novel of wartime Burma about a British pilot whose will to survive and escape after his plane crashes is inspired by his love for a Burmese girl. The novel was made into a film in 1954 starring Gregory Peck and a Burmese actress, Win Min Than. Also by Bates is *The jacaranda tree* (London: Michael Joseph, 1949. 223p.), a tense novel portraying the attempt of a small group of British civilians, an Anglo-Burmese nurse and a Burmese brother and sister to escape from the Japanese in Burma. Both novels have been reprinted by Penguin Books.

668 Look down in mercy.
Walter Baxter. London: Heinemann, 1951; London: Hutchinson
Library Services, 1975. 288p.
A compelling novel of the moral and physical breakdown of a British officer during the harsh and brutal conditions of the retreat from Burma into India in 1942.

669 The orange robe.
Dorothy Black. London: Robert Hale, 1960. 175p.
A love story and treasure hunt set against a background of uneasy postwar days in Burma. Also by Black is *Burmese picnic* (London: Michael Joseph, 1943. 196p.), a novel depicting the social pursuits and preoccupations of the European community in colonial Burma. Authorship of the anonymously published *Letters of an Indian judge to an English gentlewoman* (London: Peter Davies, 1934; London: Futura Publications, 1979. 255p.) – a charming, if improbable, series of letters mostly set in Burma in the 1920s and early 1930s – can also be attributed to Dorothy Black.

670 Three rivers to glory.
Sidney Butterworth. London: Hutchinson, 1956. 224p.
A powerful war novel based on the first, unpublicized campaign of the 81st (West African) Division in Arakan. Another novel which features a company of African troops and British officers fighting the Japanese is *The charm of the Mambas* by George Brendon (London: Heinemann, 1959. 279p.). Also published under the title, *The fighting Mambas* (London: Four Square Books, 1961).

671 Man for men.
Tim Carew. London: Constable, 1955. 221p.
This war novel about the Fourteenth Army in Burma pays tribute to the work of the American Field Service Ambulance Troop. Also by Carew is *The longest retreat* (London: Hamish Hamilton, 1969. 276p. 2 maps. bibliog.), a skilful compilation from

the harrowing accounts of both army and civilian survivors of the retreat from Burma to India in 1942.

672 **Love in Burma: a tale of the silken East.**
Ray Carr. London: Geoffrey Bles, 1928. 319p.

The first of several novels written by E. C. V. Foucar under this pseudonym with the theme of the 'water-tight compartments' of colonial society – the European, Eurasian and the Indians and Burmans – and what happens when these are breached. His other novels are: *The red tiger: an adventure in Rangoon* (London: Skeffington, 1929. 288p.) *The cluster of gems* (London:Skeffington, 1930. 288p.); *Moonshine: an adventure in Burma* (London: Gerald Howe, 1932. 287p.); *Rose of Asia* (London: Skeffington 1933. 288p.).

673 **Never so few.**
Tom T. Chamales. London: Allan Wingate, 1958. 351p.

An American war novel which tells of American and Kachin guerrilla units' activities behind Japanese lines in Upper Burma.

674 **A marriage in Burmah: a novel.**
M. Chan-Toon. London: Greening, 1905. 306p.

An accomplished novel about an unhappy marriage between an English girl and a Burmese barrister in colonial days. Mrs. Chan-Toon wrote other novels of which one *A shadow of Burmah* (London: Digby, Long, 1914) touches tangentially upon Burma.

675 **Forests of the night.**
Jon Cleary. London: Collins Fontana Books, 1965. 253p.

The hero of this novel flies to Burma to visit his father who is British consul in Mandalay, meets a colourful Australian Catholic missionary and becomes caught up with local rebels and intrigues.

676 **A battle is fought to be won.**
Francis Clifford. London: Hamish Hamilton, 1960. 189p.

Set against a vivid background of vicious warfare in Japanese-occupied Burma, this novel centres on the relationship between a young British officer and his Karen second in-command.

677 **She was a queen.**
Maurice Collis. London: Faber & Faber, 1937. 301p. map.

A historical novel set in the closing years of the Pagan empire, based on the Burmese *Glass Palace Chronicle* account of these events. There is a less lavishly illustrated second edition (London: Faber & Faber, 1952. 248p.) to which Collis has added some explanatory notes at the end. Collis also wrote a dramatized version, *Lord of the three worlds* (London: Faber & Faber, 1947. 107p.), printed with designs for the stage by Feliks Topolski. Collis' other Burma novels are *Sanda Mala* (London: Faber & Faber 1939. 328p.) which blends colonial officers and Burmese royal descendants and draws on Collis' own experiences in Mergui; *The mystery of dead lovers* (London: Faber & Faber, 1951. 160p.), a historical novel about a Shan princess, based on a Burmese play; and *The dark door* (London: Faber & Faber, 1960. 296p.) which has a colonial

Burma setting and was classed by Collis as a 'comedy' and by his publishers as a thriller'; while his *Descent of the god* (London: Faber & Faber, 1948. 147p.) is a retelling of a Burmese legend of the scented mountain on the Arakanese island of Manaung (Cheduba), with an epilogue describing Collis' own experiences there in 1920. Details of Collis' life in Burma and his pursuit of a literary career can be found in his autobiographical trilogy beginning with *The journey outward* (q.v.). The article by Dagmar Novakova, 'Maurice Collis and his novels on Burma', *Journal of the Burma Research Society*, vol. 42, pt. 2 (Dec. 1959), p. 15-23, is also relevant.

578 Four days.
William Crook. London: Eyre Methuen, 1979. 172p.

A novel of a Japanese patrol's relentless hunt for a severely wounded British officer and his pilot who refuses to abandon him after their plane crashes in the Burmese jungle, set against the background of the Fourteenth Army's crossing of the Irrawaddy River.

579 A kind of fighting.
Patrick Cruttwell. London: JM Dent, 1959. 272p.

This novel told through the eyes of a retired British colonial is set in the invented land of Sagha and tells the story of its national hero and his assassination. It is obviously based on the life and death of General Aung San of Burma.

580 The hātanee: a tale of Burman superstition.
Arthur Eggar. London: John Murray, 1906. 244p.

A novel set in Burma at the turn of the century.

581 Foxes have holes.
Donald Cuthbert Eyre. London: Robert Hale, 1949. 287p.

This is a war novel of Chindits trapped in the Burmese jungle. Among other war novels featuring the Chindits are *Burma story* by Sidney Charles George (London; New York: Frederick Warne, 1948. 255p. 2 maps.) and *We too can die: tales of the Chindits* by Paul Le Butt (London: Robert Anscombe, 1947. 163p.).

582 Incident at Badamyâ.
Dorothy Gilman. New York: Fawcett Crest, 1989. 216p.

An engaging novel set in Burma in 1950 about a group of Westerners captured by Communist insurgents whose respective *kan* (fate) brings about their rescue with some help from a friendly dacoit and a mysterious puppeteer.

583 I fall on grass.
Ian Gordon. London: Robert Hale, 1952. 220p.

This adventure novel, set in 1946 portrays life in the remote Kachin Hills. The author draws on his own experiences in Burma, and has published under his full name of Fellowes–Gordon two accounts of military operations in the Kachin Hills, *Amiable assassins* (q.v.) and *The battle for Naw Seng's kingdom* (q.v.).

684 **The lacquer lady.**
Fryniwyd Tennyson Jesse, with a new introduction by Joanna
Colenbrander. London: Virago, 1979. 383p. (Virago Modern
Classics).

First published in 1929 (London: William Heinemann), this historical novel is based on
the true story of Mattie Calogreedy (renamed Fanny Moroni in the book), at the court
of Mandalay. It is a fascinating evocation of the atmosphere and life at the court of
King Thibaw and Queen Supayalat and of the British and French rivalries and intrigues
that led to the British annexation of Upper Burma in 1886. For a biography of
Tennyson Jesse (1888-1958) and brief details of her visit to Burma in 1923 and the
sources of inspiration for her novel, see Joanna Colenbrander, *A portrait of Fryn: a*
biography of F. Tennyson Jesse (London: André Deutsch, 1984. 305p. bibliog.).
Tennyson Jesse also wrote *The story of Burma* (London: Macmillan, 1946. 206p.), an
outline of Burmese history, politics and religion in which the British are 'we' and the
Burmese 'they'.

685 **Mandalay.**
Alexandra Jones. London; Sydney: Macdonald, 1987. 607p. New
York: Villard, 1988. 485p.

An epic Oriental swashbuckling novel with a vast array of real and fictional characters,
set against the background of events at the royal court of Mandalay before and after its
capture by the British in 1885-86.

686 **Barrack-room ballads and other verses.**
Rudyard Kipling. London, Methuen, 1989. 208p. (Methuen
Centenary Edition).

Originally published in 1892 and reprinted many times, Kipling's *Barrack-room ballads*
was dedicated to 'lives such as fought and sailed and ruled and loved and made our
world'. The collection includes *Mandalay*, one of Kipling's best known poems which
became a popular song. Among other Kipling poems associated with Burma are *The*
grave of the hundred dead and *The ballad of Boh Da Thone* (1888). The inspiration for
these poems can be traced through Kipling's accomplished travelogues, published
under the title *From sea to sea: letters of travel* (New York: Doubleday & McClure,
1899. 2 vols.) where he describes (vol. 1, p. 202-22) the 'golden mystery' of the Shwe
Dagon in Rangoon and the 'old Moulmein pagoda' (saying 'I should better remember
what that pagoda was like had I not fallen deeply and irrevocably in love with a
Burmese girl at the foot of the first flight of steps'). For a literary appreciation, see
G. H. Webb's article, 'Kipling's Burma: a literary and historical review', *Asian Affairs*
vol. 15 [new series], pt. 2 (June 1984), p. 163-78.

687 **The coffin tree.**
Wendy Law-Yone. New York: Alfred A. Knopf, 1983. 195p.

This psychological novel evokes a childhood in Burma and exile to the unfamiliar and
terrifying new world of New York City. By the same author is an article on life with
Burmese refugee students and Karen and Kachin insurgents, 'Burma: life in the hills'
Atlantic Monthly (December 1989), p. 24-36.

88 NTR: nothing to report.
James Leasor.   London: Werner Laurice, 1955. 224p.
A vivid novel of army life and the battle for Kohima in 1944.

89 The treasury-officer's wooing.
Cecil Champain Lowis.   London: Macmillan, 1899. 508p.
Lowis (1864-1918), superintendent of the Ethnographic Survey of Burma in the 1900s, found time to write a series of novels set in Burma, of which this is the first. His novels splendidly evoke life in British Burma with a varied cast of British colonial officials and Burmese, an emphasis upon the isolation of life in remote out-posts and a mixture of romance, intrigue and murder. His other Burma novels are: *The machinations of the myo-ok* (London: Methuen, 1903, 320p.); *The Ava mining syndicate* (London: Greening, 1908. 317p.); *Fascination* (London: John Lane Bodley Head, 1913. 339p.); *Four blind mice* (London: John Lane Bodley Head, 1920. 318p.); *Snags and shallows* (London: John Lane Bodley Head, 1922. 320p.); *The runagate* (London: Jonathan Cape, 1924. 351p.); *The grass spinster* (London: Jonathan Cape, 1925. 320p.); *Green sandals* (London: Jonathan Cape, 1926. 352p.); *The district bungalow* (London: Jonathan Cape, 1927. 350p.); *The penal settlement* (London: Jonathan Cape, 1928. 320p.); *The Huntress* (London: Jonathan Cape, 1929. 285p.); *In the hag's hands: an affair of the Burma delta* (London: Jonathan Cape, 1931. 251p.); and *The dripping tamarinds* (London: T. Werner Laurie, 1922. 254p.).

90 The living lotus.
Ethel Mannin.   London: Jarrolds, 1956. 320p.
This novel has a reasonably authentic Burmese background and centres on the life of an Anglo–Burman girl who becomes separated from her parents during the Japanese occupation of Burma and is rescued by a Burmese family. After the war, she is reluctantly reunited with her English father who attempts to Anglicize her in London, but the pull of Buddhist Burma proves irresistible to her. Ethel Mannin has also published *Land of the crested lion* (London: Jarrolds, 1955. 256p.) describing her tour of Burma made in 1954 as guest of the Union Buddha Sasana Council.

91 Naw Su.
Harry I. Marshall.   Portland, Maine: Falmouth, 1947. 351p.
Set just after the Third Anglo–Burmese War, this novel depicts the clash of cultures and faiths arising when a Karen girl is converted to Christianity.

92 The peacock throne.
Trevor Molony.   London: Herbert Jenkins, 1935. 312p.
A novel of adventurre and intrigue set in British Burma and of a plot to restore the Burmese monarchy. Also by Molony is *The house of the dragon* (London: Herbert Jenkins, 1934. 312p.), a mystery novel set in Burma and the Nicobar Islands with a cast of English colonial traders, Chinese and Anglo–Indians.

693 Rubies.
Louis Moresby. London: George G. Harrap, 1927. 288p.

A novel of mystery and adventure set in Cornwall and British Burma. The author has published works on Buddhism under her real name of Lily Beck Adams, and a volume of short stories, *The ninth vibration and other stories* (London: T. Fisher Unwin, 1928; New York: Arno Press, 1976. 313p.) which includes one set in ancient Pagan: 'The hatred of the queen: a story of Burma' (p. 175-202).

694 South of Fort Hertz: a tale in rhyme.
Martin Moynihan. London: Mitre, 1956. 162p.

An epic poem on the war in Burma.

695 Burmese days.
George Orwell. London: Penguin, 1989. 300p.

This, the most famous novel of Burma, was George Orwell's first novel to be published (New York: Harper & Brothers, 1934). Its subsequent publishing history and textual changes are explained in a 'note on the text' prefacing the 1989 Penguin edition. Orwell drew on his own experiences in the Indian Imperial Police in Burma from 1922 to 1927, to produce a powerful novel of colonial Burma and the bigotry of its social and racial relationships. In *Shooting an elephant and other essays* (London: Secker & Warburg, 1950. 212p.), Orwell includes two on Burma 'Shooting an elephant' (p. 1-10) and 'A hanging' (p. 11-17) with the theme of the 'futility of the white man's Dominion in the East'. Bernard Crick's definitive biography of George Orwell (1903-50) – born Eric Arthur Blair – *George Orwell: a life* (London: Secker & Warburg, 1981. 2nd rev ed. 473p. bibliog.) contains a chapter 'An Englishman in Burma, 1922-27' (p. 76-103), while *The unknown Orwell* by Peter Stansky and William Abrahams (London: Constable, 1972. 270p.) provides an excellent description of imperial police service work and Orwell's life in Burma 'as a police-officer who was a writer-in-embryo' (p. 123-76). Htin Aung's essay 'George Orwell and Burma' in *The world of George Orwell*, edited by Miriam Gross (London: Weidenfeld & Nicolson, 1971, p. 19-30) contains personal memories of an encounter with Orwell in Burma and maintains that Orwell in *Burmese days* 'set out to destroy the conventional picture of Burma as a green and pleasant land, and the Burmese as a charming, carefree and childlike people'. Also relevant is a thesis (PhD, University of Washington, Seattle, Washington 1957) by Arthur Wilber Stevens, *George Orwell and contemporary British fiction of Burma: the problem of 'place'* – which also discusses the work of H. E. Bates and Ethel Mannin – (available from University Microfilms, Ann Arbor, Michigan, order no. UM 22,188).

696 Stranger in the land.
Michael Pereira. London: Geoffrey Bles, 1967. 217p.

An accomplished novel with many strands, set against the background of the Burma Army fighting the Shan insurgents in the early 1960s.

697 The next best thing.
John Ralston Saul. London: Grafton, 1986. 241p. map.

A novel about the theft of art treasures from the temples of Pagan and of smuggling on the Burma–Thailand border and the Shan States.

698   'Neath Burmese bells.
Ella M. Scrymsour.   London: T. Fisher Unwin, 1925. 318p.
A novel, reflecting the racial prejudices of its colonial Burma setting, with an Anglo–Burmese tragic heroine who can find a place neither in the West nor the East.

699   **The chequer board.**
Nevil Shute.   London: William Heinemann, 1947. 316p.
This novel of a dying man's last months is partly set in Burma in the immediate postwar period with flashbacks to the war.

700   **You'll walk to Mandalay.**
John Sibly.   London: Jonathan Cape, 1960. 253p.
A novel set on board a hospital ship on the Irrawaddy against the background of the onset of war in Burma in 1942.

701   **Burma through the prism of western novels.**
Josef Silverstein.   *Journal of Southeast Asian Studies*, vol. 16, no. 1 (March 1985), p. 129-40.
A discussion of thirteen novels on Burma from which Silverstein identifies four major themes: colonial rule and its impact on Burmans and Europeans alike, religion and the clash of culture, war (especially the Second World War), and Burmese history at moments of great change. He concludes that the era of Westerners writing fiction set in Burma is over and looks forward to more translations of Burmese novels so that foreigners can get to know independent Burma better. Also relevant is Clive J. Christie, *A preliminary survey of British literature on South-East Asia in the era of colonial decline and decolonisation* (Hull, England: Centre for South-East Asian Studies, University of Hull, 1986. 52p. bibliog. [Bibliography and Literature Series, no. 1]).

702   **The pass.**
John Slimming.   London: John Murray, 1962. 256p.
A powerful novel of Kachin hill peoples attempting to escape persecution in Communist China by crossing the mountains to join Kachins in northern Burma.

703   **Harp of Burma.**
Michio Takeyama, translated from the Japanese by Howard Hibbett.
Rutland, Vermont; Tokyo: Tuttle, 1966. 132p. (UNESCO Collection of Contemporary Works, Library of Japanese Literature).
A haunting novel of a group of Japanese soldiers in Burma during the closing stages of the war and the decision of one of them, the harp-playing Mizushima, to stay behind as a Buddhist monk in order to bury the scattered bones of his many dead comrades-in-arms. *Harp of Burma* was first published in 1946 under the title *Biruma no tategoto*, and made into a film of memorable moral ferocity by Kon Ichikawa in 1956.

704 The Chindits and the stars.
Thiha.   London: Regency, 1971. 232p.
This novel has realistic Burmese characters and background and its theme is the liberation of Burma from the Japanese, and the insurgencies that followed independence in 1948.

705 Burmese silver.
Edward Thompson.   London: Faber & Faber, 1937; Pan, 1948. 246p.
A novel set in the Upper Chindwin valley, during the post-1886 'pacification' period, about the search for an Englishman who had become ruler, 'Raja Gabriel', of a shadowy kingdom rich in silver mines.

706 The city of gems.
Joanna Trollope.   London; Melbourne, Australia; Auckland, New Zealand; Hutchinson, 1981. 301p. map.
An accomplished historical romance set in Mandalay in the period 1879 to 1885 with a mixed cast of real and fictional characters and a good evocation of the splendour and menace of life at the Burmese court and capital.

707 The weeping jungle.
Patrick Turnbull.   London: Robert Hale, 1983. 158p.
In this tense psychological novel a former British officer, haunted by an ugly wartime incident, returns to Upper Burma in an attempt to expiate a past crime. Also by Turnbull is *One bullet for the general* (London: Collins, 1969. 224p.), a war novel about the conflicting loyalties of a small group of soldiers whose mission is to infiltrate the Japanese lines and to kill a Japanese general and an Indian National Army commander. The author's *Battle of the box* (London: Ian Allan, 1979. 144p. maps.) is a military account of XV Corps' fierce campaign to drive the Japanese forces from Arakan and of the twenty-days' long 'Battle of the Box' which inflicted the first major defeat of the war on the Japanese Army and marked a turning point in the Burma campaign.

708 The golden stairs.
Monica Wadley.   Garden City, New York: Doubleday, 1968. 286p.
A sensitive novel set during the trek from Burma to India in 1942. The novel focuses on the ambivalence and tensions of those of the British and Burmese cultures during a period of change, with vivid descriptions of remote areas of northern Burma and of the evacuees' struggle.

A bachelor girl in Burma.
See item no. 74.

Scott of the Shan Hills: orders and impressions.
See item no. 323.

The square egg: and other sketches, with three plays and illustrations with a biography by his sister.
See item no. 325.

Burma retrospect and other sketches.
See item no. 330.

Reverie of a qu'hai and other stories.
See item no. 331.

Quiet skies on Salween.
See item no. 332.

Children's literature

709 **Images of Southeast Asia in children's fiction.**
Lai Nam Chen. Singapore: Singapore University Press, 1981. 114p.
bibliog.

A critique of fictional and evangelistic English-language works for children set in
Southeast Asia (and dominated by Western writers) and of folk tales retold in English.
The annotated bibliography of 150 titles includes crisp evaluations of the following
works with a Burma setting: *Told to Burmese children* by Maurice Russell (London:
Epworth Press, 1956); *Shan's lucky knife* by Jean Merrill, illustrated by Ronni Solbert
(New York: William R. Scott, 1960); *High, wide and handsome and their three tall tales*
by Jean Merrill, Ronni Solbert, illustrated by Ronni Solbert (New York: William R.
Scott, 1964); *A kingdom lost for a drop of honey and other Burmese folktales* by Htin
Aung, Helen Trager, illustrated by Paw Oo Thet (New York: Parents' Magazine Press,
1968); *Burma boy* by Willis Linquist (New York: McGraw Hill, 1952); *Elephant bridge*
by Jeffrey Potter, illustrated by Robert Moynihan (London: Hutchinson, 1957);
Elephant boy of Burma by Robert R. Harry, illustrated by Matthew Kalmenoff
(London: Odhams' Press, 1960); *The rogue elephant* by A. R. Channel, illustrated by
D. Watkins-Pitchford (London: Dobson, 1962); *Elephant boy* by Susan Williams,
illustrations by Peter Chadwick (London: William Kimber, 1963); *Jungle foster-child*
by Florence Agnew, Robert Agnew (London: Blackie & Son, 1961); *The springing of
the rice* by Erick Barry (New York: Macmillan, 1966); and, *Orange-robed boy* by
Patricia Wallace Garlan, Maryjane Dunstan, illustrated by Paw Oo Thet (New York:
Viking Press, 1967).

710 **The white elephant: or the hunters of Ava and the king of the golden
foot.**
William Dalton. London: Griffith & Farran, 1860. 416p.

This adventure story set in Burma in the 1850s displays a lot of local knowledge and
must rank as one of the first children's books or 'ripping yarns' about Burma. The
illustrations accompanying the story are by Harrison Weir, and R. H. Moore. The
work was reissued in 1888 (London: Griffith, Farran, Okeden & Welsh) to capitalize,
no doubt, on the 1886 British annexation of Upper Burma.

711 **Khyberie in Burma: the adventures of a mountain pony.**
Colin Metcalf Dallas Enriquez. London: A. & C. Black, 1939. 216p.

A children's story about a hill pony and his life in the household of a captain of the
Burma Military Police, and his adventures during the 1930-32 rebellion in Burma.
K. F. Barker provided the illustrations.

712 **The road to Mandalay.**
James Thomas Gorman. London: Blackie, 1950. 256p.
An adventure story for children set in British Burma, originally publihsed in 1929. Another story by the same author and set primarily in Kachin country is *Through the air and the jungle* (London: Blackie, 1931. 256p.).

713 **Scouts in the Shan jungle.**
Sercombe Griffin. London: George G. Harrap, 1937. 253p.
An improbable adventure story for juveniles – full of 'tally-ho' and 'topping' type language – about a Scout troop's rescue of a young Shan prince. Also by Griffin are *The treasure of gems* (London: George G. Harrap, 1934. 255p.), an adventure story set in 16th-century Burma; and, *Burma road calling* (London: George G. Harrap, 1943. 206p.), set at the beginning of the Second World War and featuring Nazi and Japanese spies and a journey through Burma.

714 **On the Irrawaddy: a story of the First Burmese War.**
George Alfred Henty. London: Blackie, 1897. 352p.
A stirring adventure story in Henty's high imperialist style.

715 **Corrigan and the white cobra.**
Reginald B. Maddock. London: Thomas Nelson, 1956. 247p.
A children's adventure story, illustrated by Robert Hodgson, about a group of Europeans whose plane crashes in the Burmese jungle and their encounters with dacoits. Other adventure stories by Maddock set in post-war Burma are *Corrigan and the golden pagoda* (London: Thomas Nelson, 1958. 212p.) and *Corrigan and the green tiger* (London: Thomas Nelson, 1961. 209p.), while *One more river* (London: Thomas Nelson, 1963. 150p.) features two children and a group of British soldiers escaping from Japanese-occupied Burma.

716 **Marching to Ava: a story of the First Burmese War.**
Henry Charles Moore. London: Gall & Inglish, 1904. 318p.
A well-researched adventure story for juveniles that refights every battle of the First Anglo-Burmese War (1824-26). Also by Moore is *The dacoit's treasure or in the days of Po Thaw: a story of adventure in Burma* (London: W. H. Addison, 1897. 432p.), a novel about fighting dacoits in Upper Burma.

717 **The tiger-man of Burma: and other adventure yarns.**
Argyll Saxby. London: 'Boy's Own Paper' Office, 1923. 245p.
A collection of children's adventure stories in which the first, from which the book takes its title, is about dacoits in Burma (p. 1-80).

718 **Drummer boy of Burma.**
William Oliver Stevens. London; Glasgow: Collins, 1946. 242p. map.
An above-average children's novel set in Burma in the 1880s.

The Arts

General

719 **Oriental art: a handbook of styles and forms.**
Jeannine Auboyer, Michel Beurdeley, Jean Boisselier, Huguette
Rousset, Chantal Massonaud, translated from the French by Elizabeth
and Richard Bartlett. London; Boston,; Massachusetts: Faber &
Faber, 1979. 608p. maps. bibliog.

Designed for Western travellers to the East, and for visitors to museums and sale-
rooms, this handbook provides a basic introduction to Oriental art. Each region or
country chapter has a short introduction giving a brief account of its art and history,
followed by line drawings illustrating temples, architectural decoration, sculpture,
ceramics, decorative arts, etc. A concise bibliography, map, and listing of museums is
provided for each section. The Southeast Asia section entries have been written by
Professor Jean Boisselier and Burma is covered on p. 131-59, while a further section
'The Buddha's gestures' (p. 365-80) by Professor Boisselier is useful for understanding
the iconography of Buddha images.

720 **Burmese art and its influences.**
London: Beurdeley Matthews, 1981. 60p. map. bibliog.

This is an illustrated catalogue of an exhibition of Burmese art held in London from 8-
25 April, 1981. Its value lies in its excellent bibliography on Burmese art with
approximately 200 entries.

721 **The temples and sculptures of Southeast Asia.**
Louis Frédéric, foreword by Jeannine Auboyer, translated from the
French by Arnold Rosin. London: Thames & Hudson, 1965. 435p.
maps. bibliog.

This handsome art history volume has two chapters on Burma (p. 22-142) covering
from the earliest Pyu period to the late 19th-century Mandalay period, with over 100
black-and-white plates illustrating temples and art of Hmawza, Pagan, Pegu,
Mrohaung, Sagaing, Mingun, Amarapura and Mandalay.

722 **Burma, Korea, Tibet.**
Alexander B. Griswold, Chewon Kim, Peter H. Pott. London:
Methuen; New York: Crown Publishers, 1964. 277p. maps. bibliog.
(Art of the World).

The Burma section of this attractive book is written by Alexander B. Griswold and the
text and ten colour plates occupy a disproportionately small number of pages (p. 12-
60) in comparison with the Korea and Tibet sections, with a bibliography (p. 255-56)
and maps in the appendixes. Griswold concentrates almost entirely upon Pagan and its
architecture, with only a brief consideration of the evolution of Pagan painting and
sculpture.

723 **Burmese art.**
John Lowry. London: Her Majesty's Stationery Office, 1974. [n.p.].

This short introduction to Burmese art reproduces, (mostly in colour), and describes,
fifty works of art from the collection of the Victoria and Albert Museum, London.
Objects illustrated include Buddhas and other images, pottery, gold and lacquer
ornaments and receptacles, wood carvings, swords, and an embroidered hanging
(*kalaga*). See also the article by Lowry, 'Burmese art at the V & A Museum', *Arts of
Asia*, vol. 5, no. 2 (March–April 1975), p. 26-37. Also relevant is Lowry's illustrated
article, 'A Burmese Buddhist shrine', in *Victoria and Albert Museum Yearbook: 3*
(London: Phaidon Press, 1972, p. 116-32), which describes an elaborate gilded shrine
from Mandalay palace and the figures and objects associated with it, and compares its
motifs and style with Burmese royal thrones and Buddhist iconography.

724 **In praise of Buddhist art in Burma.**
Marg, vol. 9, no. 3 (June 1956). 64p. maps.

The entire issue of this lavishly illustrated Indian magazine of the arts is devoted to
Burma, and contains the following miscellany: 'The cultural background of Burma' by
Reginald Le May (p. 5-19); 'Ananda temple at Pagan: architecture' by Charles
Duroiselle (p. 21-44): 'Frescoes' by Niharanjan Ray (p. 45-50); 'The fantastic world of
the thirty-seven nats' by Richard Carnac Temple (p. 51-59); 'A Buddhist building for
20th century Burma: the International Institute of Advanced Buddhist Studies,
Rangoon' by Benjamin Polk (p. 61-64).

725 **Kunst in Burma: 2000 Jahre Architektur, Malerei und Plastik im
Zeichen des Buddhismus und Animismus.** (Art in Burma: 2,000 years of
architecture, painting and sculpture in the context of Buddhism and
animism.)
Nine Oshegowa, Sergej Oshegow, translated from the Russian by
Christian Heidemann. Leipzig, GDR: VEB E. A. Seemann, 1988.
337p. map.
There is to date no popular book on the art of Burma in English that can rival this
German publication which describes and illustrates Burma's ancient temples,
architecture and iconography, wall paintings, manuscripts, wood carvings and
lacquerware illustrated by line drawings and sixty-five colour and eighty-nine black-
and-white photographs. Originally published in Russian under the title *Iskusstvo
Birmy*; the authors' names also appear romanized as Ozegova and Ozegov.

726 **Art of South East Asia: Cambodia, Vietnam, Thailand, Laos, Burma,
Java, Bali.**
Philip Rawson. London: Thames & Hudson, 1990. 288p. bibliog.
(World Art Library).
This profusely illustrated general introduction to Southeast Asian art devotes a long
section (p. 161-202) to Burma, with colour and black-and-white plates and some Pagan
temple plans.

727 **Survivors from a Burmese palace.**
Noel F. Singer. *Arts of Asia*, vol. 18, no. 1 (Jan.–Feb. 1988), p. 94-
102.
The author, drawing on Burmese sources regarding court ceremonies, etiquette and
sumptuary laws, describes and illustrates objects and symbols associated with the
palaces and thrones of the kings of the Konbaung dynasty (1752-1885), and attempts to
trace objects from Mandalay palace surviving today in museums and private collections
worldwide. Also relevant is the detailed illustrated account of royal ceremonies, titles,
dress and regalia by Yi Yi, 'Life at the Burmese court under the Burmese kings',
Journal of the Burma Research Society, vol. 44, pt. 1 (June 1961), p. 85-129, together
with her earlier article, 'The thrones of Burmese kings', *Journal of the Burma Research
Society*, vol. 43, pt. 2 (Dec. 1960), p. 97-123. Photos of the 'goose' and 'lily' thrones at
Mandalay palace can be found in the handsome photographic album by Martin
Hürlimann, *Burma, Ceylon, Indo–China, Siam, Cambodia, Annam, Tongking,
Yunnan: landscape, architecture* (London: The Studio, 1930. 288p. maps.) which
contains altogether seventy-nine full page black-and-white plates (p. 49-127) of Burma.
A useful listing of the Burmese royal regalia, with a folding black-and-white drawing of
the throne of King Thibaw and surrounding regalia showing each item's disposition and
name, is Richard Carnac Temple's 'Notes on a collection of royal regalia of the kings
of Burma of the Alompra dynasty', *Indian Antiquary*, vol. 31 (Nov. 1902), p. 442-44.

**Essays offered to G. H. Luce by his colleagues and friends in honour of his
seventy-fifth birthday.**
See item no. 2.

Special Burma Studies Issue.
See item no. 7.

The world of Buddhism.
See item no. 469.

Buddhism: art and faith.
See item no. 494.

The Buddhist Art Museum of the Department of Religious Affairs.
See item no. 796.

Some observations on libraries, manuscripts and books of Burma from the 3rd century AD to 1886.
See item no. 797.

The Burmese collection at Denison University.
See item no. 798.

Arts of Asia.
See item no. 803.

Painting, sculpture and architecture

728 **Some Burmese paintings of the seventeenth century and later.**
Jane Terry Bailey. *Artibus Asiae*, vol. 38, pt. 4 (1976), p. 267-86;
vol. 40, pt. 1 (1978), p. 41-61; vol. 41, pt. 1 (1979), p. 41-63.
This three-part series of articles describes and illustrates late 17th-century wall paintings at Tilawkaguru Cave (a monastic complex south of Sagaing), early 18th-century paintings at Pagan, and 19th-century murals at the Taungthaman Kyauktawgyi temple at Amarapura.

729 **Traditional Burmese architecture, Pagan period.**
Rangoon: Department of Higher Education, Ministry of Education,
1986.
A portfolio volume (sixty-seven leaves, 38 × 52 cm) of architectural drawings of Buddhist temples and shrines at Pagan, built in the period 1044-1314. The plans have legends in Burmese and/or English. Also relevant is the article by Than Tun, 'Religious buildings of Burma, AD 1000-1300', *Journal of the Burma Research Society*, vol. 42, pt. 2 (1959), p. 71-80.

730 **Buddha images from Burma.**
Sylvia Fraser-Lu. *Arts of Asia*, vol. 11, nos. 1-3 (Jan—Feb;
March–April; May–June 1981), p. 72-82; p. 62-72; p. 129-36.
A three-part survey of Burmese Buddhist images in consecutive articles, subtitled as follows: part one, 'Sculptured in stone'; part two, 'Bronze and related materials'; part three, 'Wood and lacquer'. The articles are profusely illustrated with black-and-white

photographs of images from the earliest Pyu period through to the 20th century, including many from collections in Burma. Also relevant is the article by Nancy H. Dowling, 'Five nineteenth-century Burmese bronzes', *Journal of the Siam Society*, vol. 66, pt. 2 (July 1978), p. 172-78, which describes some dated images with a translation of their inscriptions.

731 **L'armée de Māra au pied de l'Ānanda (Pagan, Birmanie).** (The army of Mara at the base of the Ananda [Pagan, Burma].)
Emmanuel Guillon. Paris: Editions Recherche sur les Civilisations, 1985. 108p. bibliog. (Mémoire, 60).

A detailed iconographic and palaeographic analysis of the plaques portraying the Buddha's defeat of the army of Mara on the west facade of the Ananda temple basement at Pagan. Guillon discusses and translates the plaques' Mon inscriptions and considers the textual sources for the scenes, and makes comparisons with other depictions and temples. Illustrated with black-and-white plates of thirty-two plaques. For an account of a different series of plaques on the Ananda's east face, see Harry L. Shorto's article in *Essays offered to G. H. Luce by his colleagues and friends in honour of his seventy-fifth birthday* (q.v.).

732 **Two Burmese manuscripts of the life of the Buddha.**
Patricia M. Herbert. *FMR*, no. 15 (1985), p. 130-39.

This article in a de luxe art magazine published in America reproduces in fifteen full-colour plates scenes from the life of the Buddha, with a description and part translation of the manuscripts which are in the collection of the British Library. Another illustrated (with one colour and fourteen black-and-white plates) manuscript study is that by Charles Duroiselle, 'Pageant of King Mindon leaving his palace on a visit to the Kyauktawgyi Buddha image at Mandalay (1865): reproduced from a contemporary and rare document', *Memoirs of the Archaeological Survey of India*, no. 27 (1925), p. 1-16 (+ fifteen plates), describing a particularly fine Burmese folding book manuscript once owned by Rodway Swinhoe, author of *The incomplete guide to Burma* (Rangoon: [s.n.], [1925]), and now in the British Library's collection.

733 **The 550 Jatakas in old Burma.**
Gordon H. Luce. *Artibus Asiae*, vol. 19, parts 3-4 (1956), p. 291-307.

Luce contributed this article to a special number of the journal *Artibus Asiae* (Ascona, Switzerland) dedicated to the memory of the French scholar Pierre Dupont (1908-55). In it Luce examines the series of Jataka plaques and paintings at the Ananda, West and East Hpet-leik, Gu-byauk-gyi, Naga-yon, Abe-yadana, Pyat-sa-shwe and Mingala-zei-di temples in Pagan, with particular reference to the ordering and numbering of the Jataka and to name variants. He signals the need for further research to establish links between textual sources and the popularity of the Jataka stories as a subject for depiction at Pagan. See also the detailed analysis of Jataka paintings from one Pagan temple given in the article by Ba Shin, K. J. Whitbread, and G. H. Luce, 'Pagan Wetkyi–in Kubyaugyi', *Artibus Asiae*, vol. 33 (1971), p. 167-218 which also includes an account of the activities of Thomann, author of *Pagan: ein Jahrtausend Buddhistischer Tempelkunst* (q.v.).

734 **The iconography of Avalokitesvara in mainland South East Asia.**
Nandana Chutivongs. Leiden, The Netherlands: [s.n.], 1984. 616p.
bibliog.
Written as a thesis for the Rijksuniversiteit te Leiden, this study examines the
iconography of the Bodhisattva image in Indian and Sinhalese art, and its development
in the art of Burma, Thailand, Cambodia and Champa. Chapter three (p. 95-211)
covers Burma and provides an iconographical and statistical analysis of images of
Avalokitesvara in Burma, illustrated with black-and-white plates and line drawings at
the end of the book.

735 **Pagan: mural paintings of the Buddhist temples in Burma.**
Toru Ono. Tokyo: Kodansha, 1978. 254p. 2 maps. bibliog.
The quality of Takao Inoue's photographic plates (135 in colour, 132 in black-and-
white) make this an invaluable source book on Burmese wall paintings. Most
illustrations are from temples in Pagan, but examples from other regions of Burma are
also included. The text is in Japanese, but all plates are captioned in English and
Japanese and an English summary of the book's six chapters is provided (p. 211-29).

736 **Buddhist book illuminations.**
Pratapaditya Pal, Julia Meech-Pekarik. New York; Paris; Hong
Kong; New Delhi: Ravi Kumar, 1988. 339p. bibliog.
A lavish art book published in a limited edition of 500 copies. Burma is briefly covered
in the chapter 'Sri Lanka and Southeast Asia' (p. 181-224) and some comparisons
made with Indian and Thai art. Although there are several illustrations of Burmese
manuscripts, the quality of the colour reproduction is often poor and some plates are
printed upside-down or in reverse.

737 **Les monuments sur plan pentagone à Pagan.** (Pentagonal plan
monuments at Pagan.)
Pierre Pichard. *Bulletin de l'Ecole Française d'Extrême-Orient*, vol. 74
(1985), p. 305-367.
An examination and description of sixteen temples built on a pentagonal ground plan
in Pagan and of one in Salé, constructed in the 12th and 13th centuries, and claimed as
the first regular five-sided buildings in the world. The temples' construction
architecture and dimensions are detailed, with forty supplementary pages of temple
plans, cross-sections and black-and-white photographs.

738 **Brahmanical gods in Burma: a chapter of Indian art and iconography.**
Niharranjan Ray. Calcutta, India: Calcutta University Press, 1932.
99p.
An examination of Visnu, Siva, Brahma and other gods in Burmese art with examples
from Arakan, Hmawza, Thaton and Pagan. Twenty-two additional plates complement
the text.

739 **The Buddhist art of ancient Arakan: an eastern border state beyond ancient India, east of Vanga and Samatata.**
San Tha Aung. Rangoon: Daw Saw Saw [1979]. 128p. bibliog.
Detailed archaeological work on the ancient kingdom of Arakan remains to be done. However, this study, including fourteen pages of plates, looks at early remains as well as the later Buddhist temples of the 15th to 17th centuries.

740 **The Peimpathara parabaik.**
Noel F. Singer. *Arts of Asia*, vol. 18, no. 6 (Nov.–Dec. 1988), p. 128-37.
The focus of this article is an incomplete Burmese folding-book manuscript (*parabaik*) of c. 1823 illustrating the life of the Buddha. In describing this important manuscript, the author provides much helpful information upon dating Burmese painting styles (from such features as hair styles, costumes and architecture) and draws comparisons with Burmese wall paintings and other illustrated manuscripts. The article is well illustrated with colour and black-and-white plates. For another study of individual manuscripts see the articles by Vivian Ba, 'Court life and festivals in King Mindon's palace', *Guardian*, vol. 14, nos. 10-11 (Oct.-Nov. 1967), p. 20-24; p. 16-20, and 'A Burmese painting of the Nimi-Jataka 1869 by Saya Ko Kya Nyun in the Musée Guimet of Paris', *Guardian*, vol. 13, no. 2 (Feb. 1966), p. 33-43.

741 **King Dhammaceti's Pegu.**
Donald M. Stadtner. *Orientations* (Feb. 1990), p. 53-60.
This illustrated article investigates the symbolic significance and textual sources for a series of Buddhist monuments built in the 15th century by the Mon King Dhammaceti (1472-92) at Pegu. By the same author is 'A fifteenth century royal monument in Burma and the seven stations in Buddhist art', *Art Bulletin*, vol. 63, pt. 1 (March 1991), p. 39-52.

742 **Pagan: art and architecture of old Burma.**
Paul Strachan. Whiting Bay, Scotland: Kiscadale, 1989. 159p. 3 maps. bibliog.
This beautiful art book on Burma's ancient capital, Pagan, helps fill the great gap that exists between Gordon H. Luce's monumental study *Old Burma – early Pagan* (q.v.) and the brief guide, *Glimpses of glorious Pagan* (q.v.). The author conducted research in Pagan in 1986 and 1987 and his book provides much to interest both scholars and general readers. In part one, Western explorations and scholarship on Pagan are outlined, and the rise of the Pagan dynasty and the stylistic evolution of its temples, stupas and mural paintings are described. In part two, over seventy monuments are presented, grouped into three periods, with a detailed analysis of their architecture and iconography. A number of well-known monuments have been reappraised while some significant late temples which have not previously been published, are also featured. With 35 colour and 160 black-and-white photographs, and 32 line drawings of temple plans. Published in America under the title *Imperial Pagan: art and architecture of old Burma* (Honolulu: University of Hawaii Press, 1990).

The Arts. Painting, sculpture and architecture

743 **Pagan: ein Jahrtausend buddhistischer Tempelkunst.** (Pagan: a thousand years of Buddhist temple art.)
Th. H. Thomann. Stuttgart: Heilbronn, Germany: Verlag Walter Seifert, 1923. 186p. map.

Thomann's work represents the first major Western study of Pagan. The first part of the book (p. 1-109), and most of the black-and-white plates, are devoted to the temples of Pagan. The book also contains Thomann's description and photographs of the Shwe Dagon in Rangoon and of Burma's minority ethnic groups and the Andaman Islanders. Thomann was responsible for hacking large chunks of paintings from the walls of Pagan's temples, and some of these are now in the Hamburg Ethnographic Museum, but the fate of many of the treasures looted by Thomann remains unknown. For an account of Thomann's activities and a fascinating study of the paintings which reconstructs the original order of some 260 Jataka wall paintings and transcribes and translates the ink glosses beneath them, see the article (including five pages of plates) by Kenneth J. Whitbread, 'Mediaeval Burmese wall-paintings from a temple at Pagan now in the Hamburgisches Museum für Völkerkunde, Hamburg', *Oriens Extremus*, vol. 18, pt. 1 (July 1971), p. 85-122.

744 **Old Burmese painting.**
Tin Lwin. *Oriens Extremus*, vol. 21, pt. 2 (Dec. 1974), p. 237-59.

A translation of a Burmese work published by the Burmese Ministry of Culture in 1967 under the title *Shei-yo Myan-ma baji*. It describes Burmese wall paintings from the Pagan period to the late 19th century. Tin Lwin's translation is published without the illustrations included in the original Burmese edition. See also the article by Pe Maung Tin, 'A handbook of old handicrafts', *Journal of the Burma Research Society*, vol. 45, pt. 1 (1962), p. 109-16, which gives extracts from Burmese works on painting and carpentry.

745 **Early Burma – old Siam: a comparative commentary.**
Horace Geoffrey Quaritch Wales. London: Bernard Quaritch, 1973. 188p.

This study of the artistic traditions of Burma and Thailand concentrates on the art of Pagan and of Sukhotai, illustrated here by thirty-nine pages of plates. The author draws on, and pays homage to, Gordon Luce's work, especially his *Old Burma – early Pagan* (q.v.), while challenging some of his interpretations. Wales pays particular attention to decorative motifs, especially the stucco decoration of Pagan temples, and also deals with 13th-century Pagan temples not included in Luce's study. Among other studies by Quaritch Wales – who primarily writes on Thailand – is *The universe around them: cosmology and cosmic renewal in Indianized South-East Asia* (q.v.) and *Dvaravati: the earliest kingdom of Siam* (London: Bernard Quaritch, 1969. 149p. bibliog.) which examines archaeological findings on the ancient Mon empire of the first millennium AD.

746 **Murals in Burma: volume 1, paintings from Pagan of the late period, 18th century.**
Klaus Wenk, with a contribution by Tin Lwin. Zurich, Switzerland: Verlag Inigo von Oppersdorff, 1977. 267p. bibliog.

This lavish and costly art book has been produced to the highest standards. It contains sixty-six colour plates of 18th-century wall paintings from seven temples in Pagan, capital of Burma from the 11th to the 13th centuries. The plates are fully described, and the subject of Burmese painting from the Pagan period to the 19th century is surveyed in three introductory chapters. The photography was done before the severe earthquake that damaged Pagan in July 1975 and the book thus provides a record of much that has been lost. To date, no further volumes have appeared.

Perspective of Burma: an Atlantic Monthly supplement.
See item no. 15.

Historical sites in Burma.
See item no. 90.

Glimpses of glorious Pagan.
See item no. 91.

Guide to the Mandalay palace.
See item no. 92.

Ancient Arakan.
See item no. 94.

Mandalay and other cities of the past in Burma.
See item no. 95.

Shwe Dagon.
See item no. 96.

Old Burma – early Pagan.
See item no. 172.

Southeast Asia in the 9th to 14th centuries.
See item no. 173.

Sanskrit Buddhism in Burma.
See item no. 483.

The thirty-seven nats: a phase of spirit worship prevailing in Burma.
See item no. 490.

History of Buddhism in Burma, AD 1000-1300.
See item no. 492.

Pagan Newsletter.
See item no. 819.

Ceramics

747 **Burmese ceramics.**
Sumarah Adhyatman. *The Ceramic Society of Indonesia Bulletin*
(*Himpunan Keramik Indonesia*), (May 1985), p. 1-41.
This well-illustrated (in colour and black-and-white) article reviews Burma's ceramic
trade, particularly in large Martaban jars, from the 13th to the 17th centuries and
describes early wares found at sites in Burma. The present pottery production of
Burma is also described.

748 **The ceramics of South-East Asia: their dating and identification.**
Roxanna M. Brown. Singapore; Oxford; New York: Oxford
University Press, 1988. 2nd ed. 130p. 6 maps. bibliog. (Oxford in Asia
Studies in Ceramics).
The publication of the first edition of this book (Oxford: Oxford University Press,
1977) did much to stimulate interest and research in Southeast Asian ceramics. This
revised and updated edition incorporates the results of recent research and discoveries
and has many new illustrations and maps depicted on 113 supplementary pages of
plates. The original edition omitted Burma altogether, but for this revised edition a
chapter on Burmese ceramics (p. 99-112) has been added together with colour and
black-and-white plates of Burmese wares. In the case of Burma the most important
recent findings have been early glazed ceramics and the excavations of burial sites in
Tak province along the Thai–Burmese border which have yielded a new type of green-
and-white ware. The chapter on Burma also discusses the Martaban storage jars.

749 **Ceramic traditions of South-East Asia.**
John Guy. Singapore; Oxford; New York: Oxford University Press,
1989. 68p. map. bibliog. (The Asia Collection).
This introduction to the ceramics of Southeast Asia discusses the wares, kiln
technology and the evolution of forms and glazes, and features the findings of recent
archaeological work. The chapter on Burma (p. 5-14) indicates the pre-Pagan origins
of glazed ceramics, discusses glazed architectural ceramics at Pagan, and glazed
earthenware at Pagan, Pegu, Martaban and other production centres. There are black-
and-white illustrations of Burmese ceramics and a colour reproduction of a Burmese
glazed tile on the cover of the book.

750 **Introducing Thai ceramics also Burmese and Khmer.**
John C. Shaw. Chiang Mai, Thailand: Duangphorn Kemasingki,
1987. 111p. 2 maps. bibliog.
So little has been written on Burmese ceramics that, although the Burma section of this
book is very brief (p. 98-108) and, in the author's words, 'highly speculative', it does
help throw some light on Burma's 'ceramic blank'. The author concentrates on the
recent discovery of Burmese tin glazed and celadon wares at hill top burial sites in Tak
province, near Thailand's border with Burma. Three pages of colour plates illustrate
some of these wares.

751 **Ceramic sites in Burma.**
Noel F. Singer. *Arts of Asia* (Sept.–Oct. 1990), p. 108-17.
This wide-ranging article discusses ceramics in Burma and Pyu, Mon and Burmese pottery sites and production from the Pyu period (to 832 AD) through to the present day. The names of Mon sites are given in their original Mon form rather than their more familiar Burmese form (i.e. Sudhuim for Thaton; Bago for Pegu). Illustrated with line drawings, black-and-white and colour photography.

752 **Monograph on the pottery and glassware of Burma, 1894-95.**
Taw Sein Ko. Rangoon: Government Printing, 1895. 13p.
A description of the production of earthenware pottery in Burma, with illustrations of different types of pottery and stages of production on twenty-three supplementary pages of lithographs. The only mention of glassware is a statement to the effect that it is not an indigenous industry. See also Dawn F. Rooney, *Folk pottery in South-East Asia* (Singapore; Oxford; New York: Oxford University Press, 1987. 73p. 2 maps. bibliog. [Images of Asia]) which has brief references to Burma in sections on glazed wares and on contemporary pottery production.

Crafts and costume

753 **Opium Gewichte/Opium weights/Poids d'Asie.**
Rolf Braun, Ilse Braun. Landau, GFR: Pfälzische Verlagsanstalt, 1983. 239p. map. bibliog.
The first half of this book (p. 9-115) has parallel texts in English, French and German arranged on facing pages so that the interspersed photographs and line illustrations can immediately be related to the text. Very little has been written about opium weights which are mostly associated with Burma, but are also found in Thailand, Cambodia and Laos. Although best known and sought after as 'opium weights', these animal shaped weights were used throughout the region for weighing all kinds of produce. This detailed study traces the history of the weights, discusses standardization and gauge marks and seals, lists and classifies all the various shapes used, and gives advice on distinguishing genuine from reproduction weights. The second half of the book (p. 119-239) consists of black-and-white plates with photographs of 631 weights, captioned in German only. Also relevant is the article by Sylvia Fraser-Lu, 'Burmese opium weights', *Arts of Asia*, vol. 12, no. 1 (Jan.–Feb. 1982), p. 73-81.

754 **Indian and Oriental armour.**
Wilbraham Egerton, 2nd Baron Egerton of Tatton, introduction by H. Russell Robinson. Harrisburg, Pennsylvania: Stackpole Books, 1968. 178p. map.
This is a facsimile reproduction of Lord Egerton's *A description of Indian and Oriental armour* (London, 1896) which was a revised and slightly expanded version of his *An illustrated handbook of Indian arms* (London: William H. Allen, 1880). The work is in two parts: the first gives a sketch of the military history of India and concludes with a short account of the First Anglo-Burmese War (1824-26), and the second contains a

descriptive illustrated catalogue of Indian arms. The arms of Burma are described on p. 92-95 in a section headed 'British and native Burmah and Siam'. Egerton's 1880 publication *An illustrated handbook of Indian arms* has also been recently reprinted (by White Orchid Press, Bangkok, 1981).

755 Burmese lacquerware.
Sylvia Fraser-Lu. Bangkok: Tamarind, 1986. 164p. map. bibliog.
This book constitutes the first definitive study of all aspects of Burmese lacquerware with chapters on its origins, on the lacquer process, different techniques of decoration and moulding, design motifs, lacquerware objects for secular use and for religious use, lacquer craft centres in Burma, and on lacquerware collections in Burma and abroad. The book is richly illustrated with 35 black-and-white plates, numerous line drawings and 165 colour illustrations. Also by Fraser-Lu is an article, 'The government lacquer school and museum of Pagan', *Arts of Asia*, vol. 16, no. 4 (July–Aug. 1986), p. 104-11. A brief German study with plates illustrating the lacquerware collection of the Hamburg Ethnographic Museum is Gernot Prunner, *Meisterwerke Burmanische Lackkunst.* (Masterpieces of Burmese lacquer.) (Hamburg, Germany: Hamburgisches Museum für Völkerkunde und Vorgeschichte in Selbstverlag, 1966. 64p. map. bibliog. [Wegweiser zur Völkerkunde, vol. 9]).

756 Frog drums and their importance in Burmese culture.
Sylvia Fraser-Lu. *Arts of Asia*, vol. 13, no. 5 (Sept.–Oct. 1983), p. 50-63.
An illustrated study of the bronze drums of Burma. See also Richard M. Cooler, *The Karen bronze drums of Burma: the magic pond* (PhD thesis, Cornell University Ithaca, New York, 1979. 401p. bibliog. Available from University Microfilms, Ann Arbor, Michigan, order no. UM 8003915) which examines over 400 drums, describes their place in Karen culture, and attempts to trace their evolution on the basis of certain key decorative motifs. For an exhaustive illustrated study of Southeast Asian bronze drums which reviews pioneering scholarship and analyses the typology decoration, function, musicology, geographical distribution and dispersion of the drums, with a chronological categorization of drums from the early Bronze Age and their subsequent history ('aftermath'), see A. J. Bernet Kempers, *The kettledrums of Southeast Asia: a bronze age world and its aftermath* (Rotterdam, The Netherlands Brookfield, Virginia: A. A. Balkema, 1988. 599p. bibliog. [Modern Quaternary Research in Southeast Asia, edited by Gert-Jan Bartstra, Willem Arnold Casparie vol. 10]). Bernet Kempers' work has sections describing the drums' role in Karen and Shan culture (p. 389-402) and some details of the modern manufacture of drums.

757 Handwoven textiles of South-East Asia.
Sylvia Fraser-Lu. Singapore: Oxford University Press, 1988. 229p. 3 maps. bibliog.
This spendidly illustrated study of Southeast Asia's diverse textile traditions begins with an historical overview and an introduction to the materials, equipment, weaving techniques and uses of the textiles. The rest of the book gives a country-by-country survey of textiles, past and present. The chapter on Burma (p. 85-103) provides detailed information on the woven textiles of the Burmans and of the minority ethnic peoples. Illustrations and indigenous names of different design patterns are given and there is a map showing Burma's main textile centres.

758 **Silverware of South-East Asia.**
Sylvia Fraser-Lu.   Singapore; Oxford; New York: Oxford University
Press, 1989. 124p. map. bibliog. (Images of Asia).
After introductory chapters on the background of silverware and on silversmithing
techniques, the book has separate chapters on each Southeast Asian country. The
chapter on Burma, p. 23-35, gives a description of Burmese and Shan silverware from
ancient to modern times, with line drawings of objects and motifs and black-and-white
and colour plates. See also the illustrated article by Fraser-Lu, 'Burmese silverware',
Arts of Asia, vol. 10, no. 2 (March–April 1980), p. 77-83.

759 **Some costumes of highland Burma at the Ethnographical Museum of
Gothenburg.**
Henry Harald Hansen.   Gothenburg, Sweden: Elanders Boktryckeri
Aktiebolag, 1960. 81p. bibliog. (Etnologiska Studier 24).
A description of costumes collected in the Shan States in 1934 by Ebba and René
Malaise. Costumes of twelve different groups inhabiting the area – the Kachin, Maru,
Lisu, Intha and Taungyo, the Yang Hsek and Yang Lam, and the Sgaw Karen,
Taungthu, Karen-ni, Zayein and Padaung – are represented in the collection.
Altogether sixty-seven garments are illustrated and described with special considera-
tion given to their cut.

760 **Costumes of Upper Burma and the Shan States in the collections of
Bankfield Museum, Halifax.**
R. A. Innes.   Halifax, Nova Scotia: Halifax Museums, 1957. 58p.
A catalogue of a collection of costumes formed by E. C. S. George while working on a
commission for the delimitation of the Burma–China frontier at the end of the 19th
century and presented to Bankfield Museum in 1900. As well as a description of the
individual garments of different ethnic groups (Shan, Jhinghpaw, Palaung, Lahu, etc.),
there are brief sections, with photos and illustrations, on fabrics, weaving, dyeing and
embroidery.

761 **Monograph on ivory carving in Burma.**
H. S. Pratt.   Rangoon: Superintendent, Government Printing, 1901.
6p.
A brief survey of Burmese ivory carving which at the time of writing was, the author
asserts, an insignificant industry practised only in the towns of Moulmein and
Pyinmana. Also published in the *Journal of Indian Art and Industry*, vol. 9 (1901-02),
p. 59-60.

762 **Tattoo weights from Burma.**
Noel F. Singer.   *Arts of Asia*, vol. 18, no. 2 (March–April 1988),
p. 79-79.
This article describes and illustrates not only the tattoo instruments used in traditional
Burma but the whole history of the practice in Burma and the types of tattoo designs
used over the centuries.

The Arts. Crafts and costume

763   **Kalagas: the wall hangings of Southeast Asia.**
Mary Anne Stanislaw.   Menlo Park, California: Ainslies, 1987. 64p.
bibliog.

An introduction is given to the history and making of Burmese appliqué and embroidered hangings (*kalaga*), and to the modern-day revival of the art in Burma. The author describes the principal stories and motifs of Burmese *kalaga* and includes over thirty colour photographs by Robert Stedman of (mostly new) *kalaga*. A useful article on the same subject is Sylvia Fraser-Lu's 'Kalagas: Burmese wall hangings and related embroideries', *Arts of Asia*, vol. 12, no. 4 (July–Aug. 1987), p. 73-82, which has lavish illustrations of many antique *kalaga*. Also relevant is the thesis (MA, California State College at Fullerton, 1967) by Helen L. D. Breunig, *Burmese embroidery: an historical and illustrated study of the 'kalaga'* (Ann Arbor, Michigan: University Microfilms, 1980. 89p. bibliog. order no. M-1237) which discusses the history, use, methods of manufacture and stylistic motifs of Burmese *kalaga*, with data on their modern production. The microfilm, however, omits the illustrations on p. 1-8, 254-61.

764   **Glass mosaics of Burma.**
Harry L. Tilly.   Rangoon: Superintendent, Government Printing, 1901. 12p.

A description of the preparation and use of this elaborate form of decoration known in Burmese as *hman-zi shwei-cha*, with fine photographs, on thirty-one pages of plates, of glass mosaic decorations at the Shwe Dagon pagoda. Also published as an article in the *Journal of Indian Art and Industry*, vol. 9 (1901-02), p. 61-65 (+ 7 plates).

765   **Monograph on the brass and copper wares of Burma.**
Harry L. Tilly.   Rangoon: Government Printing, 1894. 12p.

The author notes that, in marked contrast to India, brass and copperware are not extensively used in Burma, nor highly ornamented. An account is given of the Burmese method of brass casting, and a list of articles produced and of brassworkers' tools is provided in Burmese and English.

766   **The silverwork of Burma.**
Harry L. Tilly.   Rangoon: Superintendent, Government Printing, 1902. 22p. [+16p. of plates].

A record of the best examples of traditional Burmese silverwork, excluding the European-influenced heavy silverware with designs in high relief which became increasingly popular in the late 19th century, together with a description of silversmiths' methods. The book was later translated into Burmese and came to serve as a textbook for silversmiths. Tilly provides information on dating Burmese silverware and on the evolution of styles, with a detailed description of each plate and, where possible, the name of the silversmith and date of production. The excellent photographs were taken by Philip Adolphe Klier who worked as a trader and photographer in Moulmein and Rangoon in the period from the 1870s to approximately 1915. Tilly's monograph was also published with illustrative plates as an article in the *Journal of Indian Art and Industry*, vol. 10 (1903-04), p. 31-35. Again by Tilly, with photographs by Klier, is *Modern Burmese silverwork* (Rangoon: Superintendent, Government Printing, 1904. 8p. [+14p. of plates]) illustrating and describing prize-winning exhibits at the annual Provincial Art Competitions held in

Burma and pieces made for government exhibitions in Delhi and Calcutta in the period 1900-04.

767 **Wood-carving of Burma.**
Harry L. Tilly.   Rangoon: Superintendent, Government Printing, 1903. 14p.

A succinct guide to Burmese woodcarving design and techniques, with twenty fine black-and-white plates (by P. Klier) illustrating the best of Burmese woodcarving in Mandalay and Rangoon. Much of the architectural woodcarving featured in the book no longer exists.

768 **Indian art at Delhi, 1903: being the official catalogue of the Delhi exhibition, 1902-1903.**
George Watt.   Calcutta, India: Superintendent, Government Printing, [1903]. 546p.

The British regularly held exhibitions of Indian art, entries for which would usually be selected by district officers and other local officials from all areas of the Indian empire (including Burma), as a means of encouraging local craftsmanship and ensuring that artistic traditions continued. This catalogue contains much of relevance to Burmese art, with photographic plates of prize-winning exhibits and details of the work and craftsmen, the main areas covered being as follows: niello ware (p. 29-31), silverware (p. 39-42), pottery (p. 94-94), woodcarving (p. 135-39), ivory carving (p. 192-93), lacquerware (p. 218-25), silk weaving (p. 317-18), and appliqué embroideries (*kalaga*) (p. 413-14). The exhibition at Delhi featured a Burma Room and included items lent from museums in Burma and by the South Kensington (Victoria and Albert) Museum. Burmese art was also exhibited at major international exhibitions in the late 19th and early 20th century, many of which were illustrated in the magnificent journal sponsored by the Government of India, the *Journal of Indian Art and Industry* (published from 1884-92 under the title *Journal of Indian Art* and from 1893-1916 under the title *Journal of Indian Art and Industry*).

Burma.
See item no. 11.

Bhamo expedition: report on the practicability of re-opening the trade route between Burmah and Western China.
See item no. 35.

Sunny days in Burma.
See item no. 59.

Gazetteer of Upper Burma and the Shan States.
See item no. 111.

Performing arts

769 **Theatre in Southeast Asia.**
James R. Brandon. Cambridge, Massachusetts: Harvard University Press, 1967. 370p. 6 maps. bibliog.

Based on a year's research in Southeast Asia (1963-64), attending and recording theatrical performances and interviewing performers and scholars, the author ambitiously attempts to survey theatre from Burma to the Philippines. The author's data is presented under thematic headings such as 'Theatre as art', 'Theatre as an institution', and 'Theatre as communication'. Burma is less well-covered than other areas and the author's account, based on English language sources, makes no indication of the range of indigenous literature on the Burmese theatre. Also by Brandon is *Brandon's guide to the theater in Asia* (Honolulu: University Press of Hawaii, 1976. 178p. bibliog.) which has a brief section on Burma (p. 9-14) – 'a pristine country for the theatergoer to explore'.

770 **Birmanisches Marionettentheater.** (The Burmese puppet theatre.)
Axel Bruns, Hla Thamein. Berlin: Firma Mandalay, 1990. 163p. bibliog.

A detailed study of the Burmese puppet theatre, its history and decline, with data on the construction of the puppets and the stage, performance techniques, characters and stories, biographies of puppeteers, a glossary of puppet terms, and black-and-white photographs of different types of puppets and portraits of famous figures associated with this art form. Hla Thamein is the author of a Burmese language study of the Burmese puppet theatre, *Myan-ma yok-thei thabin* (Rangoon: In-wa Htun sa-pei, 1968. 339p.).

771 **Burmese culture: general and particular.**
Khin Zaw. Rangoon: Sarpay Beikman, 1981. 155p.

A collection of articles, originally published between 1946 and 1981, under the pen name of 'K', on the Burmese performing arts. Khin Zaw (1905-89) was literary editor and a leading luminary of the *Guardian* (q.v.) in which he published a series 'Burma in my lifetime' and much else over more than thirty years and was at one time director of the Burma Broadcasting Service. His collected articles cover the puppet theatre, films, drama, music and folk songs, and the Burmese orchestra – providing much more information on Burmese musical instruments than is to be found in Eric Taylor, *Musical instruments of South-East Asia* (Singapore: Oxford University Press, 1989. 84p. [Images of Asia]).

772 **Burmese music: a preliminary enquiry.**
Khin Zaw. Rangoon: Burma Research Society, 1941. 44p.

A pioneering study, including thirty-six pages of music, of 'a virgin field for research'. This work is reprinted from the *Journal of the Burma Research Society*, vol. 30, pt. 3 (Dec. 1940), p. 387-466, and also published in the *Bulletin of the School of Oriental & African Studies*, vol. 10 (1940), p. 717-54.

773 **The Asian film industry.**
    John A. Lent.   London: Croom Helm, 1990. 310p. bibliog.
The section on Burma (p. 221-23) describes both the historical background to the
Burmese film industry and the contemporary scene. A brief description of the growth
of the Burmese film industry can also be found in Roy Armes' *Third world film making
and the West* (Berkeley, California; London: Univesity of California Press, 1987. 381p.
bibliog.). Descriptions of Burmese film and the film scene can sometimes be found in
the annual *International Film Guide* (London: Tantivy, 1963-.).

774 **Die Musik Birmas.** (Burmese music.)
    Kurt Reinhard.   Würzburg, Germany: Konrad Triltsch Verlag, 1939.
    105p. map. bibliog. (Schriftenreihe des Musikswissenschaftlichen
    Seminar der Universität München, 5).
An analysis of Burmese melody, harmony, rhythm and form, with a forty-page
supplement of musical notations from different parts of Burma.

775 **The Ramayana at the Burmese court.**
    Noel F. Singer.   *Arts of Asia*, vol. 19, no. 6 (Nov.–Dec. 1989), p. 90-
    103.
This article traces the history of dramatic performances of the *Ramayana* epic at the
Burmese court – from their introduction from Thailand after the Burmese conquest of
Ayutthaya in 1767 to the British annexation of Upper Burma in 1886 – and gives
details of the royal theatres and of dance costumes and masks. The article is splendidly
illustrated with old prints and photographs, and with colour reproductions from
Burmese manuscripts.

776 **Seven decades of Burmese film.**
    Tetkatho Laypway.   *The Guardian* (Rangoon), vol. 34, no. 12 (Dec.
    1987), p. 10-15.
A brief survey of Burmese cinematography from its pioneering days to the early 1980s,
with illustrations and details of actors, directors, cameramen and screenwriters.
Tetkatho Laypway also writes a monthly review of the latest Burmese films in the
Guardian magazine. Also relevant is Thoung Sein's *Problems of Burmese film*
(Rangoon: Bamathit, 1950. 52p.).

777 **Ramayana in Burmese literature and arts.**
    Thein Han, Khin Zaw.   *Journal of the Burma Research Society*,
    vol. 59, pts. 1-2 (Dec. 1976), p. 137-54.
This article looks at Burmese literary versions and adaptations of the Indian epic, at
dramatic presentations, and depictions of the Ramayana in Burmese art and
handicrafts. It includes two pages of musical notation for dance and drama
performances. The article was reprinted, with the addition of sixteen black-and-white
plates of stone reliefs from a 19th-century Upper Burman temple, in the *Silver Jubilee
Publication* of the Department of Burma Historical Research (Rangoon, 1982, p. 159-
70). Black-and-white photographs of Ramayana performances and of all the other
dances of Burma (276 photographs in all) can be found in the Burmese-language
publication, *Pyei-daung-su a ka padei-tha* (Dances of Burma.) by Min Naing
(Rangoon: Union of Burma, Ministry of Culture, 1959).

778 **A medieval Burmese orchestra.**
Denis Crispin Twitchett, Anthony H. Christie. *Asia Major: A British Journal of Far Eastern Studies* [new series], vol. 7, pts. 1-2 (1959), p. 176-95. (Arthur Waley Anniversary Volume, edited by R. Schindler).

A translation from, and discussion of, Chinese sources describing the dancers and musicians presented to the Chinese emperor in 802 AD by a mission from the Pyu kingdom in Burma. The sources include the earliest known description of an orchestra which gives specifications for the tuning of instruments. Included are illustrations of instruments and a comparative table of Pyu orchestra and Mon and Burmese musical instruments of the Pagan period.

779 **The iconography of arched harps in Burma.**
Muriel C. Williamson. In: *Music and tradition: essays on Asian and other musics presented to Laurence Picken.* Edited by D. R. Widdess, R. F. Wolpert. Cambridge, England: Cambridge University Press, 1981. p. 209-28.

This detailed study deals with the evolution of the arched harp in Burma and compares its changing features from the mid 7th-century Pyu harp through to the modern Burmese harp. The author draws on all published iconographical representations of the harp from the Pyu, Pagan and later periods and points out the large gaps – often of several centuries – between examples of harp iconography in Burma.

240

Recreation

780 **Games and children's play.**
  R. B. Dennis.   Rangoon: Burma Research Society, 1952. 113p.
  bibliog.
An illustrated study of fifty-five children's games as observed and taught to the author
in Burma, with full explanations, words of chants etc. (in Burmese script and in
translation). A description and diagram of Burmese chess is included. Originally
published as an article in the *Journal of the Burma Research Society*, vol. 35, pt. 1
(1952), p. 1-113.

Our trip to Burmah: with notes on that country.
See item no. 45.

Philately and Numismatics

781 India used in Burma.

Jal Cooper. Bombay, India: [s.n.], 1950. 65p.

An enthusiastic and well-illustrated postal history of Burma from 1824 until the administrative separation of Burma from India in 1937, with a supplementary section on Burmese postage stamp issues from 1937 to 1948. Reproduced are the texts of letters sent by British participants in the First and Second Anglo–Burmese Wars, with illustrations of their postal covers. Details and illustrations of the many handstruck cancellations used in Burma are given, together with a section on ship, railway and miscellaneous other postmarks, and a note on the postal history of the Andaman Islands (used by the British as a penal settlement for life and long-term Indian and Burmese convicts).

782 Burma postal history.

Gerald Davis, Denys Martin. London: Robson Lowe, [1987]. 204p. 38p. 10 maps. bibliog.

Originally published in 1971, this book has been republished with a thirty-eight page supplement of extensive additions and connections. It is the definitive work on the postal history of Burma from the early 19th century until 1937, when the Government of Burma was separated from the Government of British India. The Andaman and Nicobar Islands are included because they were under the Provincial Government of Burma from 1864 until 1937. Although it contains much information on postage stamps, its main focus is on the vast number of handstamps, cancellations and miscellaneous postal marks used in Burma. These are investigated in minute detail and with a wealth of illustrations. Appendixes give the numbers of stamps sold and items of mail carried, postal establishment statistics, a list of post offices, and tables of scarcity factors.

'83 The matchbox label collectors encyclopaedia.
John Henry Luker. Camberley, England: Vesta, 1984. 3rd ed. 840p. bibliog. (World Matchbox Label Series).

This compilation is in three parts: alphabetical by name of match manufacturer/company; by name of country; and miscellaneous (phillumeny news etc.). Burma matchbox labels are illustrated and described in the countries section (p. 347-51), and individual company details (for example, Muslim Match Factory, Mandalay Match Co., Dawood & Co., Finlay Fleming & Co.) are listed in the alphabetical section.

'84 The coins and banknotes of Burma.
Michael Robinson, Lewis A. Shaw. Manchester, England: The Authors, 1980. 160p. 3 maps. bibliog.

Very little has been published in any language on Burmese numismatics and this book stands as the standard reference work on the subject. It covers all the issues of Burma and Arakan (an independent kingdom until the Burmese conquest of 1784), concentrating particularly on the period from the 16th century to the present, and gives a detailed classification of Burmese coins, based on specimens in museums and private collections. A great deal of hitherto unpublished material from chronicles, reports and letters is included, and the text is fully illustrated, with colour reproductions of the banknotes. Two chapters deal with British and Japanese Second World War banknotes, and an appendix gives valuations as a guide for collectors. Robinson and Shaw have also published a short illustrated classification of copper coins minted by King Mindon (1853-78) and King Thibaw (1878-85), *The die varieties of nineteenth century Burmese copper coins* (Sale, England: The Authors, 1986. 13p.), while Michael Robinson's *The lead and tin coins of Pegu and Tenasserim* (Sale, England: The Author: 1986. 83p. map. bibliog.) is a detailed analysis of the subject, supplemented by eighteen black-and-white plates. These publications are distributed by M. Robinson, 1, Priory Road, Sale, Cheshire, M33 2BU. Also obtainable from the same source is *Arakanese coins* by San Tha Aung, translated from the Burmese by Aye Set (Sale, England: M. Robinson, 1986. 2nd ed. 66p.) which contains much information from Arakanese chronicles and other sources and includes thirty pages of plates reproduced from the original Burmese publication.

85 Philately and politics in modern Burma.
Warren Sykes. *The American Philatelist*, vol. 102, no. 8 (Aug. 1988), p. 750-57.

The subject of this forthright article is the effect of political and bureaucratic decisions on the design, issue and printing of stamps in Burma. Burmese philatelic issues from 1948 to 1986 are described and illustrated, with details of printers and the role of the State Philatelic Advisory Board.

86 The ancient coinage of mainland Southeast Asia.
Robert S. Wicks. *Journal of Southeast Asian Studies*, vol. 16, no. 2 (Sept. 1985), p. 195-225. map.

This careful study evaluates other studies of the subject – including those by Pamela Gutman, 'The ancient coinage of Southeast Asia', *Journal of the Siam Society*, vol. 66, pt. 1 (Jan. 1978), p. 8-21, and by Michael Mitchiner, 'The date of the early Funanese, Mon, Pyu and Arakanese coins ("symbolic coins")', *Journal of the Siam Society*,

Philately and Numismatics

vol. 70, pts. 1-2 (Jan.–July 1982), p. 5-12 – and provides illustrations of coins and dynastic tables of Candra and post-Candra rulers of Arakan (c. 320-729 AD).

Profile of a Burma frontier man.
See item no. 300.

The Burma Peacock.
See item no. 809.

Cuisine

787 Seafood of South-East Asia.

Alan Davidson. Singapore: Kuala Lumpur; Hong Kong: Federal Publications, 1976. 366p. map. bibliog.

This work is in two parts: the first (p. 13-198) is a detailed, illustrated catalogue of edible marine fish, crustaceans, molluscs and other sea creatures of Southeast Asia; the second (p. 201-335) consists of recipes from the countries of the region, with recipes from Burma given on p. 219-32. Indexes of names (scientific, English and in vernacular languages) and of recipe titles and ingredients are provided. The work includes drawings by Banjong Mianmanus, Thosaporn Wongratana, Elian Prasit, and Soun Singha.

788 Burma.

Patricia M. Herbert. In: *The encyclopaedia of Asian cooking.* Edited by Jeni Wright. London: Octopus Books, 1980, p. 86-99.

This contribution to a richly illustrated cookery book contains twenty recipes and an introduction to Burmese food.

789 The Burmese kitchen.

Copeland Marks, Aung Thein. New York: M. Evans, 1987. 275p. map. bibliog.

This is the most extensive English language recipe book for Burmese cookery available with over 200 recipes, helpful introductory comments, clear instructions and a glossary of ingredients.

790 Cook and entertain the Burmese way.

Mi Mi Khaing. Rangoon: Daw Ma Ma Khin/Student Press, 1975; Ann Arbor, Michigan: Karoma Publishers, 1978. 192p.

A discourse on Burmese meals, family life and entertaining as well as a recipe book giving more than 100 recipes; with an appendix listing Burmese names of fruit, vegetables, spices and fish.

Cuisine

791 South-East Asian cookery.
Sallie Morris. London: Grafton, 1989. 256p. map.

South-East Asian cookery contains a description of the author's enjoyable trip t Burma and gives thirty Burmese recipes collected there (p. 75-106). By the sam author is *Oriental cookery* (London: Apple, 1984. 223p.) which contains eleve Burmese recipes (p. 174-85).

792 The complete Asian cookbook.
Charmaine Solomon. Sydney; Auckland, New Zealand; London:
Summit, Paul Hamlyn, 1976. 511p. map.

The author's mother and aunt were born in Mandalay while she herself grew up in S Lanka. The section on Burma (p. 263-91) has an introduction to Burmese food an over fifty family recipes.

Libraries, Museums and Archives

93 Art museums of Southeast Asia: with travel notes.
Brenda Duncombe.   Sydney: Crafts Council of Australia, 1988. 28p. maps.

The section on Burma (p. 5-6) provides a brief introduction to the country and a listing of sixteen museums with addresses, opening times and a sentence on their holdings.

94 A brief guide to sources for the study of Burma in the India Office Records.
Andrew Griffin.   London: India Office Library & Records, 1979. 25p.

A helpful guide to the wealth of archival material on Burma held in the India Office Records (now part of the British Library). Also briefly covered are official publications, maps and European manuscripts and a summary list of official archives and a select list of collections of private papers are given in the appendixes. For further details on the administrative background and history of the records and their contents, see Martin Moir, *A general guide to the India Office Records* (London: British Library, 1988. 331p.). Other archival sources and private papers on Burma in British collections can be found in the detailed compilation by Mary Doreen Wainwright and Noel Matthews, *A guide to western manuscripts and documents in the British Isles relating to South and South East Asia* (London: Oxford University Press, 1965. 532p.) and its updating supplement compiled by James D. Pearson, *A guide to manuscripts and documents in the British Isles relating to South and South-East Asia: a supplement* (London: Mansell, 1989-90. 2 vols.), while for military material a useful guide is that by S. L. Mayer and William J. Koenig, *The two world wars: a guide to manuscript collections in the United Kingdom* (London; New York: Bowker, 1976). Archival material on Burma in American collections can best be accessed through the index volume five) of the massive compilation edited by G. Raymond Nunn, *Asia and Oceania: a guide to archival and manuscript sources in the United States* (London, New York: Mansell, 1985. 5 vols.).

795 **Some reflections on the library scene in Burma today.**
Michael Hill. In: *Michael Hill on science, invention and information.*
Compiled by Purabi Ward. London: The British Library, 1988, p. 50-
62.

The author, a former director of the Science Reference and Information Service of the
British Library, spent three weeks in Burma in 1976 surveying library resources for the
support of science and technology. His article, originally published in *Information*
Scientist (vol. 11, no. 2, 1977) contains general observations on library matters in
Burma and useful information on some of the twenty-four libraries visited, including
major non-science libraries such as the National Library and the Sarpay Beikman
Library. A useful earlier report by a UNESCO consultant to Burma in 1968 which
surveys twenty-two libraries is that by Palle Birkelund, *Report on the development of*
Burmese university and research libraries (Paris: UNESCO, 1969. 21p. [Serial
No. 1186/BMS/RD/DRA]). A historical survey of libraries in Burma and of post
independence developments is given by Paul Bixler under the heading 'Burma
libraries in' in *Encyclopaedia of library and information science*, edited by Allen Kent
Harold Lancour (New York: Marcel Dekker, 1970, vol. 3, p. 494-508) and reprinted in
the *Guardian*, vol. 17, no. 12 (Dec. 1970), p. 14-21.

796 **The Buddhist Art Museum of the Department of Religious Affairs.**
Maung Maung Lay. *Light of the Dhamma*, vol. 1, no. 2 (Aug. 1981),
p. 49-52.

A brief introduction to the collections of this research museum inaugurated in 1962 and
attached to the Institute of Advanced Buddhist Studies at the Kaba Aye Pagoda
(World Peace Pagoda), Rangoon. The author also includes some details on the
iconography of Burmese Buddhas.

797 **Some observations on libraries, manuscripts and books of Burma from**
the 3rd century AD to 1886.
E. Pauline Quigly. London: Arthur Probsthain, 1956. 34p. map.
bibliog.

The main focus of this illustrated essay is on the manuscripts of Burma, based mainly
on items in the collection of the British Library. See also the colour illustrated article
by Patricia M. Herbert, 'The making of a collection: Burmese manuscripts in the
British Library', *British Library Journal*, vol. 15, no. 2 (Spring 1989), p. 59-70, and by
Noel F. Singer, 'Palm leaf manuscripts of Myanmar (Burma)', *Arts of Asia*, vol. 21
no. 1 (Jan.–Feb. 1991), p. 133-40. Also relevant is the article by Wun, 'Notes on
Burmese manuscript books', *Journal of the Burma Research Society*, vol. 30, pt. 1
(Dec. 1933), p. 224-29. The article by Sylvia Fraser-Lu, 'Sadaik: Burmese manuscript
chests' *Arts of Asia*, vol. 14, no. 3 (May–June 1984), p. 68-74, has colour and black
and-white illustrations of different manuscript storage chests and a description of their
main decorative motifs. Stretching the definition of books somewhat, *The world'*
biggest book by (Ludu Daw) Ahmar (Mandalay, Burma: Kyipwayay, 1980. 2nd ed
57p. bibliog.) describes the 730 marble slabs at the Kuthodaw temple in Mandalay
which were inscribed between 1860 and 1868 with the text of the Buddhist canon.

798   **The Burmese collection at Denison University.**
Ursula Roberts.   *Arts of Asia*, vol. 18, no. 1 (Jan.–Feb. 1988), p. 132-35.

Denison University (Granville, Ohio, USA) has a long association with Burma where some fifty of its graduates have worked as American Baptist missionaries. Its Burmese collection was started in the 1960s by Helen K. Hunt, who was dean of women at Judson College from 1919 to 1951. This article outlines the collection's history and growth and describes and illustrates a wide range of items from the collection. Also relevant is the irregularly published *Burmese art newsletter* (Granville, Ohio: Denison University, Dept. of Visual Arts, 1968-), edited by Jane Terry Bailey, which features news and articles about the collection at Denison University and about Burmese art in general.

The World of Learning.
See item no. 642.

Publishing and
Mass Media

799 **The media in Burma and the pro-democracy movement of July–September 1988.**
Anna Allott.   *South-East Asia Library Group Newsletter*, no. 34-35 (Dec. 1990), p. 17-24.

A review of the media in Burma and of Burma's brief period of press freedom, with a chronology of events. The article is supplemented in the same issue by a 'List of Burmese pro-democracy (Aug.–Sept. 1988) publications in the British Library', compiled by Patricia M. Herbert (p. 25-38).

800 **Prose writing and publishing in Burma today: government policy and popular practice.**
Anna J. Allott.   In: *Essays on literature and society in Southeast Asia: political and sociological perspectives*. Edited by Tham Seong Chee. Singapore: Singapore University Press, 1981. p. 1-35.

This interesting essay explores the complexities arising from the Burmese government's support for literary development and language promotion (through literary seminars, the Burmese Language Commission, etc.) and the implications this has for literary creativity and freedom of expression. It contains a lot of information not readily available elsewhere on publishing and censorship in Burma, and reproduces government guidelines for printers, publishers, writers, and those working in the media.

801 **Burma.**
Paul P. Blackburn.   In: *Newspapers in Asia: contemporary trends and problems*. Edited by John A. Lent. Hong Kong, Singapore, Kuala Lumpur: Heinemann Asia, 1982, p. 177-90.

This survey describes the change from a 'golden age of journalism' in Burma in the 1950s into a 'tamed, government-dominated press' of the 1960s onwards. See also Blackburn's study of the media, *Communications and national development in Burma*,

Malaysia, and Thailand: a comparative systematic analysis (PhD thesis, The American University, Washington, DC, 1971. 440p. Available from University Microfilms, Ann Arbor, Michigan, order no. UM 71-24938).

802 **Broadcasting in Asia and the Pacific: a continental survey of radio and television.**
Edited by John A. Lent. Hong Kong, Singapore, Kuala Lumpur: Heinemann Asia, 1978. 429p. bibliog.

This compilation has contributions from thirty-five specialists and surveys broadcasting in general, the media country-by-country, and cross-system functions of the radio and television media. There is a section on the radio in Burma written by Paul P. Blackburn (p. 188-95) and brief references to religious (Christian) broadcasting to Burma (p. 344-45) in the section on religious broadcasting in Asia by Constantino E. Bernardez and William E. Harvey.

Burma Press Summary.
See item no. 810.

Myanmar Press Release.
See item no. 818.

Summary of World Broadcasts: Part III – Far East.
See item no. 820.

Asian mass communications: a comprehensive bibliography.
See item no. 843.

Burmese and Thai newspapers: an international union list.
See item no. 846.

Periodicals

803 **Arts of Asia.**
Hong Kong: Arts of Asia Publications, 1970-. bimonthly.

This handsome, glossy art magazine has in recent years featured many articles on aspects of Burmese art, contributed for the most part by Sylvia Fraser-Lu and Noel F. Singer. Forthcoming (1991-92) are articles by Noel F. Singer on Kammavaca manuscripts and binding ribbons, Jentung bowls, and rhino horn and elephant ivory carvings.

804 **Asian Survey.**
Berkeley, California: University of California Press, 1961-. monthly.

This review of contemporary Asian affairs has in each February issue a useful survey of the major, mainly political, developments in Burma in the previous year, contributed by Burma specialists.

805 **Bulletin du Cédok.**
Lausanne, Switzerland: Centre d'Etude et de Documentation sur le Karenni, 1982-. annually.

This periodical concentrates on the Karenni peoples of Burma. The Centre d'Etude et de Documentation sur le Karenni (CEDOK) also publishes separate monographs and bibliographical compilations including the following by Jean-Marc Rastorfer, *Sources anciennes sur la langue Kayah et les autres langues du Karenni* (1983. 115p.), *Karenni: une courte bibliographie avec des commentaires* (1984. 115p.), and *Ethnicité et écriture au Karenni* (1988. 42p.). CEDOK's address is Case Postale 27, CH 1000 Lausanne 22, Switzerland.

806 **Bulletin of the Burma Studies Group.**
Cobleskill, New York: Burma Studies Group, 1979-. irregular.

This *Bulletin* is edited by John P. Ferguson and Hugh MacDougall and provides news of academic activities in the field of Burma studies. Since the foundation of the Center for Burma Studies at Northern Illinois University, DeKalb, Illinois, in 1987, the Burma Studies Group has held an annual colloquium at DeKalb, and also meets during the annual conference of the Association for Asian Studies. The Center for Burma Studies issues its own *CBS News* while also distributing the *Bulletin of the Burma Studies Group*, the *Pagan Newsletter* (q.v.) and the *Burma Newsletter* (q.v.). All four are available through a combined annual subscription to the Center for Burma Studies, 140 Carrol Avenue, Northern Illinois University, DeKalb, Illinois 60115, USA.

807 **Burma Affairs Bulletin.**
London: Burma Affairs Monitor, 1991-. bimonthly.
This is one of the more recent, and more substantial, of the many newsletters and journals that have started up outside Burma to campaign for a democratic form of government and to monitor Burma issues. It is the successor to an earlier journal, *Burma Newsletter* (1988-90) issued by the UK Committee for the Restoration of Democracy in Burma. It works in close cooperation with the US-based bilingual (English and Burmese) publication, *Burma Review* (Rego Park, New York: Burma Review Committee, 1990-. monthly. Edited by Khin Ny). The first issues have highlighted the award to Daw Aung San Suu Kyi (Burma's leading opposition leader) of the 1990 Rafto Human Rights Prize and the Sakharov Prize for Freedom of Thought and her nomination for the Nobel Peace Prize, and Amnesty International's special campaign on Burma (December 1990–April 1991). Among the articles published have been, in vol. 1, no. 2 (Mar.-April 1991), 'The problem of economic development in Burma' by Tzang Yawnghwe and 'The Ne Win regime: 29 years on (a giant step backwards)' by Aung Kin which concentrates on the role of the Military Intelligence Service in Burma. Also by Aung Kin (in vol. 1, no. 3 (May-June 1991, p. 14-15) is a review or synopsis of the Burmese work entitled *U Ne Win nhin let-ma-yun a-na-shin mya* ('U Ne Win and his unflinching henchmen') (New York: Khin Nyo in International Network for Democracy in Burma, 1990) by Thaung (Aung Bala) describing MI5 activities. *Burma Affairs Bulletin*, together with such other publications produced by Burmese exiles as *Burma Review* and *Burma Alert* is a good source of information on the current economic situation in Burma, reporting forestry, logging, mining, oil exploration and other contracts made by the current military regime with foreign companies, and reporting arms deals with China, and highlighting ecological consequences and other matters which in general are not widely reported. *Burma Affairs Bulletin* is available on subscription from 3A Chatto Road, London SW11 6LJ; *Burma Review* from PO Box 7726, Rego Park, NY 11374, USA; and *Burma Alert* from Associates to Develop Democratic Burma, c/o Harn Yawnghwe, RR4, Shawville, Quebec JOX 2YO, Canada.

808 **Burma Newsletter.**
New York: [Maureen Aung-Thwin], 1987-. irregular.
A compilation of Burma news culled from newspaper and journal articles worldwide on aspects of contemporary Burma, with details of recent publications and Burma-related matters in general. It is a good source of information on Burmese current affairs, reprinting news and articles on the human rights situation, refugees, oil company activities in Burma, teak extraction, opium traffic, etc. It is a revival of an earlier periodical of the same name issued from 1979-82 by the Asia Society, New York, and is obtainable on subscription from the Center for Burma Studies at Northern Illinois University, DeKalb, Illinois.

Periodicals

809　The Burma Peacock.
Edmonton, Alberta: Burma Philatelic Study Circle, 1979-. quarterly.
This slender journal of the Burma Philatelic Study Circle (7127-87 Street, Edmonton Alberta, Canada T6C 3G1) contains a mass of philatelic information and research relating to Burma. A bibliography of Burma philately is currently in preparation by the journal's editor, Alan Meech.

810　Burma Press Summary.
Cooperstown, New York: Hugh C. MacDougall, 1987-. monthly.
This provides a summary of selected items from the English-language *Working People's Daily* newspaper published in Rangoon. It is compiled for the Burma Studies Group of America and can be obtained on subscription from Hugh C. MacDougall, 32 Elm Street, Cooperstown, NY 13326.

811　Contemporary Southeast Asia.
Singapore: Institute of Southeast Asian Studies, 1979-. quarterly.
This journal specializes in politics, international relations and security-related issues in Southeast Asia. As well as original articles and book reviews, it publishes 'documentation' to provide an up-to-date source of information. For example, vol. 10 no. 4 of March 1989 published (p. 430-31) the texts of the Political Parties Registration Law (Burma), Law Relating to Forming of Organizations (Burma), and the Union of Burma Foreign Investment Law.

812　Country Report: Thailand, Burma.
London: Economist Intelligence Unit, 1986-. quarterly.
This is one of a series of reviews covering some 150 countries produced by the Economist Intelligence Unit, an international business research and advisory organization providing information on political and economic trends. It is a successor to the EIU's earlier publication, *Quarterly Economic Review: Thailand, Burma* (London: EIU, 1971-). There is an annual supplement entitled *Country Profile Thailand, Burma* (London: Economist Intelligence Unit, 1986-) which presents basic data and statistics across a wide range of subjects and is designed primarily for business people. A new periodical by a subsidiary of the Economist Group which focuses on investment opportunities and provides a concise monthly analysis of business economic and political developments in Vietnam, Laos, Cambodia and Burma is *Insight Indochina* (Hong Kong: Business International, 1990-. monthly).

813　Far Eastern Economic Review.
Hong Kong: Far Eastern Economic Review, 1946-. weekly.
This informative journal focuses on political, economic and commercial news with feature articles on all aspects of Asia. Its Bangkok-based correspondent Bertil Lintner has largely been responsible for giving Burma high profile coverage, especially during the pro-democracy uprising period from 1988 onwards. It is the best source of news on all aspects of Burmese current affairs, carrying an increasing number of articles on Burma as the military régime (SLORC) opens up Burma to international commercial ventures while at the same time exercising rigorous political control over its citizens

314   The Guardian.

Rangoon: Guardian Press, 1953-. monthly.

This magazine has distinguished origins, being the inspiration of Thein Han ('Zawgyi', 1908-90), Burma's foremost literary critic, and having many eminent names associated with it in its early years. It has featured covers and illustrations by the artist Ngwe Gaing, and its literary editor for many years was Khin Zaw ('K'), while Dr. Maung Maung took an active interest in it, contributing in particular in the 1950s an illustrated biographical series of 'profiles' on Burmese politicians and other personalities. Early issues even included articles by Ne Win and Nu, as well as by foreigners such as G. H. Luce, J. S. Furnivall and C. J. Richards. In scope *The Guardian* embraces current affairs, literature and the arts and includes book and film reviews. After the 1962 military coup and with the nationalization of private enterprises, advertisements disappeared from the *Guardian*'s pages, and the magazine has struggled to maintain standards, declining into a bland shadow of its former self. A loyal contributor over the years has been the monk/poet Ashin Ananda (the Buddhist name of Friedrich Lustig), while a review of the Burmese cinema by 'Tetkatho Laypway' is a regular feature.

315   Journal of Asian Studies.

Ann Arbor, Michigan: Association for Asian Studies, 1956-. quarterly.

This is the premier American academic journal in the field of Asian studies, with an excellent book review section. The *Journal* succeeds the *Far Eastern Quarterly*, published November 1941 to September 1956. The Association for Asian Studies also publishes an invaluable annual *Bibliography of Asian Studies* which, although sometimes running in arrears (e.g. the 1985 *Bibliography* was only published in 1990), is an excellent location source for books and articles on Burma and even lists the myriad, and sometimes trivial, articles appearing in two of Burma's English language periodicals, the *Guardian* (q.v.), and *Forward* (published by the Burma Socialist Programme Party from 1962-88).

316   Journal of the Burma Research Society.

Rangoon: Burma Research Society, 1911-77. biannual.

The Burma Research Society was inaugurated on 29 March 1910 at a meeting held at the Bernard Free Library, Rangoon. Its aims were 'the investigation and encouragement of Art, Science and Literature in relation to Burma and the neighbouring countries'. From the start the Burma Research Society represented a fusion of the energy and initiative of a generation of both Burmans and Europeans – early leading luminaries being John S. Furnivall, Charles Duroiselle, May Oung, Gordon Luce and Pe Maung Tin – and the Society's meetings and *Journal* were a forum for enthusiastic debate and research on Burma for seventy years. As well as publishing the *Journal*, the Burma Research Society played a leading role in the publication of rare Burmese historical and literary manuscript texts and in the publication of prescribed school textbooks. In the wartime period, the Society sponsored the publication in India of a useful series of eleven 'Burma Pamphlets', as follows: *Burma background* by B. R. Pearn (1943), *Burma setting* by O. H. K. Spate (1943), *Buddhism in Burma* by G. Appleton (1943), *Burma rice* (1944), *Forests of Burma* by F. T. Morehead (1944), *The hill peoples of Burma* by H. N. C. Stevenson (1944), *The Burman: an appreciation* by C. J. Richards (1945), *The Karens of Burma* by Harry I. Marshall (1945), *Burma facts and figures* (1946), *The Burma petroleum industry* (1946), *The birds of Burma* by B. E. Smythies (1946). The Society also published its *Fiftieth Anniversary Publications* (Rangoon: Burma Research Society, 1960-61. 2 vols.) of which the first volume consisted of papers read at the Society's fiftieth anniversary conference, with photographs of all past presidents of the Society, and the second, and most useful, volume reprinted a selection of articles on history and literature from earlier issues of the *Journal* (including articles by D. G. E. Hall, G. H. Luce, Kaung, and Pe Maung Tin). There is an *Index to the Journal of the Burma Research Society (1911-1977)* compiled by Than Aung (Rangoon: Department of Library Studies, Diploma in Librarianship, 1978. 138p.) covering vols. 1-59 and the Fiftieth Anniversary Publications volumes, with entries listed by author and subject. This supersedes the earlier 'Index to JBRS, vols. 1-30, 1911-1930' by Suleiman Meer (published in the *JBRS*, vol. 20, 1931). In 1980 the Burma Research Society celebrated its seventieth anniversary with a conference at Rangoon University, but following the surprise attendance of Ne Win at one session of this conference, the Society was closed down, its *Journal* ceased and the contents of its library discarded. The abrupt end of this distinguished Society and *Journal* makes a sad comparison with the still flourishing and near contemporaneous *Journal of the Siam Society* (Bangkok: The Siam Society, 1904-) which although focused on Thailand sometimes includes articles on Burma.

817 **Journal of Southeast Asian Studies.**
Singapore: McGraw Hill Far Eastern Publishers, 1970-77; Singapore University Press, 1978-. semi-annual.

This periodical succeeds the *Journal of Southeast Asian History* (Singapore: University of Singapore, Department of History, 1960-69) and its new title indicates its wider orientation and policy of facilitating scholarly discussion and debate of various topics and issues in Southeast Asian studies. It carries articles on Burma from time to time and has a regular book review section. Some issues are devoted to a specific theme, for example vol. 15, no. 2 (Sept. 1984), of *JSEAS* published a 'Symposium on societal organization in mainland Southeast Asia prior to the eighteenth century' (p. 219-329) which included two papers on Burma: 'Hierarchy and order in pre-colonial Burma' by Michael Aung-Thwin (p. 224-32) and 'Freedom and bondage in traditional Burma and Thailand' by Frederick K. Lehman (p. 230-44).

818 **Myanmar Press Release.**
London: Embassy of Union of Myanmar, 1988-. irregular.

This publication, distributed abroad through Burmese embassies, represents an attempt by the Information Committee of SLORC, which has ruled Burma since 18 September 1988, to hold regular press conferences to publicize its point of view, issue 'clarifications' and reply to outside criticisms. As such it offers insights into the preoccupations, prejudices and mentality of Burma's ruling junta. Its predominent tone is strident and a recurrent theme is that the international community must refrain 'from interfering or exerting pressure in any shape or form in the internal affairs of Myanmar'. The early issues (from 15 November 1988–May 1989) appeared under the title of *Burma Press Release*. SLORC also publishes *Press conferences* (Rangoon: Union of Burma State Law and Order Restoration Council, Information Committee, 1989-), a series of volumes containing the proceedings of its regular press conferences. Two further publications contain the texts of special press conferences given by SLORC Secretary and Director of Defence Services Intelligence, Major General Khin Nyunt, with biographies and photographs of 'traitorous' individuals (including some foreigners) and reproductions of photographs and documents exhibited at the press conferences, as follows: *Burma Communist Party's conspiracy to take over state power* (Rangoon: Ministry of Information, 1989. 174p.) and, *The conspiracy of traitorous minions within the Myanmar naing-ngan and traitorous cohorts abroad* (Rangoon: Ministry of Information, 1989. 332p. map). Also relevant is *The Working People's*

Daily: collected articles (Rangoon: Guardian Press, News & Periodicals Enterprise of Ministry of Information, 1988-. 8 vols. to date), reprinting articles appearing in Burma's English-language state-controlled newspaper from 25 September 1988 onwards, supplemented by some items translated from its Burmese language counterpart *Lok-tha pyei-thu nei-zin*. The foreword to this series claims that the articles are 'constructively criticising and objectively reviewing and assessing the changing political, economic, social and public management affairs of the state' and a constant theme is that the Tatmadaw (the Burma Army) has saved the country from an 'abyss'. Lastly, there is a compilation of rambling speeches, in Burmese and English translation, by General Saw Maung entitled *State Law and Order Restoration Council Chairman Commander-in-Chief of The Defence Services Senior General Saw Maung's addresses* (Rangoon: Ministry of Information, 1990-91. 3 vols. [to date]).

819 **Pagan Newsletter.**
[Bangkok]: UNDP/UNESCO, 1983-. annual.
In 1975 Burma's ancient capital Pagan, which contains over 2,000 temples, was damaged by a severe earthquake. To undertake restoration work a UNDP–UNESCO Project (BUR/81/032) on the Conservation of the Cultural Heritage of Burma was agreed with the government of Burma and Pierre Pichard of the Ecole Française d'Extrême-Orient, was appointed the project supervisor. The *Pagan Newsletter*, published for the duration of the project, contains a record of the progress of the restoration work, technical details, news of archaeological discoveries made in the course of the work and circulates news of stolen art objects. Since 1988, international work at Pagan has ceased as approval of the next three-year phase of the UNDP–UNESCO project has been delayed by the political situation in Burma. The last issue to appear was that for 1989 and it took the form of a reduced scale archaeological map of Pagan – the first such to be produced – showing 2,230 monuments' precise location. Publication of a full 'Inventory of Pagan Monuments' with scale drawings and ground plans of temples is planned. Also relevant is a report by Than Tun on the preservation and study of Pagan briefly describing forty-eight temples at Pagan, published in *Cultural heritage in Asia: study and preservation of historic cities of Southeast Asia*, edited by Y. Ishizawa, Y. Kono (Tokyo: Institute of Asian Cultures, Sophia University, 1986), p. 67-84.

820 **Summary of World Broadcasts. Part III – Far East.**
Caversham Park, England: Monitoring Service of the British Broadcasting Corporation, 1949-. daily.
This provides a selection from Asian home and foreign radio stations' broadcasting output monitored by the BBC, supplemented by extracts from press articles and official reports. The summary is divided into (A) 'International affairs' and (B) 'Internal affairs', with most reports from Burma included in section B. It provides a useful means for journalists and others to follow events in Burma on the occasions when it is in the news, as during the pro-democracy uprising of 1988 and its aftermath. There is an equivalent United States publication, *FBIS Daily Report: East Asia* (Springfield, Virginia: National Technical Education Service, 1974-. daily).

Yearbooks, Directories and Statistics

821 Asia Yearbook.

Hong Kong: Review Publishing, 1960-. annual.

Compiled by the editors and correspondents of the *Far Eastern Economic Review* (q.v.), this contains a good overview of Asian developments and a country-by-country survey from Afghanistan to New Zealand. The Burma chapter is informative and well-presented with illustrations and maps, a 'databox' of basic statistics and a list of members of the government, and provides a review of politics and social affairs, foreign relations and the economy.

822 The Far East and Australasia.

London: Europa Publications, 1969-. annual.

A comprehensive guide to political events and economic developments. Part one provides a general review of the region, with details of population trends, commodity markets, and current political trends; with a directory of international organizations and research bodies active in Asia and the Pacific. Part two examines regional organizations and looks at the work of the United Nations and its agencies (UNDP. FAO, IMF, WHO, etc.). Part three consists of country surveys with sections contributed by different specialists: the 1988 edition's Burma section had Harvey Demaine writing on physical and social geography, Josef Silverstein on history, and Richard Vokes on the economy. Also included is a statistical survey (of area and population, agriculture, forestry, fishing, mining, industry, finance, trade, transport, communications media, tourism and education) and a directory of Burma's constitution, government, legislation, political organization, diplomatic representation, the media, trade and industrial organizations.

823 Southeast Asian Affairs.

Singapore: Institute of Southeast Asian Affairs, 1974-. annual.

This excellent annual review of significant developments in the region has introductory background chapters surveying the region as a whole, followed by chapters on individual countries. The Burma chapters have in recent years included contributions from visiting Burmese research fellows at the Institute of Southeast Asian Affairs. The level of contributions is high and the publication provides a useful and accumulative review and analysis of developments in Burma. A list of the relevant entries from the 1985-91 annual issues follows: 'Burma in 1984: unasked questions, unanswered issues' by David Steinberg (p. 111-30); 'Burma in 1985: a nation on hold' by Josef Silverstein (p. 55-67) and, 'Burma's energy use: perils and promises' by Tin Maung Maung Than (q.v.); 'Burma in 1986: the year of the snake' by Mya Than (p. 105-28); 'Burma in 1987 – twenty-five years after the revolution' by Tin Maung Maung Than (p. 73-93); 'Burma in 1988: perestroika with a military face' by James F. Guyot (p. 107-33); and (1990 issue), 'The Burmese way to capitalism' by John H. Badgley (p. 229-39) and 'Agriculture in Myanmar: what has happened to Asia's rice bowl?' by Mya Than (p. 240-54); and lastly, 'Myanmar 1990: new era or old?' by Robert H. Taylor (p. 199-219).

824 **Statistical Yearbook for Asia and the Pacific/Annuaire Statistique pour l'Asie et le Pacifique.**
Bangkok: United Nations, Economic and Social Commission for Asia and the Pacific (ESCAP), 1966-. annual.

Prepared by the Statistics Division of ESCAP, this provides a wide variety of statistical information on such subjects as population, manpower, national accounts, agriculture, forestry and fishing, industry, energy, transport and communications, internal and external trade, wages, prices and household expenditures, etc. It is a more convenient way of accessing statistical information on Burma than tracing and consulting the government of Burma's official reports such as the annual *Report to the Pyithu Hluttaw on the financial, economic and social conditions of the Socialist Republic of the Union of Burma* (Rangoon: Ministry of Planning and Finance).

825 **Statistik des Auslandes: Länderbericht: Birma 1984.** (Foreign statistics: country reports: Burma 1984.)
Wiesbaden: Statistisches Bundesamt, 1984. 99p. 2 maps.

This statistical compilation covers Burma's population, health, education, employment, agriculture, forestries, fisheries, industries, foreign trade, transport and communications, tourism, public finance, wages, prices, national accounts, balance of payments, development planning and development co-operation. The data is taken from reports published by the government of Burma. This publication, part of an irregular series of country statistical reports, is distributed by W. Kohlhammer GmbH, Publications of the Federal Statistical Office, Phillipp-Reis-Strasse 3, D-6500, Mainz 42, Germany.

826 **Who's who in Burma.**
Rangoon: People's Literature Committee & House, 1961. 220p.

Contains approximately 450 biographical sketches of prominent Burmese personalities from all walks of life. A colonial period compilation giving biographical details and photographs of prominent residents of British Burma is *Who's who in Burma: under the distinguished patronage of HE Sir Harcourt Butler* (Calcutta, India; Rangoon: Indo–Burma Publishing Agency, [1927]. 262p.), while there are short biographies of seventy-seven individuals in the wartime official publication, *Burma handbook* (Simla, India: Government of India Press, 1943). S. Chatterjie's *Meeting the personalities: Burma series* (Rangoon: Rasika Ranjani Press, [1956]. 70p.) provides chatty profiles of twenty individuals from the 1920s-1950s period.

827   **Who's who in medicine in Burma.**
      Khin Thet Htar.   Rangoon: Department of Medical Health, Ministry
      of Health, 1973. 203p. (Burma Medical Research Council Special
      Report Series, no. 9).
This work is both a biographical dictionary of medical specialists and other health-
related scientists (dental surgeons, pharmacists, biochemists, etc.) and a directory of
Burmese health institutions, laboratories, medical associations and periodicals.

Bibliographies and
Research Guides

828   **A Burma bibliography.**
  J. R. Allan.   *Dekho!*, no. 101 (Winter 1986), p. 30-33.
A selective listing of books on the Burma Campaign. *Dekho!* is the journal of the
Burma Star Association for veterans of the Burma campaign and it often reviews
books on the war in Burma and is full of news and reminiscences.

829   **Burma: a study guide.**
  Asia Program, Woodrow Wilson International Center for Scholars.
  Washington, DC: The Wilson Center, 1987. [208p.].
This guide has three separate sections of which the two last, and largest, are
unpaginated. It consists of (1) *Burma studies worldwide*, edited by Ronald A. Morse
and Helen A. Loerke; (2) *Burma: a selective guide to scholarly resources*, edited by
Anita Hibler and William P. Tuchrello; (3) *Burma: a selective guide to periodical
literature (1970-1986)*, edited by Anita Hibler and William P. Tuchrello. These works
arose out of an international conference on the state of Burma studies, held in June
1986 by the Asia Program of the Woodrow Wilson International Center for Scholars,
The *Burma studies worldwide* (59p.) section is an edited version of delegates' reports
on the then state of Burma studies and research in Russia, Japan, France, Federal
Republic of Germany, German Democratic Republic, Czechoslovakia, Burma, United
States, and United Kingdom. The second section, *Burma: a selective guide to scholarly
resources* constitutes a useful supplement to Trager's *Burma: a selected and annotated
bibliography* (q.v.) but is actually a listing of 1,080 publications on Burma that were
acquired and catalogued by the US Library of Congress from 1970 to 1986. For
accessions since that period, the latest issues of the *Library of Congress Accessions
List: Southeast Asia* (Jakarta, Indonesia: Library of Congress Office, 1979-.
bimonthly), should be consulted. This was published earlier under a different title, but
entries for Burma only began to appear from the July–Sept. 1979 issue onwards; an
annual cumulative index is published in the Nov.–Dec. issue and a separate cumulative
list of serials is issued periodically. The third section, *Burma: a selective guide to
periodical literature* lists 1,618 articles selected (somewhat erratically) from an

261

impressive list of 250 periodical titles. A subject index is provided to both these sections.

830 **Southeast Asian research tools: Burma.**
Michael Aung-Thwin. Honolulu: Southeast Asian Studies, Asian Studies Program, University of Hawaii, 1979. 67p. (Southeast Asia Paper, no. 16, part. 3).

A bibliographical listing of existing reference and research tools on Burma for scholars, with a very brief evaluation under the headings 'scope', 'comprehensiveness' and 'usefulness' of some, but by no means all, entries. The information is arranged by subject categories. The listing is not comprehensive, and its chief value lies in its inclusion of Burmese-language research tools and in its recommendations for future bibliographical compilations and cataloguing projects to fill gaps in the coverage provided by existing reference tools.

831 **A guide to Mon studies.**
Christian Bauer. Clayton, Australia: Monash University, Centre of Southeast Asian Studies, 1984. 84p. bibliog. (Monash University, Centre of Southeast Asian Studies, Working Paper, no. 32).

A useful review of previous studies on Mon language and culture and of their present state, with a bibliography (p. 41-76) of Mon studies, arranged by subject, with approximately 230 entries. Also by Bauer is 'Language and ethnicity: the Mon in Burma and Thailand' in *Ethnic groups across national boundaries in mainland Southeast Asia*, edited by Gehan Wijeyewardene (Singapore: Institute of Southeast Asian Studies, 1990), p. 14-47.

832 **Bibliographie birmane: années 1950-1960.** (Burmese bibliography: years 1950-1960.)
Denise Bernot. Paris: Editions du Centre National de la Recherche Scientifique, 1960. 228p. (Atlas Ethno-Linguistique: Recherche Cooperative sur Programme 61, Troisième Série Bibliographies).

This bibliography, compiled from Burma items in Paris libraries, is arranged in two sequences: by subject, and by alphabetical order of author. Only minimal annotations of some entries in the author section are given. It includes periodical articles and has a good coverage of items in Russian. There is a continuation, *Bibliographie birmane: années 1960-1970*. (Burmese bibliography: years 1960-1970) compiled by Denise Bernot, with the collaboration of Gilles Garachon, Liêu Mignot, Jean-Pierre Scribnai, Laurent Tchang (Paris: Editions du Centre National de la Recherche Scientifique, 1982-83, 2 vols.) which is unannotated and arranged by subject divisions, with a good coverage of Burmese titles and of periodical articles.

833 **The economic conditions of East and Southeast Asia: a bibliography of English-language materials, 1965-1977.**
Compiled by Virginia Chen. Westport, Connecticut; London: Greenwood, 1978. 788p.

The Burma section (p. 81-85) has approximately sixty entries listed under selected subject headings (cotton industry, fish, investments, rice, etc.).

834 Bibliotheca Indosinica: dictionnaire bibliographique des ouvrages relatifs à la péninsule indochinoise. (Bibliographical dictionary of works relating to the Indochinese peninsula).
Henry Cordier. Paris: Lerous, 1912-15. 4 vols.; New York: Burt Franklin, 1967. 3 vols. (Burt Franklin Bibliographic and Reference Sources, no. 106).

This is a meticulous and, for its time, comprehensive bibliographical compilation. Burma is covered in volume 1 (columns 1-516), with entries arranged by detailed subject divisions. It includes references to reviews of books and lists many obscure periodical articles, with coverage of publications in a wide range of languages including Pali and Burmese. A volume index by M.-A. Roland-Cabaton was originally published in Paris in 1932, later to be included in the 3-volume 1967 edition.

835 **Burma.**
Alan Gledhill. Brussels: Editions de l'Institut de Sociologie, Université Libre de Bruxelles, 1970. 42p. (Bibliographical introduction to legal history and ethnology. Edited by John Gilissen. Section E/7. Etudes d'Histoire et d'Ethnologie Juridique).

A bibliography and survey of Burmese law and legal sources, listing law reports, law digests, acts and codes, gazetteers and indigenous law codes (*dhammathat*).

836 **Burma.**
Patricia M. Herbert. In: *South Asian bibliography: a handbook and guide.* Compiled by the South Asia Library Group, general editor J. D. Pearson. Hassocks, England: Harvester; Atlantic Highlands, New Jersey: Humanities, 1979. p. 328-51.

This contribution to a bibliographical compilation on countries of the South Asian region surveys bibliographical sources of information on Burma and includes Burmese-language items. It has 156 annotated entries arranged into the following broad subject categories: general bibliographies; catalogues of printed books; catalogues of manuscripts and microfilms; theses; arts; sciences. A subject index is provided.

837 **South-East Asia languages and literatures: a select guide.**
Edited by Patricia M. Herbert, Anthony C. Milner. Whiting Bay, Scotland: Kiscadale, 1988. Honolulu: University of Hawaii Press, 1989. 182p. map. bibliog.

This bibliographical guide provides a concise introduction to the history, major languages, scripts, dating systems, manuscripts, printing and publishing histories, and literary genres of the different countries that constitute Southeast Asia. Full bibliographical references are provided at the end of each country chapter. The Burma chapter (p. 1-22) has been compiled by Anna Allott, Patricia M. Herbert and John Okell.

838 **Bibliotheca Catholica Birmana.**
Rev. H. Hosten, Rev. E. Luce.   Rangoon: British Burma Press, 1915.
122p.

This rare publication contains valuable bibliographical information on the work of Roman Catholic missionaries in Burma. It is arranged in five parts: publications by missionaries, publications having reference to the Burma Catholic Mission, indexes to Burma references in the Annals of the Propagation of the Faith, and of the Holy Childhood, index to Bengal Catholic periodicals, and index to Burma Catholic periodicals.

839 **Bibliography and index of mainland Southeast Asian languages and linguistics.**
Franklin E. Huffman.   New Haven, Connecticut; London: Yale University Press, 1986. 640p.

This monumental bibliography comprises some 10,000 entries, arranged by author and chronologically under each author (p. 1-514), with a language and subject index (p. 517-640). The author's aim was to attempt to list 'everything ever written in any lanugage about any language of mainland Southeast Asia'. The key to the use of the bibliography is the index which provides alternative names and cross-references in abundance. Also, each language is followed by various subject categories (dictionaries, grammar, idioms, etc.) in the index. Thus, a search under the names of any of the languages and dialects of Burma provides an exhaustive listing of entries and cross-references.

840 **Southeast Asian literature in translation: a preliminary bibliography.**
Philip N. Jenner.   Honolulu: University Press of Hawaii, 1973. 198p.
(Asian Studies at Hawaii, 9).

The section on Burma (p. 1-46) has 855 listings of translations and of expository works, arranged under topical headings (folk literature, inscriptions, chronicles, poetry, etc.), but the work is in need of updating.

841 **Annotated bibliography of medical literature on Burma (1866-1976).**
Khin Thet Htar.   New Delhi: World Health Organisation South-East Asia Regional Office 1981. 484p. (WHO Regional Publications South-East Asia Series, no. 13).

This vast bibliography of over 2,000 entries covers all medical literature (books, articles, pamphlets, reports, theses) written in English relating to medicine, and allied subjects such as zoology and botany, in Burma. Subject and author indexes are provided, together with a thirty-five page supplement up to 1980.

842 **Land tenure and agrarian reform in East and Southeast Asia: an annotated bibliography.**
Compiled by staff of the Land Tenure Center Library, University of Wisconsin, directed by Teresa J. Anderson.   Boston, Massachusetts: G. K. Hall, 1980. 557p.

This bibliography has been compiled to assist those concerned with the problems of rural development and agrarian reform. The section on Burma (p. 244-54) contains forty-six well-evaluated entries.

843 **Asian mass communications: a comprehensive bibliography.**
John A. Lent.   Philadelphia: School of Communications and Theater, Temple University, 1975. 708p.

The Burma section (p. 248-51) of this bibliography covers film, printed media, radio and television. There is from the same source a 619-page *1977 Supplement* giving additional listings, with Burma entries on p. 269-70.

844 **Scholars' guide to Washington, DC for Southeast Asian studies.**
Patrick M. Mayerchak.   Washington, DC: Smithsonian Institute Press, 1983. 411p. bibliog. (Woodrow Wilson International Center; Scholars' Guide to Washington, DC, no. 9).

Over 400 collections, organizations and agencies have been surveyed for this guide which describes and evaluates Southeast Asian resources in Washington, as well as providing a lot of useful background information on the collections and institutions. Part one examines resource collections (libraries, archives and manuscript repositories, art, film, music and map collections, and data banks); part two covers Washington-based organizations, both public and private. Sources on Burma can be located through the subject index.

845 **Selected bibliography on education in Southeast Asia.**
Kenneth L. Neff.   Washington, DC: US Department of Health, Education & Welfare, Government Printing Office, 1963. 16p. (Studies in Comparative Education).

Contains twenty-two annotated entries on all aspects of education in Burma (p. 4-6).

846 **Burmese and Thai newspapers: an international union list.**
Compiled by G. Raymond Nunn.   Taipei: Ch'eng-Wen, 1972. 44p. bibliog. (Chinese Materials & Research Aids Service Center, Occasional Series, no. 13).

A listing of thirty Burmese newspapers is given on p. 1-5, with a listing in the appendix on p. 41-44 of seventy-five newspaper titles for which no holdings information is available. More detailed listings of holdings of Burmese newspapers and periodicals can be found, under the title entry, in Brenda Moon's *Periodicals for South-East Asian studies: a union catalogue of holdings in British and selected European libraries* (London: Mansell, 1979. 610p.). For periodicals see also G. Raymond Nunn's *South East Asian periodicals: an international union list* (London: Mansell, 1977. 456p.).

847 **Burma: an annotated bibliographical guide to international doctoral dissertation research on Burma 1898-1985.**
Frank Joseph Shulman.   Lanham, Maryland; New York; London: University Press of America, in association with the Asia Program, the Wilson Center, 1986. 247p.

This is the first authoritative reference guide to thesis literature on Burma. It is a comprehensive, interdisciplinary, annotated listing of 707 dissertation entries for work in the humanities, social sciences, medicine, and the natural sciences. A lot of care has been taken to include dissertations that treat Burma within a comparative framework, as well as dissertations about Western literary interest in Burma. The entries are arranged under subject headings, and liberal cross-references are provided. Within each subject section or sub-section, entries are grouped into two categories: theses concerned primarily with Burma and theses concerned secondarily or tangentially with Burma. Five sets of statistical tables summarize a wealth of data (distribution of dissertation by country and year of degree, etc.) and reveal much about long-term trends in doctoral research. Author, institutional and subject indexes are also provided. The annual volumes of the bibliographical journal *Doctoral Dissertations on Asia: an Annotated Bibliographical Journal of Current International Research* (Ann Arbor, Michigan: Association for Asian Studies, 1975-) can be used as an update for post-1985 dissertations on Burma.

848 **Burma: a selected and annotated bibliography.**
Frank N. Trager, assisted by Janelle Wang, Dorothea Schoenfeldt, Ann Riotto, Mary Parker, Aung San Suu Kyi, Robert Bordonaro and Frank Simonie.   New Haven, Connecticut: Human Relations Area Files, 1973. 356p. (Behavior Science Bibliographies).

An updating of an earlier bibliography by Frank N. Trager, John K. Musgrave and Janet Welsh, *Annotated bibliography of Burma* (New Haven, Connecticut: Human Relations Area Files, 1956). It has 2,086 entries arranged into eight sections: bibliographies; books and other separates; journal articles; documents; English-language serials concerning Burma; Burmese lanuage sources; Russian and Eastern language sources; dissertations. In addition there is a list of Western-language periodicals and an author and topical index (p. 265-356). The annotations are very brief and not every entry is annotated. In spite of some inaccuracies it remains a major bibliography of pre-1970 publications on Burma.

849 **Furnivall of Burma: an annotated bibliography of the works of John S. Furnivall.**
Compiled and edited by Frank N. Trager.   New Haven, Connecticut: Yale University Southeast Asia Studies in cooperation with University of British Columbia, Department of Asian Studies, 1963. 51p. (Bibliography Series, no. 8).

Furnivall (1878-1960) was a pioneering scholar and foremost economic historian of Burma. His ICS career in Burma spanned the period 1902-31, while through the Burma Research Society, founded in 1910, and his Burma Book Club, the *Gandalawka/World of Books* magazine encouraging translations into Burmese and reviewing literature, and the Burma Education Extension Association founded by Furnivall in 1928, and his subsequent lecturing career and postwar position as advisor to the government of Burma, Furnivall made an unparalleled direct intellectual contribution to Burma. This bibliography lists 220 published and unpublished works by Furnivall and includes articles and official papers prepared for the governments of British Burma and independent Burma. The entries are arranged chronologically and by topic, with useful summaries and comments upon each item. Also provided is a brief *curriculum vitae* and appreciation of Furnivall.

850 **Southeast Asian references in the British Parliamentary Papers, 1801-1972/73: an index.**
Compiled, edited and introduced by Thomas F. Willer. Athens, Ohio: Ohio University Center for International Studies, Southeast Asia Program, 1978. 88p. (Papers in International Studies Southeast Asia Series, no. 48).

This index facilitates access for researchers to the Parliamentary Papers, which consist of official proceedings, debates, reports and background papers presented before the British House of Commons. The vast amount of material they contain on Burma is listed on p. 16-41.

Special Burma Studies Issue.
See item no. 7.

A brief guide to sources for the study of Burma in the India Office Records.
See item no. 794.

Journal of Asian Studies.
See item no. 815.

Indexes

There follow three separate indexes: authors (personal and corporate), translators and illustrators; titles; and subjects. Title entries are italicized and refer either to the main titles, or to other works cited in the annotations. The numbers refer to bibliographic entries, not to pages. In conformity with standard usage, Burmese (and also Thai and Lao) names have been entered in direct order. Honorific terms of address (U, Maung, Daw etc.) and other qualifiers have not been included except where necessary to distinguish between authors.

Index of Authors

A

Abbott, G. 301
Abrahams, W. 695
Adams, L. B. 693
 see also Moresby, L.
Adamson, C. H. E. 32
Adas, M. 216, 232
Adhyatman, Sumarah 747
Adloff, R. 440
Aflalo, F. G. 329
Agabeg, A. 214
Agnew, F. 709
Agnew, R. 709
Ahmad, N. 97
Ahmad, Z. H. 561
Ahmar, Ludu Daw 797
Aitken, D. J. 642
Alexander, J. E 353
Allan, J. R. 828
Allen, L. 253
Allott, A. 441, 643-44,
 658, 799-800, 837
Ames, M. M. 481
Amin, H. M. 593
Amnesty International
 522, 523
Ananda, Ashin
 see Lustig, F. V.
Anders, L. 254
Anderson, C. 341
Anderson, J. (1833-1900)
 33, 411
Anderson, J. 85

Anderson, T. J. 842
Andrew, E. J. L. 437
Andrus, J. R. 225
Appleton, G. 816
Archer, M. 215
Aris, M. 536
Armes, R. 773
Arumugam, R. S. 607
Ashton, S. R. 212
Asia Society 148
Asia Watch 524
Atkins, D. 362
Atwool, D. C. 351
Auboyer, J. 719, 721
Aung Aung Thaik 280
Aung Bala
 see Thaung
Aung Kin 807
Aung San 209
Aung San Suu Kyi 1, 6,
 182, 281, 536, 562, 848
Aung Than Batu 430
Aung Thaw 90, 135-36
Aung Thein 789
Aung Thein (Yodaya) 177
Aung Tun Thet 218
Aung-Thwin, Margaret 658
Aung-Thwin, Michael 10,
 137, 143, 148, 165,
 178, 217, 556, 817, 830
Aye Hlaing 224, 620
Aye Kyaw 7
Aye Saung 282, 541
Aye Set 784
Ayoob, Mohammed 561

B

Ba, V. 498, 639, 740
Ba Han 445
Ba Kyaw ('MBK') 608
Ba Kyi 16, 657
Ba Lone Lay 296
Ba Maw 142, 283
Ba Shin 2, 495, 733
Ba Than 525
Ba Thann Win 632
Ba U 284
BACSA
 see British Association
 for Cemeteries in
 South Asia
Badgley, J. H. 278, 526,
 533, 546, 555-56, 566,
 600, 645, 823
Bagshawe, L. E. 639, 646
Bailey, J. T. 728, 798
Baker, A. D. 255
Baker, E. C. S. 114
Baker, T. T. 354
Ballou, R. O. 349
Bandyopadhyay, S. 594
Bandyopadhyaya, K. 567
Banerjee, A. C. 236
Banjong Mianmanus 787
Bannert, D. 98
Barber, C. T. 302
Bareigts, A. 412
Barker, K. F. 711
Barker, R. 595

Winston, W. R. 352
Winter, C. T. 340
Withey, J. A. 296
Wohl, J. 554
Wohlgemuth, P. 581
Wolin, S. 316
Wolpert, R. F. 779
Wolters, O. W. 147
Won, Z. Y.
  see Yoon, Won Zoon
Woodcock, M. W. 121
Woodman, D. 164
Woodrow Wilson
    International Center
    for Scholars 829
Woodside, A. 143, 146
Woodward, M. R. 7
Wootton, W. H. 320

World Health
    Organization 521
Wright, A. 214
Wright, J. 788
Wun 2, 797
Wun Tha 15
Wurfel, D. 566
Wyatt, D. K. 143, 146, 313

Y

Yabu, S. 155
Yalman, N. 481
Yegar, M. 497
Yi Yi 50, 154, 181, 727
Yin Yin Myint, Marie 447

Yin Yin Nwe 790
Ying Sita, Sao 541
Yitri, M.
  see Moksha Yitri
Yoji, A. 257
Yoon, Won Zoon 279
Young, K. R. 578
Younghusband, G. J. 60
Yule, H. 39, 44, 215, 444

Z

Zawgyi
  see Thein Han
Ziegler, P. 188
Zwalf, W. 494

Index of Titles

D

E

290

293

N

301

U

Index of Subjects

orchids 119, 124
plant hunting
  expeditions 115, 122,
  131
rhododendrons 115
rubber plant 131
Southern Shan States
  125
Tenasserim province 340
trees 16, 120
vegetables 16
vernacular names 120,
  123
Flowers
  see Flora
Folk songs
  see Songs
Folk tales and folklore 2,
  29, 31, 475, 653, 659,
  709
  Chin 300
  Kachin 419, 509
  legal element 586
  Palaung 428
  Shan 429
Force 136
  see History (Burma
  Campaign)
Forchhammer, Emil 139,
  591
Foreign policy 15, 162,
  552, 566-67, 569-70,
  575, 579
  and United Nations 581
  neutralism 15, 535, 555,
  569-70
  Soviet 573
  towards China 574
  towards India 575
Foreign relations 184, 552,
  572-73, 578-79, 587
  periodicals 821
  with Bangladesh 568
  with Britain 153, 190,
  192-93, 206
  with China 162, 439, 578
  with France 175
  with India 575
  with Russia 162
  with Sri Lanka 2, 177
  with United States 162,
  571
Forests and forestry 23, 97,
  112, 225, 629, 816

reminiscences of life in
  314-15, 317, 327, 336,
  339
deforestation 197
Forsythe, Sir Douglas 32
Fossils 142, 185
Foucar, Emil C. V.
  reminiscences 311
France
  relations with 175
Frog drums
  see Drums
Fruits
  see Flora
Funerals 11, 27
Furnivall, John S. 216
  bio-bibliography 849
Fytche, Albert
  reminiscences 192
  career 338

G

Gallo, Luigi 498
Game hunting 8, 36, 126,
  331
Games 45
  children's 780
Gandalawka 849
Gas 102
  exploration 101, 616
Gazetteers 111-112
  bibliography 112
  see also Maps and atlases
Gebhard, John 264
Gems 99
  annual emporium 614
  see also Mineral
  resources
Geography 1, 4, 28, 33,
  100, 112-13, 179, 187
  economic 97
  marine 101
  physical 99, 111
  see also Maps and
  atlases, Mineral
  resources
Geology 33, 97-99, 112,
  142, 214-15
  bibliography 98
  glossary of terms 104
  Irrawaddy Basin 142
  petroleum 105

see also Mineral
  resources
George, E. C. S. 760
Glass, Sir Leslie
  memoirs 312
Glassware
  see Crafts
Godwin, Henry T.
  letters 358
Goes, Benedict de 47
Gokteik viaduct 80
Golden Triangle 71,
  527, 513, 539
Gothenburg
  Ethnographical
  Museum
  costume collection 759
Gouger, Henry 185
Government 3, 531, 562
  Anti-Fascist People's
  Freedom League
  (AFPFL) of Nu
  (1948-58; 1960-62)
  145, 531, 546
  'Caretaker Government'
  of Ne Win (1958-60)
  531, 546, 588
  colonial 196, 213
  'Constitutional'/Burma
  Socialist Programme
  Party of Ne Win
  (1974-88) 535, 552,
  562
  Revolutionary Council
  of Ne Win (1962-74)
  30, 285, 528
  separation from India
  194
  State Law and Order
  Restoration Council
  (SLORC) (1988-) 523,
  528, 533-34, 537, 543,
  558, 560
  under kings 179
  see also History, Ne
  Win, Nu, Political
  parties, Politics
Grant, Colesworthy 46,
  215
Grasses
  see Flora
Gribble, R. H.
  diary 378
Guerreiro, Fernao 47

315

Medicinal plants
see Flora
Medicine 45, 515-16, 521
  bibliography 841
  periodicals 827
  see also Health and
    welfare, History
Mergui 95, 308
Merrill's Marauders
  see History (Burma
    Campaign)
Middleton, J. R. 53, 95
Midwifery 287
Mien people
  life and customs 425
Military coup, (1962) 28,
    143, 222
  see also Ne Win, Politics
Military coup (1988)
  see Politics, State Law
    and Order Restoration
    Council (SLORC)
Military Intelligence
  Service 807
Military rule 145, 156,
    549-50, 552, 556, 562
  see also Government,
    Politics, Ne Win
Min Yaza 646
Minami Kikan 272, 279
  see also History
Mindon, King 207, 246
  audience with 56-57
  reforms 235
Mineral resources 26,
    97-99, 104, 106, 111,
    124, 194, 214, 225
  bibliography 104
  glossaries of terms 104
  maps 104
  see also Geography,
    Geology, Oil
Minorities 440
  see also Chinese,
    Christians, Ethnic
    groups, Eurasians,
    Indian people, Jews,
    and under names of
    individual ethnic
    groups, e.g. Chin
    people
Minority problems 535
  and constitution 592
  see also Politics

Missionaries
  see Christian Missions
    and Missionaries
Mogok 67
Mogok Sayadaw 477
Mohnyin Sayadaw 477
Molluscs 787
Mon language 420, 831
  grammar 459, 461
Mon literature 420, 461
Mon people 420
  culture 831
  history 139
Monasteries 59, 491-92
  architecture 111
  ornamental motifs 35
  see also Buddhist
    monks, Buddhist
    Order
Money lending 235
  see also Chettiar,
    History
Mon-Khmer languages
    140, 443
Moral Rearmament
  movement 295
Morshead, Henry
  biography 324
Moses, Joannes 472
Mountbatten, Earl
  biography 188
Mru language
  see Tibeto-Burman
    languages
Mru people
  history 140
Mughs 247
Munro, H. H. ('Saki')
  biography 325
  letters 325
Museums
  Bankfield Museum 760
  Buddhist Art Museum
    796
  directories 642, 719, 793
  Hamburg Ethnographic
    Museum 743, 755
  Pagan Archaeological
    Museum 91
  Pagan Lacquerware
    Museum 755
  Victoria & Albert
    Burmese collection
    723

Music 15, 26, 771-72, 774
  notation 11, 361, 774, 777
Musical instruments 771,
    778
  harp 779
  Karen 427
  Pyu 778
Muslim Match Factory 783
Muslims 497, 541
  acculturation 496
  Arakanese 495, 497
  Indian 497
  see also Islam
Myitkyina
  recapture in Second
    World War 255, 268

N

Naga language 443
Naga people
  and the British 436
Names 14, 27
Narcotics 514
  see also Golden
    Triangle, Opium
Nash, P. G. E. 212
Nat (Spirits)
  see Spirit belief and cults
Nation 199
Nationalist movement
  see History
Naw Seng, General 268
Ne Win, U 9, 30, 285, 528,
    531, 546, 550, 555,
    564, 588
  biography 291
  style of rule 542-43
  see also Government
    (Caretaker,
    Revolutionary
    Council)
Negrais
  British settlement at 167
Neutralism
  see Foreign Policy
Newspapers 801
  bibliography 846
  Muslim 497
  press summary 810
  pro-democracy 799
  Working People's Daily
    810, 818
  see also Mass media

Map of Burma

This map shows the more important towns and other features.

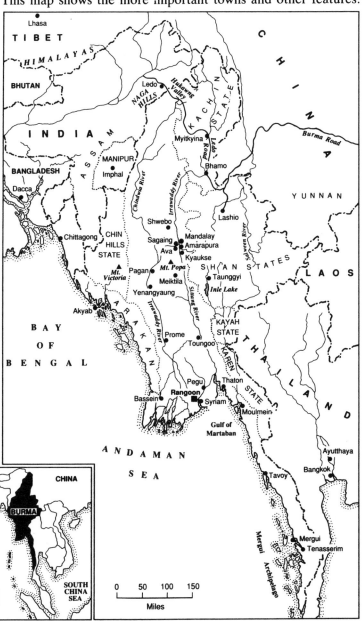